Also by David Rothkopf

Superclass: The Global Power Elite and the World They
  Are Making

Running the World: The Inside Story of the National Security
  Council and the Architects of American Power

Cuba: The Contours of Change (coauthor and coeditor with
  Susan Kaufman Purcell)

The Price of Peace: Emergency Economic Intervention and U.S.
  Foreign Policy

The Big Emerging Markets (editor and principal author)

The Common Market (coauthor with Carol Zeman Rothkopf)

Power, Inc.

Power, Inc.

The Epic Rivalry Between Big Business and Government— and the Reckoning That Lies Ahead

David Rothkopf

Farrar, Straus and Giroux ■ New York

Farrar, Straus and Giroux
18 West 18th Street, New York 10011

Library of Congress Cataloging-in-Publication Data
Rothkopf, David J. (David Jochanan), 1955–
    Power, Inc. : the epic rivalry between big business and government—and the reckoning
that lies ahead / David Rothkopf. — 1st ed.
        p.   cm.
    Includes bibliographical references and index.
    ISBN 978-0-374-15128-7 (cloth : alk. paper)
    1. Big business.   2. Business and politics.   3. Industrial policy.   4. Capitalism—
Political aspects.   I. Title.

    HD2350.8 .R68 2011
    322'.3—dc23

                                                                    2011036672

Designed by Abby Kagan

www.fsgbooks.com

10   9   8   7   6   5   4   3   2   1

For my brother and sister
and siblings everywhere
who are the first to teach us about
the great rivalries we cannot do without

It's the best possible time to be alive when almost everything you thought you knew is wrong.

—Tom Stoppard, *Arcadia*

Contents

Power, Inc.

Introduction: Bodies but No Souls

Where possessions be private, where money bearethe all the
stroke, it is harde and almost impossible that there the weal pub-
lique may justeleye be governed, and prosperously floryshe.

—Sir Thomas More, *Utopia*

Corporations have been enthroned and an era of corruption in
high places will follow, and the money power of the country will
endeavor to prolong its reign by working upon the prejudices of
the people until all wealth is aggregated in a few hands and the
Republic is destroyed.

—Abraham Lincoln, letter to Col. William Elkins

In most countries of the world today, there is a central tension that divides populations and helps define the shape and success of societies. At issue is how we balance public and private power. Differing national and regional approaches to resolving this tension will go a long way toward determining who leads and who follows in the global society of the twenty-first century, the role of evolving international institutions, and the very nature of how we organize ourselves as human beings on this planet.

The challenge is that the power of the people and the governments that represent them must harness, enable, and yet regularly offset the power of private actors and corporations that seek the maximum freedom to pursue their self-interests. It is an ancient struggle but one that has, in recent years, taken surprising turns that have forced many to question what have come to be basic assumptions about governance.

In the United States, the balance between public and private power is the defining political issue of the moment. Is government too big, a burden to society, and a threat to individual liberties? Or is it too ineffective a protector of average people, having been co-opted by big business and moneyed interests? Is it contributing to the general welfare or has it become a means of institutionalizing inequality, serving the few rather than the many?

In Europe, such controversies also roil furiously but they are joined by an intense argument over how much of the power of individual countries should be passed on to a collective European Union government, and about whose interests are best served by such collaborative governance—a departure from the traditional idea and role of the nation-state.

In China, this public-private tug-of-war is visible at every level of a society that is reinventing itself at such a breathtaking pace that stability and growth often seem as irreconcilable as they are essential to each other. It is a challenge faced elsewhere in the emerging world as well, from the battles between Russia's oligarchs and its government leaders and the sub-rosa relationships those battles sometimes obscure, to the social tumult we have recently seen in the Arab world, in which uprisings were as much against cronyism and governments that served the economic interests of elites as they were for individual freedoms and opportunities.

If the bloodshed, social experimentation, and ideological polarization of the twentieth century have offered us one lesson, it is that extreme solutions do not work when trying to balance public and private power. No society can effectively thrive without a balance between the two. When the balance between public and private power is lost, problems—often large ones—ensue.

Recent developments demand we rethink issues that were widely discussed—and, we thought, resolved—just a few years ago. The end of the cold war did not bring the expected triumph of American capitalism. The marketplace and its dominant actors, while constantly gaining influence, have, as recent scandals and crises reveal, clearly overreached and abused their power.

In the United States in particular, but in many other countries that have adopted a U.S.-like model as well, those abuses have led to a sense that the balance has become far too tilted in favor of private power. Inequality has grown in terms of both economic outcomes and apparent privileges and prerogatives of a super-empowered elite within—and beyond—the law. The result has produced a backlash and fueled the emergence of other alternative models of capitalism, each of which is based on a different kind of public-private balance as well as on different philosophical, cultural, and historical foundations.

This book, then, is about the epic rivalry between public and private power that has taken place over the centuries, and about how it has entered a new stage. It is about how essential it is to strike a balance between the two while avoiding collaborations that are too cozy between those empowered by the people and those seeking private gains. It is about the new approaches to achieving that balance that are emerging as legitimate rivals and even likely successors to an American model that has, at least temporarily, lost its equilibrium and a not inconsiderable measure of its legitimacy. And it is about the emerging world order that turns not primarily on the interplay between states, but on that between a new collection of actors: a handful of traditional states and a majority of states so weakened that they are now effectively semi-states, an emerging class of increasingly empowered private global actors that might be called super-citizens, and of all the rest of us.

Ultimately, therefore, it is about the challenges we face and the choices we must make to achieve the right balance between public and private power in the rapidly changing international environment of the decades ahead—and how history can help us gain the insights we need in order to do that.

The Evidence Is in the Headlines

In April 2010, in the wake of the financial crisis, Goldman Sachs's CEO, Lloyd Blankfein, and several other top officials of the firm were summoned to testify before Congress. More than any other company, Goldman had come to symbolize Wall Street clout. Like previous hearings involving financial executives who had played significant roles in the meltdown of global markets in 2008 and 2009, this one followed a traditional script.

The executives could barely conceal their contempt for the Congress that had called them to Washington. They read carefully worded prepared statements that denied wrongdoing. They spoke of the market collapse as if it were something like a turn in the weather. "Unfortunately," said Blankfein dryly, "the housing market went south very quickly. So people lost money in it."

Members of the Senate committee before which they were testifying derided the "fundamental conflict" in Goldman's selling financial products that its own executives characterized as "shitty" or "crap." The executives didn't flinch. One primly denied that they used that kind of language. For eleven hours the Congress attacked and the Goldman executives squirmed but argued that the products they sold were nothing but tools to reduce client risks, despite all evidence demonstrating that they had actually increased them.

America had been rocked by a financial crisis that had triggered the worst economic downturn since the Great Depression of the 1930s, and Congress, playing to angry Main Street constituencies, was talking tough. Senator Carl Levin, who chaired the hearing and whose home state of Michigan had been hard hit by the economic tsunami, condemned the fact that firms like Goldman had been having their way with government thanks to the armies of lobbyists the banks deployed who "fill the halls of Congress, hoping to weaken or kill legislation." That was going to have to come to an end. Washington was going to have to crack down on the practices that had brought about the devastating global downturn. Levin characterized the behavior of Goldman and similar big Wall Street investment houses as "unbridled greed in the absence of the cop on the beat to control it."

There would be a reckoning, promised the senators. Reforms were coming. Wall Street couldn't get rich shrugging off regulators for years, then both trigger a financial calamity and simultaneously demand a costly bailout without suffering lasting consequences. Changes were around the corner. New regulations would be imposed. A national crackdown on speculators and greed was inevitable. Washington was going to flex its muscle.

And then it blinked.

Even before the hearing, Wall Street had already begun another bonanza year. In 2010, Goldman Sachs doled out $15.3 billion in pay and bonuses to its staff. It added 3,200 more employees. Blankfein said, "Market and economic conditions for much of 2010 were difficult, but the firm's performance benefited from the strength of our global client franchise and the focus and commitment of our people."

Meanwhile, new financial reforms that had been passed in the middle of the year hung in limbo. Detailed regulatory provisions had yet to be written. Much-needed new staff had yet to be hired. Oversight agencies were too poorly funded to effectively implement the new laws. At the Securities and Exchange Commission (SEC), commissioners complained that many elements of the new laws simply couldn't be enforced because Congress hadn't appropriated the resources they needed for their computers to do even the basic tracking of key transactions. Washington had talked the talk, but when the cameras were turned off, it had shied away from walking the walk.

Resentment boiled over around the world. In the United Kingdom and across Europe, anger also welled up thanks to the latest wave of bonuses in financial districts, coming even as countries were squeezed by harsh austerity programs from their governments. Matters were not helped by the fact that the governments were soon scrambling to contain a deepening E.U. financial crisis created by a different kind of toxic collaboration between the public and private sectors. Politicians won office by promising voters benefits that the countries could not afford but had nonetheless been financed thanks to too-loose lending practices engineered by big banks—practices that, for example, enabled countries like Greece to overborrow by keeping some debts off their balance sheets. A similar cycle of public and private sector risks was generated through government officials looking the other way when it came to bankers and bankers looking the other way when it came to governments—at least until crises broke—breeding economic and social hardships from Washington to Tokyo, from Islamabad to Buenos Aires. Similar patterns were followed as giant global financial institutions played national governments against one another while helping to fund and influence candidates who helped create advantageous business conditions—even if that meant compromising everything from the health of the public to that of the planet itself.

Two thousand eleven became a year in which anger with the global and national systems that seem deliberately gamed to serve the interests of a privileged few spilled out into the streets.

In Tahrir Square in Cairo, the "Arab Spring" demonstrations protested not just the Mubarak dictatorship but the unfair concentration of power among the members of the country's crony-dominated elite. In Athens, while a government debt crisis triggered nationwide protests and strikes, the anger that motivated people to march on government buildings was triggered by a sense that the system in one of the birthplaces of democracy now had them working not just for the few in their own country but to repay bankers across Europe. England witnessed its most violent street clashes in decades.

In Zuccotti Park in lower Manhattan, not far from the offices of Goldman Sachs and other leading financial firms, the "We are the 99 percent" chants of "Occupy Wall Street" protesters highlighted the unsettling way wealth has become concentrated in the hands of the top 1 percent of American and global society—40 percent of all U.S. wealth is held by this relatively small slice of the U.S. population. The top four hundred Americans have, according to *The Wall Street Journal* in March 2011, a collective net worth almost equaling that of the bottom 50 percent of the U.S. population. At the same time, even though they were ideological worlds apart from the Wall Street demonstrators, members of the right wing's Tea Party movement were another manifestation of America's politics of alienation who mobilized to decry the degree to which the U.S. system had become broken and was no longer working for the average person. The Tea Partiers blame the concentration of too much power in the government. The "99 percent" blame the concentration of too much power in big business and the government officials whose votes have been bought.

Many of the members of these angry, restive groups around the world would argue they had little to do with one another. Many, no doubt, are completely unknown to one another. Nonetheless, the convergence of so much unrest worldwide with such a similar set of issues at its core cannot be dismissed as coincidence. In a matter of just a few short weeks, "Occupy" protests had spread to more than nine hundred cities worldwide.

A cascade of questions began to flow from the media, experts, and average citizens alike in countries around the world: Who is in charge here? Who makes the rules? The people who write the laws, or the ones who write the checks? Where did the greater good fit into all this? The global economy, it seemed, was at a watershed in terms of the relative and changing roles of public and private power. But what were its origins and its implications?

The Crisis Produces an Unexpected Winner

At about the same time global anti-establishment protests really began to gain momentum, I had breakfast with a senior official of the Obama administration at the Four Seasons Hotel in Washington. He had a provocative perspective on one of the unexpected consequences of the financial upheaval.

"Here's what you have to understand," he said to me with the authority of someone immersed every day in the ebb and flow of transpacific geopolitics. "The Chinese feel that they won the financial crisis."

The thought hung in the air for a moment. It was one of those unfamiliar ideas that nonetheless made immediate sense. I asked him to elaborate on the observation.

"Here's how they see it: Their growth didn't really suffer. They grew stronger while other major powers struggled. And perhaps most important, the American system was revealed to be profoundly corrupt and dysfunctional." The United States, therefore, lost ground while China gained. American criticisms of China's management of its economy and society were deflated. In other words, while America was trying to persuade China to devalue its currency, we were the ones who got devalued—politically and, more important, in terms of the role we had played since the end of the Second World War as an example to the world.

He described how the Chinese "victory" was almost immediately institutionalized when, in an effort to respond to the crisis, first the Bush and then the Obama administrations embraced the G20 rather than the G8 as the central coordinating mechanism of the global economy. China was now at the head table of the international system. What is more, it had gained further clout not only because it was joined there by other emerging powers but also by virtue of the fact that the established Western powers were back on their heels. China had trillions in reserves, the fastest growth rate of any major country, huge investment inflows, and it had ascended to be the world's second-largest economy. Within the Chinese government, advisers around President Hu Jintao who advocated a more aggressive international stance had gained traction. China's diplomats and treasury officials had rapidly become masters of the international game.

He paused and added, "I'm not sure if some of my colleagues in the U.S. government fully understand what has happened yet. Most of them are lawyers. They are used to getting briefed and then dealing with the next issue on the agenda. Far too few have well-developed worldviews." He was acknowledging a seismic shift in the way the world works and in the way the American system was viewed. Not only was the West blindsided by this shift, but many Westerners in key positions were still not fully aware of what was happening.

China was in its ascendancy, and the missteps of Western bankers and

politicians were helping them. At the same time, other emerging economies were also benefiting, growing faster, claiming a new role on the
international stage. Seeing the flaws in the approaches America had
promoted for decades, they too began to chart much more independent
courses in terms of how they managed their own markets and politics.
Even within Europe, some of America's closest allies, top officials in the
German, French, and British governments, were assailing the "American
model" as the root of recent economic problems. Even former senior U.S.
government officials like the former chairman of the Council of Economic Advisers and Nobel Prize winner Joseph Stiglitz sensed the shift.
Said Stiglitz: "People around the world once admired us for our economy,
and we told them if you wanted to be like us, here's what you have to do—
hand over power to the market. The point now is that no one has respect
for that kind of model anymore given this crisis. And of course it raises
questions about our credibility. Everyone feels they are suffering now
because of us."

A decade and a half ago, we in the United States were celebrating
the triumph of American capitalism and the defeat of state power by the
forces of the marketplace. This came in the form of a victory dance on
the grave of communism and socialism. What is clear today is that our
celebrating was premature.

We have since gone from a battle between capitalism and communism
to something even more complex: a battle between differing forms of capitalism in which the distinction between each lies in the relative role and
responsibilities of public and private actors. As the freewheeling market
model promoted by Washington is reeling from self-inflicted wounds,
other approaches are succeeding. At the same time, those rising models
are vying with one another for influence—from the "capitalism with Chinese characteristics" of China to the "democratic development capitalism"
of India or Brazil, from Northern European approaches to capitalism built
around a strong public-private compact to new entrepreneurial models
found in such places as Singapore, Israel, or the United Arab Emirates.

Listening for Echoes of History

After the 2008–2009 crisis and in the midst of its aftershocks, political
debate in the United States has returned to old familiar themes as though

nothing fundamental has changed in the world or within the way modern economies and societies work. Yet the current argument that is so central to America's national conversation at the moment—and to that of so many countries around the world—about pitting the dangers of "big government" versus those of "big business" is much more than a tired cliché or a distorting oversimplification. It is an unwitting argument both about how the United States will position itself to compete economically in a rapidly changing world and about whether the American system which has for almost a century been seen as a model for the world will continue to influence other countries. That argument is also the latest manifestation of a struggle between public and private power that has gone on for at least a millennium. This struggle is not just about who has influence or who gets the biggest piece of the economic pie, it is about deeper issues like the changing role of national governments in the global era and how they work with, relate to, and sometimes vie for power with rapidly growing multinational corporations and other big private entities such as NGOs or terrorist networks. And make no mistake about it, history demonstrates that when the power of states is reduced, with alarming regularity, it does not benefit average citizens so much as it does big private actors well positioned to swoop in and take best advantage of the opening.

To accept recent headlines merely on their face is to misunderstand them. For example, China's rise may be new, but it is also a return to the status China held as the world's largest economy for most of history, until the early years of the Industrial Revolution. For all that time, through the early nineteenth century, India was second after China. Their current ascendancies and the differences in their two approaches on how to best organize their societies are tied to those long and very different histories.

In the same way, the contest between public and private power, between the power of the check writers and the power of the lawmakers, has been a central engine of change in countries worldwide for centuries. As a consequence, almost everywhere we look, from Europe to Asia to the Americas, we can see historical resonances between today and this seemingly unending effort to balance the interests and roles of states and private actors. In addition, by examining the past we find telling parallels between this millennium-long struggle for political, economic, and social power and the one that preceded it—the battle between church and state.

———

Writing for *Rolling Stone* in the midst of the financial crisis, Matt Taibbi vividly captured the feeling of a seething, abused public by describing Goldman Sachs as "a great vampire squid wrapped around the face of humanity, relentlessly jamming its blood funnel into anything that smells like money." It was potent language. But it also uncannily echoed the imagery of books written more than a century earlier in response to what was then perceived as the overreaching power of the first generation of American corporate giants. There was Ida Tarbell's landmark muckraking history of the Standard Oil Company, Upton Sinclair's *The Jungle*, and Frank Norris's novel about the ruthless expansion of the railroads in the West that was explicitly titled *The Octopus*.

Norris, basing his book on a real bloody land war between California farmers and railroad men, had described the railroad as "the galloping monster, the terror of steel and steam, with its single eye, Cyclopean, red, shooting from horizon to horizon ... the symbol of vast power, huge, terrible, flinging the echo of its thunder over all the reaches of the valley, leaving blood and destruction in its path; the leviathan, with tentacles of steel clutching into the soil, the soulless Force, the iron hearted Power, the monster, the Colossus, the Octopus."

More than simply evoking imagery from the past, however, the Taibbi article and the wave of books, documentaries, blog posts, and cable television shouting matches provoked by the crisis all unearthed much deeper concerns that had preoccupied philosophers and statesmen since the beginning of recorded history.

From Plato, who saw the impulse to do business as a threat to virtuous society, to Thomas More's views expressed in the epigraph to this introduction, doubts have endured about reconciling the pursuit of wealth and the pursuit of a just and equitable society. Within two centuries of More's *Utopia*, as England was recovering from a financial crisis called the South Sea Bubble (see chapter 3), the government of Prime Minister Sir Robert Walpole engineered a bailout of the shareholders of an enterprise called the South Sea Company, many of whom also happened to be members of Parliament. Two Whig critics of Walpole, John Trenchard and Thomas Gordon, wrote a series of 140 essays between 1720 and 1723 under the pseudonym "Cato" in which they bitterly attacked what they saw as the corruption of Great Britain's political class due to their too-close association with leading merchants like those who ran the failed South Sea enterprise. In so doing they revealed that a central, recurrent manifestation of the public-private power struggle would see government and business leaders coverage in what might seem a partnership but actually was more like a conspiracy to undercut the rights of citizens at large.

Trenchard and Gordon continued the theme framed by Plato and More when they wrote, "Very great Riches in private Men are always dangerous to States, because they create a greater Dependence than can be consistent with the Security of any sort of Government whatsoever . . . [they] destroy among the Commons, that Balance of Property and Power, which is necessary to Democracy." Later, they added scathingly, "It has been justly observed of Corporations, or Political Combinations of Men, that they have Bodies but no Souls, nor consequently Consciences."

Set aside conventions of usage, capitalization, and punctuation, and their critiques unerringly presage those of the past few years. Almost three hundred years ago they asserted, for example, "The last parliament were as much Representatives of the South-Sea Company as of the rest of the Kingdom." In 2009, the U.K. newspaper *The Guardian* published a column that was among many at that moment with a very similar message, stating, "By all accounts the UK government has bowed to corporate interests and meaningful reforms have been postponed . . . It is often claimed that Britain has the best democracy that money can buy."

Trenchard and Gordon observed that "Companies . . . alter the Balance of our Government, too much influence our legislature and are ever the Confederates or Tools of ambitious and designing Statesmen." *The Financial Times* carried a column at around the time of Taibbi's article stating, "The influence of finance over political life was reinforced by money. Wall Street bankers regularly appeared at the top of the giving lists for the political parties . . . Now is the time for change . . . Wall Street and the City need to be grown up about this. They might not like the prospect of losing their grip on government and exposing themselves to new ideas. But unless they do, they might just find that the page has indeed been turned and they are no longer on it."

In fact, for all the freshness and urgency of the financial crisis that, at the time of this writing, still buffets the globe, we find a wide array of today's great issues uncannily foreshadowed in events and commentaries from the past. Central elements of our contemporary political debates recur throughout history. Take globalization, for example, and read the stated concern of one of Trenchard and Gordon's admirers, Thomas Jefferson, who wrote a generation later, "Merchants have no country. The mere spot they stand on does not constitute so strong an attachment as that from which they draw their gains." How does that sound in the context of today's debate when even a pro-market publication such as *BusinessWeek* wrote just a couple of months before the fall of Bear Stearns, "In effect, U.S. multinationals have been decoupling from the U.S. economy in the past decade. They still have their headquarters in America, they're still listed on U.S. stock exchanges and most of their shareholders are still American. But their expansion has been mainly overseas."

The echoes of history remind us that much of what we are grappling with today is not just about today's players or today's big companies or today's attitudes but is really about the tension between the age-old desire for a perfect society and the equally ancient impulse to obtain wealth and the influence it brings. They also upend some of the assertions of today's leaders that they are somehow following in the footsteps of their often-cited ideological heroes.

"Leave-it-to-the-markets" conservatives who argue that they are the only true keepers of the spirit of freedom's forefathers would be made as uneasy by rereading Adam Smith's clear statements of discomfort with the power of big corporations. They might also be made more than a little uncomfortable by discovering the close ties between champion of personal liberties and property rights John Locke and the slave trade. (For more on this, see chapter 2. For more on Smith, see chapter 3.) Jefferson later also wrote, "I hope we shall crush in its birth the aristocracy of our moneyed corporations, which dare already to challenge our government to a trial of strength and bid defiance to the laws of our country." Lincoln, another venerated figure, also cited with an epigraph in this chapter, expressed a similar view. So too did other American presidents, both Democrats and Republicans, from Theodore Roosevelt to Woodrow Wilson, who lamented the rise of big corporations and the huge power they had accumulated. Wilson wrote, "We are in the presence of a new organization of society. Our life has broken away from the past."

Within a few years of Wilson's comments, U.S. Supreme Court justice Louis Brandeis would write in his opinion for the case of *Louis K. Liggett Co. et al. v. Lee*, "Through size, corporations . . . have become an institution . . . an institution which has brought such a concentration of economic power that so-called private corporations are sometimes able to dominate the State. Such is the Frankenstein monster which states have created through corporation laws." And soon after, Franklin Roosevelt would write, "The liberty of a democracy is not safe if the people tolerate the growth of private power to a point where it comes stronger than their democratic state itself. That, in its essence, is fascism— ownership of government by an individual, by a group."

Like every generation, we live in a moment that is constantly shaped by the interaction between a past most of us have forgotten and a future no one knows. We have only two useful tools in negotiating such circumstances. The first is to ensure that we understand the past, especially when there is so much evidence to suggest that it contains important lessons for our own time and much to suggest that some of the most important issues of our era have roots that extend back centuries. The second is that we then utilize what we have understood from studying that history to see what is different about today and likely to be different about tomorrow.

The objective of this book is to provide some of that perspective, to set this roiling moment in context and then to look forward at what is new and even unprecedented about the future that is unfolding.

An Essential Relationship in Search of an Elusive Balance

Any such study of the evolution of public and private power demonstrates that both have been repeatedly guilty of deep excesses and both have offered undeniable and enduring benefits. Both have evolved in tandem over time, sometimes seeking to crush each other, sometimes feeding deep mutual dependencies, sometimes allies, sometimes rivals. And such a study suggests that for all societies the most persistent and central challenge associated with this power struggle is defining a proper balance between public and private power.

It is also clear that since 1980, in the United States that balance has been lost. The results have been so damaging that they threaten America's ability to lead both economically and politically. They have, as many from the Chinese government to Joe Stiglitz have accurately concluded, undercut American legitimacy. And they have opened the door for other nations with different models that offer a different balance of public-private power and a different set of associated values to set the terms for the next great period in international social and economic development. The distortions that have taken place within the United States have been packaged and sold worldwide like toothpaste or shampoo by the federal government and other representatives of the U.S. system. And like many other products similarly marketed, they come with misleading claims.

The first of these is that democracy and free markets are somehow two sides of the same coin, both not just promoting but institutionalizing opportunity for the average citizen. While both have undeniably vital and complementary roles to play, this assertion goes too far. The reality is that markets promote efficiency, which in turn rewards scale, which in turn leads to a concentration of economic and therefore political power. (Indeed, the term "markets" implies a degree of organization or social purpose that is regularly offered as a cover for activities that amount to little more than the narrow, sometimes rapacious pursuit of self-interest in ways that harm rather than benefit the greater population.) The second distortion is that striking a blow against the allegedly "overreaching" power of government is a victory for personal freedoms, when in fact it often simply clears the way for power to accrue elsewhere, to private institutions that are less accountable than governments and whose interests do not align with most people's . . . and sometimes to private institutions well equipped and even designed to co-opt the application of power on behalf of the public.

Based on these misconceptions, policies have been promoted and adopted that have had the effect of weakening governments and putting massive segments of the population at risk. Some of these are prescriptions that have been known under the rubric of the "Washington Consensus"—promoting in the name of "liberalization" a retreat or withdrawal of government from the marketplace that has enabled major corporations to gain an unprecedented foothold on the global stage and to play the central role in defining the great historical trend of our time, globalization. Other elements of this liberalization have included opening the door to waves of financial "innovation" that have had massive unintended consequences, from the financialization of core commodities that enables speculators to push higher the price of basic foodstuffs and energy, to the proliferation of derivatives that have swamped all other forms of value-bearing instruments on the planet including, many times over, government-issued money itself. These "liberalizations" have therefore reduced in substantial ways the power of governments to fulfill their historically accepted obligations to their people while at the same time shifting power to those often invisible, largely unaccountable, typically (although not exclusively) private actors who possess the greatest means to influence market outcomes.

Studying history, however, also enables us to see that the rebalancing—the tug-of-war—between public and private power is not just a recent trend, not just a part of a consensus formed in Washington or anywhere else during our lifetime, but has gone on for centuries, and the result has been a gradual, sweeping, systematic redefinition of the role of the state and an unmanaged, not terribly well understood remaking of the international order that impacts the interests of billions. Whether those changes result in a healthy, equitable balance; a backlash against private power in the form of autocracy, communism, or fascism; or, alternatively, in a system where the power of states continues to be undercut both from within and from without by private forces with agendas that are blind to national interests, remains to be seen. It is one of the great pregnant questions of our time.

We have moved from a system in which nation-states were the fundamental building blocks of global society to one in which their most fundamental powers are both constrained and evolving. New global challenges exist far beyond the ability of any one individual nation to respond to them. The basic characteristics that made a state a state—such as the ability to control borders, print and manage a currency, levy taxes, project and use force, or even make and enforce laws—have been chipped away to the point where states are unrecognizable today compared to how they behaved in the past. It is important to understand to what degree this erosion of state prerogatives is the result of natural historical forces and to what extent it is the result of the ongoing political efforts of private actors seeking to constrain or reshape the role of national governments. It is also essential to understand how growing government budgets do not necessarily reflect enhanced government power, as when those budgets merely reflect the meeting of obligations and prior commitments rather than any exercise of choice of influence by leaders or electorates.

Within this altered international system, some states are so diminished they hardly measure up to our old ideas of what a state is supposed to be, or do. They are now just semi-states. And the reality is that this category of diminished actors is so large that it encompasses perhaps 70 to 80 percent of all the countries on the planet. At the same time, private actors have grown so large that perhaps two thousand of them are more influential than those 70 to 80 percent. These private actors are a new class of supercitizens, entities that can marshal and project to their advantage the economic, human, natural, or political resources that once were available only to nations. Ask why the world can't or won't address concerns from global warming, to embracing new forms of energy, to containing global diseases, to regulating global derivatives markets, and you will see the not-so-invisible hand of these megaplayers. These enduring private actors, which were built on an idea once created to serve national interests—the idea of the corporation—have morphed into a group that plays a leading role shaping national and international priorities often without regard for the interests of any one society anywhere—a group with the money and power to institutionalize their ideologies and serve their interests by successfully supporting efforts to translate their ideas into laws or, alternatively, carefully carve out legal and regulatory voids.

Losing Our Way by Losing Perspective

A personal reason led me to write this book. I am drawn by both conscience and curiosity to figure out where we went wrong. I mean this in two ways. In the first instance, I approach this as a former government official who had an international economic portfolio during the Clinton administration. I was among those traveling the world advocating free trade, free markets, and the rising tide of globalization during the salad days of the 1990s boom. Subsequently, I have come to the conclusion that we underestimated the dislocations associated with these processes, just as we overestimated the virtue of private actors to whom we thought we could bequeath major economic and social decisions by "leaving it to the markets."

This is not to repudiate the benefits that global trade and economic liberalization have brought to the world, or to minimize the profound failings of most experiments in centrally planned economies. Rather, it is simply to note the fact that during the years from 1980 to 2008, during which free-market ideologies spread rapidly around the world and governments pulled back from traditional regulatory roles, the benefits of rising income levels worldwide were accompanied by growing inequality. As I noted in my last book, *Superclass*, the gap between the bottom fifth of society and the top fifth grew larger during that period than it had been at any time in history, and it continues to grow worse in many nations, including the United States, today.

In a world in which the richest one thousand people have assets that are equivalent to the wealth of the two billion poorest, or in which the reckless overreach of superpowerful financial corporations can trigger global recessions that impoverish hundreds of millions, or in which giant energy producers can influence climate policies that put the planet itself at risk, it is urgent that we constantly reassess how we balance the legitimate desire to grow the global economy and the moral responsibility of doing so with some semblance of fairness.

I do not think it is entirely an accident that during the era of the rise of corporate powers, nations have come to regularly measure their success in terms of a gross metric of wealth creation rather than in terms of their higher objective of improving the general well-being of their citizens. In the same way, we must ask how, during the financial crisis, although big banks caused great damage to society—often as a direct result of misrepresentation, concealment, and rapacious pursuit of their narrow self-interests—they were able to wield the power both to be rewarded for their wrongdoing in the form of bailouts and, for the most part, to avoid prosecution. It is a phenomenon that seems closely related in its roots to the recent decision by the U.S. Supreme Court to enable corporations to spend more to influence the outcomes of elections, which further gave supercitizens an unfair advantage over "ordinary" citizens. It is not so much that justice is blind, but that we have established its price.

This is related to the second half of my "Where did we go wrong?" question: Where did the certainty that "leave it to the markets" was the right answer to so many questions come from? Were we convinced or co-opted by decades of extraordinary U.S. success and the creation of the most prosperous economy in the history of the world? (Not a small thing, of course. But it is a title that has been held by many nations throughout history.) Were we too focused on the recent past, blind to what was happening elsewhere? Were we, in this respect too, missing broader historical trends, the historical perspective that is particularly useful at times like these that are fraught with emotion and that are seen as possible breaks from the past?

Much of value has already been written on the subject covered by this book. But many previous books either were too colored by their time or have been, to a degree, for all their considerable merits, overtaken by events that variously undercut or amplify points they made.

In the 1970s, Richard Barnet and Ronald E. Muller's *Global Reach* asserted that "corporations are far from the 'engines of development' that they claim to be, abusing their leverage and duping their customers." They went on to say that multinationals undermine the "power of the nation-state to maintain economic and political stability within its territory." Their view was echoed in other books of the era, notably Raymond Vernon's *Sovereignty at Bay*. Vernon believed that the relationship between multinational companies and national governments was inherently fraught with tension. He argued that managing the tension would be of special importance going forward but that it had tilted in favor of multinationals in a way that was likely to produce a backlash. This was due in part to the fact that at the time, big global companies were seen primarily as American enterprises, a trigger for some of the pushback they felt.

Between the 1970s and the 1990s, a major transformation occurred. The welfare state and the intellectual currents of the midcentury were supplanted by the market-driven ideas of Ronald Reagan, Margaret Thatcher, Milton Friedman, and other proponents of the Chicago School of economics. Globalization had come to be seen as a defining trend of the time, aided as it was by technological breakthroughs in information and transportation technologies. And of course, the primary economic-political struggle of the twentieth century, between capitalism and communism, had also been resolved. State-dominated economies were destined for the ash heap of history. And the literature of the times reflected that perspective, notably Daniel Yergin and Joseph Stanislaw's *The Commanding Heights: The Battle for the World Economy*. Their book masterfully told the story of how the private sector and the forces of the market had, since the Second World War, seemingly achieved decisive superiority in their rivalry with the state. Smaller but equally influential books such as John Micklethwait and Adrian Wooldridge's *The Company: A Short History of a Revolutionary Idea* were infused with a certain degree of triumphalism. Anglo-American capitalism's apotheosis had inspired the literary component of that premature victory celebration mentioned earlier. Even Vernon, writing his last book, *In the Hurricane's Eye: Troubled Prospects for Multinational Enterprises*, in 1991 acknowledged how much had changed to the advantage of multinational enterprises.

Another thread among writers interested in this topic has been visible in the recent profusion of books seeking to interpret the rise of big emerging markets such as China, India, and Brazil, and what this might mean for America, the West, and corporate interests. These have ranged from Ian Bremmer's *The End of the Free Market: Who Wins the War Between States and Corporations?* to John Kampfner's *Freedom for Sale: Why the World Is Trading Democracy for Security.* And of course there have been a host of other books on the lasting impact of globalization on government and society, including two of Thomas L. Friedman's terrific books, *The World Is Flat* and *Hot, Flat, and Crowded,* as well as Anne-Marie Slaughter's smart and provocative *New World Order.*

There is considerable overlap between these other books and mine, and indeed, even though I have benefited greatly from the work of all these other authors and learned much from them, it was striking to me that in the case of all but *The Company,* the focus was primarily on the recent, rather than the remote, past. But as I read through them all, it seemed to me that the roots of all the big questions posed by recent circumstances reached much farther back in time.

I can't help but recall that the question of properly framing our own moment in history came up in one of my very first interviews for this book. I was meeting with Lawrence Summers while he was still President Barack Obama's chief economic adviser. I asked him whether the recent economic crisis had produced a political sea change that would reverse the more market-friendly trends of the past thirty years.

He shifted in his seat and didn't answer for a bit. "You know," he began, "I think that's why I would have made a terrible journalist. While I understand the impulse to see every development as a watershed, as a big turning point, I tend to see things more in a longer-term historical context, as a product of slower-moving fundamental trends." I remember thinking this was the kind of attitude that might lead to actually missing watersheds when they happen. But while I believe the Obama team has been guilty of clinging to old economic formulations for too long and not recognizing or responding to fundamental structural changes and flaws in our economy, Summers's overall instinct on this particular point matched my own views. It was an antidote to the kind of temporal narcissism from which we all suffer: the desire to view the period in which we live as a unique moment in history, above and apart from all that have come before.

From the Age of the Vikings to a Looming Reckoning

The first section of the book that follows starts at a genuine watershed in history, this one ancient, with the story of the rise of the oldest corporation still in existence. That company, born a thousand years ago in the age of the Vikings amid the rolling hills of medieval Sweden, will serve for us as a kind of "everycompany," a character to which we will regularly return because its history serves as such a useful touchstone over the centuries during which corporate power evolved and grew. Part I then looks at four pivotal years and eras in which revolutionary thinking transformed the world and our views of public and private power. The first such year is 1288, the year in which the oldest corporation's first stock transaction was recorded. This period allows us to consider the pivotal power struggle that preceded and in some ways presaged that between companies and states: the contest between church and state. The next period we'll consider centers on 1648, the year of the Treaty of Westphalia, a development important to the emergence of the modern nation-state. The third key year is 1776, the year of the American Declaration of Independence and Adam Smith's *Wealth of Nations*. The final year examined in the first part of the book is 1848, a year of political revolution in Europe and the year of *The Communist Manifesto* as well as the arrival of Andrew Carnegie in America, and of the acceleration of the Industrial Revolution. The purpose of this section is to investigate the development of our foundational ideas about the relative and specific roles of governments and private enterprises.

Next, the middle section of the book, "The Contest: The State Constrained, the Corporation Unbound," explores several of the most significant powers and privileges that have historically defined the role of the state and its special status. These privileges range from the right to legitimately use force to the right to print money or to control borders. This section examines how in each case history has worked to diminish and in some cases erase those prerogatives, often with the active collaboration of private sector actors who directly benefited from the changes. It will also consider how the private sector began to take advantage of the power vacuums created by each new constraint on the state.

The final section, "The Reckoning: Forging a New Order," examines where we are today in this time of financial crises and uncertain relationships. This section looks at the recent events in the trends revealed in the first two parts of the book and looks forward. It explores what it means to live in a world of a comparative handful of traditional major powers, of semi-states that are now only shadows of what states once were, and of a rising class of private powers, massive, influential, enduring supercitizens with global interest and growing clout with roles far greater than any ordinary, individual participants in society. It also looks at how companies, in order to adapt, are behaving more like countries, and how countries, likewise, are behaving more like companies. This section will also look ahead and describe how companies and countries must adapt their strategies to this new reality, what seems to be working and what does not, and how our theories and international structures must also be updated to reflect the new order.

In concluding, the final chapter will explore the coming ideological reckoning among the competing capitalisms, each of which seeks a different balance between public and private power often guided by very different social goals and views of the roles not only of states and companies but also of individuals and communities.

It should be noted that one could write a very different version of this book using as primary touchstones, for example, developments in China, Japan, or India that paralleled and often preceded those in the West. For the purposes of this story, in light of the fact that many of the inner workings of modern capitalism developed in the Western world, I have tilted the balance slightly in the direction of Europe and the United States— although much of the final portion of the book deals with the rise of Asia and with the likelihood that Asian views on the balance between public and private power as well as on the overall organization of society are likely to be ever more important, indeed central, in the years ahead.

Naturally, no single volume can hope to cover such a complex issue as thoroughly as the subject warrants. But with some luck, through spending a little time exploring history in the company of some of its most interesting actors—including, very shortly, an inquisitive Swedish goat—we can gain some new insights into the current challenges we face and thus perhaps come to a few good conclusions about how to repair our fractured, fragile international system and the nation-states in which we live, and how to avoid the consequences suffered in the past during those eras when rules and realities did not align.

Part 1

The Roots of Modern Power: The Rise of States and Corporations

1 ■ The Goat with the Red Horns

In the abyss itself lie in wild confusion—pell-mell—stones, slag
and scoria, and an eternal, stupefying sulphurous vapour rises
from the depths, as if the hell-broth, whose reek poisons and kills
all the green gladsomeness of nature, were being brewed down
below. One would think this was where Dante went down and
saw the Inferno, with all its horror and immitigable pain.

—E.T.A. Hoffmann, "The Mines of Falun"

The Past, Present, and Future of the Power Struggle That Defines Our Times

Throughout the writing of this book, I have had an image in my mind. It
is of one of those charts showing the evolution of mankind. You know
the type: they begin with an ape, heavy-browed, bent over, walking on all
fours. They end with us, *Homo sapiens*, walking upright and looking
somewhat brighter. The chart in my imagination however, illustrates
another side of the story of human evolution. Rather than presenting us
from a purely biological perspective—from the point of view of where, for
example, in our family trees we picked up those useful opposable thumbs
or the ability to digest frozen yogurt—it is describing a much more recent, still-unfolding aspect of our collective development. The imagined
diagram, like this book, focuses on stages of our social evolution. More
specifically, it describes the evolution of some of the most important organizations by which we bring order and productivity to our societies.
As it happens, these are also the mechanisms by which power is distributed and wielded, by which rules are formulated and enforced, by which
human collaborations and conflicts are facilitated.

Studying these organizations closely, you begin to wonder whether
they themselves are actually the alpha organisms on the planet, the life
forms that rule here on earth and of which we individuals make up only

the temporary and replaceable working parts—much like the giant interconnected families of *Armillaria ostoyae*, also known as honey mushrooms, can grow to cover thousands of acres and live for millennia. A mushroom here or there gets lopped off, tossed into a salad, or eaten by some charming woodland critter, but the rest of the organism goes on about its business, sucking the water and nutrients out of great forests of trees that tower above the largely unseen fungus but that ultimately succumb to *Armillaria*'s superior organization.

After all, we individual human beings are fragile, small, and—at least for the moment—not even capable of reproducing while acting alone. Our time here is limited, and unsurprisingly, this unfortunate twist in the rules of nature has weighed heavily on us. Almost all human societies have cooked up higher powers that we define as higher first and foremost because they are immortal. And one of the things that distinguish us from the organizations we have created to live within is that they too are designed to be immortal, to outlast us and thus in some important respects to be above us like the gods themselves . . . or like large, enduring fungal networks.

In my imagined chart, the great-ape phase of evolution is the family, the basic social building block of every stage of human civilization. Then comes the tribe, and then the village. After that we see the development of ever larger, stronger, more complex products of organizational evolution until we reach one of those forks in the road, a little bit like the one that occurred during the period during which Neanderthals and *Homo sapiens* lived simultaneously. Grappling with the choice we face at that crossroads is where we have been these past few hundred years. On the one hand, there is an organizational approach that often seems to have much in common with the Neanderthals, better suited to the past but still strong and with much to recommend it. At the same time, we can see the irreversible rise of another one, not fully formed perhaps, suggesting several evolutionary steps to come, but clearly better suited to the global environment that is developing and changing around it.

On this timeline, however, the Neanderthals are national governments (this illustration was not created, I should hasten to say, because governments are on the verge of extinction, but rather because they are not as well suited to thrive in their current environment as some of their contemporaries on the organizational evolutionary chart), and the *Homo sapiens*, the ones that seem to have the evolutionary edge, are corporations—or at least global structures that are a lot more like multi-national companies than they are like the traditional images of countries that we have today. No doubt some might say this is comparing humans to apes—apples and oranges as primates go—evolutionary cousins but clearly not the same species. But tell that to the companies and the governments. They have been locked in a power struggle with each other since the earliest days that companies were ushered into being by sovereigns who used them for economic purposes. They are different, but they are often compelled to occupy the same space. They are different, but in order to survive, it may well be that each must become more like the other. They are different, but they are both facing major evolutionary hurdles that must be addressed if they are to continue to exist in a rapidly changing international environment.

Also, as with the story of human evolution, this one is not without controversy. Just as the idea that men descended from the same ancient grandma as lemurs and chimps is offensive to those who take the Bible as literal truth, so too is the idea that somehow corporations are usurping the traditional place of countries on the international stage, thus upsetting some deeply ingrained, very nearly theological intellectual conventions. For example, to that group of political scientists who call themselves "realists," this idea undercuts a central tenet of their worldview. Of course, one must always be skeptical of groups that give themselves a name that implies that only their adherents "get it" and that everyone else is by definition out of touch with "reality." And in this instance, the skepticism is warranted despite the fact that "realists" trace their intellectual origins back thousands of years to venerable characters whose names are now inscribed on library friezes, such as Thucydides. Because while realism is purportedly built around the study of power, "realist" theory suggests that international power is solely concentrated in the hands of states. Private actors don't really have a role in the realist cosmology. This despite the fact that today private organizations often and obviously wield power in ways that once only countries could, and in some cases in ways that many countries no longer can.

Many companies have greater economic resources at their disposal than many countries. Countries once derived power from their ability to print money, but now most can't or don't or have ceded the power to set the value of their currencies to markets. In fact, most of the value-bearing instruments in today's financial markets are actually created by private organizations, traded in private markets, and only very lightly if at all regulated or understood by governments. And recently governments have concluded that the fate of private financial institutions is so important to the well-being of society that when those institutions falter—even as a result of greed and, in some cases, malfeasance—it is incumbent upon states to prop up the private entities even as private entities have from time to time propped up states.

Countries once controlled borders, but now borders are no longer the effective barriers to commerce or cultural exchange they once were, and while states are weakened by this, global private actors are strengthened. Multinational corporations effortlessly move capital, products, services, and production facilities across borders that are far more porous now than they were in the past. As has been the case almost since their very inception, private actors also have the ability to project force and influence political outcomes, and many have far more developed mechanisms of international persuasion than do the vast majority of countries. Think about the private military companies that the U.S. government employs to fight in the Middle East, or the influence that corporate lobbyists wield in democratic legislatures, or the success that some major energy companies have had in forestalling action on climate change and other environmental issues.

To be fair, even more recently developed theories of international relations such as liberalism (which is similar to realism but stresses the pacifying effects of free trade, democracy, and international institutions) and constructivism (a theory that focuses on cultural factors and asserts that the international system is a social construct) mention private actors only in passing despite their growing influence and role in the global era. In short, most theories of how international society works—the supposed focus of the academic discipline of international relations—are state-centric. Which, as I suggest, is either to miss or to grossly undervalue an important part of what is shaping today's world and will shape tomorrow's.

Such intellectual blind spots lead, not surprisingly, to some pretty important flaws in theories on which some pretty important decision making is based. For example, they lead to the thought that the central work involved in advancing national interests involves diplomacy between states. They also assume that national borders define sovereign bubbles in which there is considerably more unity of purpose among resident actors than there actually is. Yet as we all can see from recent headlines, nonstate actors from giant corporations to terrorist groups act in their narrow self-interest and in ways that are often at odds with the policy of the states in which they live and operate. While states are at no risk of disappearing, as the Neanderthals did, many weaker states are nowhere near as influential as the emerging class of globally active "supercitizens," private mega-organizations that wield great clout on economic, social, environmental, and a host of other issues (far beyond that of ordinary people operating in national political systems—hence the term "supercitizens"). Whom would you pick in a one-on-one contest to influence, say, global climate talks—ExxonMobil or Morocco? Who has more clout in an effort to impact global financial markets—JPMorgan Chase or the Central Bank of Thailand? If you were the U.S. governor in postinvasion Iraq, whom would you have chosen to protect you—the Iraqi army or Blackwater?

In addition, while the international relations theories taught in most schools assume that the biggest security threats to states come from other states, it has also been clear for quite some time that nonstate actors pose real risks. But some of the risks to the security and soundness of states that have been posed by the private sector are much more insidious and slow-moving. Over the past several centuries, the accumulation of power on the part of private actors has been, as we will see, slowly, often invisibly, but directly linked to the atrophying of states' muscle, role, and prerogatives.

For a number of years now, observant students of the world have noted important aspects of these problems associated with many of the mainstream ideas about how the world is organized. From my colleague Jessica Mathews in her 1997 article "Power Shift" in *Foreign Affairs* to perceptive academics like Princeton's Anne-Marie Slaughter in her book *A New World Order* or Harvard's Joe Nye in his book *The Future of Power*, political analysts have explored different dimensions of the changes that are afoot. These authors and others have noted that most "modern" ideas are based on a notion of a world of nation-states that dates back to the middle of the seventeenth century. They have made the case that in order to be truly realistic, contemporary theories need to take into consideration that power is more dispersed and more complex than previously thought. They also suggest that we are in a transitional period that will be marked by the continuing transfer of power from governments to nonstate actors.

In an era like ours, of emerging transnational threats and challenges from global warming to combating the proliferation of weapons of mass destruction, nation-states will have to develop new and more effective forms of international cooperation in order to achieve their objectives and maintain their relevance. Public-private partnerships will become essential to offset public-private rivalries. Indeed, public-private partnerships are already absolutely essential for handling global financial markets, managing our shared climate, or even projecting force halfway around the world. In some cases, countries may have to become more like companies. And at the same time, as the latter grow and their impact amplifies, companies may well have to become more and more like states in recognizing that a tacit social contract exists between them and a civilization that allows them to play such a central role.

In other words, we live in a world in which the old rules don't apply and we don't have a fully developed set of new ones. Changes are happening rapidly, and each major development of the past decade—from financial crises to wars to global warming—suggests that as has happened in the past, periods of transition in which there is broad disagreement about how the world is or can or should be ordered are very dangerous indeed. And for all these reasons, this is a story that must be told in a book rather than as a chart.

The Goat with Red Horns

There is one other important difference between my image of the chart of human organizational evolution and the conventional one featuring our knuckle-dragging forefathers. My chart tells a story that begins not with an ape, but with a goat.

The story of human evolution, we are told, began in the hot, humid landscapes of Africa. Our goat, however, first appears in a much colder place, in what today you would call Sweden. One can't be precisely sure when it took place; perhaps it was during the reign of Sweden's first king, Olof Skotkonung. But our story has less to do with Olof than with an anonymous goatherd who was tending his flock in central Sweden in the region then known as Dalarna or Dalecarlia. The goat belonged to a farmer whose name has been lost to time. But according to local lore, the goat was named Kare, and one day it wandered off onto the forested slopes near the town of Falun, which until the goat's adventure was an unremarkable rural village located between two lakes. After no doubt causing his owner considerable consternation by his absence, Kare eventually strolled back home. That is when he created an even bigger stir. Because now, the previously perfectly ordinary goat's previously perfectly ordinary horns had turned red.

Shocked, the farmer retraced Kare's steps looking for something to explain his goat's transformation. Ultimately he came across a bog that the adventurous animal had apparently explored. There he noticed a rust-colored puddle atop a vein of reddish-orange soil. And this, according to the stories they have told for a millennium, is how copper was first discovered in Sweden in a place that would someday be known as Stora Kopparberg, the Great Copper Mountain.

For most of the past thousand years, Stora Kopparberg was also the name taken by the enterprise devoted to mining that mountain. Its story is important to us because it so closely traces the rise of business and the twists and turns in the relationship between business and government, both the symbiosis and the tug-of-war between public and private power.

Enter the Everycompany

The business that grew up from the discovery by that wayward goat is considered by many experts to be the oldest continuously operating corporation in the world. There are documents from an early share transaction involving Stora that date back to 1288. Today, the company, renamed Stora Enso, is a booming multinational with operations in more than thirty-five countries—an important but not terribly well known enterprise that controls half as much territory as Belgium and has annual sales that are larger than the GDP of almost a hundred countries. Stora is among the world's oldest companies, and for the purposes of this book it can usefully serve as the "everycompany," both as an independent entity and in terms of its relationship with Sweden and ultimately, inevitably, other nation-states, a touchstone for those seeking to understand how the structure of the world economy came to be what it is today.

As a consequence, the horns of Kare the goat are, in some respects, the nibs of a pen, and the reddish liquid into which they were dipped are the ink with which we will write an important part of our story. And the business that grew from the copper mountain and the country that spawned that business are among that story's most important protagonists, characters to which we will return throughout because key events in their history illustrate so well the evolution that we seek to understand.

You could hardly pick a place that would seem less likely to be an Eden of free enterprise than the terrain around Falun. It lay at the northern frontier of European civilization in a region that for half of the year is typically bitterly cold and inhospitable. In that area much of the terrain was too rocky or rough to be useful for farming. Few people lived in the area, and during the Viking Age that preceded the discovery of copper by several hundred years, what few historical records there are suggest that those people were pretty tough customers. Indeed, residents of Dalecarlia have continued to be known as an independent breed, a fact that would lead both to the impulse to hew great riches from unyielding rock and to regular conflicts with Swedish kings who sought to impose their sovereign will upon them.

But under the region's typically cold and often forbidding landscape lay an extraordinary resource, one so great that it would ultimately become not only the linchpin of Sweden's economy when the country was one of the world's foremost powers during the seventeenth and eighteenth centuries, but a vital driver of Europe's economy from the late Middle Ages through the Industrial Revolution. It was home to Europe's most abundant supply of copper, producing at one point in the seventeenth century 70 percent of the entire continent's copper. Mining activity is thought to have begun in the region around the time of King Olof. Initially, the "mining" was pretty superficial—locals scraping out a little of the precious metal near the surface and smelting it for use around their farms and in their daily activities. But within decades the mining became more organized, and within two centuries, the approach to tapping the riches took a turn that marked a bright line in history, the moment when a new way of organizing human activity took root in that rocky, rust-colored soil.

It is important to note, of course, that while the corporation today known as Stora Enso may be the oldest business so organized to still be in operation, it is hardly the first corporation, nor is it anything like the world's oldest business. The Japanese construction company Kongo Gumi, now part of Takamatsu Corporation, was reportedly founded in 578. Several dozen other businesses still in existence are known to predate Stora, including a rather remarkable number of restaurants, hotels, breweries, and wine- and liquor-making establishments in Europe and Japan.

Because of Life's Uncertainty and Doubtful Course

What makes Stora so relevant is that it is the oldest example still in operation of a corporation, a legal entity owned by shareholders that had a status all its own. The idea of incorporation—literally meaning embodiment, giving an idea legal standing on its own—has evolved greatly over time. Many of the legal features of the modern corporation have their origins in ancient Rome, where the Romans pioneered the idea of the business corporation as a legal "person" with shareholders and limited liability. Initially, the corporation was seen as something endowed with its status by the sovereign, beholden to that sovereign and very limited in the scope of its undertaking and rights. How the idea has developed since, and how corporations have over time come to be seen as the full legal equivalent of citizens and then as entities sometimes rivaling states, is the subject of this book.

From its earliest days, Stora was organized in a way that lent itself to the corporate shareholder structure. Miners had rights to particular portions of the mine based on their efforts and capabilities to bring up and melt down the ore. Agreements had to be drawn up among those who had such rights to protect their collective interests. Ultimately, those rights were reflected in share documents that themselves had value and could be bought and sold.

Stora's claims to being the oldest continuously operating corporation in the world are tied to the document that offers the first evidence of its existence. That document is a Deed of Exchange dated June 16, 1288. This mottled and now brittle sheet of parchment, bedecked with massive wax seals attesting to its official nature, records a deal between a man named Peter, Bishop of Vasteras, and his nephew, Niccolai Kristinesson, by which Peter purchased back from his nephew a one-eighth interest in the copper mountain. He had previously transferred the share to his nephew in exchange for some cash that the cleric needed to serve his bishopric.

Despite the fact that the document suggests Peter grappled with cash flow problems, it also attests to his elevated status within society and his keen eye for business opportunities. Living on a large estate featuring its own little subeconomy of mills, pastures, fisheries, and forests, Peter was a man of Sweden's upper class. As such, he was aware of the latest news about economic developments throughout Northern Europe. The mine at Falun had already been a going concern for two hundred years when he bought into it, but Peter got wind of some important technological developments that he concluded improved its chances of future profitability.

A group of monks had tipped him off to the fact that Stora Kopparberg had made some improvements in the waterwheel technology used to power the mine. (A literal and figurative grace note as far as our story is concerned, as in many ways the Catholic Church was really the world's first global "private" enterprise and, as we shall later see, the Reformation was in many ways the first nationalist backlash against globalization.) As a consequence, Peter felt it important to purchase back from his nephew the share in the mine, which he did in exchange for an estate, mills, and fishing rights. One journalist has cited this first recorded corporate transaction as also being the earliest recorded case of "insider trading."

The fact that Bishop Peter's share exchange was sanctioned by Sweden's king is further evidence not only of his place in society but also of the place of this transaction in the country's economic life. The document reads:

> We, Peter, by the grace of God bishop in Vasteras, greet all who see this letter in the name of the Savior of all men. Because of life's uncertainty and its doubtful course, even those proceedings carried out in a legal manner are at times obscured by the darkness of oblivion. The endurance of truth should, therefore, be strengthened for posterity by letters and witnesses. Led by this wise consideration, we wish to make known to all through this letter that we assigned to our nephew, Niccolai Kristinesson, an eighth share in the copper mountain . . . which as is known, had been acquired throughout our care; and this in return for a loan which we in our first year in office, with its many needs, had received from our nephew . . . Later . . . we made such an exchange with the said Niccolai that the possession of the above-mentioned eighth share shall return to us and our church. And he in its place shall have the Froslunda estate . . . together with the mills . . . and also all that lawfully belongs thereto, to occupy freely in perpetuity . . . And in order that in the future no false statements can be made concerning this, we have had this letter written and have had it sealed with the seal of our Exalted and Illustrious Lord, Magnus, King of Sweden.

The signature and seal of King Magnus Ladislaus ensured that the transaction would be recognized as sanctioned and would deter future challenges to the ownership rights it transferred. But it also was indicative of the fact that the Swedish crown was deeply involved in the activities of the mine from its earliest days. The reasons are severalfold. First, at the time, the rights of sovereigns were pretty much unlimited throughout Europe, as monarchs not only controlled the means to impose their will but were seen as the sole legitimate legal forces, endowed by divine providence with their power. But beyond this, Sweden's kings quickly came to see the great copper mountain as one of the vital economic organs of their society. The copper from the mines was used to forge weapons for Sweden's armies. The copper was also exported throughout Europe by merchants, including prominently those from the Hanseatic League (an alliance of cities from what we now think of as northern Germany). Through what might be seen as an important surge in the movement toward "globalized" markets, these traders saw to it that Falun's copper made its way to virtually every corner of Europe, thus providing important hard currency for Sweden's treasury, as well as for Bishop Peter and the other owners of the mine.

The copper went to local uses as well. It was made into cannons for the Royal Navy. It was used by the upper crust of Swedish society for the roofs of their homes, for kettles, for bathtubs, for kettle drums and church bells. It was used as collateral to pay off foreign debts, finance wars, and defray other pressing expenses. For all these reasons, the involvement of the state in the development of the business of the miners from Dalecarlia was significant and growing, consistent with the role other states would play in the development of early "big businesses," and would ultimately be a source of contention between the power of the Swedish crown and the private owners of the mine. In fact, throughout the Middle Ages and the Renaissance, while the crown played a central role in controlling Sweden's copper trade, it was also so very dependent on the work of the hardscrabble men who worked beneath the surface of the copper mountain that it was often very difficult to tell who was controlling whom. In this respect, even in the early days of its existence, Stora Kopparberg illustrates both the norms of early public-private sector relations and also the central tension that would shape those relations for the ensuing eight hundred years.

A Royal Charter for Hell Signed on the
First Saturday in Lent

By 1336, when he was about twenty years old, Sweden's king Magnus IV, also known as Magnus Eriksson, was monarch of Sweden, Norway, and a substantial chunk of Denmark called Scania. He had also married a member of the French aristocracy and legitimately saw himself as being in the first tier of European rulers. But ruling such a far-flung kingdom meant putting down costly rebellions, dealing with challenges at his borders—from those with Russian principalities in the East to those with the Danes in the South (also costly)—and ensuring that the nobility who had granted the king the right to rule felt that their economic interests were being served through growth at home (not surprisingly, also a burden on the royal coffers).

For all these reasons, Magnus took an increasing interest in the mines at Falun, ultimately determining to visit them in 1347 with the objective of reasserting royal authority over them by issuing a royal charter setting up a new, more clearly delineated set of rules by which the miners could prosper and yet serve the interests of the kingdom. What Magnus found when he got to Falun in 1347 was unlikely to have been very appealing. Rolling hills and glistening lakes aside, the deeper the miners dug into the mountainside, the grimmer the enterprise became. And although we have no contemporary descriptions of the mine from the mid-fourteenth century, visitors from ensuing centuries offer up a number of descriptions that are so consistent and unvarying that they help suggest a picture of what Magnus saw in 1347 when he visited Falun and the enterprise that had made it a boom town.

While Falun and the mine were not seen to resemble the "peaceful communities filled with the familiar smells of meadows and farmyards" that more or less defined the rest of the Swedish landscape, visitors did regularly suggest it resembled another place that also happens to be located well below the surface of the earth. An Englishman who visited in 1708 wrote:

> The traveler on his way here is seized by terror even from afar when he sees the dark and heavy smoke which the city ceaselessly spews forth in such quantities that the stranger is inclined to believe that he has come to the cave of Cyclops rather than to a city. The smoke derives from the fur-

naces that are spread out over an area of a square mile around the Varpan and Runn lakes. When the wind is from the west, this smoke darkens the city so that there is twilight at midday, and the inhabitants must light torches to be able to go about their business. All the private and public buildings in the city are blacked by soot, and all the brass ornaments out of doors are covered by verdigris.

While the residents of the town rationalized the situation by developing the belief that the black smoke that emanated from the mine was actually good for their health, they could hardly have helped but notice that it gradually killed off all plant life in a wide radius around the town. Perhaps it was the desolation that led renowned Swedish botanist Carl von Linne to remark after having visited the mine in 1734 that it was "Sweden's greatest wonder, but as terrible as Hell itself." Linne continued:

> No *theologus* has ever been able to describe Hell so frightfully as it appears here. Down in the crowded passageways, buried like moles, the laborers go like black assistants of Satan, surrounded by soot and darkness, smoke and fumes, naked to the waist, with a woolen rag in front of their mouths to keep from breathing in smoke and dust by the heap; the sweat runs out of their bodies like a woolen bag . . .

The abysmal working conditions were also treacherous. From the moment they approached the mine, miners risked falls from great heights, the collapse of tunnels, being crushed by falling debris, or being burned by the constant fires that were lit to soften the stone so that ore could be carved out. Linne wrote, "A cave-in, in which everything might crumble in a heap in less than an instant, was feared at any minute, without the least hope of safety . . . Fear of being so far underground and of such darkness and danger, raised the hair on my head, so that I desired nothing more than to once more be able to stand on the surface of the earth." Others echoed the netherworldly theme. A visitor in 1662 wrote of the miners, "Since they are rather black, and grope around in the blue haze like goats on rocks, those who go down there in the dust and smoke and darkness look like mountain trolls and small devils, so that a stranger may become dizzy when he regards the men with torches."

About a century and a half later, it was clear that word of the appalling conditions had spread so far that E.T.A. Hoffmann, the famed German author of *The Nutcracker* and the subject of Offenbach's famous opera *The Tales of Hoffmann*, took it upon himself to memorialize them in his short story "The Mines of Falun." The story is based loosely on the sad tale of a young miner named Mats Israelsson, who not only suffered a horrible fate but also had to suffer the indignity of being known to history as "Fat Mats." Israelsson was setting fires deep underground in 1676 when a large cave-in buried him alive. Quickly forgotten, he joined the ranks of the countless others entombed within the mine. Then, forty-two years later, a new generation of miners was digging in the area in which he had been lost and came upon the chamber in which Mats had been sealed. In it they found the body of a young miner. Although such discoveries were fairly commonplace, the boy's appearance was not. Mats's body was still soft, his clothes intact. But when he was brought to the surface no one could think of anyone who had been lost fairly recently—which was their assumption because of his well-preserved appearance.

Then, an elderly lady, Margareta Olsdotter, heard about the discovery and took it upon herself to investigate. When she saw the body she immediately recognized the face of her lover of four decades before—Mats, the man who proposed to her shortly before he disappeared into the mine. Preserved by the mine's copper sulfate, "Fat Mats" was subsequently laid to rest in a nearby cemetery, but his story became so widely known that he was commonly thereafter referred to as "the world's most famous" resident of Falun.

Like other writers, Hoffmann was captivated by the romantic and tragic nature of the story (and like others he overlooked the fact that Margareta actually ended up being married twice after Mats's disappearance). But he too could hardly resist the familiar metaphors when describing the environment in which his miner hero lived and died:

> In the abyss itself lie in wild confusion—pell-mell—stones, slag and scoria, and an eternal, stupefying sulphurous vapour rises from the depths, as if the hell-broth, whose reek poisons and kills all the green gladsomeness of nature, were being brewed down below. One would think this was where Dante went down and saw the Inferno, with all its horror and immitigable pain.

Despite the clear consensus that the mine was a dangerous, putrid, and filthy place to work, there are also many references from Hoffmann's fiction and reports from Linne and other visitors that the miners were happy to have the work they did. Linne observed, "In these dark chambers where a cave-in is constantly feared, this condemned people carried on; happy beings; for they claw and fight to come there. How dark and horrible it ever may be, workers are never lacking; but rather people seek with force and the greatest energy to come to work there."

In fact, the same thing that drew the workers to the mine also drew Magnus Eriksson: the opportunity to tap into the riches nature had left beneath Falun's soil. Miners made more on average than any other comparable group in Sweden. Those who owned shares in the mine or who had permanent concessions grew wealthy. And the king came to town to ensure he was guaranteed his piece of the pie. His vehicle was a royal charter that outlined the rules and responsibilities for the miners. But it is worth noting that the king recognized even in the mid-fourteenth century the importance of protecting certain of the miners' rights and prerogatives, granting them among other liberties the right to own private property in exchange for their labor. This was an important first concession. It assured the king that the enterprise would continue running smoothly, but it also gave the miners a taste of independence that would grow over time. Those who gained the concessions would later use them as the foundation to claim additional privileges and ultimately, five centuries later, to break away from state ownership altogether. It was a story that may have begun with Stora but would be repeated countless times during the next half millennium.

Magnus however, was simply looking to ensure cash flows and his authority for the moment. His charter decreed that master miners would oversee production in exchange for royalties and that they would be overseen by a royal bailiff who reported directly to the king. In return, the enterprise was granted a number of unusual privileges that underscored its unique role within Sweden's economy. The charter states, in language echoed by other such documents throughout Europe that clearly communicates the great and unquestioned power of the sovereign over all aspects of life at the time:

> We, Magnus, by the grace of God King of Sweden, Norway, and Scania, greet you Mastermen and all the common people on the copper mountain, in the name of our Lord . . .
>
> First, we grant that everyone who clears by burning and puts the

timber axe over the forest and is a day laborer who goes daily to the mine . . . possesses the ground without paying rent . . .

We also graciously vouchsafe, as has previously been done, that any man who is outlawed in Sweden, wherever it may be in the kingdom, who is a man willing and able to work for his bread, may and shall all have sanctuary among you and remain there in peace, unless he be a murderer of his master, a traitor, a proven thief, or a molester of women . . .

In all matters all the people at the mine, each in his place, shall do as the [royal] bailiff orders . . .

Over the next several decades the mine boomed, and the importance of asserting control over it became a central concern for the monarchs of Sweden. In 1396, Queen Margarita followed Magnus's example and reasserted royal authority over the mine, as did many of her successors over the centuries that followed. During those centuries, royally chartered enterprises, semiautonomous businesses that were granted special privileges in exchange for advancing the interests of the state, became more and more common throughout Europe. As we shall see, Stora's example presaged those of much better known companies, widely acknowledged predecessors of today's multinationals such as the Muscovy Company, the British East India Company, the Dutch East India Company, and the South Sea Company—each a key player that redefined the relationship between the seats of public power and their private counterparts.

Stirrings of Independence and a Brutal Reply

As it happens, the twists and turns in the relationship between the men of Falun and their kings well illustrates the on-the-ground reality associated with many of the defining moments in the evolution of Western political and economic history.

For example, as the Reformation arrived and many of the most prominent of Europe's monarchs began to assert their primacy over a church that had overreached, grown corrupt, and threatened to impose its "universal" laws over their national ones, a similar story was unfolding in Sweden.

The nature of carving bits of precious metal out of the unyielding earth and of living with the constant fear of being crushed to death amid the gloom of billowing smoke and settling soot had a powerful effect on the personalities of the miners. It amplified those traits that Swedish historians have described as special to the "men of Dalarna . . . men who are independent and unafraid, men prepared—once upon a time—to reach for their weapons . . ." This independence was both a blessing and a curse, as is illustrated by the story of the miners' relationship with one of Sweden's greatest kings, an accomplished, brutal, and rather twisted leader named Gustav Vasa.

King Gustav has been described as having "an almost pathological greed for power, he was utterly unscrupulous and ruthless and his word was decidedly not to be relied on. He was litigious, but had scant respect for the law and still less for truth. His mendacity was beyond belief, his greed for wealth bottomless." In these respects, he shared much with his contemporaries, including Henry VIII of England, Louis XII of France, the Holy Roman Emperor Charles V, and an assortment of popes. The rulers of the day were, for the most part, noble in name only. In fact, one of the comforts of reading history is that the leaders of the past make their flawed successors today look benign by comparison.

Despite this, or perhaps because of it, the men of Dalarna supported the rise to power of Gustav Vasa. However, being the sort of man he was (which is to say, someone in a line of work in which political success involved not being poisoned or overthrown by your friends or family—for further reference see that notable, almost contemporary view of Scandinavian royalty, *Hamlet*), Vasa did not exactly reward those closest to him or those who had backed him for their support. In fact, among other things, he put one of his closest advisers to death for disagreeing with him, and he periodically rolled loaded cannons into parliament in order to tilt the electoral balance in his favor. In fact, it probably became clear after not too long that the king was not going to provide the miners with change they could believe in. He was fond of administering beatings with whatever wrought-iron household implement was handy, once beating a goldsmith to death for taking a day off without permission, and in at least one instance he chased one of his secretaries through his palace with a knife.

He asserted his will in other ways, consistent with the fashions of the statecraft of his day. In an effort to consolidate power and ensure that he could meet the costs of running a kingdom, he introduced a host of reforms that strengthened the state's control over the economy. He declared the church subordinate to the king and seized its assets throughout Sweden. If in order to consolidate his power he was willing to shrug off centuries of deference to Rome, and by extension the God he was raised to believe in, it should have come as no surprise when he decided also to tighten his grip on the mine that was the very heart of his country's economy and the font of its wealth.

The miners were resistant to his policies and were not shy about expressing disagreement with his views on everything from new mining technologies to how the smelting houses should be managed. Ultimately, a decision by the king to give a group of foreign traders from what is now Germany a monopoly over managing Swedish trade with Europe in exchange for a war loan proved to be the last straw. The German traders took advantage of the arrangement in a way that cut deeply into profits at the Great Copper Mountain.

With both their political freedoms and their economic livelihood encroached upon, the Dalesmen revolted, not once but three times. The first effort, in 1524, was led by a couple of Catholic clergymen who had been dispossessed. The king easily and unhesitatingly quashed the uprising and ultimately appropriated the last thing the prelates had left: their lives. Three years later, after a harsh tax was imposed (again, to fund the king's wars), a substantial number of the region's men determined to replace Gustav with another candidate. But support was spotty, and the outcome was the same: Gustav won, and the leaders of the rebellion lost their heads.

Despite Gustav's blunt methods, however, he had not successfully quelled the irrepressible spirit of the miners. Again in 1531 they rose up. The king was determined that this time he would deliver a lesson that would not be forgotten. In the bitter cold of a Swedish January, Gustav made his way up the copper mountain to Falun. There, summoning the leaders of the community together, he assailed them, asserting that they were traitorously trying to subvert his efforts to form a centralized state, a modern Sweden. He was particularly infuriated that the miners had claimed earlier that to travel through the region, the king would have to receive a safe-conduct from them. They had so long been unburdened or unconcerned with the demands of the nobility that they simply didn't know how to deal with this assertive king.

To punctuate his scathing words to a crowd that was the contemporary equivalent of the Great Copper Mountain Chamber of Commerce, the king then sent his men into the gathered crowd, where they seized the five master miners who had led the rebellion. As you might expect, given Gustav's predilections, they were then publicly beheaded, and their bloody noggins were placed on a wooden plank and displayed as a message to all that further uprising would not be tolerated and that the state's authority was not to be challenged.

Quickly following this with strong measures to assert his economic control over the mine, Gustav seized and bought up shares until, two decades after the final uprising, he controlled two-thirds of the smelting houses in Falun. He directed the copper from the mine into the munitions, cannons, anchors, horseshoes, armor, and weapons with which he consolidated and extended his power and Sweden's. Moreover, he established central-government control over the mine for two centuries to come, a period during which the application of Falun's wealth would elevate Sweden to one of Europe's and the world's greatest powers. During those centuries, the crown viewed the mine as a source of hot and cold running resources, mining without much of an eye toward sound practices. The frenzy to produce and support the rapidly growing needs of the state led to more and more accidents, more loss of life, and more resentment of the state among the miners. But there was no letup.

In 1613, Gustavus Adolphus, a successor to Vasa, chose to "monopolize the sales of copper from the mine in the hands of the state; to use the proceeds of an indemnity tax to pay the miners; and, lastly, to sell the metal to merchants against silver dollars, which they had to bring in from the Continent, through their sales of copper there." He then used these proceeds to pay off an obligation to the Danes, a ransom that was 80 percent funded by proceeds from the mine. He also sought to create mining operations that would be more efficient than Stora Kopparberg, but both of his competing companies were failures and Stora remained central to Sweden's fate. In exchange for its primacy, Stora helped Gustavus Adolphus create a Swedish empire that girded the Baltic. Indeed, in 1625, five years before Sweden entered the Thirty Years' War—the decisive conflict in determining the centrality of the power of nation-states—Gustavus Adolphus actually put Sweden on the copper standard. Not only was this expedient in a country with an abundance of the precious material, but it was also an effort to raise prices for copper throughout Europe. The policy was not terribly successful, but the move illustrates that when Sweden achieved its pinnacle of global influence during and immediately after the three-decades-long conflict that was the worst to ravage Europe in its history, it was a pinnacle built atop a copper mountain.

In fact, Gustavus Adolphus's daughter, Queen Christina, said as much. "The greatness of the realm," she asserted without fear of contradiction, "rises and falls with the Falun mine." She spoke in 1640, eight years before the Peace of Westphalia, at a time when Sweden had been engaged in the great European conflict for a decade and when Stora was by far its leading enterprise and its chief source of export revenue. Evidence of its output was found from the copper at the tips of the pikes that distinguished Swedish troops as they seized German territories and parts of Denmark, to the cash that was one of the nation's most important assets when Sweden negotiated the Treaty of Westphalia. As a consequence, Stora Kopparberg's creation seven hundred years before was not only partially responsible for the lands that Sweden claimed at the war's end (which made it the third-largest country in Europe in land mass after Russia and Spain), but ironically, the enterprise also played a central role in shaping the Treaty of Westphalia, the turning point in history after which the primacy of the nation-state was clearly and finally established.

By the end of the Thirty Years' War, the Catholic Church had been subordinated (the pope was excluded from negotiations at the Treaty of Westphalia), the Holy Roman Empire had been shattered, and the concept of *cuius regio, eius religio* was enshrined. (It means "whose realm, his religion" and gave sovereigns the right to determine the religion of their own states—provided they chose from a menu limited to Catholicism, Lutheranism, and Calvinism.) Further, it established secular state sovereignty as a core principle of the international system. The treaty not only brought an end to centuries of fighting between church and state, it also brought peace to a continent that had been in turmoil because there had been no widely accepted political order. A patchwork quilt of varied political, religious, and private actors was constantly rent with tensions and the lack of an equilibrium or agreed-upon rules. But the "rules" of Westphalia were so clear, and the cost by which they had been established was so great, that they have stood, in key respects, until today. And key ideas framed there—such as the irreducible, inalienable primacy of sovereignty—came to be accepted over time in every corner of the globe.

The world being what it is, we find even in the immediate wake of the moment that brought order and clarity to Europe and defined the role of the nation-state the first stirrings of changes that would ultimately complicate and then challenge that new reality. Those changes came as the newly confident nation-states sought to expand their power through international trade and exploration. In order to support those efforts, those countries created next-generation private enterprises, enterprises modeled on the experience of companies such as Stora. Chartered joint-stock corporations such as the British East India Company, the Dutch East India Company, the Hudson Bay Company, and La Compagnie des Habitants rose up in the decades just after Westphalia. They were evidence of new prosperity, and engines of new conflicts. And not only would these companies continue the evolution begun by Stora, but Stora would change and reinvent itself as they did.

Mercantilism was the dominant economic school of thought in this period, and nation-states that had recently consolidated themselves protected their new prerogatives by introducing protectionist policies that discouraged imports and actively promoted exports. The Age of Empire was one consequence of mercantilism, since countries sought to expand their domains in search of the resources they needed for growth. Spanish ships that had first crossed the Atlantic a century and a half earlier now plied established trade routes, as did their British competitors. Portuguese, Dutch, French, and English ships made for Asia. Overseas trade built economies and also helped fuel a prosperity that led to a growth in Europe's population of over 100 million from a century before. The Peace of Westphalia had not only created a new world order that stabilized Europe, but once the European powers branched out in search of new territories and markets, it created the first genuinely global economy. That economy relied on joint-stock companies to expand into new markets and impose European views about how they should grow. Presaging complications that would seem quite familiar today, they not only fueled booms and busts but were seen as closely linked with political elites and, moreover, in some instances as actors behaving very much like independent states themselves.

Thus, around the time of Sweden's pinnacle of copper-gilded power and the Treaty of Westphalia, both states and corporations began an evolutionary fugue in which each developed capabilities and modalities that would sometimes draw them together so closely as to make them parts of a whole and would sometimes set them at odds with each other over the control of riches, influence, or both. An event that was supposed to simplify the global power scene, ending centuries of tension between church and state, marked the beginning of a new such power struggle, one that we would come to see as being between the public and private sectors.

As we shall see at almost every turn in the history of nation-states and corporations, the oldest corporation still in existence rode the shifting tide. Often, as Stora Kopparberg evolved into Stora and eventually Stora Enso, transitions in its relations with the Swedish government or other governments worldwide, or later with companies it acquired or even NGOs with which it jousted, led the way for changes that were coming to society worldwide. It is striking that many of the biggest transformations came at watershed moments in history when revolutions of one sort or another were in the air. The greatest of these moments—Stora's birth at the end of the Middle Ages, its growth as a nationally important enterprise during the beginning of the Renaissance, and the central role it played in the changes associated with the Reformation and the Thirty Years' War, the Treaty of Westphalia, the Enlightenment, the Industrial Revolution, and the global era—were accompanied by others in the area of science, art, technology, and of course political philosophy and economics.

2 ■ 1288: The Battles That Gave Birth to Modernity

The condition of man . . . is a condition of war of everyone
against everyone.

—Thomas Hobbes

Between the time that Kare the goat wandered off in the direction of that bog near Falun and the era during which Bishop Peter concluded his deal to buy back his share of the mine that was Kare's legacy, Europe churned. During those five or so centuries, the Continent remade itself over and over again in what many saw as an effort to restore the stability of the Roman era that itself had ended half a millennium before the beginning of mining at the Great Copper Mountain. But the eyes of the great actors of that era were not on the past. Nor can it fairly be said that they were fixed on some future horizon. No, like the leaders of every period in history, the men and women who drove Europe's fitful progress through what we think of today as the Middle Ages and early Renaissance produced history by happenstance. What they were doing is what the people of every era do: they were single-mindedly and often ruthlessly pursuing their narrow self-interests.

They draped their greed and their ambition in some glorious ideas, and once they had accumulated enough wealth, they ensured that the bards and chroniclers and artists and tapestry weavers of the day told their stories as if they had nobler objectives. Some framed their goals in political terms. Others chose to characterize their work as service to the deity or to virtue itself. Some—those who rose particularly high and were particularly deft or particularly craven or both—claimed both sorts of elevated justifications for their brutality, thievery, and worse.

But if you look beneath the superficial characterizations that conventional histories tend to proffer, what you find in the Europe of this period is a society in search of order and organizing principle. To say that the defining power struggle of the time was a battle between church and state is a gross oversimplification, because political and economic and military power was so diffuse, distributed among many levels of nobility and clergy—although given the behaviors of both groups as they grappled with each other for power and spoils, we can only view characterizations of most of the prominent players as "noble" or "men of God" as among history's bitter ironies. Nonetheless, for our purposes, it is important to understand the church-versus-state and related dynamics because they offer a revealing prelude and striking parallels to the public-private power struggles that followed.

As we shall see, in the Scandinavia of this era, the same sort of struggles that rattled and bled the Continent were also dividing and reordering the relationships between Sweden's ruling families and the representatives of the church. At the same time, as the first bits of ground were scraped from the surface at the mines of Dalecarlia, more than just copper ore was unleashed. So too was another force that would define world history: private power, business, or what would gradually become known (thanks to innovations not just in mining or the legal structure of businesses but also in the technology of agriculture, transportation, and other nascent enterprises) as a "third estate," one powered by labor and capital to take its place alongside the ones powered by the sword and the cross.

As a consequence of this development, even as most of the attention of the era was focused on seeking an equilibrium in the endlessly destabilizing local and regional contests among those who would advance their own interests in the name of church or of state, the roots of the public-private struggle that was to succeed that one centuries later were creeping ever downward, expanding, growing more robust, mimicking the tunneling at Falun. It was during this era that many of the ideas, institutions, and conflicts that define our own time were shaped. It was in the battles of this period that modernity was born and great trends with then unimaginable consequences were set in motion.

Of Popes and Emperors Prostrate in the Snow

Given the primacy achieved by Roman emperors, the battle to claim their throne was among the most momentous of history. In many ways, the fall of Rome resulted in over a millennium's worth of attempts to restore and thereby harness its former glory.

As often happens in history, the seeds of the rifts and turbulence of one era were planted in the prior period. Even as Rome was in decline and emperors seldom spent much time in the "eternal city," one of the last of the great emperors, Constantine, converted to Christianity and through the Council of Nicea granted the church his imperial sanction. Although popes had existed for more than three hundred years as reputed successors to the apostle Peter, it took a nod from an emperor whose predecessors had once outlawed Christianity to nudge the church to the status that would allow it to outlive the empire and, ultimately, in many ways succeed it.

Indeed, among the early popes of the era that followed the fall of Rome, one of the most notable was Gregory the Great, who hailed from a family that had once been prominent among Rome's senators. But he and his successors were weakened by the fact that their political patrons had moved eastward out of Rome. By the time that Kare the goat began sniffing around that bog, say in the year 800 or so, the popes had a problem. Despite their divine authority, they faced regular earthly challenges from princes who claimed papal land or revenues to which they felt entitled. And it's worth noting that throughout all the battles that follow between church and state, it is the right to land and revenue that drives the actions of the main actors. We talk about the political organization of Europe, but what we mean is the economic divvying up of the Continent by those with enough power to make any sort of claim on any source of wealth at all. In fact, many actions with seemingly "higher" motives have very compelling economic explanations. For example, the prohibition against clerical marriage—promulgated a couple of decades before the Council of Nicea at the Synod of Elvira—had the advantage of ensuring that the wealth accumulated by the clergy would always be passed on to the church. That way there would be no conflict of interest on the part of priests and bishops who might seek to pass on at least some of the fruits of their labors to their children.

The "Dark Ages" that followed the fall of Rome in A.D. 410 can be seen as a period of what might be called political entrepreneurism. Other than the Catholic Church, there were few enduring strong national or international institutions. Consequently, a feudal system emerged in which those who were strong enough claimed as much as they could defend, although even then there were often overlapping claims among competing families and between such families and the church. Despite the differences in their "callings," both local feudal lords and their clerical competitors, usually bishops like Peter of Vasteras, were chosen and survived through political intrigue, the sword, bribery, and the taxation of common citizens. Wherever weakness was perceived, one of these figures would scramble to fill the void. In this respect, the period was much like the current global era in which there are few effective international institutions and large private enterprises seek to take advantage of institutional and legal voids.

During the eighth century, just as Sweden was ruled by a shifting mix of Viking chieftains, in continental Europe warrior kings sought to concentrate power. One of the most successful at this was the founder of what would become the Carolingian dynasty, Charles Martel. His nickname was "the Hammer," which tells you roughly all you need to know about what it took to establish and maintain a kingdom during the Middle Ages. Charles made his name in part from doing what Europeans have in one way or another been focused on doing to this day: keeping out Islamic invaders. Charles repelled the Muslims at the Battle of Poitiers in order to preserve his holdings. It is worth noting, however, that those holdings, while they comprised a goodly chunk of modern France and Germany, were not exactly a kingdom. The official title was still held by a dynasty, the Merovingians, established in the middle of the fifth century by a ruler named Merovech and his son Childeric, who had considerable success defeating some of the tribes that had previously beaten up on the Romans, including the Visigoths and the Saxons.

Charles's victory, however, established the Carolingians as the most powerful clan in Europe. So when, in 751, Pope Zachary needed help holding on to his papal territories, which were being threatened by the Lombards of northern Italy, he faced a conundrum when the Byzantine emperor—theoretical heir to the throne and responsibilities of the Caesars—was unable to protect him. Zachary's solution presented itself when Charles Martel's son Pepin III approached the pope to seek his blessing on his intent to depose the last Merovingian king and assume royal authority.

In exchange for having the pope send an archbishop to anoint him king of the Franks, Pepin—known to history as "Pepin the Short," a nickname that must make all sons of powerful men wince—would later provide the Papal States with military assistance in their tussle with the Lombards. In leading his men across the Alps to repel a Lombard invasion of Rome, Pepin not only returned Zachary's favor on behalf of his successor, Stephen II, he also crisply illustrated the mutual dependency of the secular and clerical leaders of the era (a non-zero-sum relationship that again is evocative of the current rivalry-riven but collaboration-dependent relationship between companies and countries). He added to the good light in which the pope saw him by returning to the Holy See a goodly portion of the northern Italian lands he had conquered. This "Donation of Pepin" was seen as a foundation of a new alliance between the king of the Franks and the church based on "a bond of love and devotion and peace" but also clearly based on something else that translates better in the language of the church: quid pro quo.

Almost certainly, Pepin's biggest donation to history was not the land he won in northern Italy, but rather his son, a man who would transcend his father (and every other ruler of his era) in every definition of stature. The son, known today as Charlemagne (Carolus Magnus, or Charles the Great), was not only an imposing figure of six foot three with fair hair and a flowing beard, but he extended the family's kingdom to the plains of Hungary and thus united Europe to a greater degree than anyone had since the Romans. To this day he is seen as having presided over a kind of pre- or mini-Renaissance in the midst of the Middle Ages and as being the founder of both the French and German royal lines.

Charlemagne continued his father's policy of assisting the pope, working initially to support Pope Hadrian I during a Lombard onslaught in 773. (It's worth noting that the Lombards didn't much like Charlemagne to begin with, as he had a couple of years earlier briefly married and then dumped the daughter of their king, Desiderius. To add injury to insult, Charlemagne beat the Lombards so decisively that he assumed their Iron Crown as king of Italy.) Pope Hadrian was succeeded by Leo III. Leo was supposedly born a commoner, a fact which didn't sit well with Roman upper-crusters. His admirers ultimately prevailed with his canonization nine centuries after his death. But during his lifetime, the detractors—who accused him of everything from adultery to perjury and corruption—made his papacy a tumultuous one. While Charlemagne had sent his hopes that Leo would be a worthy pope upon his election, he was soon among those disappointed by reports that the pontiff was "hard and cruel."

In 799, an angry Roman throng attacked the pope, reportedly attempting to gouge out his eyes and cut off his tongue, and imprisoned him in a monastery. Leo escaped after shinnying down the monastery's walls on a rope and made his way to a meeting with Charlemagne at Paderborn, a city in northwest Westphalia in modern-day Germany. Charlemagne listened as Leo enumerated the injustices that the "accursed sons of the devil" had inflicted upon him. Charlemagne had also listened carefully to emissaries sent by Leo's detractors, who made accusations against the pope. The latter group demanded that the pope step down or clear his name via oath. Neither option would exactly strengthen the institution of the papacy, so Charlemagne sought another solution.

The Frankish king sent Leo back to Rome accompanied by a contingent of his soldiers. When they arrived, the conspirators against Leo were placed on trial. They failed to prove that the pope had done as they alleged, and they were sentenced to prison in Francia. These moves, however, did not stabilize the situation in Rome, and ultimately Charlemagne felt he had no choice but to go there himself, which he did in late November of the year 800. He helped broker a decision in which the pope would offer a voluntary oath to clear his name and dispel any suspicions against his character; because the oath was voluntary, it didn't weaken the pope's legitimacy. Since this decision was enough for the most powerful man in Europe—Charlemagne—it was enough for everyone else in Rome, and the pope's authority was restored.

In exchange, on Christmas Day A.D. 800, Leo placed an imperial crown on Charlemagne's head in front of an assembly of Romans. The symbolism worked its magic, and the Roman crowds shouted "Hail to Charles the Augustus, crowned of God, the peace-bringing emperor of the Romans!" This cry says it all: Charlemagne was legitimized by God, and as Holy Roman Emperor he was the undeniable successor to the Caesars. This didn't sit well with the empress Irene, sitting on what was allegedly the throne of the Caesars in Constantinople, but she did not have the power to challenge the heir to Charles the Hammer.

Of course, at the time, no one saw the implicit problems that this bold step raised. Leo had elevated his protector to a status that left Charlemagne feeling as though he were Europe's highest authority in any practical sense. At the same time, Charlemagne had not only strengthened the papacy at a critical moment, but he had also reaffirmed the idea that only the pope could grant legitimate power to a secular leader. Thus, while the alliance proved beneficial in the short term, it raised manifold problems associated with the dual and competing nature of all thrones.

As Northwestern University professor Hendrik Spruyt has written:

Despite all the benefits that cooperation between church and king yielded, however, their alliance was ultimately based on divergent interests. At the heart of the king's endeavor lay an attempt to obtain sole control over the resources within his domain and to expand the area of that domain. This clashed with the church's claim of jurisdiction over all clerical affairs and of ultimate superiority over rulers on secular matters as well.

The challenges associated with this tension manifested themselves with special clarity almost three centuries after Charlemagne's investiture, during the Reformation. During the intervening years, the dependence of the emperors on the popes who crowned them led them, not surprisingly, to become deeply involved in Roman and papal politics. In part this was explained by their economic interests in Italy, but it was mostly the inevitable consequence of seeking to protect their self-interest. The result was that the invisible hand of the emperors could be seen in rigging papal elections, deposing and replacing corrupt popes, and ensuring that bishops within their empire were satisfactory by simply appointing them directly.

The power to appoint bishops was especially important to the emperors because, while top positions in the nobility were hereditary, top clerical posts could be filled by emperors with loyal supporters or those to whom they owed a debt or from whom they might someday want a favor. The result was a system in which the line between interdependence and too much dependence, between secular and clerical centers of power, was very blurry. Later, and repeatedly, we will see just such a fuzzy and contentious relationship evolve between centers of public and private power.

A crisis arose with the inevitable conflict between a pope who believed in a strong and unchallengeable papacy and an emperor who saw a similar role for himself. The pope in question was Gregory VII. He "conceived of Christendom as an undivided state, of a state as a polity dominated by a sovereign; of a sovereign as a ruler who must be either absolute or useless. And who, he asked, but their heir to the Prince of the Apostles could presume to claim a power so tremendous?" He believed only the church was competent to give authoritative interpretations of Christianity's sacred writings—the observance of which was the only way any man could be saved—and to trust the church's privileges to impure lay rulers was nothing short of condemning mankind to hell. While past popes, including Gelasius, had noted that the world was ruled by two different powers—the sacerdotal and the secular—they left it ambiguous whether those powers were equal or one was greater than the other. Gregory made it clear which of these he thought was superior.

Gregory did this through a papal bull he circulated in 1075 called *Dictatus Papae*. In it he asserted—despite all evidence to the contrary—that the papacy was completely independent of the emperor. He then went on to claim and assert powers that were relevant to the emperors, particularly the then current one, Henry IV. Among the powers Gregory claimed were that the pope alone could depose or reinstate bishops, that he might depose emperors, that the Roman church was incapable of error, and that the pope may "absolve subjects of unjust men from their fealty." These assertions meant more than the simple rivalry that resulted from his claim that "the Roman Pontiff alone is rightly to be called universal." Denying emperors the right to appoint bishops also meant that the control of all the church's land and revenue went straight to the pope. The issue therefore went well beyond a question of prestige or legitimacy. It went to the bottom line.

In response to the bull, Henry IV asserted his authority by appointing a supporter to the post of archbishop of Milan, a key position with regard to his Italian holdings. He gave the archbishop the church and the land that went with it, signifying that the property was the emperor's to administer as he saw fit and not the pope's. The pope protested, and Henry responded with a letter that did not mince words:

> Henry, King not by usurpation but by pious ordination of God, to Hildebrand [Gregory's birthname], now not Pope, but false monk: . . . Our Lord, Jesus Christ, has called us to kingship, but has not called you to priesthood . . . I, Henry, King by the grace of God, together with all our bishops say to you, Descend! Descend, to be damned through the ages!

Gregory responded by excommunicating Henry, releasing all his subjects from allegiance to him, and forbidding anyone to serve him as king. The excommunication wasn't just rhetoric: it was all that some of Henry's insubordinate subjects needed in order to justify rebellion against an emperor that their infallible spiritual leader said they simply could not heed. Henry's back was against the wall, and he blinked first. In the midst of the frigid winter of 1077, he crossed the Alps and rode to the castle of Canossa in northern Italy where Gregory was residing under the protection of Countess Matilda of Tuscany while en route to Germany, where a council of bishops and magnates had gathered to elect a successor to Henry IV if the emperor failed to have his excommunication lifted within a year.

At the castle walls, Henry dressed himself as a humble penitent and promised he would abide by papal rulings in the future. To underscore his change of heart, he walked barefoot through the snow and prostrated himself beneath the pope's window. Initially, Gregory was unmoved. But as a priest, he could not refuse to forgive a penitent Christian. Besides, the image of the emperor lying in the snow was a powerful one, not to mention a notable personal victory. After three days the pope emerged from the castle to find Henry lying before him in the shape of the cross. They then celebrated mass together and Gregory lifted the excommunication.

That would have been the end of the story had Henry actually meant any of it. But it was all politics, the latest melodramatic episode in the story of the central rivalry of the age. Once threats of rebellion had been quashed, Henry resumed appointing bishops. Furthermore, the German nobility were alienated when the pope forgave the emperor—which was a problem for Gregory when he tried to excommunicate Henry again three years later. Without the support of the German princes, the move was a political dud. Seizing the moment, the emperor marched on Rome and oversaw the election of a new pope, who placed the imperial crown on his head. Gregory, in turn, was forced to flee, and he died a year later in the city of Salerno, his last words being, "I have loved justice and hated iniquity, that is why I die in exile."

Even after Gregory's death, the core conflict between the Holy Roman Emperor and the papacy boiled on. In the near term, it was resolved in 1122, when one of Gregory's successors, Calixtus II, and Henry's son, Henry V, reached a compromise called the Concordat of Worms. The document basically split the baby right down the middle in symbolic terms, creating a two-part investiture ritual in which a church official would first give a soon-to-be bishop the symbols of ecclesiastical office—a ring and a staff—and then a secular representative would touch the bishop with a scepter, signifying the land and other earthly possessions that went with the office. This compromise ultimately sowed the seeds for the future separation of church and state. Now that religious and secular authorities were separate, kings had to justify their sovereignty on secular terms alone. This justification would eventually evolve into the doctrine of territorial sovereignty, a crucial tenet of the nation-state system that would eventually drive the last nail in the coffin of the church's pretensions to universal authority six centuries later. The territorial basis for sovereignty of course raises new complications in a global era in which some great entities, including multinational corporations, have neither territorial allegiances nor limitations. And the entire episode illustrates the linkages between our own times and seemingly distant points in history, reminding us that very often today's headlines started to be written centuries earlier, that the first drafts of Twitter feeds about twenty-first-century crises and issues were sometimes written with a quill pen.

In countries across Europe, however, the tug-of-war would be played out at different speeds and with different points of contention dominating. In part this was due to the different speeds of development of national and theological institutions. For example, in Sweden, it was only in the twelfth century that Christianity began putting down real roots. King Sverker the Elder was a major proponent of the church and, in 1152, instituted a tax on Rome's behalf that had been known previously only in England as "Peter's Pence." A dozen years later, a Cistercian monk, probably of English origin, was consecrated with the permission of King Karl Sverkersson at the cathedral of Sens in northern France to become archbishop of Uppsala, a community no doubt chosen in part because it was one of the last remaining strongholds of paganism in Sweden. This would be the first archbishop to reside in Sweden, and his appointment was seen by the king as a way of helping to provide more order and stability within the kingdom, a fact underscored when Karl's successor, Erik Knuttson, became the first Swedish king anointed with holy oil and crowned by the pope.

Not surprisingly, the church sought to consolidate economic power in Sweden in fairly short order. By the year 1200, it had received its first major charter from the new king, Sverker the Younger. The charter, negotiated by representatives of Rome, granted the church freedom from taxation on all church lands and released the clergy from the jurisdiction of temporal criminal courts. Importantly, through the charter, "a privileged clerical class came into being and churchmen now had a firm foundation on which to build." Their independence grew through the Convention of Skanninge in 1248, at which it was determined that all clergy owed obedience to the pope and the pope alone. A great illustration of that class and its political clout was the soon-to-be Bishop Peter of Vasteras, who, in exercising his clerical prerogatives, would become an example of the wealth that clergy quickly accumulated as well as the opportunistic appreciation of the clergy for the just-emerging third set of actors on the scene: businesspeople, the miners of Falun.

Even as the power of the pope had diminished vis-à-vis the Holy Roman Emperor and certain key tenets of papal authority had been challenged successfully, the church found other ways to assert its authority and was even embraced by local rulers. Tension occurred when those rulers were challenged by the church, whose approval was critical to their survival. One such set of challenges was brought against the legal authority of kings; another was clearly brewing on the front of taxation. The conflicts around these issues produced resolutions that were central in defining what made a state a state—key to our understanding of the challenges coming today to states from a completely different set of actors, but ones who also have interests and powers that rival those of political leaders and the states they represent.

Of Lawyers, Death, and Taxes

Gilbert Becket was the son of a knight but chose the trade of a mercer (a textile merchant) to support his family. He lived at the beginning of the twelfth century in Cheapside, London, with his wife, Matilda. There, hoping for the best for their son, Thomas, and his sisters, they regularly sought to expose their children to the world of their wealthier friends, of hunts and, in young Thomas's case, a serious education in languages, religion, and the law. Thomas took well to the training and traveled to the great intellectual capitals of Europe, from Paris to Bologna, preparing himself for what life might bring. He did brilliantly, and as a young man, back in England, he won a position working with the archbishop of Canterbury. The archbishop was the most important representative of Rome in the country, and Thomas won his trust and with it important appointments within the church. Recognizing that Thomas's gifts were worthy of even greater challenges, Theobald, the archbishop, suggested to England's king, Henry II, that when he had an opening for a new chancellor, he should consider Thomas for the job. Henry did, and the two formed not only a formidable partnership but a fast friendship.

King Henry II was one of those rare monarchs who make contributions that resonate through the centuries. The actions he took and the values he promoted not only transformed England almost a thousand years ago but also affect our daily lives in countless ways. Henry was canny in legal matters, smart enough to form a potent alliance through marriage to the equally formidable Eleanor of Aquitaine. He was also an effective administrator who took special interest in the king's and the state's role as determiner and enforcer of justice within society.

Early in his reign, Henry sought to both strengthen himself and enhance the effectiveness of the British legal system by promoting profound reforms. At the core of these reforms was the idea of common law: laws applicable to all citizens throughout England. He sent royal justices on regular trips to every locality throughout the kingdom and required twelve representatives of the nobility to meet with them and hand over accused criminals for trial. In addition, Henry's royal courts undertook to adjudicate property cases. Thanks to Henry's innovation, litigants could file a property claim with the royal court if refused a trial locally. Despite the costs of such a system, the benefits to the kingdom were clear. The common law system was more transparent, more centralized, and a great source of revenue as a consequence of the penalty fees imposed on criminals, which were transferred directly to the royal treasury. The problem was that those penalties used to be collected by the nobility or the church, each of which administered its own system of justice, or some facsimile thereof.

Those who had been the beneficiaries of these customary legal systems, now superseded by Henry's courts, were angered. They had lost both money and the prerogatives of power. Furthermore, clerics who had enjoyed the gentler justice of church courts were also resistant to change. The church courts had actually grown during the reign prior to Henry's, that of King Stephen, and as such they had encroached on what had once been an important element of previous kings' powers. But Henry was not only interested in reclaiming powers lost during the reign of his feckless predecessor. He also wanted to expand his own authority in ways that would make his government the undisputed primary seat of power within his kingdom. This impulse brought him into direct conflict with Becket, a man who had once been so much like a brother to him that Henry sent his namesake son to live with Becket and his family. Indeed, it's possible that some of the acrimony that would poison this once warm relationship came from the fact that the younger Henry reputedly felt he was the beneficiary of more fatherly love in a day with Thomas Becket than he enjoyed from his father in a lifetime.

Quite apart from such personal tension, there were practical rivalries in play that echoed others from across Europe. The king saw the church encroaching on his power and his sources of revenue. His loyal friend Becket had at one time been part of his solution to this problem. Henry appointed him archbishop of Canterbury, seeking to bring the church further under his direct control. But Becket, who had lived the high life as chancellor, underwent a fairly profound change as he undertook his new clerical duties. He had what has been characterized as an ascetic transformation. But regardless of the reasons for or the nature of the change, the consequence was that Henry's handpicked man for the job soon became less pliable and even an active opponent of Henry's proposed reforms.

In fact, Becket resisted when Henry sought to codify reforms that would bring the church more under his control. In 1164 Henry saw to it that a set of sixteen specific reforms were passed to limit the sway of the papacy, the church, and the church's courts in England. Of special importance in the reforms were provisions underscoring the authority of royal courts to try "criminous clerks"—church officials who had broken the law and who were likely to escape serious consequences if the only law they faced was the one administered by their employer. Unsurprisingly, Becket refused to accept these reforms, known as the Constitutions of Clarendon, and the resulting power struggle with Henry led Becket to flee into exile in France. There he did what any self-respecting theocrat would have done: he turned to the pope for assistance, calling for Henry's excommunication and punishment. For six years, the recriminations flew back and forth. The pope declared Henry's reforms null and void. But Henry feared worse was in store, and in an effort to avoid excommunication, he lured Becket back to England in the hope that some kind of an understanding would be reached.

But Becket was unyielding despite the king's demands. Indeed, he made matters worse by excommunicating an archbishop and two prominent bishops who had played along with Henry, presiding at the coronation of Henry's son despite the fact that this right was technically that of the archbishop of Canterbury alone. Weeks later, fuming, Henry, infirm and in his sickbed, asked loud enough for men of action in his court to hear, "What miserable drones and traitors have I nourished and promoted in my household who let their lord be treated with such shameful contempt by a low born clerk?" Four knights took the king's complaint to mean something more, and they made their way to Canterbury, arriving on December 29. They asked Becket to come with them to be called to account for his actions. He refused. What followed is described in an eyewitness account:

> . . . The wicked knight leapt suddenly upon [Becket], cutting off the top of the crown which the unction of sacred chrism had dedicated to God. Next he received a second blow on the head, but still he stood firm and immoveable. At the third blow he fell on his knees and elbows, offering himself a living sacrifice, and saying in a low voice, "For the name of Jesus and the protection of the Church, I am ready to embrace death." But the third knight inflicted a terrible wound as he lay prostrate. By this stroke, the crown of his head was separated from the head in such a way that the blood white with the brain, and the brain no less red from the blood, dyed the floor of the cathedral. The same clerk who had entered with the knights placed his foot on the neck of the holy priest and precious martyr, and horrible to relate, scattered the brains and blood about the pavements, crying to the others, "Let us away, knights; this fellow will arise no more."

Becket may have been brutally killed, but he continued to play a role in the struggle between the church and the English royal court. Within three years he was canonized and venerated as a martyr. In fact, he became so powerful a symbol to the faithful (the path from London to Canterbury became such a popular pilgrimage that it was immortalized in literature such as Chaucer's *Canterbury Tales*) that even Henry, just four years after the death of his former friend, traveled to Becket's grave site to do penance. Becket would forever symbolize the threat that powerful bishops pose to kings. That is why, four hundred years later, when Henry VIII sought to finally finish the business the second Henry had started, one of his most important acts while destroying monasteries across the kingdom was to obliterate the tomb and all remnants and relics of Thomas Becket.

The friendship and falling-out of Henry and the man now known as Saint Thomas Becket was such a compelling human drama that even twentieth-century playwrights and poets such as T. S. Eliot and Jean Anouilh created major works about it. But behind that drama is an even greater story that impacts people everywhere, the story of a rivalry between institutions, between two visions of how society should operate and who should set the rules. It is a struggle that seemed to take place with similar fury and often with similar results over each and every one of the prerogatives and privileges that secular and clerical elites jealously aspired to or guarded. In the case of Charlemagne and the popes of his era, it was a question of determining legitimacy, of establishing from which source authority flowed. In the case of Henry and Thomas Becket, it was over which courts had ultimate authority, over whose justice would be meted out. And in the case of King Philip IV of France, known as Philip the Fair, and Pope Boniface VIII, it was over who controlled the lifeblood of any state or church: the ability to set and raise taxes.

In this last instance, through conflict came progress in clarifying just what determined a state and how it related to the other powerful actors that might be rivals. This was one of the most important—if bloody, frustrating, and convoluted—tasks and outcomes of the Middle Ages. And while the final issues involved were not resolved until centuries later, the critical questions were framed and advanced. As is the way with most forms of giving birth, the advent of the modern state not only took what seemed to be an excruciatingly long time but was also a bloody mess. Virtually all issues were resolved with violence or the threat of it. Any hint of weakness was an invitation to further mayhem. And given that throughout the Middle Ages the church was undergoing what must be described as one of the most protracted crises of confidence and leadership in history, it was a particularly battered target. Long after the scuffles with the Lombards, the Papal States continued to face threats, increasingly from the heirs to their former protectors from the north. Frederick Barbarossa, Henry VI, and Frederick II all made efforts on behalf of the empire to unite Sicily, the Papal States, and the northern Italian city-states under their rule. While they were unsuccessful, and periodically and predictably excommunicated by the popes they threatened, their disregard for the popes as anything other than rival princes—workaday warlords with a little extra religious mojo—is revealing.

These kings from Northern Europe were not the only heirs to Charlemagne who showed such contempt. In fact, it was their French cousin, King Philip the Fair, who dealt the papacy one of the most devastating blows—and one with especially important consequences in terms of the gradual accumulation of centralized power on behalf of the secular state. As kings and princes across Europe saw the church being challenged, they grew bolder and increasingly sought to levy taxes on the clergy, many of whom controlled significant lands and wealth. Although this was not unheard of—one way popes could get men at arms to wage crusades was by allowing them to tax local churches for "the defense of the faith"—the spread of tax levies on the clergy and church property that were not associated with papal objectives had grown so widely by the mid-thirteenth century that it produced a backlash and a confrontation.

The pope who sought to draw a line in the sand was one who was not unaccustomed to confrontations. His name was Pope Boniface VIII. History knows him primarily for two reasons. One is that as a consequence of his bare-knuckles style of handling papal and Italian politics he made an enemy of, among many others, Dante Alighieri. Much as it is said today that politicians shouldn't make enemies of people who buy ink by the barrel (a reference to newspaper publishers), it is probably equally good advice not to make enemies of people who write enduring works of literature that are likely to shape your reputation for time immemorial. Boniface was seen as a schemer who won and kept the papacy through intrigue and brutality, and although Dante's *Divine Comedy* was published while the pope was still alive, the author nonetheless placed Boniface in the ring of Hell reserved for priests who sold clerical positions and favors, a sin known as simony. That Boniface was also unpopular with many for his brutal handling of local feuds—such as one with a prominent Italian family that led the pope to lay waste to an entire Italian city, producing a death toll in the thousands—made Dante's audacity all the more palatable to his broader audience.

The pope's political weaknesses had the added effect of undercutting his primary area of real accomplishment. He, like England's Henry IV, had the mind of a lawyer and was a prolific producer of opinions regarding canon law. In addition, he promulgated several important opinions via papal bulls that had the intent, if not the effect, of strengthening the church's authority. One of these bulls addressed the issue of taxation. In his *Clericis Laicos* he asserted that kings could only tax the clergy with the permission of the pope, and he automatically excommunicated any who disobeyed.

Needless to say, this did not sit well with Europe's ruling class. In France, Philip responded decisively by banning the export of any monies out of the country, effectively denying Rome any revenue it might have been hoping for from France. He also tossed one of the pope's emissaries into prison. When Boniface reacted as might be expected, excommunicating Philip, the French king reacted as he might also be expected to do, given the utter devaluation of the threat of excommunication when it is seen as a tool of economic bullying rather than one of great sacred import: Philip burned the bull of excommunication. Boniface in turn responded with another papal declaration, one that framed the issue at stake in the clearest possible way. The document was called *Unam Sanctum*, and its thrust was that it was "altogether necessary to salvation for every human creature to be subject to the Roman pontiff." It asserted without ambiguity the argument that the pope was the highest authority on earth and that the price for disagreeing was eternal hellfire (thus adding a choice element of irony to *The Divine Comedy*).

To translate his assertion into action, Boniface summoned the leaders of the church in France to meet with him in Rome in order to shape a potent response to Philip. It was here that Boniface began to sense his gambit was not going to work. Thanks to both a rising tide of French nationalism—which would prove over time to be a potent solvent, very effective at breaking down the influence of Rome—and careful calculation as to which leader was likely to have more influence over their earthly futures, the prelates of France decided to stay home and side with their king.

Cannily, Philip sought to amplify this national feeling through even broader national political outreach. In 1302, he convened the First Estates Assembly, at which he addressed an audience that included not only nobles and clergy but also prominent townspeople. This was a watershed because it introduced the "third estate"—the rising class of merchants, freehold farmers, and tradesmen—into the political equation (in another part of Europe, Stora Kopparberg's miners would also come to constitute this third estate). King Philip recognized that to stand up to the eternal power of Rome, he had to marshal all available sources of temporal authority.

Once he had won his political victory at home, resulting in the outright rejection of both *Clericis Laicos* and *Unam Sanctum* and establishing the king's primacy on the issue of taxation, Philip sought to punctuate it in a more practical sense. He sent an emissary, his chief minister, Guillaume de Nogaret, to Rome to conspire with the Colonna family, the one that Boniface had targeted and against whom he had directed armies of mercenaries with bloody results. Together they stormed the pope's summer residence in Anagni. There they confronted the sixty-eight-year-old pope and subjected him to all manner of abuse, including a slap across the face with a steel glove. They showed some restraint, contemplating but then rejecting the idea of executing him. Providence interceded then, and Boniface was given the opportunity to discover whether Dante had it right after all when he died less than a month after the intrusion at the palace.

The Great Transformation: The Third Force Enters the Fray

More than the old pope died when Boniface expired in October 1303. So too had an important prerogative of the church and many old ideas about the true political structure of Europe. Kings and nations were in their ascendancy, and central to their power was the alliance they would forge with the merchant class. The rise of this class had, of course, been underway for several centuries. It literally began with events like the initiation of mining in central Sweden and the evolution of an association of independent miners who, through their labors, developed resources that made both them and their kingdom strong. In this sense, the organization of that mine as revealed in the share document signed by Bishop Peter in 1288 represents as important a watershed as many of the higher-profile battles that were taking place throughout Europe at that moment in history, including the one between Philip and Boniface that would take place only eight years later with the publication of *Clericis Laicos*.

Of course, not every corner of Europe moved at the same speed. Events would happen in parallel, sometimes decades or even a few centuries apart. But the cumulative effect over the period between the eleventh and the sixteenth centuries was transformational. In fact, in the longer-term context of history—in political and in economic terms—it may well be that schoolchildren would be better off studying this social transformation rather than the more narrowly defined and religiously focused Reformation. The locus of the change was not the castles or palaces of Europe but the towns of its countryside. In England, for example, at the turn of the millennium, trading centers emerged as villages began trading in goods such as pottery. Waterways, the God-given thoroughfares of the era, helped define which areas would prosper in Europe. The Crusades helped fuel the growth of these trading routes as knights who were willing to venture to the Holy Land were granted land or booty. As they passed toward the Middle East and they and their goods passed back, trading relationships with the region grew, and city-states such as Genoa and Venice prospered. And as traders moved the goods of the Mediterranean up into Italy via its rivers and ancient Roman roads and other byways, they developed and refined ways to strengthen their businesses.

Key to the growth of business—as evidenced by the share structure of Stora—was managing risk. While the owners of the companies still bore complete liability for their enterprises, they sought to create a mechanism by which that liability could be spread among several owners, and then those owners could spread their risk among several enterprises. In Italy, the structural approach was called the *compagnia* (plural *compagnie*). These were primarily family ventures, but they also embraced outside investments. They allowed, through their legal structure, for investors' shares to be precisely described (as in the Stora agreement) in terms of both their value and other provisions. There were also multiple classes of liabilities through which these enterprises could be underwritten, ranging from retained earnings to supplementary partner contributions to loans from outsiders that would be repaid within a set period. These *compagnie*, many of which were banks, were innovative, establishing everything from techniques for managing complex overseas operations to networks that could handle rapid wealth transfers. Some banking ventures lent money to kings in exchange for preferential treatment. The Bardi family made loans to courts in France and Naples in exchange for unrestricted trading privileges. The Peruzzi family lent money to the king of Naples to enable him to buy the port of Chiarenza, where the bank was then allowed to set up a branch operation. Venetian bankers helped the pope finance his ongoing battles with the German emperors.

In Northern Europe, new technologies also played an important role in shaping the rise of this merchant class. More sophisticated mining approaches—from cracking the earth to refining the ore to digging deeper—helped in places such as Falun. Along northern rivers and streams, water mills sprang up and revolutionized the European economy. Cloth and paper production—the current focus of Stora as a world leader in packaging—were utterly transformed by the ability to perform repetitive tasks using the mechanics of a mill rather than backbreaking human labor. This was a direct threat to a feudal system built on the advantages accrued by lords who held sway over armies of serfs. In fact, there have been few more destabilizing developments in history than the transfer of power from those whose edge was in marshaling massive human resources to those who could use the combination of capital and technology to achieve similar outcomes.

In one instance, reported by the chronicler Joceline of Brakelond, the rise of a member of the "third estate" triggered a squabble between an Abbot Samson and a local dean named Herbert. Herbert had built a wind mill to grind his corn, thus threatening Samson's business. The abbot was not amused. "When the abbot heard of this," according to the chronicler, "his anger was so kindled that he would scarcely eat or utter a single word. On the morrow, after hearing mass, he commanded the sacrists, that without delay he should send his carpenters thither and overturn it altogether and carefully put by the wooden materials in safe keeping." Herbert argued the wind was a public good, adding that "he only wants to grind his own corn there and no one else's, lest it be imagined he did this to the damage of the neighboring mills." Samson would not relent. "His anger not yet appeased," he responded, "I give you as many thanks as if you had cut off both my feet. By the mouth of God I will not eat bread until that building be plucked down. You are an old man and you should have known that it is not lawful even for the King or his justicar to alter or appoint a single thing within the [area] without the permission of the abbot and convent and why have you presumed to do such a thing?"

He then got to the heart of the problem: "Nor is this without prejudice to my mills, as you assert, because the burgesses will run to you and grind their corn at their pleasure, nor can I by law turn them away, because they are free men . . . Begone, begone. Before you have come to your house you shall hear what has befallen your mill." Herbert was cowed and tore down his own windmill. But ultimately the business done among the freemen that Abbot Samson so feared undid the world he was trying to preserve. Mill owners were, of course, often feudal lords, and they usually forced their serfs to work in their mills. This gave the owners a double bang for their buck—one that was often further leveraged by their monopoly status within their local economies. Mill owners' abuse of the advantages gained by those who controlled technology produced some resentment, as is expressed in *The Canterbury Tales* in Chaucer's condemnation of an abusive miller. And, given the patchwork political and social structure of Europe at the time, some of the mills were also owned by rich clergy—who themselves were not above abuse, or at least also sought profit. But in the end, the result was a flowering of free enterprise in a Europe that grew from 42 million people in A.D. 1000 to 70 million in A.D. 1300. Indeed, it was the spread of new technologies for growing and distributing food that helped support this flourishing.

At the same time, the rising classes of merchants produced economic change and important political shifts. They moved away from traditional strongholds of feudalism into new towns, or "newburghs"—hence the name by which many members of this class were known: burghers. These towns became trading centers and sources of new revenue that didn't fit into the old system. But while feudal lords were threatened by it, kings saw it as an opportunity, since the new towns deliberately lay outside the realms of lesser lords but still within the purview of the monarchs. What's more, businesspeople invariably seek a comparatively transparent, predictable environment. Kings can provide this through centralized authority, which includes a single system of taxes, tariffs, and laws. The burghers got predictability and a single individual with whom to negotiate, and the kings got dependable income streams from a community that was more likely to support them rather than local or foreign potential rivals. The idea of national sovereignty advanced with increasing success from Charlemagne onward to Philip the Fair and beyond, dovetailing with the interests of merchants and traders. A bond was forged between royal heads of state and the business class that remained powerful, albeit fraught with tension, for almost a millennium—until today, in fact. As we shall see, it is the growing disconnect between the interests of business and national leaders in the global era that is likely to be an increasing source of tension in our times and could create the same kind of systemic changes that were produced during the volatile era in which both nation-states and an independent business community were born.

This affinity between the emerging third estate and national leaders is part of what propelled Philip the Fair to his political triumph. And, as similar power struggles were replayed across Europe, the power of the emerging class was decisive. In fact, in the biggest battle of the era, a family contest for the right to control the Duchy of Limburg—an area known for the past century or so primarily for the smells associated with its two most famous exports, Limburger cheese and eau de cologne—the tide of the Battle of Worringen turned on the ability of the victor, Duke John of Brabant, to harness the support at arms of the merchants, traders, peasants, and other free citizens of the surrounding communities. That battle, four thousand to a side, with one side led by Siegfried of Westerburg, the archbishop of Cologne, and the other by Duke John, took place on June 5, 1288, less than two weeks before Bishop Peter bought his shares in Stora Kopparberg.

1288 and Beyond: Change from the Perspective of a Swedish Mining Community

After the battle was concluded, Cologne and its surrounding territories had won a degree of independence that would only enhance their ability to trade, winning it the understandable and revealing appellation "the German Rome." That status would play an important role in its ultimate membership with other major German cities in the Hanseatic League, a group of trading centers that would ultimately be the primary commercial lifeline connecting the miners of Stora Kopparberg to the markets of the European continent. Eleven days after Duke John triumphed at Worringen, Bishop Peter signed the agreement to reclaim his shares in Stora from his nephew in exchange for selected church lands. While the document in and of itself is primarily significant as the oldest artifact of a corporation still in operation today, it also resonates with many of the great themes and historical issues of its era: the role of kings and of clergy, the rise of enterprise and businesspeople, and the emergence of the state.

Much like the rest of Europe, Sweden had been grappling with the relative roles of the church and the state throughout the thirteenth century, as evidenced by the Convention of Skanninge in 1248. When King Valdemar Birgersson was crowned in 1266, the ceremony took place in Linkoping Cathedral in an effort to confer upon him the legitimacy that association with the church brought. Almost immediately this produced problems, since shortly after taking office, Valdemar committed adultery and had to go to Rome to seek forgiveness. The pope took the opportunity to force Valdemar to declare his fealty to him and to reaffirm Sweden's responsibility to provide a steady stream of Peter's Pence to the Vatican coffers. The fact that Valdemar went along with the pope angered his brothers, who, with aid from the Danish king, deposed him. After years of turmoil, Magnus Ladulas, one of the brothers, took power, this time holding the coronation in Uppsala Cathedral. Just to ensure that he would have the support of the clergy, he asserted that he reigned "by the Grace of God" and he extended tax immunities to the clergy.

To counterbalance the power of the church, in 1280 Magnus also issued the Alsno Decree, which gave a tax exemption that was previously reserved for the clergy—note the recurring issues and techniques for managing them—to any person who could provide himself with a horse and armor in defense of the kingdom. This primarily benefited the nobility, who thereafter were known as the *fralse*, meaning literally "the exempt." Magnus further fine-tuned the balance he sought by working to limit the abuses that "the exempt" often inflicted on the 95 percent of the population who belonged to neither of the first two estates. It is through such efforts that he gained the moniker "Ladulas," which literally means "barn-lock," a nickname that came from his efforts to keep nobles from forcing peasants to feed and house them and their retinues when they were traveling. When Magnus signed the share document for Bishop Peter, it was clear he was a leader trying to balance all the forces within society in an effort to achieve some kind of stability.

But as in the rest of Europe, concessions to the church or the nobility seldom brought stability. Swedish kings rarely lived past the age of thirty, often done in by members of their own family or communities. In the first four centuries of the new millennium, fifteen different kings or heirs were murdered. Between 1130 and 1250 alone, the two main Swedish dynasties alternated periods of rule five times. The ongoing efforts of the next major dynasty, that of Valdemar and Magnus, the House of Folkung, did not typically fare much better. When Magnus's older son, Birger, inherited the crown, his two brothers immediately began a series of efforts to overthrow him. So, with his wife, Margareta, Birger decided to invite his two siblings to a banquet at Nykoping Castle in December 1317. He fed them well and lubricated them with much wine. When they retired to their beds and collapsed asleep, he tied them up and threw them in the dungeon. When their supporters stormed the castle, Birger threw the key to the dungeon into the river and left town. By the time the dungeon doors were opened, the two brothers had starved to death.

The inability of the kings to manage their affairs with any sort of continuity undercut the one value offered by such royalty: stability. In response, local Swedish nobles assumed the balance of power in the kingdom and claimed the authority to elect kings. They also wrote into law the popular election of bishops—which didn't make the church hierarchy very happy. But the search for stability through balance did not stop. In 1319, after Birger's ouster, Magnus Eriksson took the throne. The election charter that was issued upon his ascension reconstituted the ruling class leadership into a council of nobles and clergy that possessed important formal rights and duties. This charter, argues Thomas Lindkvist, "can be regarded, at least symbolically, as the definitive end of the process through which Sweden became a state." Magnus also took, as did other leaders of the era including Henry IV in England, to creating a system of common law, promoting native literature, abolishing bondage, and, in a twist that presages political developments centuries in the future, developing a royal oath that carefully stipulated the king's duties to the people.

This was a watershed, and it placed Stora Kopparberg in the context of something like a functioning nation. The next centuries would not be easy. Within decades the plague would strike Europe, and Sweden would be hit hard. Economies were devastated and the balance of power shifted and shifted again. (The plague benefited the church in many instances, as the wealth of the deceased often passed to it.) Further uprisings and royal rivalries took their toll, and one result was a growing dependence of Swedish monarchs on their Danish and Norwegian counterparts. This led to Sweden's involvement in the Kalmar Union, an alliance among the kingdoms placing them under the control of a single monarch that lasted until 1523. Finally, this phase of Sweden's history ended with the reign of Gustav Vasa. Gustav saw that the ongoing Protestant Reformation afforded him the opportunity to create a strong national state that would be once and for all free of Rome's influence. He also understood that to achieve that independence and true territorial sovereignty, he would have to depend on domestically generated loans and revenues.

By far the greatest current and potential producer of such revenues was the mine at Falun. That is why he led his periodic forays up to the Copper Mountain. Before he was elected king he led a group of nationalists there to secure money, supplies, and the support of the Dalesmen.

Within two years of that raid, in 1523, he was elected king, and like many modern leaders, he discovered a crippling deficit linked to recent wars. He felt that if he was to create a strong state, all sectors of society would have to contribute to eliminating or reducing it. As the historian Franklin Scott explains in his *Sweden: The Nation's History*:

> The peasants balked at paying taxes for the war and wondered how they were better off. The men of Dalarna thought it was they who had put Gustav on the throne and so they wanted more voice in political affairs. The church people were distressed about the financial demands placed upon them and disturbed by the religious revolution that was spreading rapidly beyond Germany. Neither merchants nor farmers liked the rising price of salt nor the bad coinage.

The answer for Vasa was the answer that would drive the next chapter in European development, the inevitable next step following the buildup of the state by carving away the prerogatives of the church and the more recent advent of the Reformation. He would effectively nationalize the church and make it a tool of his kingdom. Alongside the burgeoning of the nation's greatest enterprise—the mines that furnished the raw materials for his weapons, the nation's farm tools and utensils, and the hard currency—this step would establish an integrated, stable, powerful Swedish state that could become the foundation for an empire. He would scheme and cajole and battle for control of both pillars of his new Swedish society, and as he achieved it, he would be collaborating in the remaking not only of Sweden but of Europe and of the entire international system.

3 ▪ 1648: The Beginning of the Great Leveling

Men and nations behave wisely once they have exhausted all the
other alternatives.

—Abba Eban

The greatness of this realm stands and falls with the Falun mine.

—Queen Christina of Sweden (1640)

The tensions between church and state descended from an uneasy mutual
dependency into a spiral of competition and conflict. The successor rivalry
between public and private power followed a similar trajectory, even if the
means of conflict were often subtler and the need for collaboration has
remained much stronger. The reasons for both the similarities and differences between this later power struggle and that which preceded it can
be traced back to the period during which the church-state battle was
coming to a head and large corporations were first coming into existence.

That period also witnessed a tectonic shift in history that resonates to
this day. That tremor might be characterized as the beginning of the
great leveling, a centuries-long process of both rethinking and redistributing public power. It reversed a system of power in the Western world that
was essentially an ongoing struggle for local and regional supremacy reflected and institutionalized via layer upon layer of constantly reordered
hierarchies. Its flaws, fractures, and collateral damage—illustrated most
clearly through the chain of conflicts we now call the Thirty Years' War—
ultimately moved not only the West but also the rest of the world to a system that has been marked ever since by a continuous redistribution of
power and an ever-increasing emphasis on the rule of law rather than that
of force. While the consequences were unintended, the primary beneficiaries of this "leveling" were not the aristocrats, or even the common citizens who championed it over the centuries, but rather private enterprises,

"artificial" individuals that used the changes to accumulate power and to challenge efforts to constrain their growing influence.

Force is still with us, of course. But as its costs have risen and legal institutions have grown stronger, a perceptible shift has occurred in how competing powers have asserted themselves and attempted to resolve their disputes. Further, as a result of the legal systems taking root and key legal principles winning universal or widespread acceptance, the old hierarchic view of the world began to crumble, as did the ancient hierarchies themselves. By the mid-seventeenth century, the notion of empires or religions possessing universal power was supplanted by the idea of a world of separate and equivalent sovereign states. By the mid-eighteenth century, the concept of sovereign rulers was undercut by the idea that the true wellspring of sovereign power was the people themselves. By the mid-nineteenth century, the rise of an industrial era saw a massive redistribution of economic power to private enterprises and a concurrent effort to shift hierarchic economic power away from capitalists to workers or shareholders. By the mid-twentieth century and continuing through to the first years of the twenty-first, all these struggles advanced further, with nation-states that had once been empires seeing colonies break off, the number of nations grow, and, simultaneously, development after development occur that either reduced the powers of the state or strengthened those of would-be challengers to states, be they private, supranational, or transnational.

As Gustav Vasa Lay on His Deathbed

Dark, cool and still, the first few hours of September 29, 1560, in Stockholm's royal palace were tense. The king, who had through the force of his will transformed Sweden into an independent modern kingdom, was taking his last breaths, and uncertainty hung in the air. In his last years, Gustav Vasa's great red beard had grown gray, and as it lay lank across his bedclothes with each rise and fall of his chest, observers wondered what would come next. Would the king's sons be able to hold together what he had fought to build? Was this dying sixty-four-year-old man personally essential to what had been made of the fragmented kingdom that had been pulled at for generations by foreign rulers and the church in Rome? Was it his genius or his own special brand of fury? His generalship? His brutality? His micromanagement, which included hundreds and hundreds of detailed letters to his subjects advising them precisely how he wanted his kingdom to be run?

Or was something else in play? Was he—like Henry VIII in England, another monarch who had also rebuffed Rome and asserted his sovereignty—part of a broader historical trend? That trend reflected the decline of the Catholic Church and the ascendancy of nations built on the back of a new economy in which merchants, millers, tradesmen, and farmers were using new technologies and growing trade to foster growth— and Gustav, like Henry, had seen and seized an opportunity to better tap into the revenues that the new economy was generating. Did Gustav's last thoughts bring him back to the days of his arrival on the national stage? To his being held hostage overseas, or to his return to Stockholm in time to witness—but avoid—the wholesale slaughter of the Swedish nobility (including his father and brothers) at the hands of Denmark's king Kristian II? Or to the uprising he then led, with the assistance of the men of Dalarna, to rout the foreign occupiers that led to his election as king a year later, when he was only twenty-five? Were his tumultuous relations with those men of Dalarna on his mind, perhaps evoked by the glint of candlelight off a bit of copper or bronze in the palace, a soldier's pike, or a servant's kettle? They had lifted him up, and when he then sought to impose his will, they had pushed back. He had asserted himself at the end of a sword, but throughout, he knew he depended upon them and their mine, gradually taking over direction of Stora Kopparberg's copper exports and much of its operations—though the mine masters were damnably difficult to control and maintained a frustrating degree of autonomy throughout his reign.

In the end, Gustav Vasa knew, success as a king was as much linked to economic fortunes as it was to cunning or ruthlessness or wisdom. Sweden was a state because he had pushed out the Catholic Church and seized the revenues that went to it, and because he had the mine producing exports to all Europe that provided much-needed hard currencies. While his translation of the Bible into Swedish and his following the formulas of the Reformation to create a Protestant nation would be seen by others as having a spiritual element, he knew that for him the transformation was most important for what it said about the state and its king, and for what it brought to the national treasuries.

Still, he recognized that for all he had achieved, the battle between the princes of the church in Rome and across Europe and the native-born princes of the patchwork of nations and duchies and free states and empires was still ongoing. He no doubt could imagine that his sons might one day battle for his throne in the same way that every man with true power in Europe battled others who coveted what he had and sought to take advantage of his weaknesses.

Shortly after the old king finally expired that early September morning, it became clear that he had thought ahead, seeking to bring at least some modicum of stability to the kingdom he had done so much to build. His funeral, carefully planned prior to his demise, was the most elaborate Stockholm had ever seen. Its size and extravagance sent a message about the strength of the state: unrest should not get out of hand. Gustav lay in bed while his sons, led by Prince Erik, helped orchestrate a two-day-long procession of symbols of the power, scope, and hierarchy of their kingdom. Effigies of the king and two of his three wives (with only three over his lifetime, this is one area in which he clearly lagged behind his English contemporary) were displayed, as were arms, armor, banners, flags, and symbols of all that was Swedish. The liturgy was that of the reformed church, but the eulogy, delivered by the latest Bishop Peter of Vasteras, a friend of the king, was carefully calibrated to send a message of both praise and defense of the idea that the kingship of Sweden should be passed on through heredity rather than election. Peter and the others close to the king were seeking to send the message that stability and the welfare of the state turned on keeping it all in the Vasa family, to convey the idea that sovereignty could and should be the birthright of a single family. While it would be two and a half centuries before this idea was successfully challenged, for the time it represented a step forward—the concept that somehow the fate of nations should be determined within the borders of those nations with a minimum of foreign interference.

Gustav was buried in the Cathedral of Uppsala with all three of his wives. His son Erik succeeded him, and almost immediately many of the problems so typically associated with hereditary rule began to manifest themselves. Gustav's three sons spent the rest of their lives grappling with one another for power. One was mentally unstable and ended his days in prison. The next was a Catholic who married a devout Pole, both of whom stirred religious resentment among Sweden's nobility. Third came Charles, who assumed the throne in 1604.

Charles is seen by history as having achieved two primary accomplishments during his seven-year reign. First, he restored many of his father's Protestant reforms. Second, he was father to perhaps the greatest of all Swedish monarchs, the man who built upon his grandfather's idea of a strong Swedish state and, with the vital assistance of the miners of Falun, turned it into one of the great powers of Europe—and, in so doing, set in motion a chain of events that would eventually enshrine into international law the idea of national sovereignty advanced by Gustav Vasa.

A Headlong Leap into Either the Arms of Mary or a Mountain of Dung

The historical moment that established Charles's son Gustavus Adolphus as perhaps the greatest of all Swedish monarchs (and as a vitally important European leader and one of the great battlefield generals of history) was also linked to the unresolved struggles that had created the opening for his grandfather, Gustav I. The Reformation had weakened the church, but it and its allies were still a formidable force across Europe. Kingdoms and principalities were divided between Catholic and Protestant. Claims and counterclaims on revenue, land, and privileges triggered conflicts apparently without end—bloodsoaked days like those at Worringen in 1288 came and went with the frequency of full moons in the three and a half centuries that followed. Some battles were framed as personal. Some were portrayed as historical grudge matches. Some were draped in religious explications and justifications. It hardly mattered. The system for determining who was in charge—which means the system for determining who got what—was unstable. Europe was swept up in economic, religious, and political tides of change, and the result was great swirling uncertainty and looming catastrophe.

For some, like the popes and the Holy Roman Emperors who were sometimes their allies and sometimes their rivals, the path to stability lay with restoring a paramount power in Europe. Both claimed do so in the name of history and of God, and by the early years of the seventeenth century, both found themselves allied again in a struggle against a counterforce that was not so much a unified power as it was a unifying desire among many to assert their independence.

Perhaps the rawest source of tension on the divided continent came in the area we think of today as Germany. It was an important part of the homeland of the Franks, the people united by Charlemagne, the man who sought to restore order to Europe through his own supremacy as the first Holy Roman Emperor in A.D. 800. And it was also the birthplace of the Reformation, thanks to the writings and activism of Martin Luther. The interests of the Catholic Church in the region were manifest in a variety of principalities including Bavaria, but the principal force on behalf of the church was still the Holy Roman Empire, led in the region by a Habsburg dynasty that harbored as one of its central ambitions the re-Catholicization of Germany. The empire had been weakened greatly by the Reformation, of course, especially now that its effects had reached places as remote as Sweden and England. At the same time, by the early years of the seventeenth century, the Protestant rivals of the empire had become emboldened.

In 1609, a forty-two-year-old nobleman and veteran officer of the empire's campaigns against the Turks named Heinrich Matthias Graf von Thurn und Valsassina, who also happened to be born of Protestant parents in Bohemia, led a group of his fellow Protestant nobles into the inner chambers of the emperor Rudolf II. The group had been explicitly forbidden to confront the emperor, but they were implacable. The empire ruled over Bohemia, and it enacted repressive policies toward Protestants. Thurn and his allies, known as the Defensors, demanded that Rudolf sign what came to be known as "the Letter of Majesty." This document guaranteed greater religious freedom to Bohemian Protestants, including the rights of Bohemian lords, knights, and towns to choose freely between Protestantism and Catholicism. It also sought to protect these rights through the election of ten defenders and the creation of a Protestant militia.

Rudolf agreed to these terms for a reason that might seem familiarly calculated and remote from the underlying religious or political-philosophical principles involved: he needed support against his older brother Matthias, who wanted his throne. As part of the deal, in order to cement the support of Thurn and those he led, Rudolf granted Thurn the position of castellan of Karlstadt, the royal office in charge of the crown jewels and the royal regalia, a position that was significant in that it gave the Bohemian nobleman a central role to play in future royal successions.

Those successions followed without much delay. Three years after

Thurn and the other Defensors barged in on Rudolf, Rudolf died and Matthias took over. Not surprisingly, Matthias alienated the group by upholding the Letter of Majesty in only the most minimal fashion. He transferred some of his lands to the church, banned Protestant worship in two towns he determined fell under Catholic jurisdiction, and prevented peasants from attending church services on neighboring estates. While not technically in violation of the letter, these actions were certainly an affront to its spirit.

But frail old Matthias was not long for the world either. After only five years in office, he was succeeded by Ferdinand of Styria, a cousin who was an even more devout Catholic. Thurn and the other nobles were worried—with good reason—that Ferdinand would be even less inclined to honor the Letter of Majesty than his cousin had been. In fact, Thurn had been one of only two delegates in the Bohemian Diet who opposed Ferdinand's accession as king of Bohemia. As a consequence of this opposition, he lost his position as castellan of Karlstadt. A loyalist supporter of Ferdinand named Jaroslav Borita von Martinitz replaced him. The Protestant leaders pressed Ferdinand for confirmation that he would honor his forebear's commitments. He rebuffed them. Thurn and others drafted a petition objecting to his stance and the policies that Matthias had imposed and Ferdinand supported. While the emperor offered to travel to meet with the Protestants, Bishop Klesl, a Catholic leader who was a close adviser to the emperor, sensed an opportunity. He wrote a letter forbidding the Protestants to reconvene, and he chose the empire's lord regents in Prague to deliver this message.

In retrospect, the lord regents of Prague may have wished he had chosen different messengers. Infuriated by the bishop's stance and the drift of policy from the most recent two emperors, Thurn ignored the ban on the gathering of his Protestant allies. He convened the group and urged them to confront the regents directly at Prague's Hradcany Castle. While the regents expected a civil exchange of views, Thurn had other plans. He arranged to have a captain of the castle guard let his men in, and on the morning of May 23, 1618, according to the recollection of Martinitz, they barreled into the council chamber "quite cheekily, and causing a great deal of importunity." The angry Protestants expected a significant number of regents to be present, but they found only four plus a secretary.

The level of discontent within Thurn's group was revealed to all present when they brandished the weapons they had concealed in the folds of their clothing. They demanded that someone take responsibility for Klesl's offending letter. Thurn himself confronted Martinitz and kicked him to the ground. Sensing the situation, two of the regents, the Lord Supreme Burgrave and the Lord Grand Prior, immediately denied having anything to do with the letter and reaffirmed their commitment to the Letter of Majesty. It was a canny move. The two were permitted to leave the room—by the door.

That left only Martinitz, another regent named Vilem Slavata, and their secretary, Phillip Fabricius. The regents assumed that the worst that would befall them would be to be dragged out of the room and arrested. But Thurn and several of his band whipped up anti-Catholic sentiment in the room. Frenzied, they picked up Martinitz and Slavata and dragged them not to the door but to an open window on the far side of the room. At this point the two men begged for an opportunity to make their last confession. The Protestants laughed and taunted the men, then tossed the two high-placed representatives of the Holy Roman Emperor out the window. Slavata managed to grab hold of the windowsill, but one of the Protestants used the hilt of his sword to hammer the regent's fingers and he lost his grip. Then, for good measure, out too went the only other Catholic in the room, the poor secretary, Phillip Fabricius.

Miraculously, despite being heaved out of a third-story window and falling a hundred feet, none of the three died. Catholics assert this was because they invoked the name of the Virgin Mary as they fell and she interceded on their behalf. Protestants pointed out that they had all landed in a pile of manure at the bottom of a dry moat. There's nothing to suggest, of course, that both assessments are not true. What is indisputable, however, is that while none of the three met his end there on that spring morning, in a real sense, medieval Europe did.

The Prague defenestration was not the first in that city's history. Two hundred years earlier, a civil uprising had ended with a dozen or so top officials being tossed out one of the city hall's windows. In fact, it is alleged that when mobilizing his men to head to the castle, Count Thurn suggested that they would throw the regents out the window "as is customary." But less important than the means by which the Protestants showed their displeasure with the rulings of the emperor and his supporters like Bishop Klesl is the fact that the event is seen to have triggered a three-decades-long conflict. The Thirty Years' War marked the real end of the efforts of the Catholic Church and its allies to assert political supremacy in Europe and the beginning of a new order based on the idea that the state rather than the church was the ultimate sovereign.

That Thirty Years' War left such a scar on Europe that even at the end of the bloody, industrialized atrocities of the twentieth century it was regarded, along with the two world wars, as the most grievous military calamity to befall the Continent in its history. (It says something about the nature of Europe and its circular history that the first of those two world wars began with the shooting of a Habsburg.) But from our perspective it also marks a turning point, the beginning of the resolution of the church-state struggle and the emergence of the successor rivalry between public and private power. What is more, as we shall shortly see, it is a turning point that would not have unfolded as it did without the output of a mine that was now entering its ninth century of operation and its fourth century as an organized corporation. The Sweden of Gustavus Adolphus and Stora Kopparberg would be the decisive factor in determining the outcome of this war, the ultimate triumph of the idea of the supremacy of the nation-state and the move toward the social, political, and economic revolutions that would follow. In fact, it's not entirely an accident that the man who could be said to have started the Thirty Years' War, Count Thurn, after several initial battlefield setbacks leading Protestant troops, ultimately found himself on the winning side as a lieutenant general in the service of King Gustavus Adolphus.

A War Won by a Company?

In reality, the Thirty Years' War was neither a single war, nor did it actually last for thirty years. It represented the culmination of hundreds of years of conflicts and their intersection on a patchwork battleground in which old and new rivalries and campaigns intersected like crowds in a city square, often becoming unintelligibly tangled and blended. It was also not entirely a war between states or even between church and state. In fact, among its key combatants and supporters were found an emerging class of global actors: corporations.

While we know that companies and even legally constituted corporations existed for centuries before the beginning of the seventeenth century, it was not until the first few years of that century that a movement began that would see a blossoming and transformation of the role companies could play. An important driver of this phenomenon had to do with one of those major periodic technological transformations that produced far-reaching social, political, and economic consequences. In this case the transformation had to do with the success that European navigators had achieved during the Age of Exploration. Advances in the design of sea-going vessels, constant improvements in navigational tools, and systematic mapping of the world made it possible to travel great distances and thus to embark on new frontiers both in terms of trade and conquest.

The problem was that expeditions overseas were expensive, risky, and slow. Significant capital had to be raised to finance missions, and while big profits were often possible, so too were great losses. What's more, it would often be several years after an investment was made before it was known which outcome fate had offered up. To offset these risks, it made sense for investors to come together, as had the master miners of Falun, to form corporations whose shareholders could collectively insulate each other from the downside and share the upside of their endeavors. Better still, risk could be offset in yet another way if such ventures could exist over an extended period and thus cover more than one expedition.

Given the nature of the times, such ventures required, as did Stora, the official sanction of ruling authorities. The authorities in turn saw these enterprises not only as a source of revenue but as a mechanism to finance their international ambitions, extending their reach in a new form of public-private partnership. As a consequence, some of the earliest companies were endowed with very nationlike powers, including the ability to raise armies, wage war, seize territory, and even govern. In fact, it has often been observed that these early companies—in their global scope and unique hybrid powers—bear a striking resemblance to many of their multinational successors of today.

Among the first of these ventures was the British East India Company, chartered on December 31, 1600, to the Earl of Cumberland and more than two hundred "Knights, Aldermen and Burgesses." The anticipated duration of the company's existence was fifteen years; it would exist for 274 years, during which time it would field one of the world's largest militaries and rule the Indian subcontinent. (The company was actually modeled in part on an earlier venture called the Muscovy Company, which was founded in 1555 and continued operating until the later years of the First World War).

Soon after, in 1602, the Dutch East India Company was created to enable the Dutch to compete more effectively with their English rivals for domination of the spice trade. It too was envisioned as lasting just twenty-one years, and yet it was a major force on the world stage for almost two centuries. It too ultimately gained the power to mint its own coins, rule colonies, and battle rivals with brute force. For a time, it was even more dominant than the British East India Company in economic terms, in the size of its fleets, in the volume of its trade, and in the reach of its trading activities. And just as the overseas holdings of the British East India Company became what is modern-day India, so too did the spice island holdings of the Dutch company become what we now know as the world's fourth most populous country, Indonesia. Other such companies soon followed, including the London Virginia Company in 1606, the Danish East India Company in 1616, the Portuguese East India Company in 1628, and the Hudson's Bay Company in 1670, which is still operating today as a Canadian corporation. All played a significant role in the geopolitical remapping that followed the Thirty Years' War.

We will look in a little more depth at two companies that revealed the emerging centrality of private power through their roles during the conflict that remade Europe. One, to which we will come back shortly, is Stora Kopparberg. The second is the Dutch West India Company. It was not the biggest or the longest surviving of these joint-stock companies, existing from 1621 to 1791, but its role in the Thirty Years' War is such that it exemplifies how such ventures were used and why they were soon favored by so many would-be global powers.

By the time Thurn was introducing Martinitz to the miracle of flight, the Habsburgs for whom Martinitz worked were fighting a two-front war against Protestantism. Part of this was due to the extent of the Reformation, and part of it was due to the extent and subdivision of Habsburg holdings. Those holdings had reached their zenith during the reign of Charles V, who, by virtue of extremely good genetic fortune, inherited all the lands of his four grandparents: Isabella of Castile and Ferdinand of Aragon (collectively, the crown of Spain), Mary of Burgundy (incorporating the Netherlands), and Maximilian of Habsburg (Austria and the Holy Roman Empire).

During his lifetime, Charles conducted wars against the Ottoman Turks (who were allied with his enemies in France), maintained the

Inquisition, led the push for the Council of Trent (which launched the Counter-Reformation), and took both military and other measures to fight the spread of Protestantism. He also oversaw the crushing of the Aztec and Inca empires in the Americas. That said, he was also reportedly uncomfortable with excessive violence (at least by the standards of contemporary kings), and he sought counsel to reconsider the moral issues associated with the conquest of the Americas. He sponsored Magellan's circumnavigation of the world, and ultimately, troubled by gout, he retired to a monastery during the last two years of his life.

When he stepped down, his brother Ferdinand succeeded him as Holy Roman Emperor, and his son, Philip II, received Spain, Italy, the Low Countries, and the Indies. This split the Habsburg dynasty into Madrid and Vienna branches. It also suggested a weakening that was bound to be tested, given the tensions associated with the Reformation. Not long into Philip II's reign, just such a test came in the Low Countries. The result was one of those conflicts that ultimately overlapped and intersected with the Thirty Years' War, this one known as the Eighty Years' War.

Protestant nobles in the northern provinces of the Spanish Netherlands began to rebel in the late 1560s, and by 1579, the seven northern provinces had formed the Union of Utrecht, which rejected Philip's authority. Less than a decade later they shifted political power to an assembly called a States General, which granted each province a vote, and this entity in turn became the United Provinces of the Netherlands, known familiarly as the Dutch Republic. Philip responded by sending troops, but at the time, Spain was engaged in wars with the English, the French, the Turks, and the Portuguese as well as its overseas military enterprises in the Americas and Asia. This overreach led Philip's treasury to declare bankruptcy three times during his reign despite the huge flows of resources that were pouring in from the New World. No money in the treasury meant no money for troops, and in 1596, unpaid Spanish troops mutinied and the rebels gained the upper hand. Philip died two years later, and while his son, Philip III, was unwilling to concede defeat, he was also unable to mount a counteroffensive. By 1609 the two sides agreed to a twelve-year truce. It wasn't exactly an acknowledgment of independence, but it amounted to much the same thing, with only a handful of the southern provinces of the Netherlands remaining in Spanish hands (these would later become Belgium).

This breather in the contest gave the Dutch a chance to consolidate their victory. They cultivated industries new and old including publishing, textiles, and arms; reclaimed land; and promoted active global trade. They initially did this under the flag of the Dutch East India Company. Of the Dutch Republic's gross national product, 5 percent came from the arms trade and the same amount came from the trading ventures of the East India Company, which soon became the first joint-stock company to have its shares traded on the open market. An exchange bank was founded in Amsterdam in 1609 that soon made that city Europe's leading financial center—which in turn enabled the Dutch to gain access to capital on much better terms than could their chronically financially strapped adversaries.

Because much of the power in Holland was held by the militant Calvinist house of Orange-Nassau, which harbored ambitions to reunify all the lowlands by taking the Spanish Netherlands as well as a commitment to spreading Protestantism, the truce was sure to unravel in the wake of the events in Prague. The Dutch, under Maurice of Nassau, architect of much of their conflict with the Spanish, quickly came to the support of the Protestant cause, which was symbolized by the election of Maurice's nephew Frederick V to assume the crown of Bohemia. Maurice's support involved arms, cash, and a careful calculation that by supporting the new conflict he would position the Dutch for success should the truce with the Spanish fail to be renewed in 1621.

The negotiations to renew the truce ultimately broke down when the Spanish made demands that the Dutch cease their trade in the West Indies and tolerate Catholicism at home. While the Spanish had little appetite for war, due to their financial challenges, the death of Philip III, and the fact that his son was only sixteen at the time of succession, tensions grew and battles erupted. Advisers to the young king argued that the cost of maintaining the Spanish army of Flanders was almost as high in peace as it was in war and that a war might reverse Dutch gains overseas that had begun to take a toll on Spanish shipping. Seeking to pin down the Dutch as they defended their homeland, Spain's general, the Italian-born Ambrosio Spinola, led the army of Flanders to what became the celebrated siege of Breda in 1624. The Dutch surrendered a year later after a loss of thirteen thousand troops.

At the same time, the Spanish changed tactics and started to squeeze the Dutch on the high seas. Close to home, they employed fleets of commercial raiding ships out of Dunkirk to attack Dutch shipping in the English Channel. In addition, they began intercepting and harassing Dutch ships from the New World. This hurt in many ways—for example, by interrupting the supply of salt that was vitally important to curing the herring on which the Dutch diet depended. (When you look at the importance of salt and trade routes to the wars of this period and the importance of spices to preserving fragile food supplies in rapidly expanding European societies, it is clear that much of the conflict of the day had less to do with spiritual conflict over religion or the hearts-and-minds battles for national identity than with keeping stomachs filled.) The Spanish finally imposed an embargo. The English and the northern German Hanseatic traders complied, and the latest phase of the Dutch-Spanish conflict truly became a trade war, with Spain able to use its fleet and its globally dispersed and hardened strategic network of fortresses to tighten the economic noose around the Dutch. Part of the response to this in the Netherlands was the formation of the Dutch West India Company.

This enterprise, modeled on the early success of its Asian-oriented cousin, within a couple of years of its founding in 1621 had made significant inroads into the Iberian-dominated sugar and slave trades and staked important new footholds in Brazil and elsewhere in the Americas. (Brazil, the property of Portugal, had come into play for the Dutch with the Spanish annexation of Portugal more than three decades before.) The formation of the company was clearly as much a matter of national strategy as it was of economic initiative. Although sugar, slaves, and spices were vitally important elements of Iberian-American trade, the most valuable individual ships on the Atlantic to the Spanish monarchs were undoubtedly the galleons of Spain's annual treasure fleet. For over a century, since the very first journeys of Columbus and those who followed in his wake, Spanish ships had been bringing gold and silver from mines in New Spain and Potosí to the port of Seville. The value of this treasure rose from over a million ducats a year between 1516 and 1520 to over thirty-six million a year a century later. The crown was entitled to its "royal fifth," but given the additional taxes that were imposed, the Madrid Habsburgs ended up with as much 40 percent of these seaborne revenues.

As the size of the treasure grew in value and as Spain's financial health faltered, the kingdom developed a very elaborate system of security measures to protect its vital lifeline. Spanish ships leaving Mexico and Panama would meet in Havana each March to return to Europe in a convoy escorted by a squadron of heavily armed warships. Initiated in the 1560s, the system worked well for almost a century, but in 1628, at a crucial moment in the Thirty Years' War, it failed. In the late summer of that year, the Spanish Council of Finance reported that the treasury was once again strapped, two million ducats short of its needs for the year. This was due again to the expense of distant military operations, in this case an intervention in Mantua, Italy, and the support for the emperor's wars in Germany. The delicate financial balance demanded a successful delivery by that year's treasure fleet.

The Dutch understood this, since they had been the victims of Spain's wreaking havoc with their trade routes for several years. Early that year, the Dutch West India Company financed a mission by Admiral Piet Hein to do what had never been done before: intercept and sack the Spanish treasure fleet. The Dutch had tried before, but between the challenges of locating a fleet on the high seas of the Atlantic and defeating the Spanish defenses, they had never been successful. But this time, Hein's patient four-month search yielded different results. His fleet of thirty-one ships found the fifteen-vessel Spanish flotilla off Cuba. The Dutch took nine Spanish ships in the first attack. Hein then pursued the half-dozen remaining ships to Matanzas Bay, near Havana, and opened fire to prevent the Spanish from offloading their cargo. The Spanish had met their match. They were vastly outgunned, and they abandoned their ships.

Hein returned to the Netherlands with almost two hundred thousand pounds of gold. The shareholders of the Dutch West India Company got a 75 percent dividend, but the people of the Netherlands got a historically even more significant return. Spain was forced to choose between paying for its Italian campaign and continuing to wage war with the Dutch. The king sent his emissaries to offer to negotiate a settlement with the United Provinces. The Dutch, emboldened, did not accept the offer, instead seeking to make advances in the southern provinces.

Meanwhile, the Spanish, chastened and eager to avoid a replay of the debacle, decided to vary the schedule of their treasure fleet shipments. While this initially worked, the 1631 fleet left so much later in the year that it found itself in the mid-Atlantic during hurricane season and was destroyed in high seas and winds off the Yucatán peninsula. Spain was squeezed even harder. The crown was forced to confiscate private silver from the fleets, alienating the private investors and seamen on whom it depended. It also set aside the religious principles that had allegedly gotten it into so many of the wars it was fighting at the moment and began to borrow money from Portuguese Jews and *conversos*. But Spain could not keep up. Financial pressures coupled with battlefield setbacks produced a vicious cycle that forced Spain to the peace tables and ultimately coerced it to rein in its imperial ambitions. The losses of Europe's greatest crown to a fledgling Dutch corporation was an important precipitating event that led to the undoing of the Spanish empire and also to the loss by Catholic forces in the Thirty Years' War. Conversely, the successes of that corporation and the others of that era—born of necessity and opportunity— helped fuel the growth of empires that would succeed the Habsburgs and lead to the birth of the private empires that would enjoy their own victories to come.

The Lion of the North Roars

From the western reaches of the Atlantic, Europe got gold, silver, salt, spices, and other essentials. But the waters of the seas to its north were also plied with ships carrying vital cargo: timber, textiles, porcelain, and— essential to war and building alike—copper. And just as the Dutch, Spanish, British, French, and Portuguese made the Atlantic trade a vital front in the Thirty Years' War, so too was trade on the Baltic vital.

In the early years of the conflict, Denmark's king Christian made a move into Northern Europe, allegedly in support of the Protestant cause. In 1624, with British and Dutch support, Danish armies made a play for enhanced power in Germany—taking momentary advantage of the fact that the Swedes were embroiled in a Vasa family spat pitting them against the Poles. While the motive for taking up arms against imperial and Catholic League armies led by Albrecht von Wallenstein and the Count of Tilly was allegedly associated with the Reformation-born rift, in reality King Christian was seeking to strengthen Danish access to northern Germany's ports and gain a trading advantage.

The initiative was short-lived and unsuccessful. The Danes were soundly defeated by Wallenstein, the empire's leading general, and Tilly, who had famously won a victory at the Thirty Years' War's first major battle at White Mountain, effectively using his better-trained troops to crush the Protestant opposition in two hours. By 1629, the Danes sued for peace with the emperor and withdrew, having made minimal gains. Their defeat in turn emboldened the emperor Ferdinand to proclaim the Edict of Restitution, demanding the return to Catholics of all church lands taken since 1552. The edict also denied Calvinism any official recognition at all. Even on the emperor's side, leaders from Philip II to Wallenstein winced, worried that the edict was overreaching. Their concerns were borne out. German Protestants feared that this was only a first step and that the emperor might go much further in his efforts at retribution.

They sought a champion and got one in the person of Gustav Vasa's grandson, Gustavus Adolphus. When asked why he intervened, Gustavus Adolphus would later minimize his religious motivation, commenting that if religion was his motive, he would have gone to war against the pope. Instead, he implied, his goal was to strengthen Sweden's hand in northern Germany, to protect the trade on which his rapidly growing kingdom was increasingly dependent. But Gustavus was more than a mere opportunist. He was a student of the Dutch leader Maurice of Nassau's innovative military techniques. Like Maurice, he recognized a need to counter the Spanish *tercio* system, which had successfully capitalized on formations involving columns of men fifty across and thirty deep. He sought a more flexible, versatile approach, and he embraced lines that were only six deep and that employed soldiers equipped with muskets and copper-sheathed pikes as well as cavalry. He also made great strides in the use of field artillery, developing a copper regiment piece that could be pulled by a single horse.

Sweden's advantage therefore lay not only in the innovations of its king but also in the resources found within the Great Copper Mountain. As king, Gustavus owned many of the mining huts of Falun and was acutely aware how valuable this precious resource was. With the Continent continuously shrouded in the smoke of cannon fire, the demand for copper was at unprecedented highs. From the time shortly after Gustavus entered the fray in 1630 until 1635, Swedish copper exports grew more than fivefold from what they had been in the same amount of time a decade earlier.

To seize the moment required not only clever battlefield tactics but smart management skills. And just as Gustavus borrowed from the techniques of Maurice of Nassau in his campaigns, he imported a Dutch manager named Louis de Geer to become his head of royal munitions.

Initially just an investor at Falun, De Geer introduced methods that enabled Gustavus to produce 20,000 muskets, 13,670 pikes, and 4,700 suits of cavalry armor from 1629 to 1630 alone. Later, De Geer went into business for himself and built a major operation that was, in revenue terms, about one-third the size of the Dutch East India Company. It is easy to see how such production could be a potentially decisive factor in the Thirty Years' War. As a result, interest in the mines grew and visitors from the Continent became more frequent. Foreign governments wanted to better understand what kind of economic engine Gustavus had at his disposal.

One such reconnaissance was conducted by a French diplomat named Charles Ogier. Visiting the mines just a few years after Gustav and his armies made their 1630 entry onto the Continent, Ogier wrote of the scope of the enterprise and the price it demanded of those who worked there:

> For those of you who wish to create a picture of the Mine in its entirety, imagine a dark hole, terrible and deep, down to 60 or 70 fathoms (a little over 110 meters), dug out and arched artificially and in different directions, held up by nothing other than itself, filled with fires in different places, filled with smoke and sulfur and the smell of metal, filled with dripping water. And then, in the depths of the earth, black people, like small devils, echoes from hammers and crowbars with which the stone is broken. The cries from the mine workers, those transporting the ore to the baskets and finally the desolation and the thunderous roar which could result, should such a terrible and weighty construction collapse. For you who think you can see this in your mind's eye you will get, if not a complete picture, at least an impression of this highly strange and remarkable phenomenon.

With the great dark pit as the origin of his army's strength in terms of copper, weapons, and hard currency, Gustavus entered the European war with special advantages his adversaries lacked, well served by his creative military mind. He landed in Germany in July 1630. Initial progress was slow. But approximately a year later, Gustavus's army of sixteen thousand was approached by a Catholic force of thirty-five thousand led by Tilly. Technically, Gustavus was constrained by a treaty with Catholic France, which had supported the Dutch and Swedes in a bid to offset the efforts at hegemony of their coreligionist rivals from Madrid and Vienna.

Gustavus was allowed to engage Catholic League troops only if he was first attacked, and that is just what happened. In these initial skirmishes, the Swedes won modest victory after modest victory, chipping away at Tilly's superior force. Gradually the bulk of the two armies began to converge on Saxony, which was ruled by the Protestant elector, Johann Georg. Johann had tried to remain neutral but could do so no longer and threw in with Gustavus; significantly, that put sixteen thousand Saxon troops at Gustavus's disposal. With the sides more evenly matched and with the Swedes boasting almost twice the artillery of their opponents, Gustavus engaged Tilly in the fields outside Breitenfeld on September 17, 1631.

The Protestant army included not just troops from Sweden and Saxony but also volunteers and mercenaries from Finland, Germany, Scotland, and elsewhere in Europe (mercenaries representing an early and enduring manifestation of private power and applying the spirit of entrepreneurship to meet the demands of the times). Gustavus kept the inexperienced Saxon troops cordoned off from his well-schooled Swedish army. Close to noon, the imperial artillery began to barrage Gustavus's army, only to be met by the more numerous, more maneuverable Swedish guns. Charge after charge from Tilly's troops was turned away as the afternoon wore on. Ultimately it was the Saxon troops that tipped the balance, though not at all in the way Gustavus might initially have hoped. Rattled by the conflict, many of them followed their leader, the elector, in retreat. Sensing victory, a major contingent of the imperial army followed in pursuit. Tilly moved to reinforce the gap left by these troops, and in so doing he spread his army too thin. Gustavus charged the weakened center of the imperial lines. He moved his lighter guns into position and blasted away at the heart of Tilly's defenses. The imperial armies began to break and retreat. Two-thirds of Tilly's hitherto undefeated army was gone—dead, deserted, or, like the count himself, wounded.

Gustavus was hailed across Europe. After thirteen years, the tide of the war had taken a turn that would prove vitally important to the Protestant cause and the ultimate outcome. He marched on, taking additional territories and weakening the empire, which he likely sought to partition. Although he would fall in the Battle of Lutzen a year later, his right-hand man, the powerful chancellor Axel Oxenstierna, kept up the Swedish initiative with such skill that by the time the time peace talks began in 1643, the balance of Europe had been shifted, and there was no doubt that the previously underrated power from the north had played a central role. Gustavus Adolphus was hailed as the Lion of the North. Sweden, in no small part due to the ancient enterprise in Falun, had won control of the trade routes it sought and of lands around the entire perimeter of the Baltic. In fact, thanks to Gustavus, the country was reaching a zenith of international influence it would never again achieve, and it had, in so doing, changed the shape of global history.

Gustavus was succeeded by his extraordinary daughter, Queen Christina, who he had ordered should be raised as a prince—that is, with all the skills a young man would have been taught. She was trained in fencing and shooting; was tutored in religion, philosophy, Greek, Latin, and the great languages of modern Europe; and was exceptionally gifted on horseback. Oxenstierna wrote of her when she was fourteen that "she is not at all like a female" in that that she had "a bright intelligence." In an effort to counteract the obviously sexist biases both of courtiers like Oxenstierna and of the era, she took the oath of office as a king rather than as a queen, thus resulting in her nickname "the Girl King."

Part of her education was an introduction to the mine at the heart of the Swedish economy. When she was about twenty, the striking young monarch rode to Falun to urge the miners on. She and Oxenstierna, who through his long and distinguished service ultimately grew to be recognized as one of the leading figures in Swedish history, knew that Sweden's gains during the war could not be maintained without ever-increasing output—a fact that led them ultimately to embrace unsustainable practices. Speaking to the gathered miners, she said, "Sweden stands or falls with the Copper Mountain." Visiting yet again a few years later, she would say, displaying a view understandably rather different from that of Ogier, that she hoped the sulfurous smoke that emanated from the smelting houses in Falun would never disappear.

At the Tip of a Copper Pike: The Nation-State Takes Center Stage

In the wake of the Swedish victories, the course of the war took several more turns. First, the emperor and many of the Protestants within the empire agreed in 1635 to the Peace of Prague, which dissolved the Catholic League, granted amnesty to many former enemies of the emperor, recognized Calvinism, and suspended for forty years the implementation of the Edict of Restitution. The peace was signed, and the archduke Ferdinand, the emperor's son, pressed for a general amnesty for anyone who agreed to the peace. Once again, the emperor miscalculated, denying amnesty for several old enemies including the Elector Palatine (who had accepted the Bohemian throne in 1620) and the Landgrave of Hessen-Kassel. This was enough for the Swedes and their allies in France, who had only recently entered the war in order to assert that they were still ostensibly fighting on behalf of some of the Germans on whose land they were battling.

In 1636, Ferdinand II died, replaced by his more peace-minded son, Ferdinand III. Four years later Spain faced revolts in Catalonia and Portugal, and soon after, the citizens of Naples and Sicily were similarly inspired to challenge Madrid. Philip IV's finances were now in such dire straits that he could barely manage a 60,000-florin loan to his Vienna cousins, one-seventh of what he had given outright just two years earlier. Then, in 1643, the French won a striking victory over the Army of Flanders at the town of Rocroi, thanks to a little bit of late-night daring, a 3:00 a.m. attack on sleeping Spanish troops led by the troops of the Duc d'Enghien. After a fierce day of battle the Spanish were down to five, then two, of their once-feared *tercios*. The Spanish surrendered and d'Enghien led his army to the gates of Vienna by 1645, thus sending the unmistakable message to both branches of the Habsburg clan that it was time to seriously negotiate the peace.

Not surprisingly, the peace negotiations that led to the conclusion of the many conflicts that comprised what is today known as the Thirty Years' War were as complex, fitful, protracted, and momentous as the conflicts themselves. Initial negotiations between France and the Habsburgs started in Cologne in 1636 but were quashed because France sought the inclusion of all its allies. The Swedes meanwhile had also engaged in preliminary negotiations in Hamburg. Ultimately, all parties acknowledged that these discussions were preparation for an overall peace agreement. This agreement would itself be negotiated in two cities in Westphalia, one Catholic—Munster—and one both Lutheran and Catholic—Osnabruck. The Lutheran Swedes took Osnabruck as the location for their negotiations with the empire, while the French did their primary diplomatic work in Munster.

The half-decade-long negotiations were extraordinary in many respects. In terms of the sheer number of participants, they were a mirror onto the Europe whose future they sought to resolve. A total of 194 European kingdoms, principalities, estates, electorates, republics, and free cities were represented by 235 official envoys. While these delegations never met in any single plenary session, the discussions were effectively managed serially over the course of the five years, with the greatest concentration of participants gathering during the year and a half following January 1646.

The simple act of convening so many different actors in a secular conference, sponsored not by the church but by political actors treating one another as equals, was revolutionary, and it proved to be a model for virtually all European peace conferences that have taken place in the centuries that followed, from Utrecht in 1711 to Vienna in 1814 to Paris in 1919. For centuries, hierarchy had been a central organizing principle of European society, but at Westphalia, as a practical matter and as a step reflecting broader social and political changes that were taking place, all participants, regardless of the size of the entity they represented, were to be referred to as "Excellency," all kings, regardless of the history of their thrones, were to be referred to as "Majesty," and theoretically all official representatives were to arrive in the two cities on equal footing, limited to coaches pulled by no more than six horses.

These aspirations to create an equitable environment were not all honored to the letter—the Swedes arrived with a delegation of 165 including "medical personnel, cooks, a tailor and a personal shopper." But status-based mechanisms and roles such as chairmen were done without, and much was achieved through the multiple, parallel negotiations. Leo Gross, the noted international legal scholar, has described the outcomes of Westphalia as follows:

> [The treaties of Munster and Osnabruck] marked man's abandonment of the idea of a hierarchical structure of society and his option for a new system characterized by the co-existence of a multiplicity of states, each sovereign within its territory, equal to one another, and free from any external earthly authority. The idea of authority or organization above

the sovereign state is no longer. What takes its place is the notion that all states form a world-wide political system, or that, at any rate, the states of Western Europe form a single political system. This new system rests on international law and the balance of power, a law operating between rather than above states and a power operating between rather than above states.

Further, the agreements enshrined the idea that each individual state's choice of religion was to be respected without foreign interference. While the only acknowledged choices were Catholicism, Lutheranism, or Calvinism, the principle that was established—making the leaders of each state sovereign in all political and theological matters—forms the basis for most modern theories of political science. From neorealism to neoliberalism, a central precept that has gone unchallenged to this day is that states are "autonomous, unified, rational actors" with total authority over a defined geographical area. Later in this book, we will consider whether this assumption needs to be revisited as a consequence of intervening events.

Specifically, the treaty recognized the advance of Protestantism deep into territories ruled for centuries by Catholic institutions. The Habsburgs would be able to suppress Protestantism only within very limited hereditary lands, the outlines of which would ultimately emerge as what was known as the Austro-Hungarian Empire. Further, Christians—living as religious minorities—would be permitted to practice their religion without interference. Spain acknowledged the full independence of the Dutch. The Dutch gave up their claims on the Spanish Netherlands and agreed to keep their trading ships away from Spain's American colonies in exchange for Spanish recognition of Dutch rights to territories formally controlled by Portugal. The Swiss Confederation gained independence. Sweden received five million *dalers* with which to pay its armies and also gained Western Pomerania, Wismar, Bremen, and Verden.

Of all the participants in the conflict, the Swedes, the Dutch, and the French emerged particularly strengthened. But territorial gains and national fortunes would continue to ebb and flow over the decades and centuries to come. What made the Treaty of Westphalia (as the two treaties were collectively known) significant was the shift in collective attitudes that it enshrined, perhaps the most significant collective adjustment in political philosophy and structure that the West had seen since the fall of

Rome. Notable in that context was the relatively minor role the pope himself and the Vatican played in the final outcome in Westphalia. Popes had for so long been pulled between the interests of Europe's various leading Catholic actors—in Vienna, Madrid, Paris, or elsewhere—that it was hard for them to take sides in the war, and they spent most of its duration tending to the development of the Holy See.

The pope's representative to Westphalia, the nuncio Fabio Chigi, was a proponent of parallel talks, which effectively eliminated the chance for the pope to play any leading role in the settlement. That point was essentially made moot by the fact that the official position of the Vatican throughout was to avoid any concessions to the Protestants. This was such a stunningly anachronistic view that it negated the influence of the pope more than any procedural, structural, or tactical undertaking could have. The official response of the Vatican to the treaty was a papal bull from Pope Innocent X that declared the agreement "null, void, invalid, damnable, reprobate, inane, empty of meaning and effect for all time." Psychologists have a term for such a statement. They call it projection, because in political terms it was the central role of the Catholic Church in European affairs that was being declared null, void, and increasingly empty of meaning and effect due to the church's failure to adapt. After all, perhaps the most striking element of the Treaty of Westphalia was its provision that granted states "territorial superiority in all matters ecclesiastical as well as political." The old battle lines were erased; the old was map remade. The hierarchies were undone. A coda was written to the epoch during which the struggle between church and state was central. The great leveling had begun—not just in the titles exchanged among diplomats, but also in the rising role of businesspeople and businesses in the affairs of the reordered sovereign states of Europe.

Coronation and Abdication, Collapse and Reinvention

The coronation of Queen Christina in 1650 in Stockholm was a kind of exclamation point attached to the country's hard-won victories in the Thirty Years' War. It was a massive, gorgeous, unprecedented, excessive celebration "with a splendor previously unparalleled in the realm." Featuring a massive parade of musicians and heralds, nobles in gilded carriages and officials of state in their best finery, and the queen herself riding in a carriage drawn by six white horses shod in silver, the procession at the center of the coronation was a far more civilized sort of political theater than her great-grandfather had used to knit the kingdom together. It was also considerably more than the recently triumphant kingdom could afford, even with the workers in the mines performing at levels never before equaled, which were ultimately unsustainable. Something would surely come crashing down.

The queen herself was a contradiction, one of the great victors in the Thirty Years' War who would within a few years renounce her throne and her religion and run off to live for years in the Vatican under the protection of a series of popes and cardinals, a striking woman who won the hearts of many men and is reputed to have had at least one woman among her great loves, a patron of knowledge and of the arts who was deeply practical, and yet a ruler and later a self-exiled queen who spent money with abandon. Under her leadership Sweden completed the transition to being a modern European power, yet at her coronation there was doubt about whether the realm had the funds to cover the salaries of the bureaucrats who ran the government.

Similarly, Sweden's golden age has other contradictory elements to it when we look at the world of the average citizen. Despite the country's victories—or perhaps in part because of the expense associated with them—the standard of living for the average Swedish peasant during the era was actually lower than it had been in the century before. Hunger and poverty were so commonplace that bread made of tree bark actually became a staple in the peasant diet. With Swedish soldiers demanding their pay for the wars, even with the big settlement that followed Westphalia, the economic pressures on the country were enormous. This in turn led to a major push at the mines, which had already been operating during the war at a fever pitch. The years immediately after the war were the most successful ever in terms of the amount of copper produced. But the need for output was such that little attention was paid to longer-term considerations such as maintaining the mine pit infrastructure properly. Safe practices were ignored, and miners worked on because on average even the lowest among them was still doing somewhat better than the average struggling Swede.

At the end of the year of Christina's grand coronation, driven as they had been to produce, forty miners at Falun stood together to evaluate the year's output. Throughout the day, the last day of December in 1650, they weighed the copper. Though they were eager to celebrate the arrival of the New Year, that had to be postponed because there was still more ore to be weighed. In the end, the numbers represented a new record for the mine: three thousand tons of raw copper. The average yield in prior years had been less than one-sixth of that. The achievement of 1650 at the mines at the time of the glittering coronation was hard to equal.

In 1654, Christina abdicated. In part, this was due to a desire to practice in public what had been her secret Catholicism. In part, this was due to the fact that she had created so many new nobles—almost five hundred overall—that she had been forced to sell or mortgage crown property to the tune of 1.2 million *riksdalers* annually. In the months after that, the reckoning for the mine's neglect finally came. The great pit collapsed on itself, dirt filling in the many chambers of the mine, bringing operations to a complete halt. It was the greatest catastrophe to that date in the mine's history. But whereas with the departure of Queen Christina, or even that of her father, it might be said that Sweden had passed its zenith, and even though the mine would never again achieve the output it achieved in 1650, it cannot be said that the enterprise called Stora Kopparberg had begun its downturn. Because, as a company, Stora was built to adapt and reinvent itself, to change and adjust with a nimbleness that a country could hardly duplicate.

In fact, Stora had begun to shift its economic foundations even as the walls of the great pit started to groan with the stresses of overmining. As the Thirty Years' War was coming to a close, a master miner from Germany named Hans Filip Lybecker recognized that a constant supply of lumber was essential to the mine. He therefore established in the late 1640s Stora Kopparberg's Wood Company, a venture that gradually grew over time and, thanks to good management, would offer an alternative growth path for the concern when, in the late seventeenth century it became clear that the glory days of the mine were behind it. Furthermore, as the Swedish crown grew strained, the miners at Stora found ways to enhance their independence, building their business in ways that over the next century would greatly increase its autonomy and diversify its sources of revenue.

Stora had played a central role in Sweden's rise, and Sweden in turn had played a central role in ending the dominance of the church and asserting the rights of the nation-state. But in the early years of the era of nation-states, Stora entered a new, increasingly independent chapter in the company's history, one that would once again track with the evolution and rise of the other companies mentioned in this chapter and indeed with an entirely new global economic structure increasingly built around the accumulation of private rather than public power. The implications for the new nation-states were more complex, and in ways more ominous, than they might have imagined, or indeed than they might imagine even today.

I hope we shall crush in its birth the aristocracy of our moneyed corporations, which dare already to challenge our government to a trial of strength and bid defiance to the laws of our country.

—Thomas Jefferson

Practical men, who believe themselves to be quite exempt from intellectual influences, are usually the slaves of some defunct economist.

—John Maynard Keynes

As noted in the introduction, Thomas Jefferson was a great admirer of Trenchard and Gordon's "The Cato Letters." Not only did he keep a copy in his library at Monticello, but he recommended that another be kept in the collection at the University of Virginia, the institution whose founding he considered among his greatest achievements. In his apparent unease with "moneyed corporations," Jefferson was hardly just manifesting the biases of America's eighteenth-century country gentry. Nor was he listening solely with the ears of a radical revolutionary to isolated kindred spirits from across the sea.

On the contrary, Jefferson was, as he was on many of the central causes of his life, swept up in a view that was increasingly mainstream. He was in fact seldom a lone wolf on anything, but rather a master interpreter of trends. Even his most famous revolutionary act, drafting the Declaration of Independence, was in his view not so much a presentation of new ideas as a restating in a contemporary voice of existing views. As he wrote shortly before his death, "Neither aiming at originality of principle or sentiment, nor yet copied from any particular or previous writing, it was intended to be an expression of the American mind, and to give that expression the proper tone and spirit called for by the occasion."

Jefferson's views on independence and the principles that should guide the conduct of governments flowed from a century of thought about the nature of states that had followed the forging of the treaties in Westphalia. Like other leaders of the American Revolution, Jefferson was shaped primarily by English and French philosophers and politicians such as Locke, Rousseau, and Montesquieu, who grappled with the new-found powers of their states, their kings, and the institutions that were created to counterbalance royal authority. He was most directly a product of a political culture that had been shaped by England's "Glorious Revolution," which enshrined the principle of Parliament above the crown as the source of English law. From the days of his education at the College of William and Mary in Williamsburg, Virginia, where he read widely among the era's leading political thinkers, he was among the large number of colonists and subjects of the crown around the world who felt that, regardless of its power, Parliament could not undo the fundamental rights of individuals.

But as influenced as he was by this political debate, he was also very much shaped by the recent economic experiences of the British Empire and of Europe. Included among those are the events that inspired Trenchard and Gordon's writings—the South Sea Bubble of 1720 and the corporate corruption they saw associated with it. It also included the remarkable, almost unimaginable, rise of those state-sponsored corporations whose birth predated the Thirty Years' War, companies such as the Dutch East India Company, the South Sea Company, and above all the British East India Company, whose involvement in the series of provocations that triggered the American Revolution was direct and of central importance. (As will be seen, the British East India Company played a substantial if utterly unintentional role in triggering the movements that ultimately led to the creation of both of the world's largest democracies—the United States and India—and the consequent downfall of the empire it was formed to help support.)

Jefferson—who, despite the benefits of his birth and his ownership of a large plantation that over his lifetime drew upon the services of more than six hundred slaves, died very nearly bankrupt—was, however, never known primarily as an economic thinker. And while his views on corporations did tap into a mainstream view of the era, they are best characterized as representing one side in what was perhaps the central economic debate of the day, one that was particularly popular among gentlemen farmers such as himself. A notable countervailing voice on the American side of that debate was Jefferson's great rival, Alexander Hamilton, America's first Treasury secretary, who saw the rise of a United States built largely around a thriving commercial and manufacturing sector as the best trajectory for the recently born country. Many of Hamilton's perspectives were in turned fueled by the ideas of the other great revolutionary of 1776, the man whose work was arguably the second most important, after Jefferson's declaration, written that year: Adam Smith. (It is worth noting that 1776 was a particularly remarkable year in terms of history-making writing. It was also a year that began with the publication of Thomas Paine's *Common Sense* and included, a month later, Edward Gibbons's *The Decline and Fall of the Roman Empire*, a landmark tome rich with political resonances for the time.)

Smith's *An Inquiry into the Nature and Causes of the Wealth of Nations* appeared in March 1776, and in the context of the moment it was certainly not seen as the equal of the other two books in terms of impact. It would be years before the book assumed the stature that it now has as a cornerstone of economic thought. Smith's book was also written in large part as a reaction against the mercantile economic system that had become so important to England and other European powers in the past century, and it was notably critical of the role of corporations like the British East India Company. But it also made the case for an economic approach that advocated leaving critical decisions to markets and individual economic actors, in much the same way that the Declaration asserted that as a matter of natural law, important national decisions should be left to the people. While there is much in harmony between these views of bottom-up governance, there is also a fundamental tension between them when the question emerges as to which set of decision makers takes precedence when the interests of those who vote with ballots are at odds with the interests of those who vote with their money. Smith wrote that when individuals were free to pursue their economic interests, the public interest was advanced as if through the workings of "an invisible hand." Yet history has shown that often that hand has been more than invisible, it has been absent. And sometimes history has also shown the alternative: an iron fist wrapped in an invisible glove.

America's uncertainty about whether to follow Jefferson's agrarian, anticorporate instincts or the industrial vision Hamilton best described in his prescient prescription for industrializing America, *The Report on Manufactures*, solidified into a north-south rift that defined the first one hundred years of U.S. history and resulted, in the end, in the bloodiest war in the history of humankind up to that point. This national agrarian-versus-industrial identity crisis also may have been resolved, in the end, less as a direct consequence of the democratic revolution Jefferson spearheaded and more as the result of the economic revolution whose beginning co-incided with the release of Smith's book. The parallels and harmonies between these two revolutions as well as the potential tensions they en-gendered mark the next major phase in the emerging relationship be-tween the newly ascendant nation-states and the private power centers they played such a central role in fostering.

The Thing's the Thing

Throughout history, there has been a need to balance the recognition that there must be some "highest" authority to resolve disputes and ensure order with the desire to limit the abuses so common to those who hold the power in their hands. Since ancient times, one method for achieving this balance has been through varying forms of what today we might call democracy but which would hardly meet any of the contemporary defi-nitions of the term. Within the smallest societies—such as tribes and tiny villages—some form of voting among members was relatively com-mon, whether it was formalized or not.

Community councils involved many voices, although typically crite-ria such as age or gender or family background or even health or stature would give some more say than others. As communities grew, so too did the need for more formal mechanisms. From the councils of elders or of those who were of an age to bear arms in ancient Mesopotamia to the *ga-nas* of ancient India in which rajas were advised by their local assemblies, there was a widespread desire to ensure that some form of pluralism trumped the always-present impulse toward autocracy of the strongest, richest, or most fortunate. Even in oligarchies such as Sparta, government was structured with dual kings, elders, and other oversight councils in order to ensure a semblance of fairness and some institutional guaran-tees for the distribution of power.

Sometimes, of course, the institutions were more clearly the ancestors of modern democracies, beginning with the Ecclesia of Athens, an as-sembly open to all citizens, and the carefully crafted system of laws within which it and other leadership groups worked. As described by Pericles:

> Its administration favors the many instead of the few; this is why it is called a *democracy*. If we look to the laws, they afford equal justice to all in their private differences; if no social standing, advancement in public life falls to reputation for capacity, class considerations not being allowed to interfere with merit; nor again does poverty bar the way, if a man is able to serve the state, he is not hindered by the obscurity of his condition.

Thanks to the work of political philosophers such as Plato and Aristotle and later to the embracing of Greek ideas by the Romans in their own republic, the basic idea of governments founded on the principle of inclusion and broad representation of views achieved a level of refinement that would not be equaled again for more than a thousand years. The fall of Rome and the Middle Ages did not see ideas about representative government disappear in the West, but certainly the core concepts were set back by a dependency on monarchical rule, rule by force, and underlying economic systems such as feudalism, which elevated landowners to the central position within an agrarian society that controlled the primary mechanisms for subsistence and wealth creation.

Nonetheless, during the Middle Ages there were institutions and traditions of communal rule that endured and periodically flourished. These extend from the oligarchic councils of the Italian city-states to the great gatherings of Northern European peoples that in many respects, despite the lack of recognition by academics who have preferred to trace modern institutions back to classical Greece and Rome, are the more direct antecedents of British and American democracies (and all those derived from them). Even around the fall of Rome, tribal societies in Northern Europe would gather in annual or even more frequent meetings that were part festival, part marketplace, and part government. At these meetings, participants would typically gather in or around a large field, often living in tents or other makeshift shelters, to resolve intratribal or clan disputes, make laws, and briefly knit together societies that were very loosely connected (due to few roads or dependable means of communication).

The oldest of the world's parliaments that is still in existence, Iceland's Althing, is derived from this tradition. It was first convened in A.D. 930

as a place for local leaders to set rules for society and resolve conflicts. The chairman of the gathering was called the lawspeaker (from which the modern term for the "speaker" of a parliamentary body is derived). One of this individual's responsibilities was actually to speak the law, to read out all the laws currently in effect or recently agreed. He did this from a perch called Law Rock. The concept of the "thing" was common throughout Scandinavia, the term being derived from an ancient Indo-European term meaning "a stretch of time for a great gathering." Later, the word came to mean a designated time, and then to refer to the fairs or assemblies themselves. It is a fascinating twist of etymology with much resonance for our story that the word "thing" first meant the source of laws and only later came to mean "object" or "possession." Today, in addition to Iceland's legislature, evidence of the enduring nature of this approach to government includes the parliament of Norway, which is called the Storting, meaning "great thing," and the Danish parliament, which is called the Folketing, meaning "thing of the people." The roots and evolution of these words suggest that property rights hold a privileged position among all laws, more ancient and more fundamental than many others, with the concept of ownership and by extension economic matters being among the earliest concerns of Western legal systems.

In Sweden, the word was used to refer to provincial gatherings called "Landsting," but before the days of the Riksdag, far back in history and extending well into the Middle Ages, a similar type of gathering took place in Uppsala toward the end of winter that coincided with a pagan celebration called Disablot, which was held to ensure a good harvest for the year ahead. Although the religious celebration focused on fertility and was performed largely by women, a larger purpose developed. There was also a festival called the Disting, and later this evolved into the broader political assembly called "the Thing of All Swedes," a great market and rudimentary parliament all wrapped up into a single event.

While the fertility celebration focused on those who possessed wombs, the political proceedings were open to all those who possessed weapons. This fact—that political participation was limited to those who could provide the force needed to secure or project the will of the group—ties to another core dimension of what makes states states: the ability to legitimately project force.

The Swedish gathering was also presided over by a lawspeaker. Later it became the mechanism by which kings were selected and at which those kings played a judicial role. But there were incidents in which these gatherings also counterbalanced and even countermanded those kings, as in 1018 when King Olof Skotkonung sought war against Norway and was rebuffed by the Thing. In this instance, Thorgnyr the lawspeaker upbraided the monarch in a speech, forcefully asserting that the real power of Sweden resided not with the monarch but with the people, who were disinclined toward another costly war. The surrounding armed throngs cheered so enthusiastically that Olof reconsidered his foreign adventure.

Similarly, two centuries later in another field at Runnymede, the Great Seal of King John of England was attached to a document that also asserted limits to the monarch's power. While the document, known to history as the Magna Carta, is celebrated as one of the turning points in the history of democracy, it is an event with fundamentally economic rather than egalitarian roots. It was not the first time an English king, for example, had acknowledged that his powers were secondary to those of the law. That was in the year 1100, in the Charter of Liberties voluntarily adopted by Henry I. By 1215, however, England's ruling landowners felt overtaxed, abused, and—like their Swedish cousins also unhappy with their king's overseas ambitions, in John's case in France—had risen up in rebellion.

King John, with great reluctance but no choice, acceded to the landowners' demands that limits on his power be codified and that the power of certain laws guaranteeing basic rights be officially acknowledged as being greater than that of the king. Thus, the Magna Carta was the first such document to be forced upon an English king. The agreement established a committee that could overrule the king if he ignored the provisions of the document and even, as punishment, seize his landholdings. While the document went through many revisions and was annulled by the pope (then later revised and reapproved), it is still seen as being a vital element of England's constitutional law and the historical thread leading from the Greeks to the democratic renaissance that started in the wake of the Thirty Years' War.

In Search of New Rules for a New World

One of the central actors who helped trigger the revival of constitutional law—although in large part unintentionally—was no great fan of the

Magna Carta. Oliver Cromwell, in fact, was so dismissive of lawyers and their efforts to use the law to constrain his authority that on one occasion he referred to it derisively as the Magna Farta. (In this he was like many others—including Thomas Jefferson—who championed freedoms and legal limitations on ruling authorities right up until the moment he assumed power, at which point his views shifted.) At the same time, it was the son of a country lawyer who served in Cromwell's army who would play a pivotal role in making the next great leap toward placing the people above heads of state, atop the monarch-centric hierarchy of power that would succeed that which had dominated since the Romans.

While the Thirty Years' War was playing out, Cromwell was the pivotal figure in the English Civil War. It was a conflict that would bring down Charles I, who himself was so dismissive of Parliament that, despite having acknowledged its precedence, he failed to convene it for more than a decade, spending recklessly, involving England in the Continental wars, and making Protestant England nervous with his marriage to a French Catholic wife. When the armies led by Cromwell ultimately took power, after two rounds of civil conflict in December 1648, Cromwell restored Parliament by ousting anyone in it who did not agree with him. Then, manipulating the Rump Parliament to his purposes, he oversaw the trial at which Charles was found guilty of treason and put to death.

A brilliant general and a pragmatic leader, Cromwell oversaw almost a decade of unprecedented social freedoms in England. It was a time in which guilds and tradesmen gained considerable traction, seizing the lands and resources of members of the aristocracy, pushing for more democracy, and getting a taste of a somewhat more level playing field. Again, confounding those who would paint him as an idealist, Cromwell also saw as a threat movements among his own army to embrace these new freedoms in a more organized, ideological way. He may have participated in the "great leveling," but one of the target groups he quashed within his own forces was in fact called the Levelers. Although Cromwell died in 1658 and his son was unable to hold power afterward, being replaced at the behest of the army by King Charles II, the terms of the new king's restoration were to make it clear that he ruled only with the consent of the Parliament. It was an important evolutionary leap forward in the power structure of England that reflected a potent post-Westphalian impulse across Europe.

If Westphalia set new international laws focused on the sovereign state, the next order of business was to set rules within those states regarding the true nature of sovereign power—in terms of both its extent and the limits placed on it. Critical to all these movements was the spirit of the ancient lawspeakers, that kings served at the pleasure of the people and within the limits of the laws established by those people. But just as some kings would continue to argue for over a century that, like the popes, theirs was an authority that was paramount because it flowed from the heavens, history would turn on the fact that proponents of constraints on royal power were by the mid-seventeenth century beginning to more effectively make the case that basic laws had more sacred, fundamental origins. Defining those origins, and framing in ever greater depth the rules in terms of God-given rights of individuals that superseded the God-given powers of kings, was a central intellectual pursuit of the century and a half that followed Westphalia, Cromwell, and the Restoration in England.

As a direct consequence of that intellectual ferment, something very near to the literal words we associate with the American Revolution were coined in the two decades after Cromwell, as England further refined the relationship between king and Parliament. As it happens, those original words not only reflected more directly on the economic issues so central to these power struggles, but were written by a man whose life itself blended elements associated with both the transforming business and political trends of the day.

That man was John Locke. Born in 1632, the son of that rural lawyer who had served in Cromwell's army, he took advantage of the ascension of his father's commander from the wars to a seat in Parliament to gain entrance into England's leading school, and from there he went on at age twenty to Christ Church, Oxford. While he began his studies in the classic way, he was drawn to a new intellectual movement focused on the observation of nature. This in turn drew him into medicine and studies at Oxford with some of the leading scientists of the time, including one who would grow to become a good friend, Isaac Newton.

By a twist of circumstance, Locke was introduced to Sir Anthony Ashley Cooper, one of England's richest men and a rising political star, who had come to Oxford seeking medical assistance. The two hit it off, and Locke was persuaded to go to London and join Ashley's household as his personal physician. Because Ashley would play a central role in the political tumult of Restoration England, leading the forces most skeptical of the efforts of the crown to reclaim authority and especially wary of those within the Royal Stuart household who were sympathetic to the Vatican, Locke was soon drawn into an important role in the next great political revolution of the era.

As political events were unfolding, Locke also won a position that gave him a unique perspective on the rise of both the modern state and global business. He was appointed secretary of the Board of Trade and Plantations and secretary to the Lords Proprietors of the Carolinas. While his contribution to the writing of the early constitution of the Carolinas is often cited in relation to this role, it is equally interesting from our perspective that Locke was so intimately involved in overseeing the evolution of the British mercantile system. This is because in this capacity, Locke was directly involved with the rise of the state-sponsored corporation; with the biggest protagonist in that system, the British East India Company; with the early administration and therefore exploitation of the American colonies; and, as it happens, with the slave trade—an especially sharp irony given his recognition today as a champion of the rights of man.

Locke made his greatest contributions writing during a period of English constitutional crisis. Reforms from those of the Magna Carta to those imposed by Cromwell were shrugged off by the restored king, Charles II, and Lord Ashley was engaged in the political struggle to keep James, Charles's brother, the Catholic duke of York, from inheriting the throne. This led to Lord Ashley, now the Earl of Shaftesbury, being arrested and eventually exiled. While Ashley suffered these misfortunes, Locke traveled through Europe and wrote a major work, *An Essay Concerning Human Understanding*, which explored the limits of human understanding, and *Letters Concerning Toleration*, drawn in part from his observations of how Protestants were treated in Europe.

However, his most important work in terms of the evolution of the state was his *Two Treatises of Government*. It was written in the prelude to what was called the Glorious Revolution, the name given to the transformational rebellion during which James, now king, was forced from office and replaced by William of Orange and his wife Mary, James's Protestant sister. William was the nephew of Maurits of Nassau, the innovative general who was so influential to Gustavus Adolphus and the armies that defeated the Habsburgs and the Catholic League during the Thirty Years' War. Central to the assumption of the throne by William and Mary was their agreement to be bound by a new set of rules that granted Parliament the right to determine the succession of English monarchs. This was the final pivot point in the six-century-long struggle to transform England into a true constitutional monarchy.

Locke's *Two Treatises of Government* offered a vital intellectual foundation on which the changes of the era were built. It directly assaulted and dismantled the arguments associated with the divine right of kings, refuting past assertions that men were not "naturally free" and thus delegitimizing monarchy as part of the natural order or anything prescribed by scriptural doctrine. More important, in his second treatise, Locke made the argument that in man's original state he was born free and with certain rights, rights that he did not transfer to government once he concluded there were merits associated with entering into a social contract. In the first chapter of the second treatise, he wrote:

> *Political power*, then, I take to be a *right* of making laws with penalties of death, and consequently all less penalties, for the regulating and preserving of property, and of employing the force of the community, in the execution of such laws, and in the defence of the common wealth from foreign injury; and all this only for the public good.

Even more fundamentally, Locke argued that God's purpose is for man to survive, and that therefore the most basic rights given to man are those associated with that purpose, which he asserted are life, liberty, health, and property: "The state of nature has a law of nature to govern it, which obliges everyone: and reason which is that law, teaches all mankind who will but consult it, that being all equal and independent, no one ought to harm another in his life, health, liberty or possessions."

The issues associated with possessions take up a considerable portion of the second treatise. Locke saw issues concerning wealth and ownership and the business of life as central drivers of the development of human rights and laws. He asserted that although the world was shared among all when it was given to men by God, soon, for reasons of practicality, men began to own what they harvested or captured for their survival. In this early state, ownership is not a threat because abundance is a natural condition. Later, as agricultural society developed, constraints that men should own no more than they could cultivate guided, but then all such rules were distorted and inequality entered into the picture when men adopted systems of money. It was largely to regulate such inequality that Locke saw the reason for the creation of civil government.

Over the ensuing centuries, and particularly recently, there has been much debate about whether Locke ultimately was arguing for a system in which unlimited acquisition of property was acceptable and governments were created to protect men's rights to their property and to adjudicate disputes, or whether he felt too much self-interest was a dangerous thing. In all likelihood, he was unclear on this point, especially given the multiple forces acting on him at the time he wrote the treatise. Not only was he doing the work of a political philosopher, but he was also seeking to justify a revolution in the conditions of a transforming England. Not only was he a propagandist, but he was also a participant in the high economic workings of English society, linked to the development of its empire. Hence, while he argues that life and liberty are natural rights, slavery can be justified as a condition of war when a conqueror chooses not to end the life of a captive but to postpone death in order to put the captive to work for him. This apparent contradiction is more easily explained in the context of Locke's subsequent professional work with regard to the Carolinas and even in terms of investments he made in the slave trade. Here again, one who has most shaped our views about self-interest has done so in the service of and influenced by his own evolving self-interests.

Locke's views heavily influenced the English Bill of Rights of 1689. This document not only described limits on the power of the monarch and the government at large, but also necessarily defined the core elements of what governments would be expected to do. So, while the 1689 Bill—seen as part of the English constitution and a model for subsequent such efforts in the United States and elsewhere—guaranteed that Englishmen were born with certain rights, including freedom from royal meddling with the law, it also defined and sanctioned the appropriate role the government might play in administering the law. It limited taxation by "royal prerogative" but acknowledged the right to tax if new taxes were approved by Parliament. It specified that there be freedom from the standing army during peacetime but asserted the right of Parliament to determine when force can be used. It granted Protestants the right to bear arms in their own defense and in so doing still implied a governmental hand in the religious affairs of their communities.

In short, the English Bill of Rights represented a major step forward toward helping to describe both the extent and limits of the post-Westphalian nation-state. But through its often noble and even profound focus on individual freedoms and property and on beginning to establish a complex system of legal restraints on the power of the state, it laid the foundation for further changes to come.

The Corporation Unleashed

During the same years that Locke was rising in prominence, so too was the influence of the British East India Company. In fact, Locke was approached by a member of Parliament named Sir John Somers to prepare counterarguments to those put forth by some East India Company lobbyists that the government should manipulate money markets in a way they thought would be beneficial to the company. This led to Locke's *Some Consideration of the Consequences of Lowering of Interest, and Raising the Value of Money,* one of his few purely economic efforts and one to which he did not affix his name. In this book, however, he argued that governments should not interfere excessively in markets, as to do so was contrary to the natural laws of those markets. In so doing, he presaged some themes that Adam Smith would develop later. In 1698, Locke was named a commissioner on the Board of Trade, which oversaw England's colonial interests as well as trade policy. He served for four years, during which time he oversaw policies of government involvement in markets that were considered quite natural—including imposing tariffs and managing the mercantile trade within the empire on which in fact the growing influence of the government's largest commercial enterprise, the British East India Company, was based.

By the time the BEIC reached a century of existence in the first decade of the eighteenth century, the scope of its operations had grown enormously. Trading in spices, textiles, dyes, and other precious goods, it had during its first one hundred years established more than two dozen outposts in India alone. It also ventured as far as the Straits of Malacca and China, developed an organized lobby in the British Parliament, and by 1670, thanks to a series of acts produced by King Charles II, was granted the power to acquire territory, mint money, command armies and forts, adjudicate the law in the territories they controlled, and make war and peace. In short, the company was both a kind of ward of the state and a state unto itself. Its power grew so great that not only was Locke enlisted in pushing back against it, others who sought to limit it established a rival company to challenge its monopoly on trade with India. Thanks to the size of the original company and an effort by BEIC shareholders to buy up the new venture, the new company lasted only a few years and was merged into a new consolidated United Company of Merchants of England Trading to the East Indies. But it was still called the East India Company in conversation, or, in the vernacular, John Company.

Indeed, in the early years of the new century, the company saw its power grow substantially as nearly 15 percent of British imports passed through it from India. Its licenses were extended and its role in the government grew—even as other business ventures such as the previously discussed South Sea Company went bust and rocked the British capital with accusations of corruption. This was due in large part to the fact that the East India Company was the most potent, successful, and valuable foreign policy weapon in the British arsenal.

In 1744, a nineteen-year-old Englishman with decidedly undistinguished family and academic credentials who was "out of measure addicted to fighting" arrived in India to make his fortune in the employ of the company. By the time he left India for the third and last time in 1767, he was renowned for his military exploits at the head of the company's army, had received the title Baron of Plassey, had been elected to Parliament and been booted out, and had set a precedent within the British Empire for treating local leaders as casually as if they were chess pieces in a Sunday afternoon game in the park. His name was Robert Clive, although to later generations he would be known by the more romantic and imposing title Clive of India. Ultimately, in twists that suggest a darker kind of romanticism, he would become a target for the critics of the company, be called before Parliament to answer charges, and, his reputation spiraling downward, become the victim of a downward spiral into drugs and depression, stabbing himself to death with a penknife just three decades after he first set foot in India.

At the tip of a sword, Clive would not only play a major role in creating the greatest empire the world had seen since the Caesars, but he would develop the state-sponsored company to such an extreme that it would dwarf anything imagined by those who fear state involvement in markets in the twenty-first century. Indeed, under his leadership, on the ground in

India, the East India Company would create what looked very much like the world's first company-sponsored state.

India in 1750 was responsible for almost a quarter of the world's manufacturing output, and its people had a standard of living that approached that of those in England (a fact that would change as a result of the East India Company's two-hundred-year despoiling of the subcontinent). Bengal, the richest province on the then Mughal-controlled subcontinent, was so prosperous that one Mughal emperor called it "the paradise of nations." Its principal output was textiles, for which it was famous around the world. Manouchi, the chief physician to the Mughal emperor Aurangzeb, said during the seventeenth century of Bengal that "it is not inferior in anything to Egypt and that it even exceeds that kingdom in its products of silks, cottons, sugar and indigo. All things are in great plenty here, fruits, pulse, grain, muslins, cloths of gold and silk."

While most Indian provinces had been controlled by two officials on behalf of the emperor—one responsible for taxes and the other for financial affairs—since 1717, Bengal had been administered by one man who held both responsibilities. His name was Murshid Quli, and the title he held was Nawab of Bengal. In the same year that Quli became Nawab, the Mughal emperor Furrukhsiyar granted the British East India Company duty-free trading rights for Bengal and thus established their most important foothold in India. The company had already been involved in the Bengal textile market for almost seven decades at that point, having secured a monopoly on Indian trade into Britain in exchange for a loan to the crown of £1.2 million at 0 percent interest. When you consider the extent of the return on this loan, it is a bargain that makes the Dutch purchase of Manhattan Island for 60 guilders seem like overpayment. It's worth noting that the Dutch "purchase" in 1626 was also made on behalf of a company, the Dutch West India Company, which employed Peter Minuit, the man which negotiated the Manhattan deal.

As soon as the British East India Company was granted its trading rights, it began illegally maximizing its profits from them by reselling rights to Asian merchants, by granting rights to its own executives so they could engage in private trading, and by trading in goods they did not actually have the legal right to trade. The Nawab protested and tried to crack down, but this only provoked resentment from the British.

At the same time that the company was inflaming its "hosts" in Bengal, it was actually in a shooting war with a competing company in southern

India. That conflict was an extension of the nearly permanent conflict between Britain and France and involved, as the commercial proxy for the French, the Compagnie Perpétuelle des Indes. Periodically during European wars over royal successions in Spain and Austria, the two competing companies would tussle and then declare truces, with the British attacking French ships and then the French seizing the British base in Madras and defeating the local Indian ruler, the Nawab of the Carnatic. Later, the British got the base back, but the two companies continued to spar for supremacy.

However, something more significant happened during that war between the two great companies: Robert Clive earned his spurs. He achieved notable victories, leading a small guerrilla force to capture French outposts at Arcot and Trichinopoly. As a consequence, he was feted by his bosses in London and given a diamond-studded sword by the directors, and he even briefly served in Parliament. However, impolitic and combative as he was by nature, he was soon voted out and headed back to the one place on earth where he seemed to excel. He returned to India in 1755, by which time Indian workers and craftsmen accounted for almost a quarter of the planet's manufactured output.

By this time, relations with the Nawabs of Bengal had reached a boiling point. Seven times during the preceding three decades, the local government demanded additional duties from the company, and they regularly pushed back against and protested the company's efforts to militarize its outpost in Calcutta, the province's leading city. Tweaking the Nawab, now a descendant of previous occupants of the job named Siraj-ud-Daula, the company even went so far as to harbor one of his leading political opponents. When the Nawab tried to negotiate, his envoy was rebuffed, and the Bengal leader determined that force was the only remaining option. He attacked the company's main garrison in Calcutta, Fort William. In so doing he caught the company unawares, and shortly before Clive's return, the company was embarrassed to have its agents sent packing from the crown jewel in their global network. The loss amounted to more than £2 million.

Something had to be done, and Clive was the man for the job. He reconquered Calcutta in February 1757 but was not content to stop there. He pushed on, next going after the French headquarters at Chandernagore, where he was also triumphant. He then collaborated with three major Bengalis, a former general, a banker, and a leading merchant, regarding their shared desire to neutralize Siraj. Although Siraj heard of the plotting before they struck, he did nothing, a costly error. On June 23, 1757, at Plassey, a Bengali force of approximately fifty thousand was defeated by a British East India Company army of only three thousand led by Clive.

Shortly afterward, Siraj was assassinated and Mir Jafar, the former general allied with Clive, was installed as the company's handpicked Nawab. Whatever illusions the new ruler may have had about his autonomy were soon dispelled by Clive's heavy hand and clear direction. The French were immediately expelled from Bengal. The company was given land around the city, and the Bengal treasury was emptied directly into company ships that were headed straight to England and company shareholders. Clive made the company more money in this one initiative than it had lost earlier from the debacle at Fort William, and he secured a neat £234,000 for himself.

Clive would later continue to up this amount, almost doubling it within a decade. Yet in retrospect he said, "When I think, of the marvelous riches of that country, and the comparatively small part which I took away, I am astonished at my own moderation." His £400,000 in 1767 would be worth approximately £559 million today. He and his fellow officers of the company took out almost £18 million for themselves in just the years 1757 to 1784. And this is only their "commission" on the vastly greater earnings of the company and by extension Britain as a whole. Said the historian William Digby at the turn of the last century, "the industrial revolution could not have happened in Britain had it not been for the loot that came in from India. It is indeed a curious coincidence: Plassey (1757); the flying shuttle (1760); the spinning jenny (1764); the power-loom (1765); the steam engine (1768)." It's the same old story: company meets country, company takes over country, company begets industrial revolution that spawns countless other massive companies. It is estimated that in the almost two hundred years between Plassey and Indian independence, Britain probably sucked as much as a trillion dollars in current money out of the subcontinent, so debilitating it that the country's standard of living did not rise during that entire period. The British actually charged back to the Indians the cost of their own wars of conquest against them.

In the years that followed, the Nawabs were maintained as puppets and the textile weavers of Bengal were essentially reduced to a state of near slavery, working for almost nothing to fill the coffers of the East India

Company and to pump revenues back to England. Company ruthlessness was such that during a drought in 1769, the company used its resources to corner local stocks of grain to feed its managers and only sold it back to the people of the region at grossly inflated prices. The result was a death toll of over a million Bengalis, a number roughly equivalent to the population of London at that time. Outraged by this brutality, and by the bursting of a bubble valuation of the company's stock (I will leave it to the reader to determine which was a greater motivator of British public opinion), an inquiry into the consequences of applying corporate principles of placing profits above all else to running a country was undertaken by a select parliamentary committee chaired by Sir John Burgoyne—who would later make his name at the Battle of Saratoga. One member of Burgoyne's committee observed: "Never did such a system exist where mercantile avarice was the only principle and force the only means of carrying on government."

While reforms in corporate and Indian governance were implemented, perhaps the greatest consequence of the actions of Clive and the company in India were that they shaped the views of revolutionaries like Smith and Jefferson and that they came at a time when the world had an especially great appetite for change.

Empires Squandered: Hats, Caps, French, Indians, and a Tea Party

Sweden once again demonstrates that the changes associated with the era were not limited to the great stages and actors who have won the most limelight. Further, it illustrates the impulse across the post-Westphalian landscape of Europe to limit power within sovereign states and to transfer power from above (God and church and divinely anointed kings) to "below," and to fight an overconcentration of power. Finally, in the context of the relationship between the state and the private sector, the weakness of the private sector can just as easily bring turmoil to a government as the strength of the East India Company brought strength in Britain. With Stora on the ropes due to declining copper output, Sweden became dependent on outside handouts, which in turn corrupted the political processes of the country and derailed it permanently from a chance to maintain the greatness it had achieved in the eighteenth century. Without its rich copper mine, the state became too dependent, budget cutbacks ("reductions") were the norm, and the people of the country were squeezed and unhappy.

Sweden's appetite for change, whether at the political level or at the level of what had been Sweden's great state enterprise, Stora, was born of a malady that has commonly afflicted great powers. While England faced the challenges of building a great empire, Sweden was suffering the burdens of having had an empire it could not afford to maintain. Wars had sapped the treasury and the will of the people to tolerate the ambitions of their kings. And those same wars had sapped the underground resources that had made Stora such a great engine of Swedish growth and international expansion. Twice in fifty years the mine collapsed and fires rivaled those collapses as threats to the miners—one that started in 1760 burned for months; another that started in 1799 would burn for twenty-one years.

The political unrest in the country had come as a result of the fact that Sweden's young king, Charles XII, only fifteen when he assumed the throne in 1697, was drawn only two years later into what became known as the Great Northern War. This was a battle between the Swedes and the Russians, Saxony, and the Danes over territories and control of Baltic trade routes that Sweden had won with its victories decades before. Charles had many opportunities to settle the war on favorable terms, but, eager to extend his reach to Poland (given old animosities), he passed them up, and when he did settle with the Poles in 1706, he received no compensation and the financial state of the country was damaged further. By 1725, Sweden had ceded Estonia, Livonia, Ingria, and key provinces of Finland to Russia. Also by this time, there was a new king, the husband of Charles's sister, crowned Frederick I. But following in the British tradition, the monarchy was extremely limited by a new constitution that invested more power in the people and the representatives of the four estates (clergy, aristocracy, burgesses, and peasants) convening in the Riksdag. This structure made it hard to get much done, because progress required three of the four diverse groups to agree, which was seldom the case.

The man who actually held the most power in this arrangement was the president of the chancery, Count Arvid Horn. Eschewing past tradition, he shifted Sweden out of the French sphere and toward that of the English, drawn to them by the political progress they had shown in the days of Locke and the Glorious Revolution. Horn ushered in a period of peace that, after a time, came to be seen as a period of decline and weakness after the accomplishments of the preceding century. Critics rose up among the aristocracy and, led by Counts Carl Gustaf Tessin and Carl Gyllenborg, derided Horn and his followers as sleepy old men in night-caps. Soon the proponents of the government were called Caps as a consequence, and their critics, identifying themselves with the stylish headwear of the prosperous, called themselves Hats.

The Hats sought to restore ties with France and to advance an international policy that would, they thought, restore Swedish glory. France returned the favor with cash and political support, a relationship fittingly taking place beneath a Versailles roof made of the best Falun copper. For the thirty years between 1738 and 1770, the Hats sought to draw Sweden closer to France and into wars with Russia and other neighbors; then, when the costs of those wars also grew intolerable, the Caps were swept back into power and sought to reverse the positions, seeking closer ties with the Russians. The French poured money into one political party; the Russians poured money into the other. And the Swedish king vacillated between being the Nawab of one empire or the other.

This was not a period that was without progress in Sweden. Indeed, it is known in Swedish history as the Age of Freedom. To placate restive citizens, in addition to seeking to contain the threats associated with the autocratic rule of kings, the republic introduced new freedoms, including a statute assuring freedom of the press that was promulgated almost three decades before the creation of the U.S. Constitution. In his authoritative history of Sweden, Franklin Scott has written, "the Age of Freedom had discovered or reinterpreted certain democratic fundamentals: sovereignty of the people, representation of all classes, freedom of expression, and the right and duty of independent judgment by elected representatives. Also temporarily established were some of the institutions natural to a democratic state, as a two-party system and at least the idea of ministerial responsibility." While he notes that this experiment was unsuccessful and was undone with a return to monarchy in 1772, it laid the groundwork for the kind of system that was later to endure.

Something else happened too: as in politics, tough straits produced business innovation at Stora that helped it move once again to the forefront of broader industrial changes that would ultimately transform the world in the next great wave of economic revolution following the political upheavals that marked the late seventeenth and the eighteenth centuries.

One of the wars in which the Swedes found themselves entangled due to the Hats' affection for all things French is worthy of a special look because it ties together Britain, France, Sweden, the East India Company, Jefferson, and Smith. It was called the Seven Years' War in Europe, but in the American colonies, its offshoots were referred to as the French and Indian War. As should be apparent from even the skimming of history that comprises the initial portions of this book, Von Clausewitz's observation in the early nineteenth century that "war is not merely a political act, but also a political instrument, a continuation of political relations, a carrying out of the same by other means" had resonances in the Europe into which he was born in 1780 that are largely lost on us today. The statement not only frames war in the context of its purpose for states, but it also gives a hint of how commonplace it was as a political mechanism, like any other in regular use. It is interesting to think of the dictum in the context of the wars of the East India Company or other national enterprises, in which case it might be paraphrased as stating that war is sometimes just a continuation of business by other means (or in the imperial and mercantile sense, perhaps it is just as accurate to say that business is just a continuation of war by other means).

The eighteenth century may well have earned the designation "the Age of Enlightenment," but it was, in Europe, an age that was also distinguished by how little had been learned from prior history. For example, the post-Westphalian reality for nation-states was not much more peaceful than that which preceded it. As noted already, the century saw the War of Spanish Succession (1701–1714) over who would take the Spanish crown after the death of the last Habsburg king, Charles II—and at the center of the conflict was the Franco-British rivalry. The two then faced off in the War of Austrian Succession (1740–1748) in a dispute over whether a female, Maria Theresa, daughter of the Holy Roman Emperor, could accede to the Habsburg throne in Vienna. Although much of the fighting in this war occurred in Europe and again involved the British and the French as well as the various states influenced by the Habsburgs—arguably the most dangerous family in history if you tally up the number of conflicts associated with their various disputes—some of the key battles in the war took place around the world. The conflicts in India's First Carnatic

War were part of this broader struggle. In the Caribbean, the War of Jenkins' Ear was an extension of it. In North America, it first manifested itself as King George's War.

During the next phase of conflict that involved England and France (1754–1763), the fighting was so widespread—taking place in Europe, the Americas, Asia, and Africa—that it is described by some as "the first true world war." In the British colonies in North America, the French and Indian War is today remembered for having provided the training ground for young officers such as George Washington and for the escalation of violence between colonists and Native Americans. However, as important to the development of our thinking about states and their roles were the decisions that the British made regarding the governance of the colonies after the war was over. At the same time that Parliament passed the Regulating Act, designed to reform the East India Company's management structure and behavior in India, it also passed Lord North's Tea Act, which removed certain customs duties that had been imposed on trade into the American colonies. One tax, however, was maintained: a tea tax.

The tax had been a nuisance to the East India Company because it was eating into sales of the Company's imports from India. Colonists were boycotting tea purchases since the imposition of the earlier duties known as the Townshend Acts, after their author, Lord Townshend, the chancellor of the Exchequer. To placate the company, Parliament granted it the right to ship tea directly to America from India, avoiding a stopover and customs duties in Britain. To take advantage of this exemption, the company sent shiploads of tea to four major colonial ports: Boston, Charleston, New York, and Philadelphia. Although the tea boycott had been losing steam, the Tea Act and the shipments reinvigorated the movement. Colonists assailed the Company's tyranny in India and its monopolistic tendencies. The Company's merchants in Philadelphia and New York resigned their commissions rather than risk conflict with protesters, but the ships in Boston were forbidden by the royal governor from leaving without unloading the controversial cargo. In response, on the night of December 13, 1773, Boston colonists organized by Samuel Adams disguised themselves as Mohawk Indians, slipped on board the East India Company's ships in the harbor, and dumped the tea overboard. Ninety thousand pounds of Indian tea ended up floating in Boston Harbor.

The British response was to punish the colonies as a whole through the Coercive Acts of 1774. These closed the Port of Boston until the tea was paid for. At the same time, the royal governor was given more power and the local legislature less. Further, the governor was granted the power to try royal officials charged with capital crimes in England and to house British troops in local private buildings. The governor was then replaced by General Thomas Gage, the commander of British forces in America. It was a post that had been offered initially to Clive. One can only imagine he would have been even more ruthless than Gage, but the end result—the battles that exploded at Lexington and Concord and triggered the American Revolution—would likely have been the same.

Ironically, the standards that flew over the Company ships in Boston Harbor would look very familiar to modern observers, because the flag used by the British East India Company from 1707 to 1801 was almost identical to the "Great Union Flag" used by Washington's armies during the first years of the war. It featured thirteen alternating red and white stripes and in the upper left-hand quadrant of the flag a replica of the Union Jack. While it is no doubt true that the stripes on the American flag were intended to represent the thirteen American colonies, the fact is that the British East India Company was flying a flag with thirteen such stripes long before the idea of American independence had crossed anyone's mind. Thus, on one level or another, the inspiration for the symbol of the United States was much more likely to have been a rapacious, profit-oriented proto-multinational rather than the structure of the colonies themselves.

The Wealth of Nations and What It Means for Governments

In 2005, U.S. Federal Reserve Bank chairman Alan Greenspan, the chief architect of the wide-open markets of the late twentieth and early twenty-first centuries, made a pilgrimage to Kirkcaldy, Scotland, to pay tribute to its most famous native son. There, Greenspan called Adam Smith "a towering contributor to the development of the modern world" and hailed Smith for having "essentially benevolent views of the working of competition [that] counteracted pressures for market regulation of the evident excesses of the factory system" that had begun early in the eighteenth century. Those excesses were decried a century later by the poet William Blake as "the dark Satanic mills" by then characterizing much of industrial England.

Greenspan then offered what at the time seemed a great compliment, although with the benefit of hindsight it seems one that might have made Smith just as uncomfortable as Greenspan's hailing the Scotsman for standing up for competition in place of regulation that would protect factory workers. The Fed chairman argued that "one could hardly imagine that today's awesome array of international transactions would produce the relative economic stability we experience daily if they were not led by some international version of Smith's invisible hand."

While today *The Wealth of Nations* is seen as a landmark work in modern capitalist thought, its initial publication, four months before America declared its independence, was inauspicious. Indeed, Smith's closest friends urged him to get the book out before the conflagration in America consumed everyone's attention. David Hume wrote, "if you wait till the fate of America be decided you may wait too long." As it was, the book came out eleven months after Lexington and Concord and just days after the British had begun preparing for the evacuation of Boston.

Smith's work, initially receiving modest acclaim, drew from other Enlightenment thinkers as well as from the views that had evolved in England in the years since the South Sea Bubble and the rise of the East India Company.

The Wealth of Nations also echoed some of the critiques that had been common in England in the wake of the abuses of the Company in India and those of the crown in the American colonies. Smith popularized the term "mercantilism" to describe the system in which trade within the empire was controlled and regulated to benefit the state and by extension the few who had the right to conduct the trade. Although he argued that Britain was more liberal in its views toward its colonies than were other European powers (a difficult view to defend, but a not uncommon one at the time), he noted that imperial policy was still "dictated by the same mercantile spirit as that of other nations." He also observed that Britain's approach to mercantilism was more restrictive than that of Spain, France, or Portugal in that Britain mandated that its colonies trade all goods exclusively within the empire and obligated merchants to trade through a particular port or trading company.

Smith felt this approach was unfair: "to prohibit a great people, however, from making all that they can of every part of their own produce, or from employing their stock and industry in the way that they judge most advantageous to themselves, is a manifest violation of the most sacred rights of mankind." In this he was clearly echoing the liberal views of Locke and developing Locke's own focus on the rights associated with property. Smith, no doubt heavily influenced by the views of British merchants that had evolved in the wake of the hardships and corruption associated with the South Sea Bubble and the privileges won by the East India Company, blamed it on the business community. "Of the greater part of the regulations concerning the colony trade," he wrote, "the merchants who carry it on, it must be observed, have been the principal advisers. We must not wonder, therefore, if in the greater part of them, their interest has been considered more than either that of the colonies or that of the mother country."

Continuing in a vein that was welcomed in the colonies as that of a kindred revolutionary spirit, Smith asserted that the colonies deserved more freedom to grow and develop without undue interference from Britain's imperial economic and political managers. His approach was not independence, however; it was making the colonies full partners in the empire, much as his native Scotland was. "There is not the least probability," Smith stated, "that the British constitution would be hurt by the union of Great Britain with her colonies. That constitution, on the contrary, would be completed by it, and seems imperfect without it. The assembly which deliberates and decides concerning the affairs of every part of the empire, in order to be properly informed, ought to have representatives from every part of it." The father of modern economics certainly was not a man for taxation without representation. In fact, he recommended that the colonies be represented in proportion to those tax revenues, and he predicted that within a century the American colonies might end up exceeding Britain in their tax revenue generation, at which time he believed that "the seat of the empire would then naturally remove itself to that part of the empire which contributed most to the general defence and support of the whole."

As to the East India Company specifically, Smith added sections dealing with what he saw as their abuses and perversion of market forces, in a third edition of the book that came out in 1783. While he believed "it was not unreasonable" to grant a monopoly for a period of years to the first group of merchants to initiate trade with a "remote and barbarous nation," he was decidedly opposed to entrenched monopolies and granting companies too much political influence. Monopolies were both inefficient and "enabled the company to support the negligence, profusion and malversation of their own servants, whose disorderly conduct seldom allows the dividend of the company to exceed the ordinary rate of profit in trades which are altogether free." He was unconvinced that the reforms of the preceding decade had done much to fix the flaws in the Company's governance of the subcontinent. Unflinchingly, he wrote that "the government of an exclusive company of merchants is, perhaps, the worst of all governments for any country whatever."

He believed that stockholders often invested in enterprises like the East India Company for influence rather than for profit and that therefore they cared insufficiently about the "prosperity of the great empire . . . No other sovereigns ever were or, from the nature of things, ever could be so perfectly indifferent about the happiness or misery of their subjects, the improvement or waste of their dominions, the glory or disgrace of their administration; as, from irresistible moral causes, the greater part of the proprietors of such a mercantile company are, and necessarily must be." Companies like the East India Company were "nuisances in every respect; always more or less inconvenient to the countries in which they are established, and destructive to those which have the misfortune to fall under their government."

He felt that the Company's monopoly should be allowed to expire and that its tale was a compelling argument on behalf of his general arguments on letting free competition and the pursuit of individual interests drive markets. His core view was not only inherently optimistic, based on the idea that individuals acting on their own will better the world, but also very much in keeping with the overall spirit of the times, seeking to contain the power of the state and to counterbalance it with mechanisms, systems, and laws that would enshrine and preserve individual rights. Just as Samuel Adams and Thomas Paine had already reacted to the king's abuses, so was Smith reacting against the economic abuses of the Company and those in the government who catered to it or were otherwise co-opted by it. Just like them, he was playing an important role in influencing the development of views about the appropriate role of the state, how state power should be constrained, and where and in what circumstances it should be applied.

Smith's ideas did provoke some unease among the landed gentry, who felt he "failed to understand the economic peril of gentlemen farmers living in an increasingly commercial society." It was a fear that was later echoed by Thomas Jefferson when he was confronted with the zeal-ous pro-Smith, pro-market ideas of his chief rival, Alexander Hamilton. But for the most part, Smith's work was generally if underwhelmingly embraced at the time of its publication. He commented, with some relief perhaps, that the book was "much less abused than I had reason to ex-pect." His publisher explained the underwhelming reaction by implying it required "much thought and Reflexion." The views of Smith's publisher have seemingly endured, every bit as fresh and apt as Smith's.

The Declaration: A Call to Arms, to Allies, and to a New Idea of the State

Three months after the appearance of *The Wealth of Nations*, Richard Henry Lee, a Virginia delegate to the Continental Congress in Philadel-phia, broke a deadlock in the discussion of American independence. He made three motions to Congress: "That these United Colonies are, and of right ought to be, free and independent states, that they are absolved from allegiance to the British Crown, and that all political connection between them and the State of Great Britain is, and ought to be, totally dissolved. That is an expedient forthwith to take the most effectual measures for forming foreign alliances. That a plan of confederation be prepared and transmitted to the respective colonies for their contribution and approbation."

While Lee's resolution and the resultant effort that would less than a month later produce the American Declaration of Independence are seen primarily as a watershed in political thinking, they had a very pragmatic component. The revolutionary colonists were concerned that the British had them outgunned, and they knew what happened to British colonies that confronted the empire. They needed assistance from other nations. They also knew that, given the nature of European politics, the French and the Spanish might provide just such assistance. But they couldn't do so if the colonies were not seen to be an independent entity. This was a consequence of Westphalia. Sovereigns could deal only with other sover-eigns. So America had to assert independence not primarily out of a need to express a native political philosophy but rather to win aid that would be essential to its survival. In exchange, the colonies felt they could offer commercial benefits to whoever their benefactors might be—through trade, through breaking free of the mercantile system and harnessing American assets for America's good.

Four days after Lee's resolution, a committee consisting of John Adams, Benjamin Franklin, Thomas Jefferson, Robert Livingston of New York, and Roger Sherman of Connecticut was assigned the task of drafting the declaration that would assert American independence and thus its eligibility for foreign support. Although it is often claimed that Adams resisted drafting the declaration himself because he was, as he himself observed, "obnoxious and disliked," it is likely that at least as compelling a reason was that he was focusing on the core business at hand: drafting a treaty that might be entered into with the French as soon as possible.

Jefferson was chosen to do the writing despite his relative youth. Although he was only thirty-three, he was already an accomplished writer. In the wake of the Coercive Acts he had written a very well received pamphlet called "A Summary View of the Rights of British America." He had also drafted the Virginia Constitution, which he used as a source for the new document. He also drew upon George Mason's Virginia Declaration of Rights. But it was clear that all these documents and much of his other thinking that went into the declaration had roots in the work of Locke. In part this was due to the core ideas of individual liberty that had been embraced through reforms across Europe; in part it was also out of a desire to echo not just the spirit of the Glorious Revolution but its bloodlessness. The colonists hoped to emulate a transition that occurred without physical conflict even as it reined in once and for all the power of the British monarch. In so doing, the colonists emphasized the foundation of their initiative in English law.

In keeping with the guidelines for interactions between states that had evolved since Westphalia, Jefferson also relied on the chief handbook of international law available at the time, *The Law of Nations* by Swiss legal scholar Emerich de Vattel. This work, unlike prior international legal books, asserted three important qualities of states: freedom, independence, and interdependence. For Vattel, "Nations being composed of people naturally free and independent, and who, before the establishment of civil societies lived together in a state of nature, nations or sovereign states, must be considered as if they were free persons who co-exist in the state of nature." He also argued that states had an obligation to contribute to the happiness and perfection of other states and should not interfere with other states' peaceful enjoyment of liberty. It was a view that not only was useful to Jefferson but would later have important echoes in the rights and responsibilities corporate actors were seen to have to each other and to people at large.

The focus on the legal core of the declaration—to assert sovereignty, to base that sovereignty on the free choice of individuals by asserting their right to make such a choice, and to define the legally prescribed role of the state—is more than a political nicety. It is, continuing in the tradition that began with the lawspeakers and continued to Runnymede and then through Locke to Independence Hall in Philadelphia, a further step toward establishing the idea that laws exist above all entities and actors. Nations are under the law. Kings are under the law. And later, as it would emerge, so too would independent actors like corporations be seen in the same way, as independent entities with rights under the law and the ability to resolve differences through the law. While this seems basic today, it asserts that more important than force or tradition in establishing order is law, and that gives actors who don't possess the means to project force a more equal footing or at least a fighting chance with those that do. When gun-toting companies like the East India Company eventually faded from the world stage in the mid-nineteenth century, this idea would seem ever more significant.

Jefferson's declaration begins immediately with the business at hand: asserting sovereignty and hinting at the reason for establishing territorial sovereignty in the first place. "When in the course of human events, it becomes necessary for one people to dissolve the political bands which have connected them with another, and to assume among the powers of the earth, the separate and equal station to which the Laws of Nature and Nature's God entitle them, a decent respect to the opinions of mankind requires that they should declare the causes which impel them to separation." As "free and independent states"—thus eligible for the international support the country so desperately needed—the new country would have certain rights that form a kind of definition of what made a state a state: "the full Power to levy War, conclude Peace, contract Alliances [and] establish Commerce."

The middle section of the document was essentially the work of Jefferson the lawyer, a legal brief arguing the offenses of the crown against the colonies that made their actions inevitable and justified. Of the listed grievances, a dozen were aimed directly at the king and another nine were addressed to both the monarch and Parliament. Following a list of five that dealt with "war atrocities," the Declaration affirms the separation and asserts, no doubt with the hope of minimizing the rift, that the new entity would view the British, "as we hold the rest of mankind, Enemies in War, in Peace Friends."

For the first few months after the Declaration was issued, it looked as though the statement would be nothing more than a footnote in history, the aspirations of a handful of men who would soon be crushed by the world's greatest army. The British took New York City and were moving across New Jersey when, in the midst of a winter storm that hit on Christmas night, George Washington surprised the main body of the British force consisting of both regulars and Hessian mercenaries. Crossing the Delaware River in the dark of night and marching toward the British encampment at Trenton, Washington achieved what the British leaders thought impossible and, suffering only a handful of American casualties, imposed a devastating defeat on the British. The tide turned. Ten months later, at Saratoga, the Americans defeated the same General Burgoyne who had overseen the investigation into the East India Company abuses at and after Plassey. This, in turn, was seen by the French as proof that the Americans were worthy of their support, and in Paris two treaties were signed—one military, one commercial. Later, Spain and the Netherlands joined on the side of the Americans. On October 18, 1781, a U.S.-French force surrounded the main British army at Yorktown, and with the redcoat band playing "The World Turned Upside Down," the American Revolutionary War was over.

By achieving victory, Washington did what was necessary to begin to give Jefferson's views global resonance. It was not just America's philosophy but its success that made the words of revolutionary thinkers even more famous than those of the antecedents from whom they borrowed.

Aftershocks, Blowback, and Unintended Consequences

Establishing a new country was, needless to say, only the beginning, and among the very first sets of conflicts that occurred within that new nation were those associated with the nature of the American economy and the role the government would play with regard to that economy. The Jeffersonian unease with corporations and industry and Jefferson's regard for an agrarian ideal for the new United States were met by a strong counter-vailing force from men like Federalist leader and first Treasury secretary Alexander Hamilton. Hamilton received a copy of *The Wealth of Nations* four years after it was published from his sister-in-law who lived in London. He used it as he was researching his idea for a U.S. national bank.

Hamilton's proposal regarding the bank echoed Smith's concern that gold and silver were worthless if locked up in the vault of a nation or individual; placed in a bank, the precious metals could serve as surety for credit, allowing capital for the creation of new enterprises and the fueling of national economic growth. In his landmark "Report on Manufactures," Hamilton again "displayed an intimate familiarity" with Smith's work, arguing that agriculture should not be privileged over manufacturing in the new economy—a direct shot at Jefferson. Hamilton suggested that the American economy's bias toward agriculture in its early years was due as much to British mercantile manipulation as it was to any inherent desire on the part of the American people. Jefferson, on the other hand, felt that industry would result in the concentration of power and wealth in the hands of businesspeople as it had in England.

While Hamilton differed with Smith on the issue of government involvement in protective trade policies, taking the view that if the other governments of the world practiced mercantilism, the United States would have to do likewise to some degree to protect itself, he clearly felt a strong affinity to Smith's work. *The Wealth of Nations* in turn played an important role in shaping policies that later led to accelerated U.S. growth and ultimately to the fulfillment of Smith's predictions about the speed and nature of U.S. economic growth relative to that of Great Britain.

While Jefferson warned about the power of corporations, the new country saw a burgeoning of new chartered enterprises with men like Hamilton at its helm. From 1790 to 1800 the states and the federal government chartered 328 corporations, almost ten times the number chartered in the previous decade. Massachusetts, for example, granted only five charters between 1784 and 1789, one for banking, three for transportation, and one for manufacturing, all to merchants linked to Thomas Russell and George Cabot, two prominent American alpha capitalists.

Eventually, in Massachusetts and elsewhere, legislatures became more comfortable with corporations and granted more charters. Given the relative lack of power of the states compared to, say, an empire such as Great Britain, there could be no granting of monopoly powers like those given the East India Company, so the entities in question would have to seek efficiencies and profits if they were to survive. Ultimately, the idea developed that those corporations that did survive could not be dissolved by the state. James Sullivan, who drafted the charter of the Bank of Massachusetts in 1784 without an express provision of time, was confident the state could dissolve it in 1792, but pro-corporate arguments had gained so much traction that by 1802 he was not so sure. Within two decades the cases of *The Trustees of Dartmouth College v. Woodward* and *The Proprietors of the Charles River Bridge v. the Proprietors of the Warren Bridge* would affirm that corporations could exist in perpetuity and begin to lay the groundwork for the idea that they themselves possessed legal rights.

Thus, while the East India Company illustrated a relationship between corporation and state that was suited to a world of concentrated hierarchical power, the push toward individual freedoms and rule of law that marked the Enlightenment would grant corporations a new and different set of rights. Corporations were initially much less like countries than was the East India Company, and while they may have had less in the way of special powers or the ability to deploy force, under the new system they would begin to acquire special privileges and prerogatives. These special rights would ultimately make corporations stronger and more flexible than the behemoth that was originally conceived of in the court of Elizabeth I to help Britain assert its power during the Age of Exploration.

Just as the reaction to the excesses of the East India Company and mercantilism produced new legal frameworks that promoted competition and asserted individual economic freedoms that would lead to a different kind of corporate flowering, so too did the multiple physical, political, and economic collapses that befell the world's oldest surviving corporation, Stora Kopparberg, produce changes that ultimately strengthened the enterprise. While the weakening of Sweden, the gutting of the resources of the copper mine, and the reduction of demand for copper all battered what had been a thriving franchise for eight centuries, they did not produce the final chapter for the copper mountain. Rather, during Sweden's Age of Freedom under a weak monarch, the miners were given the opportunity to act with greater independence. While the state remained the leading shareholder, its influence diminished, and the professional miners in Falun began to translate their own growing independence into a series of innovations that transformed the business utterly and indicated just how and why a corporation can make the case that it is actually perpetual, an entity with everlasting life.

In the case of Stora, as we shall see in subsequent chapters, the story is one of remarkable adaptation. Copper was scarcer, the quality of copper that was produced was inferior, and demand was lower. And so Stora adapted to growing global demand for iron by moving into that business. The king had, in the late seventeenth century, decreed that the roofs of Swedish houses be painted red, and red paint was made from copper-related materials, and so Stora went into the red paint business. And the timber business that was born in the mid-seventeenth century continued to grow, by the end of the eighteenth century forming a major part of Stora's business. The miners themselves, realizing the importance of professionalism and science in the spirit of the age, began to require technical training for the master miners that would help shape the innovations of the company, enhance its efficiency, and position it to seize the opportunities of the next great era of revolution to come. Thus out of hardship came innovation and the foundations for growth that would produce a world-leading enterprise two centuries later.

In the mines, far from the more familiar stories of the eighteenth century and of the Age of Enlightenment, all the forces of the era were at work. Whether it was the principles of Smith or those of the Age of Freedom or of Jefferson, whether it was the burdens of maintaining an empire or the creativity demanded by hard times or a brewing global industrial revolution, something completely new was being forged where once they made Viking swords and the pikes and cannons of Gustavus Adolphus. Such changes were not, of course, unique to the great business of Dalarna, and in the end, their consequences would rock the world as had the twin revolutions of 1776.

5 ▦ 1848: What Makes a State a State?

> I believe that right now we are sleeping on a volcano . . . can you not sense, by a sort of instinctive intuition, that the earth is trembling again in Europe? Can you not feel . . . the wind of revolution in the air?
>
> —Alexis de Tocqueville

> In bourgeois society capital is independent and has individuality, while the living person is dependent and has no individuality.
>
> —Karl Marx

Historians and students of history who like their story lines simple look for bright lines that divide epochs. But as we have seen, while history produces notable turning points, most great transitions are evolutionary. Furthermore, as if the world were an inattentive student of progress, key episodes must seemingly be repeated over and over again until they overcome the seductive familiarity of the past and true transformations can take root.

Among all the years of history, few are as widely regarded as a bright line as 1848. It was a year that not only saw revolution sweep Europe, but also saw profound economic, political, and social change worldwide. Factors driving those changes range from the Industrial Revolution to famines in Europe, from the discovery of gold in California that triggered the growth of America as the world's first continental economy to unrest in India that would force profound changes in the way the British government did business within its empire. It was a year in which once again Sweden and Stora were among the early adopters of reforms that swept across the West and that would accelerate the arrival of multinational corporations. In the year 1848, Karl Marx produced *The Communist Manifesto*. That was the year a fourteen-year-old Irish immigrant to America named Andrew Carnegie got his first job as a bobbin boy, and the year the old monarchial order of Europe was given final notice that popular rule was the unavoidable reality of the future.

As striking as the concurrence of all those changes is, it is just as striking that many of them represent the continuation of ancient struggles to resolve core issues about the shape and nature of society. Still, when those long-standing tensions are seen in the context of 1848, they begin to change their shape and look familiar to modern audiences for the first time. Contemporary themes are more recognizable. The social contract underwent another set of sweeping revisions, and public and private actors began to take on more familiar, complex roles—roles that would foment rivalry, tension, and ultimately competing theories about the balance between the two power centers that would fuel political debate, division, and conflict for more than a century and a half. And the revolutions and debates of 1848 resonate strongly with those of our own moment in history.

Metternich and the Old Way

Mark Twain wrote, "It is not worthwhile to try to keep history from repeating itself, for man's character will always make the preventing of the repetitions impossible." While he would not be born until twenty years after the Treaty of Vienna was concluded in 1815, Twain could certainly have been writing about its circumstances, forebears, and consequences. Convened as the latest in a series of attempts to restore stability in Europe in the wake of the thrusts and parries of the Napoleonic wars, the Congress of Vienna, where the treaty was hammered out, brought together representatives of more than two hundred states and principalities from across Europe. While historians have characterized the gathering as a harbinger and a model for the peace conferences and international gatherings of the twentieth century, it is hard not to see the similarities to the bustling, messy political bazaar that was Westphalia. Not only was the purpose of the conference to redraw the map of Europe, it was seen by its architects as an opportunity to redefine the nature and relations of states, addressing some of the questions about states that had arisen during the preceding century or so. It was thus also a hugely complex diplomatic symphony that could very easily have produced useless or even counterproductive cacophony had it not been guided by skillful hands.

The maestro of the Vienna negotiations was Austrian nobleman Prince Klemens Wenzel von Metternich, a forty-two-year-old diplomat, the father of what later would be seen as a school of diplomacy that remains influential to this day. His work to help bring peace to Europe—which is to say, his work to maintain as much influence as possible for his Habsburg employers and Austria—is seen as a blueprint for balance-of-power politics. Henry Kissinger made his first notable headlines on the public stage with the publication of his doctoral dissertation "A World Restored: Metternich, Castlereagh and the Problems of the Peace, 1812–1822." Later, Kissinger was seen to have emulated Metternich's strategies and values (or lack thereof) during his own career as the foremost diplomat of his era. It is an irony the twenty-first-century reader cannot help but note that Kissinger began his career with a look at balance-of-power politics just as the mid-twentieth-century world was entering an anomalously bipolar, and then briefly unipolar, period. Then, just as Kissinger's decades-long period of extraordinary influence drew to a close, the rise of new powers renewed demand for understanding the old-style game of balancing the conflicting interests of a small cluster of major players, which once again became central.

At Vienna, Metternich represented the Habsburgs, those familiar protagonists of European conflict. They were not only the effective hosts of the meeting that convened the great and the small political entities of Europe, but also among the conservative power players eager to put a lid once and for all on the aftershocks of the concurrent political, intellectual, and economic revolutions of the Enlightenment. In particular, the passionate but extremely messy French emulation of the American experiment in democracy made those traditional powers whose roots stretched deep back into Europe's feudal past extremely uncomfortable. Not only did the first manifestation of that revolution in 1789 involve the washing away in a torrent of blood of an ancient monarchy and its symbiotic partner-rivals in the aristocracy, but it subsequently unleashed utter anarchy. Paradoxically, rationalist Enlightenment thinking begat action without thought, emotional spasms that ultimately consumed many of the leaders of the first wave of revolution. Then, as if that were not enough of a threat to the other old houses of Europe, still hoping to cling to the states that were their patrimonies, industrial revolution was undoing and reshaping economies, and populations were beginning to grow and shift to cities.

At first, many felt that the return to stability in France that came in the person of Napoleon Bonaparte might be a healthy development. Soon, however, they saw that even if he did in no uncertain terms put his foot on the throat of any remaining democratic stirrings, he also sought to rechannel his country's emotions outward. Playing a hand familiar to monarchs throughout the centuries, he turned to nationalism to give his people a sense of purpose. But his brand of nationalism was guided by a personal level of ambition unseen in Europe since Charlemagne. He set out to conquer the Continent and thus turned crowned heads once worried about social unrest toward a new set of concerns about whether they could withstand French conquest.

The Napoleonic Wars were as much a consequence of the revolutions of the late eighteenth century as they were a trigger of those of the mid-nineteenth. And, when alliances among governments threatened by Napoleon finally turned the tide against him and it was time to remake the map of Europe and determine reparations, Metternich and his sponsors sought to do so in a way that would restore the monarchy and the Westphalian ideal of nation-states in balance with one another as the antidote to both liberalism and nationalism. Of course, Metternich felt that at the center of this order should be a powerful Habsburg family. Metternich would write to Czar Alexander I of Russia:

> It is in times of crisis that monarchs are principally called upon . . . to show themselves for what they are: fathers invested with all the authority that belongs to the heads of families: to prove that, in dark times, they know how to be just, wise, and, by that alone, strong, and that they do not abandon the peoples, whom they have the duty to govern, to the play of factions, to error and its consequences, which will fatally lead to the destruction of society.

It was his hope that the Treaty of Vienna—which by 1815 reset France's borders, defined the hundreds of millions in reparations it would have to pay its neighbors, and put great family dynasties again at the center of European stability—would ensure that in decades to come it would be something closer to the spirit of 1648 than to that of the Glorious Revolution, 1776, or 1779 that would prevail.

Within less than a generation, it was clear that Metternich's efforts to restore the old order would be undone. Not only had vigorous seeds of popular doubt and aspiration been sown since Locke, but two powerful economic storms were to collide and put a final end to feudalism and ultimately aristocracy, monarchy, and the "old way." One was temporal, a series of European economic crises that would have reverberations in every corner of the globe. The second was historical, the Industrial Revolution that would completely and utterly undo a geopolitical and social order in which wealth and power were based primarily on the ownership of land. The Industrial Revolution would change what was necessary to create wealth, make it more fungible, make it less tied to location, and also create new and different relationships among the business leaders it economically empowered and those who depended on them, whether for employment or for financial support of one kind or another. There were echoes of feudalism in this, to be sure, but there were new dimensions to what was happening that it can be argued we still don't fully understand or accept today—the birth of power centers that were growing in ways that would soon have them increasingly operating above or apart from national political or legal systems.

There were those who noticed the stirrings of change. Among them was Alexis de Tocqueville, who recognized on his visit to the United States to inspect America's prisons a country with an entirely different economic culture from Europe, one that he saw as threatening the old social and economic order with which he was familiar. Not only was the United States industrializing, but it was also a country in which there was so much land available that the ownership of a commodity that had already been the primary source of power in Europe for centuries was revalued as an empowerer of the many rather than the few.

This in turn produced attitudes that amplified some of the individualist ideals of eighteenth-century philosophers and revolutionary political leaders. Tocqueville expressed his concerns for the American "depraved taste for equality, which impels the weak to want to bring the strong down to their level and which reduces men to preferring equality in servitude to inequality in freedom." One of his concerns with the resulting system was that it produced the regular undermining of elites—although he also acknowledged the vibrancy it created. Most important from our perspective, however, is that he saw that a consequence of this burgeoning American capitalism was a redistribution of power that elevated commoners and civil centers of power that were quite apart from the state. Entrepreneurialism and personal ambition drove this new system and resulted in biases in the legislature that had begun to break down the old landcentric system of property and power that echoed Europe's.

Silent Revolutions Come First

Tocqueville decried America's obsession with money. He saw American democracy as a potential threat to meritocracy, giving too much sway to the common and the "merely" economically empowered. But given the turmoil that had marked his life since growing up in the shadows of the Reign of Terror—as part of a family temporarily forced into exile who were able to return only with the advent of the Bourbon restoration, when his father would assume the role and privileges of a peer—and coming of age in an industrializing Europe racked by both political and economic change, perhaps he was also uncomfortable with the fact that what was happening in America echoed threats that had stalked him and his class throughout his life.

In fact, the economic changes that were taking place were reweaving the fabric of European society in ways that would soon lead to the undoing of the social order with which the peripatetic Frenchman was most comfortable. For example, at the time his *Democracy in America* was published in 1835, Europe was seeing major changes to its economic system. Old ways dating back to the guild structures that were familiar, for example, on the Great Copper Mountain half a millennium earlier were changing. Thanks to the growing dependence on technology, capitalists who could fund factories had gained the upper hand over craftsmen as the managers of enterprises. Further, as Mike Rapport writes in his book *1848: Year of Revolution*, the social pressures associated with industrialization took other forms as well:

> Artisans and craft workers, who had formerly enjoyed existences as small-scale producers, found that their skills and independence were being threatened not only by the introduction of machinery, but by new ways of organizing production, in which unskilled or semi-skilled workers—including women—could produce the same goods in greater numbers and at lower cost, although (the beleaguered artisans argued) of poorer quality.

Under these conditions, it was easy for wealthy landowners and factory owners to take advantage of peasants and laborers. Wages plummeted, and soon workers crowded into cities, where the new factories were creating jobs even if they were low-paying and the conditions were abysmal. Typical workdays lasted fifteen hours in dark, cold, cramped, often dangerous environments. Sanitary conditions were awful and disease was common. City workers actually had shorter lifespans than those in the country, largely because their diets were poor and unvaried, consisting primarily of potatoes and bread.

These were the conditions of which Dickens wrote, burning into the conscience of history the enduring images of workhouses and poverty that we have to this day. But if anything, the situation in most European cities was worse than Dickens described. Tenements were often grimmer, less sanitary, and more dangerous than prisons. As one reporter commenting on conditions in the French city of Lille wrote, "In their obscure cellars, in their rooms . . . the air is never renewed, it is infected, the walls are plastered with garbage . . . If a bed exists, it is a few dirty, greasy planks, it is a damp putrescent straw. The furniture is dislocated, worm eaten, covered with filth."

At the same time, conditions in the countryside grew harder for other reasons. Advances in farming promoted a shift from large numbers of small family farms to larger enterprises. Those farms also embraced fertilization and land management techniques that enabled them to cultivate land constantly, thus eliminating the fallow fields on which poorer small farmers often grazed their livestock.

Industrial demand also created resource demands that added a different set of tensions. As Jonathan Sperber notes in his economic study of the era, "Iron and leather manufacture, two economic growth areas, both involved the substantial use of forest products—oak bark for tanning and charcoal to forge pig iron from the ore." These demands created tensions over land use, such as in Sweden, for example, in which Stora had become both one of Europe's pig iron producers and one of its burgeoning forestry leaders. Old systems for guaranteeing the public use of lands were breaking down. Some cities and landed gentry sold off rights. Others simply did not address the issue. Laws were promoted to curtail public "theft" of what had once been theirs by right or custom, and they were so vigorously enforced that at one point one-third of the population of Bavaria was charged with this crime. Sperber suggests the ramifications of these conflicts when he observes that Karl Marx's father was a lawyer who defended villagers in such cases and that this led Marx for the first time to consider what was called at the time the "social question." The young Marx was a journalist writing about the issue of wood theft when he first began to consider the question of property rights.

The Social Question and the Role of Government

The economic changes that threatened the order Metternich had sought to shore up in Vienna and that were uncomfortable for even comparatively open-minded aristocrats like Tocqueville were not just structural. The 1840s in Europe saw an economic calamity that also played a role in ushering in a major rebalancing of state and private power. In the middle of the decade, a microorganism arrived in Europe that would soon spread across the northern half of the Continent and into the British Isles with devastating consequences. *Phytophthora infestans* was known commonly as potato blight. After ravaging U.S. crops in 1843 and 1844, it seems likely to have been transported to Europe via the clipper ships that were revolutionizing transatlantic travel by dramatically shortening crossing times. During the harvest season of 1845, the disease took a devastating toll on the potato crops of the lowlands, France, and the United Kingdom. As much as half the crop was lost. The next year, three-quarters of Ireland's crop was destroyed and starvation began to haunt a country where as many as three million people relied on potatoes as their primary food source. A million Irish would die and another million would leave the country. Several hundred thousand others would succumb in Europe.

Further, the potato disaster naturally pushed up the prices of other foodstuffs, with agonizing consequences for poor workers who had already seen wages fall, conditions worsen, and populations (and with them family responsibilities) burgeon. For the poor of the Continent, 1846 and 1847 were years of unrelenting privation. This led to falling demand for manufactured goods and businesses failing throughout Europe. Hundreds of major mills closed.

Next, in France, where the government of King Louis Philippe had enacted legislation promoting the purchase of land to be used for a national railway network, a market bubble was created, with demand pushing up prices for iron and consequent overproduction, leading inevitably to a crash on the Bourse. Because the government had placed a 600-million-franc bet on the future of railways, there was little money to help import food to mitigate the crisis facing the country's poor.

Unrest was inevitable and soon workers' associations were forming to air a growing list of urgent grievances. In France, Louis Philippe's government enforced the provision in the Napoleonic Code that prohibited gatherings of more than twenty people. The workers—who had essentially no political clout, no rights, no vote, and zero representation in government—were left with no other choice but to strike. The government, led by the increasingly reviled prime minister François Guizot, responded with force. Guizot's position was that if agricultural conditions were bad, then people ought to find work elsewhere. He was similarly insensitive to complaints about insufficient food, arguing essentially that more prudent savings habits prior to the crisis would have avoided the problems now racking the country's underclass. Guizot was not alone in his insensitivity to the crisis. Across Europe, discontent grew, and leaders such as Metternich viewed the question as not so much one of alleviating public concerns as one of reasserting and preserving the rule of the established order. The nationalist threat that had concerned him so in 1815 had been supplanted by a new problem: the rise of "liberalism."

Metternich, Guizot, and their confreres were children of the upheavals of the late eighteenth and early nineteenth centuries and saw it as Europe's good fortune that of the Continent's five great powers, three were absolute monarchies (Austria, Russia, and Prussia) and two were constitutional monarchies. What democracy there was offered suffrage to only a small percentage of the population. But the stability that this system had once seemingly offered had suddenly grown suspect. Said Tocqueville before his fellow deputies: "I believe that right now we are sleeping on a volcano . . . can you not sense, by a sort of instinctive intuition . . . that the earth is trembling again in Europe? Can you not feel . . . the wind of revolution in the air?"

Liberals traced their views to thinkers such as Locke and the Enlightenment's attacks on all forms of arbitrary power. Monarchies and the church were particular targets. Civil freedom was a goal even if universal suffrage had been tainted by association with the violence of France's First Republic. Struggling, disenfranchised workers could not help but find appealing the combination of attacks on the callous leaders of the established order and the prospect of a greater voice in their own future.

Another strain that was also gaining in appeal was associated with a small but growing group who called themselves "socialists." The movement had emerged out of the thinking of the eighteenth century, seeking to find an alternative to what some of its early authors saw as the disorder and inequity of capitalism. The first person to use the term *socialisme* was Count Henri Saint-Simon. Saint-Simon, born an aristocrat, had come to question that system in part due to what he had seen when, as a young man, he served in America under George Washington. Like other early socialists, his goal was to find a different way to order society in which merit rather than family heritage determined social position. In a telling contrast with Adam Smith's "invisible hand," Saint-Simon wrote of his concern with "the Hand of Greed," his view that people innately seek to elevate themselves within society and that this impulse needs to be countered to achieve a society in which people will focus on serving society through productivity. Interestingly, he saw industrialization and technology as positive forces and sought a social order that would enable society to be maximally productive.

Louis Blanc was another early socialist; he later took part in the revolution of 1848 and subsequently served in the provisional government that rose up briefly out of that upheaval. He too focused on maximizing productivity, but he thought that workers should also be assisted by the state so that they could establish and then control their own livelihoods. He felt the solution to the social question lay in mitigating the negative effects of competition, especially on those too weak to counter it. His central principle, "à chacun selon ses besoins, de chacun selon ses facultés" (from each according to his abilities, to each according to his needs) has endured to this day, but what is most significant in his thinking, as well as in that of Saint-Simon and the champions of European liberalism, is the idea that one of government's central roles is to fulfill its economic responsibilities to the people. Through their writings and the upheavals they triggered, they made the case that rather than the people owing service to the monarch, the state owed service to the people. They essentially demanded a rewrite of the terms of the social contract, seeking to update it to suit the new economic realities of the industrial era.

Waves of Revolution

The first revolution of 1848 came in response to the insensitivity and callousness of Louis Philippe and Guizot throughout the period of several years of economic hardship that had taken such a toll on France and Europe. But it was political tone-deafness to the warnings of men like Tocqueville that, combined with bungling and misfortune, triggered what would be Europe's year of upheaval.

Guizot's opponents had intended to hold a dinner on February 20 to generate support for ousting him from office. In turn, Guizot's government banned the meeting. Liberal reformists called for a protest on the twenty-second. On that cold and rainy Paris winter morning, beneath the looming gray pillars of the Madeleine, hundreds and then thousands of unemployed demonstrators and political activists and their families began to congregate. They intended to march to present a petition demanding Guizot's resignation. But soon they were confronted by the National Guard, appearing under orders to break up the gathering. Like their counterparts more than a half century earlier in the streets of Marseilles, they began singing the anthem bearing that city's name. The lyrics calling the citizens to arms energized the crowd, and it swept toward the Chamber of Deputies.

The Guard pushed back, but after reorganizing, the crowd made a second attempt and then a third. Tensions grew. Stones were thrown at the troops and the National Guard responded with force. An old woman's head smashed into a paving stone and she died. A protester died under the sword of one of the guardsmen. And chaos ensued. Although the army was dispatched to protect Guizot and the government, erecting barricades throughout the city, many among its members were sympathetic to the protesters and refused to muster. By the morning of the twenty-third, a frightened and pragmatic king summoned Guizot and fired him. Guizot was outraged, feeling deeply betrayed after long years of service.

The political gambit did not work. After a momentary lull in the protests, the leaders of the mobilizing opposition sensed a chance to do more than simply depose one civil servant. Crowds surged around Guizot's residence and a troop of cavalry and infantry protecting his home fired into the mob. Fifty died. As their corpses were carted through the city, the bloody spectacle inflamed the people of Paris. One witness described "the corpse of a young woman whose neck and chest were stained with a long stream of blood" and the illumination of the passing dead by a torch held aloft by "a child of the people, with pallid complexion, eyes burning and staring . . . as one would depict the spirit of vengeance."

That spirit only grew stronger when, on the advice of Guizot, Louis Philippe turned to Marshal Thomas Bugeaud to put down the uprising. Bugeaud had earned the nickname "the Butcher" while leading French troops during the colonization of Algeria. Attempts to negotiate a peace failed, and although Bugeaud had his troops surround the Tuileries Palace, that did not deter the people. Members of the court urged the king to call in regular military from outside the city, but even he saw that as a step too far. As musket balls flew outside a palace guard post, Louis Philippe pondered his fate, and then, as the battle continued hour after hour, he contemplated his escape.

Finally, quickly scrawling his declaration of abdication on a piece of parchment, he and his wife, Marie-Amélie, made their exit. They dressed in bourgeois clothes to escape detection and made their way by carriage to the port city of Honfleur. There, given the uncreative pseudonyms "Mr. and Mrs. Smith," they boarded a ship for exile in England. In this, they established a precedent that soon many other members of Europe's elite would emulate.

Back in Paris it was the 1790s all over again. Crowds poured through Louis Philippe's palace, smashing furniture and china, taking turns sitting on the throne, and later taking that throne to the Place de la Bastille, where it was ceremoniously burned. Their message was unmistakable: monarchy was no longer acceptable. The names of the members of a new government were announced by the poet Lamartine with the words "The Republic has been proclaimed." The cheering in Paris drifted far and wide. Not only did U.S. president Polk's administration quickly recognize the new government, but its enthusiasm was apparent as it welcomed "France into the family of republics." In the American Congress, Illinois representative Abraham Lincoln and Mississippi senator Jefferson Davis proposed resolutions offering congratulations to the people of France.

In Europe, reactions were more tempered. Many of France's neighbors were understandably unnerved. Smoldering thrones were uncomfortable images for sitting monarchs. In Germany, various princes scrambled to negotiate constitutions that might preserve their hold on authority. But elsewhere, notably in Austria and Italy but also as far north as Sweden, the stirrings of revolution could neither be ignored nor reversed.

While the provisional government in France would soon fail, this first of 1848's revolutions carried with it an important message. The uprising and the provisional government's efforts—including an ultimately unsuccessful experiment conceived by Blanc to use railway income to fund a program for workers—was among the first efforts by an industrializing state to address the "social question." Men such as Blanc and his colleagues believed that problems like the unemployment that racked France were the responsibility of the government. They were among the first to attempt to weave a social safety net that might help protect average citizens against the boom-and-bust turbulence of the capitalist business cycle. The French uprisings may have failed to produce a lasting government, but they did offer an enduring legacy: the end of the idea that the state's principal purpose was to maintain peace and order even if the people starved. Instead, as Arnold Whitridge wrote a hundred years afterward, "After 1848 . . . the workers acquired a new status in the community. Never again could a politician suggest that the men in the factories and the workshops should accept their lot with humble resignation." That said, the next of Europe's revolutions had a different tone and a different focus. While fueled by many of the same forces that fed France's conflagration, the revolution that ultimately undid Metternich was more about what a state *was* than about the specific roles the state should or should not play.

The aging Metternich was seventy-four when the news of Louis Philippe's downfall reached Vienna. He was Austria's chancellor, the man at the emperor's right hand. He knew that the Austro-Hungarian Empire was held together by the idea that the Habsburgs were the state. He also sensed that the reformers within his empire were not so much after the first elements of what would become the welfare state but rather wanted to break away from the hold of the ancient family who had inherited dominion over them. In Italy and Hungary they wanted out of the empire. By striving for independence, the reformers were also effectively calling for the final destruction of the feudal ideas that had given shape to the political landscape of the Continent for a millennium.

While Metternich recognized the long-term implications of acceding to the pressures for reform and urged that they be resisted, within the court of the emperor Ferdinand there were concerns the old man had already been in office for too long. News of the French uprising, which came to Metternich initially by a letter from his friend Salomon Rothschild, did not initially upset him too much. He saw liberalism as a weakness of the French, and his police chief assured him that there were no worrisome signs of unrest in Austria.

The trouble started for Metternich when a Hungarian liberal named Lajos Kossuth seized upon news of the French developments and gave a speech in the lower house of the Austrian parliament that sounded unsettlingly like a call for independence. Kossuth's speech triggered a reform movement within the parliament that was initially rebuffed by Metternich and his supporters. However, momentum grew for the liberals, and by mid-March they presented the government with a set of demands that would roll back the power of the aristocracy, ideally with a constitution. Whereas in France much of the pressure came from the working class, in Austria there was also considerable resentment among the best-educated citizens—lawyers, teachers, customs officials—who felt that the aristocracy saved the best civil service positions for themselves.

The reformers pushed for freedom of speech, religion, and assembly and for popular representation in the government. While this is an idea Metternich had contemplated in more modest forms, he resisted. An agitated crowd gathered, and, as is often the case, an incident triggered an escalation in the political crisis. When the crowd misinterpreted a porter's regular checking of the doors of the Landhaus building as a sign that the delegates were being locked in, the crowd stormed the building. Troops were called in. The crowd grew so large it stretched across Vienna. The archduke Albert stepped outside the emperor's residence and called for the crowd to disperse only to receive a blow from a thrown rock. The troops opened fire, and Vienna caught the peculiarly "French" disease that Metternich had felt could not spread. Within hours, protesters were demanding Metternich's resignation, and by the night of the thirteenth, he was summoned to the Hofburg and forced to resign. Within a month, he and his wife had followed Guizot and Louis Philippe to exile in England.

While the Habsburg empire would last almost another seven decades, the departure of Metternich, champion of the old order, represented the beginning of the end of that order. The petition the protesters presented to Ferdinand demanded a new role for the people in the government, and as in France, although the role for the postrevolutionary government was to be a brief one, it led to some important reforms. It abolished the *robot*—a vestige of feudalism that legally bound peasants to the land they worked. It also ended many of the aristocracy's hereditary rights to local political rule. In so doing, it gave many in the empire their first taste of political life that in turn fueled the desires of many groups within the multiethnic empire for their own states and the right of self-determination. While it would be years before these desires would be fulfilled, the cracks that appeared in the edifice of the empire in 1848 ultimately fractured it completely within less than a century. And in those areas where reforms did not permanently take, new debates sprang up as independence movements wrestled with the dilemma of how to reconcile social justice with individual liberties.

New Forces in Play

Feudalism was finally dead and Europe's most repressive monarchies were held in check by constitutions. More members of society were gaining a voice. And government was seen as having vitally important economic obligations to the people rather than, as had been the case for most of history, the other way around. Tensions emerged for the first time between the liberal emphasis on political freedom and the socialist emphasis on social justice.

The revolutions also saw the redefinition of the role of the state in response to a redefinition of the role of the private sector and, in particular, the role of the kind of private power that was embodied by the increasingly important business class in European societies. The Industrial Revolution, the rise of railroads, the breakdown of guilds and smaller-scale agriculture, urbanization—all had played important roles not only in remaking Europe's economies but also in elevating both the new capitalist class and the workers they employed as political forces.

Whereas once the central tension in public life had been between church and state, by 1848 it had become between the public and private sectors. And because increasingly important public actors were earning rather than inheriting their roles, the lines became blurred further. Whereas once inherited land and titles conferred political power, now earned income and capital did so. Ideas of property and its role in the social order were being radically changed. Early socialists saw this as a positive trend and saw industrialization as a parallel and reinforcing force to democracy. But by 1848 some were not so sure. The most notable of these, of course, is Marx. His publication in 1848 of *The Communist Manifesto* offers us one of the most enduring artifacts and consequences of that year's turmoil and the issues that drove it.

The Invisible Hand versus the Hand of Greed

In considering Marx it is useful to strip away as many as possible of the ideologically charged distortions and prejudices that have been slathered on his views by both sides during the cold war and to look at some of his most important underlying ideas. Of these, for our purposes, one of the most significant relates to the implicit consequences for public power associated with the debate over how private property should be handled. While liberals interpret the granting and expansion of private-property-related rights as further empowering individuals, the converse is also true. By stripping property away from the state, private ownership also reduces the power of the state. Since states had regularly abused those rights for the few who controlled them—and states had historically been vehicles for the interests of the aristocracy—this was naturally seen as progress. However, by transferring the rights away from an entity that at least in theory was acting on behalf of society to individuals who were not, the shift in rights created the possibility of a different form of abuse. Indeed, it created, as depicted by Saint-Simon's "Hand of Greed," the likelihood that future decisions regarding property would be even less likely to take into consideration the interests of the many.

This was why Marx was so troubled by what he saw as a journalist writing about those who had been arrested for doing what had been a right of theirs since time immemorial—collecting wood in the forest to feed the fires by which they cooked and heated their homes. The "wood theft" cases were one of the direct inspirations for his view that contemporary ideas about property rights were skewing dangerously away from the interests of the majority of society. This conclusion in turn led him to develop an alternative approach. That approach, framed in *The Communist Manifesto*, sought to find a way to preserve the interests of those who could not effectively win in the competition-controlled world of capitalism. Marx did not see this as an alternative to capitalism but rather as an evolution of it into a new form that achieved, through the creation of a classless society, the justice that the liberals had sought. Writing about economic evolution, he placed progress in the context of the feudalism-to-capitalism continuum that dominated the discourse of the 1840s:

> We see then: the means of production and of exchange, on whose Foundation the bourgeoisie built itself up, were generated in feudal Society. At a certain stage the development of these means of Production and of exchange, the conditions under which feudal society produced and exchanged . . . the feudal relations of property became no longer compatible with the already developed productive forces; they became so many fetters. They had to be burst asunder; they were burst asunder. Into their place stepped free competition, accompanied by a social and political constitution adapted in it, and the economic and political sway of the bourgeois class. A similar movement is going on before our own eyes . . . The productive forces at the disposal of society no longer tend to further the development of the conditions of bourgeois property; on the contrary, they have become too powerful for these conditions, by which they are fettered, and so soon as they overcome these fetters, they bring order into the whole of bourgeois society, endanger the existence of bourgeois property.

Marx saw this process, facilitated by both the rise of industrialism and the working class it created, as ultimately leading to such an equitable distribution of power and wealth that the state would be no longer necessary. However, in the interim, he felt the state would have to play the role of midwife on behalf of the workers, ensuring that the necessary ownership shifts took place. In this respect, for some unspecified transitional period, he saw the state playing an even greater role in addressing the "social question" than his liberal contemporaries did.

Reviled as he ultimately became in the United States, it is impossible not to hear the echoes of the other cries for justice that rang throughout Western capitals in 1848 and beyond—up to and including current concerns about concentrations of wealth and power—in Marx's words. He sought to reverse or forestall the rampant inequality he felt would result if capitalism were to continue unchanged and unchecked. "These laborers, who must sell themselves piece-meal, are a commodity, like every other article of commerce, and are consequently exposed to all the vicissitudes of competition, to all the fluctuation of the market." He goes on to clearly make the point that the progress achieved in the gradual fall of feudalism was not having the desired effect:

> Not only are [the workers] the slaves of the bourgeois class, and of the bourgeois State; they are daily and hourly enslaved by the machine, by the over-looker, and, above all, by the individual bourgeois manufacturer himself. The more openly this despotism proclaims gain to be its end and aim, the more petty, the more hateful and the more embittering it is.

With words like these, accompanied by his call for the socialization of private goods through yet another wave of revolutions, Marx was seen as dangerous, even if the publication of *The Communist Manifesto* was one of the least prominent events of 1848 in the eyes of most Europeans. Still, when a citizen writes, "Let the ruling classes tremble at a communistic revolution. The proletariat have nothing to lose but their chains. They have a world to win. Working men of all countries, unite!" it's hard to be surprised by the fact that Marx was asked to leave his home country. From Prussia he went to France, and when he was expelled from France he went to Belgium, from which he was expelled for advocating open rebellion against various European monarchs. Finally, like the displaced conservative heads of Europe, he settled in London, testimony to the diversity of views that capital tolerated.

At this pivotal moment, both those who would later be associated with the untrammeled power of the state (communists) and those who would be associated with championing the power of markets (liberals) saw industrialization and the rise of the new economic order as the answer to righting centuries of injustice. Both saw the core issue as being the more equitable distribution of property. Both saw the feudal state as a failure in this regard and the redistribution of power to the masses as the answer. And as history would develop, both would end up carrying their ideas to the point that rather than eliminating the wealth concentrations of the feudal world, they would produce their own concentrations of wealth and power—in one case in the hands of government ministers and ruling parties, and in the other in the hands of the most successful capitalists. Property rights were the crowbar with which the treasure chest of kings was opened up, but they soon became a blunt instrument used by the successors of those kings on behalf of those closest to them.

The changes to the corporation that occurred in and around 1848 were as dramatic and multifaceted as those transforming the state and altering public views of its role. They ranged from sweeping systemic changes associated with industrialization to a subtle series of legal changes that had profound consequences—actually turning the term "property rights" on its ear. In this instance, the issue wouldn't be about the rights to property, but rather the rights *of* property—about how a thing, the company, would soon acquire the rights that individuals had only just started to claim for themselves, and then some. In addition, during this period, several major corporations themselves underwent significant changes that had far-reaching ramifications. Finally, the very idea of the role and limits of a business began to change in important ways, as did ideas about the role businesses played within society.

One hub of these changes was the country to which the displaced and disaffected among 1848's leaders were most drawn: the England of Victoria. While Europe trembled, the United Kingdom remained an island of comparative stability—all the more remarkable because Ireland, which would remain under English rule until 1922, was the single place in the world most devastated by the potato famine. Nonetheless, save for the relative political blip of the Chartist movement in 1848, which called for constitutional reforms, the United Kingdom enjoyed comparative stability. There was no massive political street violence, no insurgents; and there was a sense of political soundness that did not seem out of place in a capital that was at the time the seat of power of the largest empire the world had ever known. The calm was also due in part to the fact that the British government was almost certainly already the most liberal in Europe at that time. However, this stability was a facade. Britain was metaphorically as well as geographically an island. Within its own empire, England had stability, but at a price—one that was paid by its colonies. The empire not only afforded England a place to exile and imprison potential domestic political threats, it also offered vital economic resources.

The Whig government of Lord Russell and his foreign secretary, Lord Palmerston, while keeping a wary eye on developments in Europe, focused on a well-practiced sleight of hand in their intra-imperial affairs. They were able to maintain the support of Britain's growing middle class by promising to lower taxes. However, since they needed resources to maintain the military might that held together the empire, they unflinchingly taxed their colonies to make up the difference. When maintaining the vast overseas military proved too costly, they brought troops home and replaced them with cheaper indigenous mercenaries. Further, of course, they gained the benefits mercantilism had always brought: the provision of cheap goods to the seat of power and access to the resource riches of the lands they held and that entities like the British East India Company helped exploit, from Hudson's Bay to Calcutta.

While these policies brought calm to the seemingly exile-filled streets of London, they tested the cohesion of the empire. Their overseas forces not only ruled ruthlessly but were less dependable than forces from England itself. By 1848, imperial expenditures had also reached a record high. Finally, while England may have seemed immune to the political contagion of 1848, the rest of the empire was not. From British Guiana to Canada there were peasant uprisings, regular mutinies by indigenous soldiers, and growing resistance to imperial policies.

By the middle of the nineteenth century, the East India Company was at a turning point in its existence, tumbling quickly from the precipice of power to the brink of liquidation. For all practical purposes, the company had effectively become India's government. East India executives governed the subcontinent's local affairs, and company-controlled armies kept the peace, or sought to. Within less than a decade, this apotheosis of corporate power—a company that enjoyed virtually all the prerogatives of a state—was tested by a crisis that would lead to its undoing.

Although no longer a trading company in the 1850s, the BEIC was still a licensed for-profit agent of the British crown, acting at the behest of the government but always with the interests of its shareholders at the forefront of its concerns. Not surprisingly, being ruled by a company that put the interests of a distant monarch, a distant people, and a distant cadre of shareholders ahead of those of local residents did not sit well with the people of India. By 1857, tensions produced a conflict known as the Great Rebellion or the Indian Rebellion.

Tensions had run high between the British and the Indians who served in the Company's armies, called sepoys, for decades. In part this was due to the fact that the British were foreign conquerors. In fact, many of the sepoys in the eighteenth century had actually fought against the British at the battles of Plassey and Buxar. There had been periodic flare-ups in the relationship between the sepoys and their East India Company rulers for decades. Perhaps the gravest of the warning signs during this period came in 1806 with a violent uprising when native soldiers employed by the Company's army rose up to protest a new uniform dress code that explicitly prohibited the use of any markings that might indicate the caste of the wearer. Since caste was so important to the identity of the Indians, the prohibition was inflammatory—yet another sign of British social engineering that bred deep resentment.

Company officials were utterly insensitive to the concerns of these employees, and the uprising in the summer of 1806 resulted in the death of two hundred members of the British garrison. While the East India managers in India mobilized their troops and swiftly crushed the mutineers, they shrugged off some of the most important lessons that could have been learned from the experience. Although adjustments were made to take cultural concerns into consideration, they were spotty, and the wounds were regularly reopened. By midcentury, inflaming factors included a perception that British missionaries were attempting to expand their efforts to convert Indians to Christianity and a series of decisions that removed or undercut privileges or perquisites that had previously been offered to upper-caste sepoys. Further, as the ambitions of the company spread throughout Asia, sepoys were sent farther afield; they initially received additional pay for postings far from home, but over time even that benefit was withdrawn.

In 1857, tension turned to conflict. In circumstances similar to the cascading series of misinterpreted events that had triggered the rebellions of 1848, misunderstandings begot missteps from Company managers, and conflict resulted. Early in the year, a rumor spread that the new cartridges for the Pattern 1853 Enfield rifle issued to the troops were greased with animal fats. Among Muslim sepoys, the fact that the fat might have been from forbidden pork was intolerable. Among Hindus, the allegation that the grease was supposedly made from cattle was equally troubling. For troops of both backgrounds, the fact that the cartridges had to be bitten open made the issue an impossible obstacle. This led to confrontation, and although the local military secretary ordered that the troops could grease the cartridges any way they pleased, the damage had been done.

The troops began to mobilize, and as they did, they tapped into civilian anger at other Company policies that had undone some of the historical feudal structures of Indian society. Property that had passed within families for generations was lost and aristocratic privileges disappeared. In India, a private company working on behalf of the most liberal government in Europe was facing an uprising from a population angered by policies that were undoing the old order in much the same way Europeans sought to do on the Continent. Further, the Company had set up a legal system in which its own officers were almost impossible to convict for wrongdoing against the Indians. This, plus a broad array of economic policies that were deeply unfair to Indian workers and landowners, led to further tension.

When in the wake of tensions concerning the Enfield cartridges one Indian soldier named Mangal Pandey protested and announced he would rebel against the Company and his commanders, the result was a standoff at a garrison near Calcutta. Many of his fellow sepoys refused to subdue Pandey, and although ultimately one stepped up to do the bidding of the Company commanders, the resulting hanging of Pandey and a commander who failed to subdue him angered many sepoys, as did the subsequent disbanding of the mutinous regiment.

Other conflicts concerning the cartridges followed, and dissent spread throughout the sepoy ranks. When eighty-five of the men of the 3rd Bengal Light Cavalry refused to accept their cartridges during drills, the result was that all were court-martialed, with many given ten-year sentences for disobeying orders. When they were marched off to prison, tensions grew, and within a day other Indian troops of the 3rd took action, seeking to release their comrades. British commanders tried to put down the uprising, and European civilian men, women, and children were among those killed, along with approximately fifty Indians.

The fighting then rapidly spread, and the British were slow to react. Rebellious sepoys marched to Delhi, where they sought and eventually won the support of Bahadur Shah, the titular ruler of the Indians. Although he was largely powerless, his symbolic support was important, and it galvanized rebellion throughout India. Bahadur ultimately proclaimed himself emperor, asserting his authority through the issuance of coins with his image on them—a symbolic prerogative of a head of state.

The resulting conflict lasted well into 1858. When the British finally regained "control," they exercised their anger in several grotesque displays of brutality against the rebels. These included the sentencing of some to stand before cannons which, upon firing, blew them to bits. Wrote one of the commanding officers, "With all my love for the army, I must confess, the conduct of professed Christians on this occasion, was one of the most humiliating facts" related to the uprising. Some British units took no prisoners, simply engaging in the wholesale execution of those they captured. Back in liberal Britain, politicians and poets alike, including Charles Dickens, supported the cruelty, with Dickens coauthoring a call for destruction of the "race upon whom the stain of the late cruelties rested" (that would be the Indians, by the way, in his view).

Although Britain retained its hold on India for almost another century, this was the beginning of the end for its largest imperial holding. And it was the end for the "Honourable Company." Under the Government of India Act of 1858, the company was dissolved and responsibility for India's rule shifted back to the government. A remarkable early experiment in the exercise of global private sector power thus came to an end.

The BEIC did not go without a fight. It enlisted as one of its principal advocates John Stuart Mill, author of *On Liberty* and one of the great champions of individual liberties, thus providing an echo of the relationship between Locke and the slave trade. This pillar of modern liberalism presented a petition before Parliament in which he argued that the East India Company had contributed so much to Britain that it should be allowed to remain a private enterprise. In his compelling history of the Company, Nick Robins writes:

> Mill first of all argued that the Company had, "at its own expense and by the agency of their own civil and military servants, originally acquired for this country its magnificent empire in the East"—as if it was doing the nation a favor. The language became richer still, with Mill claiming that it was the most beneficent [government] ever known among mankind.

There were, of course, other, seemingly more objective voices. As Robins also notes, an MP named George Cornwall Lewis interjected a note of reality when he responded that "no civilized government ever existed on the face of this earth which was more corrupt, more perfidious, and more rapacious" than the Company was in India. Lewis's views prevailed, and on November 1, the company ceased to be and its assets were nationalized.

Like a Phoenix

While the emblem of corporate excess of the past 250 years disappeared in Britain, successors that would in many respects emulate its scope and many of its values were rising up in America. Several factors played into this profoundly important shift of the world's economic center of gravity from one side of the Atlantic to the other. Even before we detail them, it is important to note that such economic transitions are accompanied by other equally important dislocations—such as an accompanying shift in intellectual and moral influence. In short, with the rise of American corporatism also came a rise in the influence of American ideas and values about the nature and role of the private sector. This is a point especially worth contemplating given that today we are seeing a similar phenomenon, the shift of the balance of economic power from the Atlantic to the Pacific and from America to Asia.

While the industrial expansion that Hamilton had foreseen was one driver of American growth, the great resources of the country were another. There were several factors that linked directly to the turmoil of the 1840s. One was the profound surge in immigration that resulted from Europe's famine. Not only did this bring many needed workers to America, but it brought many with skills as well as a generation of entrepreneurs who, in making their own fortune, helped make that of the young country. In addition, events of the 1840s also helped clarify America's identity as a continental power blessed with land, riches, and the benefits of being isolated from the old world's problems.

On March 10, 1848, the U.S. Congress ratified the Treaty of Guadalupe Hidalgo, which ended the two-year war with Mexico and conferred over half a million square miles of territory to the United States. The war confirmed the country's burgeoning sense of its own "manifest destiny," with the American flag now flying over Pacific shores for the first time.

The West was America's future, and little time was wasted in tapping into the energies of the enterprising, market-oriented Americans who had so fascinated (and somewhat appalled) Tocqueville. Just days before the end of the war with Mexico, two men made a discovery on a riverbank in Coloma, California, that changed the world. Swiss American immigrant John Sutter and his partner James Marshall found gold, and within months, people from every corner of the globe began pouring into California to seek their own fortune and stake their own claim.

That first gold nugget changed the world as much as or more than any other event of that year. It provided the inspiration for Americans to whom Ohio was still the Wild West to venture out across the plains and the mountains. It provided the lure for putting in place the new transportation and communications technologies—railroads and telegraphy that not only knit together the continent but made large-scale enterprises possible. It even forced the new nation to grapple as never before with the issue of whether to extend slavery to the new territories. The question in turn triggered a civil war that, although brutal and briefly divisive, eventually not only made the United States into a more tightly knit nation with a single economy, but also ensured that the driving values of that economy would be those of the industrial north and that old agrarian approaches associated with the south would gradually give way.

These things made America the greatest economy the world had ever known. They created the conditions for the birth of the first great truly private companies, the ones that would give birth to the first truly private multinationals, companies like Standard Oil and U.S. Steel. The railroads led this business revolution. They not only facilitated transcontinental commerce but also led to the creation of new forms of management and corporate finance, new methods of competition, and new phases in the relationship between business and government. While the first large railroad projects of the nineteenth century required extensive government involvement (as has been the case throughout U.S. history, from the building of canals through the development of our aerospace and information technology industries), by the 1830s an economic depression forced many states to cut back their support for such ventures. As a consequence, the railroads had to turn to private investors to enable their growth. Some of this capital came from wealthy English and Dutch investors, among others, who sought to invest their money in American ventures that were less risky than those in politically volatile Europe. As European markets suffered into the 1840s, more of this "nervous" money made its way to the rapidly growing country across the Atlantic. In the decade after 1848, as the old business monolith of the East India Company met its end, new giants were rising in the West, with railway tracks tripling in length between 1850 and 1860.

For their time, the first railway companies were enormous. The east–west lines of the New York Central and Baltimore & Ohio were valued at what was then a staggering $20 million. It was the largest venture of its kind at that time. The demand for that kind of capital helped fuel the growth of Wall Street as an important financial center. New financial instruments—stocks and bonds—were produced as never before to fund new railroads, the building of new track, and the purchase of new locomotives.

At the same time, because railroads were such huge, complex systems requiring so many people, they produced challenging working conditions that led to the development of some of the most important modern labor unions. Significantly, they also triggered a rethinking of competition that rewrote the rules for business. Fierce competition among railways seeking to gain monopoly status between key cities led to price wars. This in turn created opportunities for clever businessmen to negotiate deals that would give them tremendous advantages over their competitors. This was the approach of John D. Rockefeller, almost certainly the most important figure in the history of American business. Rockefeller, an ascetic mama's boy from upstate New York, saw American markets with different eyes from his predecessors. Based in Cleveland, not very far from America's first oil fields in Pennsylvania, he learned that he needed the railroads to get oil from those fields to market. Because his company, Standard Oil, became the largest refinery in the United States only three years after its founding, it was the most logical contender in the industry to regulate production and traffic, enabling Rockefeller to negotiate excellent rates with the railroads and significantly undercut his competition. Actually, his deals with the railroads enabled him to eliminate competitive threats, which was the goal of the man who famously said "competition is a sin." He weakened competitors by undercutting their prices and then used his profits to buy them out. His goal was to centralize the chaotic fledgling petroleum industry under one mammoth corporation, and as he achieved that goal, he realized the promise of creating great national enterprises that was first presented as a consequence of the discovery of gold in 1848.

Within less than a decade and a half, Rockefeller controlled 90 percent of America's refining. It was a story of rapacious growth that was foretold by Marx. Although he got much wrong, here Marx's fears have a prescient quality. Writing in *Das Kapital*, he had observed:

> One capitalist always kills many. Hand in hand with this centralization, or this expropriation of many capitalists by few, develop, on an ever-extending scale, the co-operative form of the labor-process, the conscious technical application of science, the methodical cultivation of the soil,

the transformation of the instruments of labor into instruments of labor only usable in common, the economizing of all means of production by their use as means of production of combined, socialized labor, the entanglement of all peoples in the net of the world-market, and with this, the international character of the capitalist regime.

Of course, what Marx feared, Rockefeller celebrated. He did indeed take the advantages he crafted for his company and build what became the world's first multinational corporation, one that despite being broken up early in the twentieth century by antitrust laws is still the predecessor of the world's second-largest corporation (ExxonMobil) and four of the world's top ten companies. While size was a source of controversy for these companies, and while the federal government in the United States sought to contain the power of the giant enterprises created in the late nineteenth century to take advantage of the national economy that really began its life at the time of Europe's upheavals, the problem of size was not one that Americans or the business world ever repudiated. On the contrary, markets seek efficiency and scale produces efficiency, and so the drive to scale is one of the forces posited by early theorists of capitalism like Smith.

Another of those early giants was established by the immigrant bobbin boy who got his first job in 1848. Andrew Carnegie systematically built a steel empire—largely on the back of railroads and the urban expansion they enabled—that when unified into U.S. Steel in 1901 was worth more than $1 billion. That's hundreds of times larger than most of what would have been considered "large businesses" when he started working in 1848.

The influence of these American industrialists was not limited to their own country. For example, one of those who was greatly influenced by Carnegie and who characterized him as a mentor was a fellow member of the American Iron and Steel Institute, Erik Johan Ljungberg, the general manager of Stora Kopparberg. When Ljungberg was born in 1843, Sweden was struggling with many of the issues confronting the rest of Europe. Ljungberg's father squandered his savings and his family was forced into bankruptcy like so many others. For Ljungberg, the answer lay in the newly industrializing aspects of the Swedish economy. As a teenager, he became an apprentice in an ironworks and within a few years was promoted to the position of chief bookkeeper, following a career path very much like that of Carnegie. At the time Ljungberg was sent by his boss to attend mining school, the Swedish mining industry was dramatically changing. Stora had taken advantage of the industrial boom in Europe by shifting from copper to iron as its principal mining product. By the time of Ljungberg's birth, the company was already producing more iron than copper.

At the same time, recognizing the need for diversification and reflecting the importance of timber to its iron-smelting operations, Stora also expanded its lumber business. In 1854, the company bought a one-third interest in the newly formed Kopparberg-Hofors Sawmill Company, giving Stora Kopparberg access to large swaths of Sweden's forests and again mirroring what had been happening across Europe. By 1860, the company was producing more timber than iron and constantly seeking ways to maximize efficiency. Management was centralized and modernized.

Both iron production and timber production boomed. The company moved into the paper business and expanded its control of forest land until it extended over two thousand square miles, already an area roughly the size of Luxembourg. Somewhat disingenuously, the company argued that it took over the land to "prevent speculators from ruthlessly exploiting these resources." Although iron, timber, and chemical products were the new source of profitability for the company, activities at the ancient Falun mine continued well into the twentieth century. Copper mining took place at about one-third of the rate seen during the golden age of the 1600s, and by late in the century the company no longer manufactured copper in metallic form, using the bronze product instead for the making of vitriol to satisfy growing demand in Europe's growing chemical industries.

Stora gradually wriggled free of the last vestiges of control by the Swedish government. By 1888 it, like many of the other companies of Europe and the United States, had embraced a limited-liability share structure. (For more on this, see the next chapter.) This concept—giving the company full independence and financing flexibility but also protecting owners from personal responsibility for its losses—caught on briskly in the latter part of the century. The inflexible structures that bound the corporations to the states in which they operated disappeared, as did many of the old companies, as we saw in the case of the British East India Company. The new generation of companies—including those as flexible and creative as Stora—were bound by the laws of countries but not controlled by their governments. And as illustrated by the size of

Standard Oil and U.S. Steel, and even the relatively obscure Stora, within no time at all some were achieving an economic size or control over physical lands that made them the rivals of some states.

Ljungberg ran Stora in a way that emulated much of what Carnegie did. Both were thrifty, valued profit, and adopted a patriarchal attitude toward their workers. Carnegie built towns and schools and libraries for them. He helped pioneer a view of the company as a provider of elements of the social contract. Ljungberg too promoted education, the welfare of his workers, and a view about the well-being of the people who worked for him that was well-intentioned if self-serving:

> If our workers were aware of the situation of industry, I believe they would not ask for increased benefits without a corresponding increase of the products of labor and if they themselves knew what really fast, skilled workers could willingly and happily accomplish, their greatest desire would be to acquire a corresponding capacity, that their services to their home country would be equal to that of the Americans.

Ljungberg's admiration for America explains not only his embrace of Carnegie's mentoring but also why Stora, an ancient European company in a country with strongly socialist impulses, would remain so flexible and evolve so well in step with the emerging new ethos of global companies. America's people were, in Ljungberg's view, "trained for intensive labor in response to the prevailing social conditions. The unmanly emotional whining in our country is absent over there. A manual laborer wants to be a man, a real man and not a poor wretch who has to be taken care of and pitied." He apparently believed that, as Carnegie wrote, "The old nations of the Earth crawl forward at a snail's pace, but the Republic speeds past them like an express."

During the nineteenth century Stora completely transformed itself yet again, starting as a copper-producing state-owned enterprise and ending as one of Europe's premier privately owned iron and timber producers. Once again, the world's oldest company was one of the best illustrations of the changing nature of businesses everywhere.

Roles Redefined

The consequence of the events of 1848 and the years immediately before and after it was the establishment of many of the views that are held today, whether by proponents or critics of concentrated power in the hands of states or business. States were now defined in terms that would seem familiar to most modern readers. If asked what makes a state a state, an observer in the mid-nineteenth century and one today might answer similarly: the right and responsibility to defend its own borders, the ability to legitimately use force, the ability to set and enforce laws, the ability to manage its own financial affairs from creating currency to levying taxes, and the right and responsibility to meet the other basic requirements of its social contract with its citizens. Although the degree to which the state should fulfill these requirements, and its approach to doing so, differs from one country to another, all nations recognize that government does have social responsibilities.

Similarly, in 1848 private power began to emerge roughly as we know it today. Entities were independent, possessed their own legal status and rights, and were starting to achieve a scope and scale that gave them hitherto unimagined political power and social clout. The ideological concepts that have also largely defined our view of the respective roles of public and private power had also fallen into place as these roles were defined. While there was division about what was best, core ideas had emerged about the consent of the governed, the importance of markets, and the ways to produce the best collaboration between government and business interests.

But as we have seen, nothing remains static for long. And while many of the ideas and actors that emerged a century and a half ago may seem at least distantly familiar, in the years since, great changes have taken place. The roles of government and business have been profoundly altered. However, our understanding of the relationship between government and business has not changed, and therefore our theoretical framework is inadequate for coping with the new circumstances of the relationship.

In the next section of the book, we will look at how the idea of what makes a state a state has changed, how sovereignty has been deconstructed, and how many of the prerogatives that once belonged to governments have now been assumed by private actors. We will also examine the degree to which these changes were produced by acts of conscious application of will on behalf of private actors, to what extent they were the result of the actions of government leaders and political thinkers, and to what extent they were the result of circumstance. This will help us to understand how we have gotten to the situation in which we find ourselves today—where the international rules first set down in Westphalia or Vienna and the philosophies derived from them no longer apply.

Part 2

The Contest: The State Constrained, the Corporation Unbound

6 ▪ How the Rule of Law Backfired

It is legal because I wish it.

—King Louis XIV of France

The government, which was designed for the people, has got into the hands of the bosses and their employers, the special interests. An invisible empire has been set up above the forms of democracy.

—Woodrow Wilson

Many of the forces shaping the current relationship between public and private power were evident in the swirling eddies stirred up in the wake of 1848. In Sweden, the upheaval of the Continent was felt, but it was as if muted by distance, absorbed by crossing the Baltic. King Oscar I was moved by what he saw happening across Europe, and either out of genuine sympathy for the liberal movement or to head off potential unrest at home, he proposed a variety of reforms. One included the idea of a two-chamber Riksdag, although his not-quite-wholehearted commitment to real reform was revealed by his view that the upper house should be dominated by a large royally appointed contingent. The proposals stirred a buzz and were at least temporarily parried by opponents, as were more radical notions such as granting "universal" suffrage to the men of Sweden. But clearly political change was coming even to Europe's northern frontiers.

One reform—noted earlier—that did make it through at the time, however, had a direct impact on Stora. It might be easy to overlook, given everything else that was happening in 1848, but that was the year Sweden passed limited liability laws for the first time. A year later these laws went into effect, allowing Swedish joint-stock companies to incorporate with royal approval. In fact, with the political changes afoot, the requirement for royal assent to deals quickly became a technicality that many courts were disinclined to demand before granting limited liability status and breathing legal life into new entities. The limited liability laws also made it possible for companies like Stora to raise the capital they needed for growth. By 1872, limited liability companies employed almost half Sweden's workforce, and over 80 percent of it by World War I. The rethinking of the shape, structure, and basic concept of the role of companies in society in Sweden was again a harbinger of a trend that was sweeping Europe, the United States, and countries around the world.

At the same time, on the Continent, radicals who were inflamed but frustrated by the year of revolutions and the fragile, typically short-lived governments that came and went in their aftermath were thinking about the laws governing property and the sources of private power within society in rather different ways. There was a French philosopher who, while also a socialist, had a rather different view from Marx's about how to address the injustices of the capitalist system. His name was Pierre-Joseph Proudhon. In 1840, he published a book titled *What Is Property? Or, an Inquiry into the Principle of Right and Government.* Within it was his most famous assertion: "Property is theft."

By this he meant that capitalists or landowners who benefited from the efforts of the workers or peasants in his employ were actually stealing the fruits of their labors. He wrote, "The economic idea of capitalism, the politics of government or authority, and the theological idea of the Church are three identical ideas, linked in various ways. To attack one of them is equivalent to attacking all of them . . . what capital does to labor, and the State to liberty, the Church does to the spirit." His conclusion was that the power of anyone over others in society was an infringement of their rights and should be eliminated. Following these beliefs to their logical conclusion, he became the world's first self-professed anarchist. As it happened, these views also gave him an idea of socialism very different from that of Marx (who himself took issue with the "property is theft" formulation). Prudhon believed property should not be transferred to the state, but rather should reside within associations of workers. He also believed that workers should manage themselves. (As impractical as these ideas must have sounded in a world dependent on hierarchies like that of the nineteenth and twentieth centuries, one wonders how they might be received in the increasingly network-dominated world of the current century. For example, do the leaderless revolutions such as that in

Egypt in early 2011 suggest that Proudhon's ideal might now be slightly more within reach? In a different variation on the idea, it is also worth noting that labor participation in corporate boards, as is found in Germany, for example, has proved to be an effective structure—often credited with playing a significant role in that country's economic success.)

In the interplay between views like Proudhon's and those of Marx, the socialist movement gradually gained momentum in Europe. With 1848 demonstrating that old political and economic systems were in need of reform, the Continent and indeed the world were seeing an emerging, intensifying ferment over the political and economic rules and philosophies that should shape society.

In Sweden, new political parties were emerging that would ultimately demand a very different relationship between companies and governments. A young tailor named August Palme came to Sweden after being imprisoned in Germany for his active socialist views. By 1889—three years after the country finally adopted a bicameral legislature—Palme, something of a political entrepreneur, launched the country's Social Democratic Party. His creation, soon cultivated under the leadership of a math and astronomy student named Hjalmar Branting, took a very practical Swedish turn away from Marxist radicalism and toward a view of "social reform as a way to socialism." This more gradualist focus on finding a way to work within the government rather than through revolution was abetted by the parallel rise of labor unions, which emerged earlier in Sweden than elsewhere. The industrial workers of Sweden, like the miners centuries before, sought a stronger voice in society, and they allied with the Social Democratic Party to form a counterweight to the power of traditional aristocrats and moneyed elites. The result was the modern Swedish vision of society in which the old idea of balance among the estates is reflected in a compact between the state and workers that counterbalanced the concentrated power of the private sector.

But if Sweden was establishing itself as an incubator of what would later be known as Eurosocialism or the welfare state, and of what we shall later discuss as one of the primary alternative models of modern capitalism, throughout the nineteenth century the economic center of gravity of the world was indisputably shifting across the Atlantic Ocean, as Stora's Ljungberg had appreciated. Eurocapitalism and American capitalism were evolving along related but different lines. The role America would come to play in redefining the corporation was every bit as important as the one it played in ushering in important advances in the modern idea of democracy. And, as we shall see, the evolution of American ideas regarding not just the nature of public and private power but the relationship between the two would emerge in an American capitalist model that at the end of the twentieth century and in the first years of the twenty-first century looked as if it might transcend all other approaches—from socialism to social democratic approaches to every variation between and beyond them.

However, in order to understand why it now appears that the American model might not ultimately triumph and why new life is being bred into the alternative approaches that evolved in Sweden and elsewhere in Europe and in Asia, the middle section of this book will explore the rise of corporate power and the decline of state power during the past century and a half. The rise of corporate power—often at the expense of the state—may be among the most important yet least understood major trends affecting the modern world—despite the efforts of writers mentioned earlier, like Barnet or Vernon, to bring it to the fore.

While it is impossible to cover every nuance of the changes affecting these complex institutional structures, we will attempt to provide a look at certain major changes that are illustrative of broader trends in the historical relationship between private and public power. To do so, we will look at four of the basic components of nation-states that had come to define them by the mid-nineteenth century: the ability to pass and enforce laws, the ability to define and be defined by borders, the ability to print money and manage national fiscal affairs, and the ability to legitimately project force. In each case, we will take several specific examples of how, over the past century or so and especially in the recent past, the power of states has been chipped away and the power of companies has grown, and how there has often been a direct and intentional connection between the two. In addition, we will consider how these changes have altered the relationship between these two power centers and thereby how the functions of societies have changed.

This discussion will then lead to the final section of the book, in which we will explore how these trends have directly contributed to the great challenges we face today and, consequently, to the way the international system seems likely to change in the years ahead.

From Individual Property Rights to Property
with More Rights than Individuals

If the watershed associated with Westphalia and 1648 had to do with defining the rights and roles of states, and the liberal reforms associated with 1776 and 1848 had to do with asserting the rights of individuals, it might be argued that the most significant trend since then has had to do with asserting the relative rights and roles of private enterprises. The change in those rights has come by marrying the legal concept of the business corporation—an idea originally created to serve the needs of the state—to the individual rights that were originally asserted to define the origins and limits of state power. Whereas the battle between church and state was a battle between two sets of "lawgivers," the subsequent tug-of-war between public and private power centers has turned on the revolutionary idea that more important than the laws states could make were the laws that limited and defined the origins of state powers—an approach to lawmaking that traces its roots to the Magna Carta and the U.S. Constitution.

It was the fact that America embraced the idea of constitutional law earlier than other countries that helped make the United States the birth-place of a new form of corporate power that would dwarf even the rather remarkable rise of early great enterprises, from Stora to the British East India Company. This fueled America's remarkable ascent to its status as the world's richest and most powerful nation and, at the same time, may have—at least temporarily—compromised both its political and eco-nomic systems.

As we have discussed, medieval Europeans inherited from Rome the idea that an entity or an institution could incorporate and be granted the status of a legal person. An entity could request corporate status from the king, and the king would, if he chose, grant this status, creating an artificial legal person of the corporation. Importantly, the monarch would also retain the right to withdraw the privileges he or she had bestowed. Corporations existed at the pleasure of the state and thus clearly to serve the purposes of the state.

Just before the South Sea bubble burst, businessmen used their influ-ence to persuade Parliament to pass legislation that greatly set back the development of the corporation in England and may consequently have fatally compromised British competitiveness. As stock prices were rising sharply early in 1720, there was a boom in establishing corporations by the dozens. Many of these companies were not officially registered, but investors, seeking profits wherever they could find them, began buying stock in many of them, thus creating unwelcome competition for established and still capital-hungry entities like the South Sea Company.

Thanks to its friends in Parliament, the leadership of the South Sea Company was able to engineer the passage of the Bubble Act of 1720. This law mandated severe penalties—including infinite fines and perpetual imprisonment (which is about as severe as you can get short of legislating eternal damnation)—on any joint-stock company operating without a charter. The impact of the act, however, was not exactly what was expected by the South Sea Company leadership, since the company collapsed in scandal shortly afterward. The Whigs—whose views on businesses were exemplified by Trenchard and Gordon—became even more leery and made the existence of any corporation even more dependent on a Parliament that, postcrash, was reluctant to give its permission. In essence, in the eyes of legal scholars like Douglas Arner, a historian of early corporations, the Bubble Act "essentially cut off the growth of the private corporation in England until the nineteenth century." The joint-stock corporation was on a short leash, and the development of the modern corporation would therefore have to take place somewhere else.

The Word "Corporation" Appears Nowhere in the U.S. Constitution

Prior to the American Revolution, only seven businesses had been chartered in the United States. When one more—a bank—was chartered during the period in which the Articles of Confederation were the law of the land, the bank's officers made sure to get state charters too to ensure the legality of its existence. During the 1780s there was something of a surge in the formation of companies in the new country—ten were established during the first half of the decade and twenty-two more before 1790. While drafting the Constitution that was to replace the Articles of Confederation, James Madison proposed an amendment that would have given the U.S. Congress the power to "grant charters of incorporation where the interest of the U.S. might require & the legislative provisions of the individual States may be incompetent." Only three states voted for the proposal, however, and eight voted against it; as a result, the U.S. Constitution contains no mention of corporations.

This omission led to one of the biggest controversies of the presidency of George Washington. For all the new country's differences with the country that had until recently ruled it, the political divisions within the United States and the views of the leaders tracked with those in England. Washington's secretary of the Treasury, Alexander Hamilton, and many others from northern, more industrially inclined states were considered Tories. Jefferson, like many others with agricultural roots, was more sympathetic to Whig views about business.

Hamilton was an advocate for a U.S. version of the Bank of England, which he saw as an essential engine of British growth. He felt a U.S. central bank would increase capital availability, enable the government to gain financing when necessary, and allow for the issuing of banknotes that could facilitate payment of taxes. In his view, such a bank would best serve the public interest if it were privately incorporated and thus immunized from being buffeted by public opinion. He wrote in his *Report on a National Bank* that "to attach full confidence to an institution of this nature, it appears to be an essential ingredient in its structure that it shall be under a private and not a public direction, under the guidance of individual interest, not of public policy, which would be supposed to be, and in certain emergencies, under a feeble or too sanguine administration, would really be, liable to being too much influenced by public necessity." Despite no mention of corporations in the Constitution, Hamilton felt that the bank could be brought into existence under the provision that allowed the Congress to take such actions as are "necessary and proper." Although the primary author of the Constitution and one of Hamilton's coauthors of the *Federalist Papers*, James Madison, objected to the Treasury secretary's arguments, Congress chartered the Bank of the United States early in 1791.

Seeking advice on whether he should sign the new legislation, President Washington turned to Jefferson. Unsurprisingly, Jefferson sided with Madison, his Virginia neighbor and close friend. He argued that Hamilton was playing fast and loose with the meaning of the word "necessary" in the "necessary and proper" clause of the Constitution, going on to write: "the constitution only allows the means which are 'necessary' not those which are merely 'convenient' for effecting the enumerated powers." In his view, the bank was not undeniably essential, so the Congress had no right to will it into existence.

Washington sent Jefferson's response to Hamilton, who responded vehemently. He asserted that the power to incorporate the bank was implied if and only if chartering such a corporation would help Congress achieve one of its specifically designated duties. "It is unequestionably incident to sovereign power to erect corporations," he wrote, "and consequently to that of the United States, in relation to the objects intrusted to the management of the government." He felt Jefferson's restrictive view of the "necessary and proper" clause would severely hamstring the federal government. He also asserted that, although it was not mentioned, the power to grant corporate charters would be important for the new country going forward, given the relative benefits of limited-liability arrangements over those associated with simple private partnerships. Later Hamilton's widow said, "[Hamilton] made your bank. I sat up all night with him to help him do it. Jefferson thought we ought not to have a bank and President Washington thought so. But my husband said, 'We must have a Bank.' I sat up all night, copied out his writing, and the next morning he carried it to President Washington and we had a bank."

Despite Hamilton's persuasion of America's first president, the next four chief executives of the United States were less enthusiastic about corporations. John Adams was on the record as being particularly critical of banks. Jefferson's views were well known and greatly influenced those of his two successors—Madison and James Monroe—both of whom hailed from within a few miles of Jefferson's home at Monticello. It is an interesting and perhaps unexpected twist of fate that it was another Virginian from the same neighborhood—a relative of Jefferson's who was a friend of Washington and a political ally of Madison and Adams and would ultimately be appointed by Adams, first as secretary of state and later as a Supreme Court justice—who would play a vitally important role in granting corporations the freedoms they would use to shrug off key state controls and then grow to a size that allowed them (as the *New York Times* columnist Thomas L. Friedman has put it) to "lift off" and begin to "float above" nation-states altogether and thus have a very different kind of relationship with national laws.

That individual was John Marshall, whom Adams named Chief Justice of the U.S. Supreme Court in 1801. Over his nearly three and a half decades in office, the longest-serving Chief Justice in U.S. history handed down a series of decisions that gave shape to the modern corporation and marked a pronounced deviation away from English legal traditions regarding companies. After Marshall, America took the initiative, and Britain, Sweden, and other nations would follow the U.S. lead.

At first, the Marshall court's decisions seemed to cleave closely to British common law. Indeed, in 1804, in its first major decision on corporate law, the Court decided the case of *Head & Amory v. Providence Insurance Co.*, in which it ruled that corporations were creations not only of the charters that gave birth to them but also of the common law. Using this conclusion as a springboard, in 1809, in his opinion in the case of *Bank of the United States v. Deveaux*, Marshall used common law principles to create a universal definition of the corporation in American law, which had the effect of preventing state courts from developing separate understandings of what constituted a corporation (a first step toward the precedence of federal law that would later lead to decisions that would help create a national market and economy and thus corporations of continental scale).

A decade later, in one of the Marshall era's most famous decisions, *McCulloch v. Maryland*, Marshall underscored some of Hamilton's initial arguments by asserting that Congress could constitutionally charter corporations to achieve constitutionally permissible ends despite there being no specific incorporation power in the founding document. As important as this decision was, it primarily had the effect of increasing the influence of the Supreme Court and the federal government over corporate law. However, later in 1819, Marshall participated in a decision that would dramatically alter the balance of power between corporations and the governments that created them: *The Trustees of Dartmouth College v. Woodward.*

The origins of the case can be traced back to the founding of what became Dartmouth College in 1754. At that time, the Reverend Eleazor Wheelock founded a school in Connecticut to teach Christianity to Native Americans. After depleting the initial donations from colonists, Wheelock sent a friend, Nathaniel Whitaker, to England to raise additional monies. The trip resulted in the establishment of a fund under the direction of the Earl of Dartmouth, who gave the institution not only his money but his name. In 1769, the royal governor of New Hampshire granted the school a charter of incorporation on behalf of King George III. The charter granted the school land in New Hampshire, provided that it also be used to teach English students. Wheelock was made president of the school and given power to choose his own successor, and, most important, control of the school was granted to the trustees and "their successors forever."

When Wheelock died a decade later, he designated in his will that his son John should take over the school. A twenty-five-year-old colonel in the Revolutionary Army, the son was reluctant to assume the daunting responsibilities of managing the school but gave in to the urging of the trustees. John's tenure was marked by increasingly frequent battles with the board over a variety of issues, ranging from tax questions to where students were to sit when attending village church services. When a rival of Wheelock's father, Nathaniel Niles, was appointed to the board in 1793, matters grew more tense as Niles outmaneuvered Wheelock and began to exert control over the board.

By 1815, the two sides were issuing contentious pamphlets, and the trustees ultimately decided to remove Wheelock and elect a replacement. In response, Wheelock went to the New Hampshire legislature and got them to pass a series of laws revoking Dartmouth's corporate charter and putting the school under public control. The trustees ignored the law and continued operation of the school as before. This triggered passage of yet another act by the legislature, making it illegal to serve as a trustee or officer of the college without an appointment by the legislature.

Wheelock, elected president of the State of New Hampshire's "new" Dartmouth, moved to oust the old board and any faculty who supported them from the campus. They responded by setting up shop nearby and requesting the college's records and seal from William Woodward, a former college officer who was siding with Wheelock and the state. Naturally, Woodward refused to comply, and the trustees sued. The all-Republican New Hampshire Court of Appeals upheld the view of the Republican-dominated legislature on behalf of Wheelock and the "new" college. They held that the college was a public corporation from its inception; that the constitutional protections accorded were meant to protect private rights; and that even if the royal charter was a contract, it would be against proper principles of government to prevent the legislature from being able to amend the charter if it was in the public interest to do so.

The trustees appealed to the Supreme Court. On March 10, 1818, Congressman Daniel Webster—a Dartmouth alumnus and future senator, secretary of state, and presidential candidate, already coming into his own as one of America's greatest orators—presented arguments on behalf of the college and the original trustees. He began by noting that the corporate charter declared that "the powers conferred on the trustees, are 'privileges, advantages, liberties and immunities' and that they shall be forever holden by them and their successors." He linked these rights with the most fundamental historical rights granted to Englishmen and subsequently to Americans:

> The privilege, then, of being a member of a corporation, under a lawful Grant, and of exercising the rights and powers of such members, is such a privilege, liberty or franchise, as has been the object of legal protection, and the subject of a legal interest from the time of the Magna Carta until the present moment.

He then made his pivotal argument. States, he asserted, were within their rights to decide what privileges they might wish to confer in a charter prior to issuing it. However, "once granted, the constitution holds them [the rights granted under the charter] to be sacred, till forfeited for just cause."

Webster then made a connection as remarkable for its legal deftness as it was for its internal ironies. He declared that "the very object sought in obtaining such a charter, and in giving property to such a corporation, is to make and keep it private property, and to clothe it with all the security and inviolability of private property."

In a single sentence he linked key ideas about the nature of states and property rights that had evolved throughout English and Western history and added a new twist. The Magna Carta had been drafted for the same reasons as the agreements between estates in Sweden and other similar documents from the days of the absolute power of monarchs: it promulgated the idea of individual rights as a way of circumscribing the powers of kings. While the Magna Carta was essentially a document designed to preserve the interests of other nobles, Locke and others built on the ideas within it to assert that the individual was the ultimate authority, that the only legitimate powers of the state were those that existed in service of the individual. In both instances, property rights were of primary importance. Wealth, to whatever degree it existed, was seen as the foundation of individual independence and influence. The question of the ability of the monarch or the state to make unchallenged or unlimited claims on personal property was central to determining who would have the upper hand within a society. Therefore, guaranteeing life and liberty without guaranteeing the right to property was essentially politically irrelevant, and Locke and his contemporaries knew it.

Now Webster had gone a step further. He used the idea of property rights to limit a state's influence over a corporation once it had been brought into existence. This would open the door to the gradual accumulation of other rights and prerogatives by corporate "fictional persons" that had only recently been won by real people. As we shall soon see, the concept of property rights, which was originally developed to preserve an individual's rights to property, would as a direct result of this decision be used to grant individual rights to entities that were themselves a form of property. It is a toxic stain on all involved that while these early advances were being made on the road to granting individual rights to "fictional persons," which were in fact forms of property, real people were still being bought and sold as property with fewer protections than corporations.

Webster closed his case by arguing that the actions of the New Hampshire legislature in undoing the original charter violated constitutional provisions against taking away property without due process:

> This Court then, does not admit the doctrine, that a legislature can repeal statutes creating private corporations. If it cannot repeal them altogether, of course it cannot repeal any part of them, or impair them, or essentially alter them, without the consent of the corporators . . . A grant of corporate powers and privileges is as much a contract as a grant of land.

He later added, "In charters creating artificial persons for purposes exclusively private, and not interfering with the common rights of citizens; it may be admitted that the legislature cannot interfere to amend without the consent of the grantees."

According to witnesses, when Webster finished his arguments, he stood silently for a few moments before the Court and then addressed Marshall: "Sir, you may destroy this little institution; it is weak; it is in your hands! I know it is one of the lesser lights in the literary horizons of our country. You may put it out. But if you do so, you must carry through your work! You must extinguish, one after another, all those great lights of science which, for more than a century, have thrown their radiance over our land! It is, Sir, as I have said, a small College. And yet, there are those who love it." Webster then was consumed by emotion, his voice cracking and his passion so great that apparently even Marshall was deeply moved.

When the Court announced its decision, the Chief Justice began by stating that "the American people have said, in the constitution of the United States, that 'no State shall pass any bill of attainder, ex post facto law, or law impairing an obligation of contracts." He asserted that "it can require no argument to prove" that a contract existed in this case. The private donations of funds with future authority vested in the trustees made Dartmouth a private corporation whose rights were protected by the Constitution despite the holding of the New Hampshire court. He then defined what a corporation is:

> A corporation is an artificial being, invisible, intangible, and existing only in contemplation of law. Being the mere creature of law, it possesses only those properties which the charter of its creation confers upon it . . . among the most important are immortality, and, if the expression may be allowed, individuality; properties, by which a perpetual succession of many persons are considered as the same, and may act as a single individual. They enable a corporation to manage its own affairs, and to hold property without the perplexing intricacies, the hazardous and endless necessity, of perpetual conveyances for the purposes of transmitting it from hand to hand . . . By these means, a perpetual succession of individuals are capable of acting for the promotion of the particular object like one immortal being. But this being does not share in the civil government of the country, unless that be the purpose for which it was created. Its immortality no more confers on it political power, or a political character, than immortality would confer such power or character on a natural person. It is no more a State instrument, than a natural person exercising the same powers would be.

While Marshall's definition is famous, it contains a flaw. It fails to recognize the connection between economic and political power. It fails to note that an entity that is granted immortality has the ability to accumulate more means and thus influence than a mortal human being. Further, it fails to recognize that the decision of which it was a part would later be used to open the door to future Supreme Court decisions that would grant additional "individual" rights to these "artificial beings" that would allow them to use that economic power specifically for political purposes. Furthermore, the corporation in question was an institution of higher learning, not a profit-seeking enterprise. The decision and its subsequent interpretations seem to gloss too quickly over this fact, ignoring the critical role a corporation's mission plays in determining its value to society and consequently how it should be treated under the law.

Marshall noted that although the British Parliament was "omnipotent" and thus had the ability to annul corporate rights, the New Hampshire legislature was limited by the U.S. Constitution. The decision was not only a victory for Webster and for the trustees of Dartmouth College, it was a watershed for the corporation in America and, at the same time, a turning point for the state. When King James II had decided in 1686 that New England's states needed better central coordination to defend themselves, he easily persuaded the courts to cancel existing royal charters and to create the Dominion of New England. As we know, Parliament was also able to cancel the East India Company's charter after the Indian Great Rebellion of 1857. But in the United States after *Dartmouth*, the state was prohibited from arbitrary interference with corporate charters and the door was opened to the modern corporation.

U.S. states were naturally unsettled by the *Dartmouth* decision and tried for a number of years to work around it by either limiting the duration of charters or obligating companies to have a public purpose. But gradually they began to change their laws in ways that ultimately gave even greater latitude to companies. In 1830, Massachusetts passed an act decreeing that corporations did not need a public purpose in order to achieve limited liability status. Seven years later Connecticut created what would be a popular model when it enabled firms in almost all areas of business to incorporate without a special legislative act. This signaled the beginning of a competition among the states to offer ever more business friendly laws. New York was an early leader in this sweepstakes, then New Jersey; ultimately Delaware was viewed as so welcoming that today more than 50 percent of publicly traded corporations are incorporated in that state.

This competition for investment, of course, presaged a similar competition that would be created among nation-states for the investment of multinational corporations. While some might assert that states have the upper hand because they can issue and enforce laws, states' power is not absolute if in so doing they damage themselves economically (which in turn damages their leaders politically).

Further, while *Dartmouth* offered corporations the protections of property and contract laws pertaining to their charters, subsequent Supreme Court cases have enabled companies to obtain additional rights that had previously been thought to be available only to actual flesh-and-blood people. In 1886, in the case of *Santa Clara County v. Southern Pacific Railroad*, the Court declared without argument that the Fourteenth Amendment of the U.S. Constitution, which guarantees equal protection of the laws (and was originally intended to provide protection for actual human beings denied such protection), applied to corporations. In 1890, it used this principle to start a series of rulings over the next fifty years that were used to strike down economic and often anticorporate regulations under the Fourteenth Amendment's doctrine of substantive due process. Fifth Amendment due process and Fourth Amendment protections against unreasonable searches were added in 1893 and 1906 respectively. And then, in the 1970s, the pace picked up and some really remarkable bending of the law took place to empower the private sector in ways that would have been unimaginable to those who once saw property rights as a tool by which to empower individuals.

A Campaign to Capture the Legislature

Writing seventy years after the initial passage of the Fourteenth Amendment, the U.S. Supreme Court justice Hugo Black lamented the fact that of all the cases to which it was applied, "less than one-half of one percent invoked it in protection of the Negro race, and more than 50 percent asked that its benefits be extended to corporations." Given that the amendment was passed after the Civil War to correct the grotesque ways the law had been used to deprive African Americans of their liberties and fundamental rights, Black's shock was easy to understand. It is quite clear that corporations were never the amendment's intended subject.

The language of the amendment speaks of protections for "all persons born or naturalized in the United States." It asserts that no state can deprive such people of "life, liberty or property, without due process of law; nor deny to any person within its jurisdiction the equal protection of the laws." While Justice Marshall had noted that historically the law had viewed corporations as "artificial" beings, in the tradition of English law there was a pronounced emphasis on this fact of artificiality. Corporations were creatures of the state, figments of the legal imagination of the public sector. It is quite clear that they were not seen as part of the society of individuals that the U.S. Bill of Rights or its British forebears were meant to protect. If anything, they were seen as quasipublic extensions of the state among the kind of potentially corrupting forces from which the framers of U.S. law sought to protect the people. Corruption, in fact, weighed heavily on their minds, given their recent experience with the British Parliament and their memories of the recent history of British society. It was discussed more during the Constitutional Convention than issues such as factions, violence, or instability.

From *Dartmouth* onward, the theory of corporations evolved; they ultimately came to be seen as "natural entities" with "a separate existence and independent rights." *Santa Clara* was a major step "forward" in this process. The case was presided over by Chief Justice Morrison "Mott" Waite, a Yale-educated Ohio lawyer who was the seventh person to whom President Ulysses S. Grant had offered the job and who was derided by *The Nation* as being "in the front-rank of second-rank lawyers." Nonetheless, he presided over nearly 3,500 cases during his fourteen-year tenure, many of which involved interpretation of the Thirteenth, Fourteenth, and Fifteenth Amendments and oversight of the adaptation of American law to the booming world of a post–Civil War America increasingly dominated by national enterprises such as the railroad industry. If there was a theme during his court, it was the systematic limitation of the power of the U.S. federal government.

Even before oral arguments in the case began, Chief Justice Waite informed the participants in the case that "the Court does not wish to hear argument on the question whether the provision within the Fourteenth Amendment to the Constitution which forbids a state to deny to any person within its jurisdiction the equal protection of the laws applies to these corporations. We are all of the opinion that it does." The statement was included in the headnote to the case, and with that notation, the basis for the accumulation of ever more "rights" by corporations was established.

The initial applications of the law made by the *Santa Clara* headnote were primarily at the state level. This was consistent with a prevailing reluctance to overempower the federal government and a tendency to defer regulatory matters to the states. This preference was not only rooted in the original concept of the U.S. government in which sovereignty resided within the states, but was also due to a perception that taking a state-by-state approach to such matters impeded corruption. Justice Louis Brandeis would later write that he was skeptical of regulation at the federal level because he thought it might "lead to capture of the national legislature by the industry, but that the insurance industry could never capture every statehouse." While his fears would later be borne out, it should also have been fairly clear that if "capturing every statehouse" was what it took, then that's precisely what companies would attempt. Standard Oil's systematic cultivation of state legislatures from Ohio to New Jersey, for example, was as important to its explosive growth as was any process by which it drilled for, processed, or shipped petroleum products.

A 1905 case ushered in a boom in the application of the Fourteenth Amendment to companies. The case was *Lochner vs. New York*, in which a bakery owner who was fined for overworking an employee claimed the law violated his freedom of contract. While courts had previously acknowledged that the right to contract was a part of due process as defined by the Fourteenth Amendment, they had asserted that the right was balanced by the "police powers" of states—their ability to regulate affairs within their borders. In the *Lochner* decision, the Supreme Court asserted that the police power of states was not without limits. The Court thereby essentially identified a "substantive economic doctrine" within the Fourteenth Amendment: that of "laissez-faire and freedom of contract." Although the decision was overturned in 1937, in the intervening decades companies used it as precedent for efforts to protect themselves from regulations pertaining to labor, prices, and limitations on who can conduct business. It was this legal era of using the *Santa Clara* headnote as a bludgeon to beat back state (and sometimes federal) regulation that Justice Black was lamenting in 1938.

By 1938, the United States had undergone a major political shift in its views toward corporations, thanks to the rise of trusts during the "robber baron" era, the trust-busting efforts that followed, and later the fact that the Jazz Age excesses of the 1920s were followed by the deprivations and personal economic tragedies of the Depression years. As a consequence, the New Deal era that followed saw a willingness to reconsider federal-level regulations. Naturally, corporations challenged the new federal securities laws of the early twentieth century, as well as attempts at price regulation, with all the tools at their disposal, but it would be a couple of decades before corporations would again tailor the U.S. Bill of Rights to their advantage.

The next surge, which began in the 1960s and 1970s and has continued until the present, has corresponded with a burgeoning of what might be called the "regulatory state." Government regulations of this era differed from those of earlier eras in the twentieth century because they had more expansive social goals (such as environmental protection, consumer protection, and employee health and safety), were conducted largely on the federal level, were arguably more intrusive and systematic, and covered virtually all sectors of the economy. Between 1964 and 1977, ten new agencies of the U.S. government were created with the goal of protecting consumers, employees, or the public. (Prior to 1964, the Food and Drug Administration was the only agency with this kind of broad mandate.) It was this expansion of the role of the federal government that led corporations to more aggressively seek other protections within the U.S. Bill of Rights; and their reaction to federal government expansion is as good an illustration as there is, not only of the ongoing struggle between public and private power, but also of how the expansion of the "regulatory state" has directly and paradoxically led to the superempowerment of corporations and the nationally corrupting state of affairs that so concerned Justice Brandeis. The powers the state ceded in granting enduring "rights" to corporations were, because they carved away historical state prerogatives, an order of magnitude greater than many of those asserted through expanded regulation—especially since superempowered corporations had so much influence over what such regulations might be passed and how they might be enforced.

Of the ten amendments that make up the Bill of Rights, corporations have successfully asserted the applicability of five to win protections for themselves. These include the First Amendment right to free speech, which we will discuss in a moment in more detail; the Fourth Amendment freedom from unreasonable searches and seizures; the Fifth Amendment prohibition against takings and double jeopardy (despite the fact that the amendment clearly refers to natural persons); and the Sixth and Seventh Amendment rights to jury trials in criminal and civil matters, respectively.

For example, in a 1977 case, the Court held that a provision of the Occupational Safety and Health Act was unconstitutional because it permitted an inspector to enter the premises of an Idaho electrical and plumbing company for the purposes of performing a safety inspection without a search warrant. Any sympathies one might muster for the poor defenseless Idaho company may be tempered somewhat in light of the fact that it was backed in the case by the U.S. Chamber of Commerce, the American Conservative Union, the National Federation of Independent Business, and two legal foundations representing corporate interests.

This sort of high-paid alliance on behalf of the interests of business illustrates yet another way in which the scales of justice are balanced somewhat differently when it comes to corporate citizens rather than mere individuals with much more limited means. If this results in an uneven application of the laws or more protections for those who can afford to assert them, then the law is once again being used as a tool to advance the interest of the few in ways that reasonable critics may see as antithetical to at least its asserted purpose within "just" societies.

Other cases show similar creativity in the use of constitutional protections to push back against federal power and advance corporate interests. For example, in a 1986 case, Dow Chemical was upheld when it objected to Environmental Protection Agency overflights of its facilities to monitor compliance with the Clean Air Act because, under the Fourth Amendment, Dow had a "reasonable, legitimate, and objective expectation of privacy." Certainly, the assertion of such a right seems to be at odds with the original concept of the corporation as an entity created exclusively to advance public interests.

The Fifth Amendment protects against double jeopardy by stating that no person shall "be subject for the same offense to be twice put in jeopardy of life or limb." Nonetheless, even though a 1906 ruling asserted that corporations do not enjoy constitutional protections against self-incrimination, a 1962 case and 1977 case both asserted that companies could not be retried in cases that had previously been settled by direct verdicts. As for the Fifth Amendment guarantee that "life, liberty or property" cannot be taken by the state "without due process of law," in 1980 the Washington, D.C., Court of Appeals found that the Pentagon's decision to prohibit a dairy company from selling to the military because an audit found it had been "irresponsible" and lacked "business integrity" was a violation of the dairy's "liberty rights" in its reputation.

If Money Is Speech, Then Can Speech
Really Be Considered Free?

As has already been illustrated, in the United States, as in other countries
around the world, the law is not immutable. But not only does it evolve
to keep up with political, economic, and technological progress, it does
so also to keep pace with national moods and mores. Consequently, as
views have ebbed and flowed regarding the relative roles of companies
and states, so too have laws reflected those changes. Nowhere is this quite
as clearly illustrated as in the story of how America's most fundamental
liberty, the First Amendment right to free speech, pertains to companies.

At the beginning of the twentieth century, as public outrage grew concerning the excesses of the Gilded Age and the perception that the corporate titans atop the great trusts like Rockefeller, Morgan, and Carnegie
had far too much power, President Theodore Roosevelt channeled the zeit-
geist in asking that Congress regulate corporate contributions to political
campaigns. "All contributions by corporations to any political committee
or for any political purpose," he said in his 1905 annual message to Congress, "should be forbidden by law; directors should not be permitted to
use stockholders' money for such purposes; and, moreover, a prohibition
of this kind would be, as far as it went, an effective method of stopping the
evils aimed at in corrupt practices acts."

Within two years, Congress responded by passing the Tillman Act,
which banned all corporate contributions to any political candidate for
federal office. Later, in reflecting on Congress's reason for embracing
Roosevelt's suggestion, Justice John Paul Stevens cited "the enormous
power corporations had come to wield in federal elections, with the accompanying threat of both actual corruption and a public perception of corruption" as well as "a respect for the interest of shareholders and members in
preventing the use of their money to support candidates they opposed."

These motivations continued to guide Congress throughout the remainder of the twentieth century as it steadfastly maintained its right to
set clear limits on corporate involvement in politics. If companies could
grow to great size, then, it was assumed, they could purchase outsized
influence over the affairs of the nation, and that was an idea utterly inconsistent with the views of representative democracy that had emerged

in the seventeenth and eighteenth centuries. Similarly, in 1943, Congress sought to level the playing field in response to massive union political donations by extending the ban to them. That ban was made permanent by the Taft-Hartley Act of 1947. Concerned that either companies or unions might find a way around the ban by narrowly defining "political donations" as directly giving money to candidates, the law also banned any "expenditure" by either group from their general treasury funds "in connection with" a federal election. It should be noted that these large private entities were still allowed to make donations from political action committees that were funded by "voluntary" donations from employees or union members. This was a bit of a wink-and-a-nod approach, as both companies and unions clearly have ways of seeking donations from their employees or members that are voluntary in name only. At the same time, throughout this period, not only did Congress feel unconstrained by the Constitution in regulating corporate speech in the form of political donations, it had no hesitation about regulating it in terms of advertising or in terms of what companies could say about stock offerings or certain types of financial information. There were no perceived protections for "commercial speech," and indeed some of these constraints on such speech—for example, as those on "insider trading" or pertaining to "truth in advertising"—still exist today.

As the mood of the country began to shift with the boom era of the 1960s and the 1970s, the growth of regulatory government, and the backlash against it from big business, "rights" to corporate speech began to be more broadly defined. Some of the legal decisions that expanded those rights were driven by perceived consumer interest, as in the 1976 Virginia case in which a ban on advertising pharmaceutical prices was overturned. Four years later, at the dawn of what would later be known as the Reagan Revolution—a period in which attitudes toward reducing fetters on business translated into a fundamental ideological divide pitting "free markets" against "big government"—the Supreme Court provided a test for determining the constitutionality of the regulation of corporate speech. In another case concerning an advertising ban, in this instance pertaining to ads by electrical utilities, the Court argued that for government regulation of commercial speech to be lawful, the government must have a substantial interest in regulating the particular speech that is advanced by a regulation that is not more extensive than necessary. Given the breadth of interpretation that such a test is open to, it has produced some rather divergent and seemingly inconsistent outcomes: banning advertising by Puerto Rican casinos was okay, while blocking publication of liquor store prices in Rhode Island was not. While these decisions are confusing, one thing is certain: states can regulate commercial speech to make sure it contains truthful information. As far as political speech goes, states have no such power.

At around the same time as the new law in corporate speech was starting to emerge, a campaign finance case called *Buckley v. Valeo* produced a ruling that spending money to influence an election was protected speech regardless of whether the money was spent as a contribution to a candidate or as an expenditure on behalf of one. While this case was silent on the specific issue of corporate political free speech "rights," two years later the Supreme Court found in *First National Bank of Boston v. Bellotti* that a Massachusetts law banning companies from making contributions from general treasury funds to advocate for or against a referendum was unconstitutional. This conclusion was reached in part, in the eyes of analysts, because with a referendum, unlike with elections for political representatives, there was no perceived threat of corruption, and also because it is in the interest of voters to hear both sides of a debate. The outcome was also influenced by the facts of the situation, in which the state had tried to pass a graduated income tax, saw strong corporate opposition to it, and thus tried to pass a ban on corporate contributions in order to clear the way for the tax.

The Court would later cherry-pick elements of *Bellotti* to support a further, even more dramatic expansion of the idea of corporate political "free speech." It would ignore the fact that the case made a distinction for the unique circumstances associated with referenda. But it would build upon *Bellotti* to grant corporations broad rights to bring their money to bear in influencing outcomes in elections.

The Court would do so despite two subsequent decisions that once again limited corporate participation in elections. One, *Austin v. Michigan Chamber of Commerce*, saw the Court uphold a Michigan law preventing companies from using general treasury funds to support or oppose candidates. In the 1990 decision, the Court cited the potentially "corrosive and distorting effects of immense aggregations of wealth that are accumulated with the help of the corporate form and that have little or no correlation to the public's support for the corporation's political ideas." It added that "the unique state-conferred corporate structure that facilitates the amassing of large treasuries warrants the limit on independent expenditures. Corporate wealth can unfairly influence elections when it is deployed in the form of independent expenditures, just as it can when it assumes the guise of political contributions." A second decision, *McConnell v. FEC*, ruled that the McCain-Feingold Bipartisan Campaign Reform Act was legal even in terms of the section that blocked corporations or unions from using general treasury funds to pay for "sham issue" ads (ads that purport to limit themselves to issues but actually urge voting for or against a particular candidate) within sixty days of a primary or a general election. Again, a key factor in influencing the decision was the desire to avoid the distortions that big bank accounts could bring to elections. A later case allowed a not-for-profit organization to use its treasury to pay for a pamphlet listing candidates who might be considered for or against its position because the Court concluded that as an NGO the entity did not "pose a threat of corruption." Thus, there was at least a rationale established—the Court wanted to protect against the distortions and potential corruption associated with companies writing big checks for candidates.

A Showstopper Moment

On January 27, 2010, President Barack Obama delivered his second State of the Union address. Before him sat members of both houses of Congress, his cabinet, members of the Joint Chiefs of Staff, and six members of the U.S. Supreme Court. In the midst of his remarks, Obama broke with tradition and directed a withering rebuke toward the representatives of the most senior members of America's judiciary.

A week earlier, the Court had handed down a decision that was a game changer for both campaign finance law and the idea of corporate free speech. Obama, a former professor of constitutional law, argued that the case—*Citizens United v. FEC*—"reversed a century of law to open the floodgates for special interests—including foreign corporations—to spend without limit in our elections." Echoing Roosevelt 105 years earlier, Obama said he didn't think "American elections should be bankrolled by America's most powerful interests, or worse, by foreign entities." Setting aside for a moment the question of whether there is something especially American about the interests of multinational corporations headquartered in the United States, Obama's outrage made headlines and underscored the importance of the *Citizens United* decision. The fact that Justice Samuel Alito also broke with tradition and visibly reacted to the president's remarks by mouthing the words "not true" only emphasized the emotional nature of the philosophical divide revealed by the decision. *The Atlantic* called the Alito reaction "the showstopper moment" of the State of the Union.

Citizens United turned on whether a movie distributor could run ads promoting the release of an ideologically motivated attack on Hillary Clinton called *Hillary: The Movie* during the period in the run-up to an election. Since Clinton was a political candidate at the time, the distributor was concerned that the ads would be banned, and so it preempted a challenge to its rights and sought court approval to proceed. The district court agreed with the Federal Election Commission's assertion that the movie ads should not be permitted, so the case went to the high court.

The Court had several options before it. Of course, one was that it could have upheld the lower court's decision. Alternatively, it could have chosen a number of rulings that would have based its decision on relatively narrow grounds. It could have ruled that the video-on-demand distribution of the movie did not count as an "electioneering communication" under the applicable law. It could have based its decision on the not-for-profit exemption cited above. Or it could have done as *Citizens United* had specifically asked and ruled that the law was unconstitutional only as it pertained to the unique case and its specific circumstances. Instead, the Court chose to use the occasion to reconsider the *Austin* and *McConnell* decisions. It asserted it had no other choice than to permit the ads "without chilling political speech."

The reasoning of the majority in the case is based on a few core points. The first of these is that political speech is at the very heart of what the First Amendment is meant to protect. While this principle is largely consistent with prior court decisions, the next is not as clear. It asserts that money expended in a campaign equals speech and is therefore protected. While this is consistent with the *Buckley* decision, the majority went further and effectively abandoned the constraints within which it and other decisions had operated—those pertaining to distortion and corruption. It did so based on the view that more political speech is always better in the marketplace of ideas and that banning any of it diminishes the vitality of democratic discourse. This is directly contrary to previously held bans on distorting or corrupting speech, which imply that there are some forms of political speech that ought to be prohibited because they pose clear threats to the public interest. In its decision, the majority asserted that since wealthy individuals and unincorporated groups could spend massive amounts of money to distort the debate, corporations should not be treated differently solely because of their corporate form. The fact that this form gives them the ability to amass greater amounts of money than individuals theoretically can (because corporations are immortal, among other reasons), and thus gives corporations "more" speech than individuals, is not addressed. The fact that the corporate form was initially conceived as having constraints placed upon it because of its unique relationship to and dependency on the state was also not addressed.

The majority also literally took a page from a very common contemporary argument on behalf of the "rights" of businesses by asserting—as did the U.S. Chamber of Commerce in its brief to the Court on this case— that most of the almost six million corporations in the United States were "small corporations without large amounts of wealth." The Chamber brief pointed out that 96 percent of the Chamber's members had fewer than a hundred employees and that 75 percent of corporations whose income is taxed under federal law have less than $1 million in sales per year. This was sufficient for the Court to set aside the distortion arguments, even though its decision does not address the several thousand corporations with operations in the United States that have annual sales bigger than the GDP of most countries, the fact that those corporations were, not surprisingly, the biggest contributors to the Chamber, nor the fact that even small businesses have considerably more resources than do the vast majority of individuals.

The Court, which apparently had an appetite to take what could have been a case with limited impact and turn it into a sweeping statement, went further, suggesting that corporations' option of participating in an election through a political action committee (PAC) was inadequate because "a PAC is a separate association from the corporation . . . so the PAC exemption . . . does not allow corporations to speak." Further, they argue that even if PACs were construed as allowing corporations to speak, they were "expensive to administer and subject to extensive regulations." Supporting this rather outlandish reasoning, they offered as evidence of the burdensome nature of PACs that "fewer than 2,000 of the millions of corporations in this country have PACs."

Finally, the Court addressed the corruption concern. It argued that the government's interest in avoiding corruption—the interest that was so dominant during the discussions of the Constitutional Congress and the issue that has dogged governments throughout recorded history—is not more important than corporations' interests in participating in the political process via independent expenditures. Clearly, we have come a long way since the Bubble Act of 1720—and in the process have forgotten all the lessons learned immediately prior to that and throughout the three intervening centuries.

The court justified this last point by making a distinction between quid pro quo corruption and that which might result from giving large sums of money to candidates to support their election. For perhaps obvious reasons, the Court's arguments on this point are limited to a perfunctory "the anti-corruption interest here is not sufficient to displace the speech here in question" while adding that the government had provided no evidence that states with no limits on independent corporate expenditures were victims of corruption. The expectation that representatives of a government that was elected as part of the most expensive political campaign process in history would be the best people to make a strong case against corruption is yet another sharp irony associated with this decision.

The majority's argument went on to include a statement arguing that favoritism and influence are unavoidable in politics and that corruption does not automatically exist just because certain groups give a politician a lot of money and he or she ultimately votes in a way that is consistent with the interest of those groups. This argument went on to say:

> When Congress finds that a problem exists, we must give that finding due deference; but Congress may not choose an unconstitutional remedy. If elected officials succumb to improper influences from independent expenditures; if they surrender their best judgment and if they put expediency before principle then surely there is cause for concern . . . the remedies enacted by law, however, must comply with the First Amendment; and it is our law and our tradition that more speech, not less, is the governing rule.

Setting aside concerns that corporate giving might violate the interests of shareholders whose views are contrary to those supported by the company, the majority made the argument that "the procedures of corporate democracy" would be sufficient to remedy such a situation. It is particularly discordant that this argument could be used in the midst of a financial crisis that revealed that management often did not act in the broad interests of shareholders and that many aspects of corporate governance were inadequate or suspect.

The four justices of the Court who dissented from most of the key elements of the decision scoffed at the assertion that *Citizens United* was not a reversal of more than a century of ever-tightening regulations on corporate money in politics. They also argued that the decision was over-reaching (without making the politically piquant and accurate accusation of judicial activism that was clearly called for). After defending the prior decisions that had justified limits on corporate campaign spending when it was distortionary or an invitation to corruption, the dissent concluded:

> The Court's opinion is thus a rejection of the common sense of the American people, who have recognized a need to prevent corporations from undermining self-government since the founding, and who have fought against the distinctive corrupting potential of corporate electioneering since the days of Theodore Roosevelt. It is a strange time to repudiate that common sense. While American democracy is imperfect, few outside the majority of this Court would have thought its flaws included a dearth of corporate money in politics.

The Rule of Law in the Global Era: Next Frontiers in a World Without Borders

There is no other democracy, or country that claims to have a democratic character, that has come to grant corporations such a privileged role in its polity as has America. Over two centuries, this country has gone from a debate about whether corporations should even be mentioned in the Constitution to a situation in which these artificial persons are granted the same protection as individual citizens. But of course in granting resource-rich, immortal entities such rights, one is able to fashion an extraordinary role for them.

Nowhere is that clearer than with the idea that money is speech. One of the evils that the Fourteenth Amendment was conceived to eliminate was poll taxes that required certain groups of voters—such as African Americans—to pay for the right to vote. But in the context of modern American politics, if candidates cannot run unless they raise millions— or, in the case of presidential candidates, hundreds of millions—then there is a new form of poll tax in which the people who select the candidates are the ones who have the ability to make the donations that will determine who will run and who will not. And the "people" in the best position to do that are the actors with the greatest economic means: "artificial people"—an apparent injustice that helped trigger much of the backlash and anti-business ferment seen, for example, in 2011's Occupy Wall Street protests.

Thus there have come to be, in such a system, citizens and supercitizens with rights and characteristics that give both unique political advantages. And even as some argue that states have grown in power because of the rise of the "regulatory state" and the growing share of GDP that is represented by government expenditures, and even as the case is made that the state still maintains "coercive" powers—the ability to enforce the laws—the reality is that modern states are shaped by the influence of their most empowered citizens and that "persuasive power" often takes the upper hand because it is able one way or another to direct those with the "coercive" capabilities.

The American example is, of course, an extreme. Given the objectives of this book, which will ultimately focus on the different systems that have emerged for balancing public and private interests, it is important to understand the American example, because it has been, since the middle of the nineteenth century, the most influential in the world, thanks to America's economic, political, and military successes. Other countries have also granted growing roles for corporations, which in some cases arise from even closer relations between the state and companies. But virtually all competitive global corporations today are influenced in their shape, structure, and social role by the developments that have shaped corporations in the United States. Finally, the international influence of the U.S. corporate model is also manifest in the fact that of the world's top two thousand global corporations, by far the largest number are American, occupying 536 places on the 2011 list compiled by *Forbes* magazine.

Still, American capitalism is just one of the several options vying for preeminence in the world today (and others that are on the rise are more directly descended from the branch of capitalism that split off and developed in Europe, as in the case of Sweden, France, and Germany). Understanding how the emerging class of "supercitizens" has co-opted important powers of the state requires us to return our focus to the global stage.

The reality is that regardless of the system we see, corporations have grown in influence worldwide and in every instance have played a role in paring away key prerogatives of the state. As in the United States, they have used powers granted them within changing national laws to do so. But their ascent has not been bounded by such efforts. Indeed, their rise has transcended all boundaries, which in itself is both a symbolic and a sharply practical way in which modern corporations have been able to gain unprecedented power relative to the states that once gave life to them.

7 ■ Beyond Borders

This world is small and experience has now proved it.
                                    —Christopher Columbus, 1503

We cannot wait for governments to do it all. Globalization operates
on Internet time.
                                    —Kofi Annan

The history of globalization is the history of the world. It is not a phenomenon unique to any era, but a process that connects the centuries like the
roads and shipping lanes that first made it possible to link peoples together. But to suggest that globalization has but one form or that it is a
purely historical force that has not been shaped or helped along by self-
interested parties would be naive. Indeed, narrow self-interest has, ironically, made globalization what it is today, and it will determine whether
globalization continues to powerfully reshape the world order tomorrow.

"Globalization" has many definitions, of course. The Nobel Prize–
winning economist Joseph Stiglitz calls it "the removal of barriers to free
trade and the closer integration of national economies." Left-wing social
scientists who clearly have an ax to grind dub it "the present worldwide
drive toward [an] economic system dominated by supranational corporate trade and banking institutions that are not accountable to democratic
processes or governments." T. N. Harper, in "Empire, Diaspora, and the
Languages of Globalism, 1850–1914" called it a "recolonization" of the
developing world by the West, although you could easily find others
who might say it is the reverse. For some it is progress. For others it is a
tidal wave consuming cultures, homogenizing humankind in its churning vortices.

One aspect is undeniable: globalization weakens the power of the state.
While it may also produce forces that trigger nationalistic backlashes,
in the end it undercuts the state in several ways. It renders the borders by

which states are defined less meaningful as traffic over, under, around, and through them becomes less controllable. It undercuts the national identity that knits together peoples and has formed the basis for political unions throughout time. How can one speak of "self-determination" without having a clear sense of what "self" means?

This breaking down of national identity is acutely felt among those private-sector multinational actors who take to the global stage and whose interests cease to align with those of any one country. These actors further use globalization to undercut the state; once corporations, for example, are truly global in their operations, they have the ability to "venue-shop" and play countries against one another to win better legal, regulatory, or tax treatment. They gain leverage by "floating above" nations.

The rise of transnational issues that is an inevitable by-product of globalization also undercuts the state in several important ways. One is that the rise of transnational threats and challenges makes it increasingly difficult for states to fulfill their obligations to their citizens under the commonly accepted understanding of what the social contract entails. If a state can't control its borders or keep people safe or regulate economic activities, its value is diluted. Or, as Thomas Hobbes put it in *Leviathan*, "The obligations of subjects to the sovereign is understood to last as long, and no longer, than the power lasteth by which he is able to protect them."

Given the need to find other mechanisms by which the social contract can be met, globalization has also created the need for supranational organizations. These have further weakened nation-states by assuming— even if only modestly—some sovereign prerogatives or roles. Going forward, it seems certain such usurpation is likely to continue (as indeed it should if our primary objective is to satisfy the needs of people rather than preserve the interests of local political elites). Because these institutions are weak by design, thanks to the reluctance of states to cede sovereignty, the result is that on transnational issues there is a void. This creates a space in which multinational actors can take advantage of the absence of regulations or the inability of regulators to effectively enforce rules that allows them to grow larger and more influential and to defeat constraints they might find at the national level.

But, as noted earlier, while over a prolonged period the trend toward greater integration and less meaningful borders is clear, there are countervailing forces, periodic backlashes, and divergent paths taken by different actors. For the purposes of this book, we are most interested in how globalization has been influenced by the rise of corporate power and how it has in turn affected the role of states and of private actors. In each of the chapters in this section of the book, we will consider a few examples that make it clear that commercial interests have played a central role not only in advancing the process but in ensuring that as it unfolded, it did so in a way that benefited them even if the results were not optimal for states. Further, we will examine how, over time, different approaches to globalization have emerged from societies with differing views of the relationship between private and public interests.

Hints from Early History

There is no denying that globalization has historically been driven in large part by technological innovation. That is in part what has given us the impression that what is happening today is so new and special. A handful of relatively recent technological innovations have made the knitting together of once distant and distinct societies visible, and the pace of the knitting seems breathtaking.

From the time the Internet was developed by the U.S. military in the late 1960s until the mid-1980s, the pace of its embrace was so slow that the countries to which it connected could be measured in the single digits. The World Wide Web was introduced only a year before Bill Clinton ran for president of the United States for the first time. During his first year in office the number of connected countries reached a hundred. Today, not only does every country in the world have Internet connectivity, but people now view it as a utility like gas and electricity. For example, in January 2011, when the Egyptian government cut off Internet access to the demonstrators in Tahrir Square and elsewhere across Egypt, the protesters cried out that their fundamental right to Internet access had been compromised.

The New York Times's Thomas L. Friedman, passing through Tahrir Square, noted that almost everyone he encountered, even the poorest Egyptians, had a cell phone. These phones were also the cameras that recorded the events in the square. They were also the digital communications platforms that made the "Twitter revolution" possible. Cellular telephony had grown so rapidly around the world that, according to the World Bank, the hierarchy of need among the world's poorest by 2010 had become: food, shelter, clothing, and a cell phone. The number of cell phone users in the world didn't reach 100 million until the mid-1990s. It reached a billion in 2002. According to the United Nations, it is now nearly five billion, with almost two-thirds of people in developing countries owning cell phones. Almost two billion have Internet access.

But these are only the latest technological revolutions to accelerate the connection of peoples worldwide. During the mid-twentieth century, largely thanks to technologies developed to fight two world wars and then the cold war, transportation was revolutionized by aviation innovators, the development of radar and advanced navigation systems, and the creation of more powerful computers. Space technologies made global communication via satellite possible.

Before that wave, however, another had taken place during the nineteenth century. Advances in nautical technologies enabled a new era in global trade. Ice from frozen ponds in New England was shipped aboard clipper ships to Calcutta to prevent food from rotting in the heat of the Indian sun. Steamships replaced clippers and enhanced the safety of transoceanic voyages, cutting trips from weeks to days. The telegraph linked distant corners of nations and then continents. The pace of these changes must have seemed blisteringly fast back then as well. In the 1830s, the first working telegraphs dazzled by sending messages short distances—a kilometer in the early German demonstration of Gauss and Weber, thirteen miles in the first commercial demonstration in England, two miles in the 1838 instance of Samuel Morse's telegraph in the United States. Less than twenty years later, a transatlantic cable worked for the first time. Less than thirty years later, there was a dependable communications link between the United States and Europe. Within a decade after that, Alexander Graham Bell spoke the words "Mr. Watson, come here, I want to see you" into his experimental telephone.

In the same year that Morse invented his telegraph, the SS *Great Western* became the first steamship to ply the Atlantic on a regularly scheduled basis. A decade after Bell's telephone, Karl Benz put the first automobiles into production in Germany using internal combustion technology that was also invented during this period of remarkable creativity and innovation—a period that led to a blossoming of global trade from

1870 through the beginning of the First World War that has been called by Friedman "Globalization 1.0."

Such a characterization, however accurately it may capture the unprecedented growth in world trade that took place during that period, clearly does a disservice to the ages of empire and exploration that came before. Previously, technological breakthroughs, from the invention of oceangoing galleys to caravels, from road building to the sextant and the compass, all ushered in similarly profound accelerations in the ability to link together societies.

But in each case there had to be a reason to develop, perfect, and employ such technologies, to bring them to scale, to undertake the expense and risk of using them. More often than not it was the pursuit of economic advantage for either public or private actors. Sometimes this pursuit took the form of conquest. Perhaps more often it took the form of commerce. As we have seen, the two are often flip sides of the same coin.

The ambition to link societies, to gain access to distant resources and then to preserve that access and the benefits they bring, is what has shaped the expansion of nations, the formation of alliances, the spread of culture, the rationale for wars, and the rules that govern international behavior. In fact, the search for "more"—the fundamental human "grass is always greener" impulse—is what led the first humans to venture out of Africa, to walk across continents, to form new societies. It has shaped and reshaped societies, empires, the balance of power in the world, the flow of ideas, and the very character of eras as this book illustrates, from that of the Vikings to the Age of Exploration to the Thirty Years' War to the current "Global Era."

For our purposes we need to ask: Has something profound happened in that process that has now reset the terms by which global players interact, elevating private power, delimiting that of states, and forever changing the relationship between the two? And if so, can we better understand what has driven it so we can foresee where it may lead us and why?

To find the first of the world's "multinational" enterprises, we can go back to the Assyrians, the Romans, and the early caravan leaders who set out along the Silk Road. We can also look to the Vikings, the Catholic Church, or the Hanseatic League of traders that linked the mines of Dalarna to purchasers in London, Antwerp, Bruges, Berlin, Kraków, and perhaps as far away as Novgorod. But we can gain plenty of insight into what has changed and why by beginning again with the period roughly around 1848.

At that time, there were perhaps 1,500 to 2,500 enterprises that could be called "multinational" in the world. That is only a couple of times more than existed when the British East India Company was incorporated in 1600. While such estimates are rough and depend on a very loose definition of the term "multinational," this much we know: the number probably did not double again until the middle of the twentieth century. In 1969, there may have been just over 7,000 such companies. By 2000, there were 63,000, with over 820,000 foreign subsidiaries. They employed almost 100 million people and perhaps directly supported as many as half a billion people. Add the local companies that were dependent on them for business and the number of people whose economic destiny was directly influenced by these entities, and the total number of people dependent on these multinationals may have been between one and two billion in 2000, a third of the world's population. Current estimates for the number of multinationals are over eighty thousand. It is estimated that just the top three hundred companies control over a quarter of the earth's productive capacity.

At the same time, the world has seen the number of countries grow from fifty-seven in 1900 to more than two hundred today. While the burgeoning of multinational corporations and the dramatic growth in the size and influence of the largest of them clearly enhances their influence, the proliferation of countries—much of it due to the end of colonialism and the breakup of empires—has the opposite effect, creating many very small, weak states that are independent in name only and linked to the fates and policies of larger neighbors or other actors, such as major resident corporations.

One of the key examples of how globalization has limited the role of the state is the degree to which economic activity has shifted from being contained within national borders to taking place outside them. While the revolutions of 1848 were churning, global exports equaled less than 5 percent of global economic output. By 2007, they accounted for over one-third of global GDP. That means more countries were dependent on each other and the corporate intermediaries controlling the flows between them for their well-being (and that does not take into account other vital global flows heavily influenced by corporations, from capital to information).

Controlling borders and levying tariffs on trade were important ways for sovereign states to exercise their authority. But, perhaps not surprisingly, as trade began to grow in importance and multinational actors began to wield ever greater influence, they began to use their economic and political leverage to reduce barriers that increased their costs and undercut their competitiveness. As a direct consequence, the rules of world trade and prevailing attitudes toward it on the part of political leaders began to change in ways that ultimately even more dramatically reduced the influence of countries over their own economic destinies.

The Pivot of 1848: Landed Gentry Give Way to Industrial Elites

From the beginning of time through the middle of the nineteenth century, the economic formula was fairly simple: land plus people equaled wealth. The land was the source of sustenance and shelter, and people were the engines that added value to what it produced and defended it. While this equation was in place, calculating global wealth and power was a straightforward task. Throughout this period, the two most populous countries were number one and number two in terms of their economic output. As noted earlier, until the Industrial Revolution built up a head of steam in the mid-1830s, China and India were the world's economic leaders. The fact that they have not been for the past 180 years is actually an anomaly, and their rapid rise as they have harnessed the new fundamentals of wealth creation of the industrial and postindustrial eras—which turn on the availability of capital and technology to boost productivity and output—is not a new development so much as it is a return to the status quo.

Political and economic power during this initial period of human history—a period that might be referred to as the Age of Agroeconomies— were related to the control of land and people. For Swedish kings and later for the shareholders of Stora, it was access to the mines of Falun and then the country's abundant forests. For English aristocrats like those across Europe, it was more often than not the control of farmland. Politi-

cal divisions arose in the early eighteenth century as the parties of English country landowners—or of the likes of Jefferson in America—faced
off against those who represented the rising economic centers associated
with new forms of commerce and wealth creation. This fault line, representing the growing divisions between landed gentry and emerging capitalist elites, was particularly fraught with tension in the years immediately
before 1848.

While the defeat of Napoleon marked one of the great triumphs in the
history of the British Empire, it also produced a debt crisis of staggering
proportions. England's national debt soared to over £4 billion, 237 percent of the nation's GDP. It was considerably larger (in relative terms) than
the current debt of Japan, which is widely considered the most grossly
overextended nation in the contemporary developed world at a time of
widespread and grave debt problems. In order to help preserve the economy in that time of great stress, the British Parliament adopted the Corn
Laws of 1815. Parliament, still dominated by the country's landed class,
once again embarked on a policy that served that group's interests directly and transparently. The Corn Laws prohibited imports of grain
when domestic prices fell below a certain level, keeping prices artificially
high and keeping revenue from flowing out of the country at a time when
every last farthing of hard currency was required at home.

By midcentury, though, as a consequence of a changing economic picture marked by the rising influence of the country's urban industrial elites
and following the deprivation associated with the famines of the 1840s,
the protectionist policies that might have made political sense in the
wake of Waterloo were encountering serious opposition. Reformers argued that the Corn Laws benefited agriculture at the expense of the
manufacturers and the rest of British society and so, in the name of a
freer and fairer economy, they sought to have the laws repealed. Unsurprisingly, they met vigorous opposition from the protectionist-minded
champions of British agriculture (and landowners). The debate pitted the
old England against the new and thereby provides a good illustration of
how the forces of the old agrarian economy worldwide were giving way
to the emerging industrial forces.

The man who had nominal responsibility for the deal that ultimately
undid the protectionist laws and created one of the major early watersheds in the history of free trade was a leader of Britain's Conservative
Party, Prime Minister Robert Peel. He was by no means a natural ally of

the forces of reform. Rather, he concluded that if he gave in to them on this one issue, it might placate them enough that they would not seek other, more threatening reforms. This was a strategy that ultimately won the endorsement of François Guizot, who, when entering England in exile after the 1848 debacle in France that resulted in his downfall, agreed that the move might have alleviated some of the grievances that had triggered unrest on the Continent. Ironically, this came from a man who in 1841 made the famous proclamation to the French people "enrichissez-vous," or "enrich yourself"—through work and savings—to earn voting rights, and who expelled Karl Marx from Paris in 1845.

But Guizot was still in France and the revolutions of 1848 were as yet unimagined when the Corn Laws reform political battle was taking place. Manchester, England, was already, in those early years of the industrial revolution, the heart of the nation's growing manufacturing economy. There, at the helm of one of the textile businesses that were the leading symbol of the new era, was a businessman with wide-ranging intellectual interests named Richard Cobden. While Peel ultimately marshaled enough of his party to bring down the Corn Laws, it was Cobden who was not only the force behind the push to reform, but also a model for business leaders and pro-business thinkers for two centuries to come, one whose thinking on the issue of trade and markets was to become the prototype for many of the theories today that are seen as central to modern Anglo-U.S. capitalism.

Cobden's first work, *England, Ireland and America by a Manchester Manufacturer*, published in 1835, included reflections on a tour he made of North America and on several core themes with which he would later be closely identified including, notably, free trade. Bringing some of his thoughts to bear politically, for seven years Cobden led the Anti-Corn League—an alliance of those who felt protectionism was artificially pushing up food prices, harming the competitiveness of British industry, and provoking countermeasures abroad that made it harder to sell to the world the goods Cobden's factory and others produced. He believed that, thanks to its lead in technology and productivity, Britain would be able to compete as an industrial power and win, if it were only given an opportunity to do so worldwide.

Cobden became a member of Parliament and almost immediately undertook an attack on Peel and his party, blaming them for the condition of British workers and demanding the repeal of the Corn Laws.

While his initial speech was controversial for its harshness toward Peel in a period in which popular violence was a periodic threat in Great Britain (Peel's personal secretary was gunned down in the street by a man who mistook him for the prime minister), Cobden recovered and marshaled the support of others across the British business community around a philosophy of free trade and government noninterference in markets that would later become known as laissez-faire. He drew on Adam Smith and especially David Ricardo, whose ideas on comparative advantage shaped Cobden's thoughts on why British businesses could win if the government and other governments would only get out of the way.

Three years after that initial speech, in May 1846, Cobden's arguments and the broad support he had marshaled prevailed and the first Corn Laws were repealed. Within a month, Peel, who had embraced the reforms in part as a political move but in part, he would later say, because of the persuasiveness of Cobden, was out of office. The final, total repeal of the Corn Laws took place two years later. But Cobden's victory would have ramifications for many decades to come.

Reading Cobden's arguments, one is struck by the parallels with the views of modern pro-market politicians. His ideas led to a tariff reform movement that took root and has been influential in England ever since. "We advocate nothing but what is agreeable to the highest behests of Christianity—to buy in the cheapest markets and sell in the dearest," he said, using the language of higher justice so common in subsequent entreaties over the years.

In words even more similar to those of later followers who openly embraced his views, such as Margaret Thatcher, he wrote, "Peace will come to earth when the people have more to do with each other and governments less." More apposite to the issue of international trade was his statement that "The great rule of conduct for us in regard to foreign nations is—in extending our commercial relations—to have with them as little political connection as possible."

Cobden's name ultimately came to be synonymous with free trade and laissez-faire policies in England, to the point that "Cobdenism" was considered a derisive expression by those who opposed his views and championed more government intervention in the marketplace. In the midst of the rise of British socialism, he was held up by the onetime *Economist* editor F. W. Hirst as the antithesis of Karl Marx. Hirst wrote of Cobden that he "believed in individual liberty and enterprise, in free markets, freedom of opinion and freedom of trade. [His] whole creed was anathema to Karl Marx."

Drawing a further parallel between Marx and Cobden, Hirst, in the midst of the Second World War, said that the two

> stand out before the civilized world as protagonists of our two systems of political economy, political thought and human society . . . when this war is over, we in Britain will certainly have to choose whether our Press and Parliament are to be free, whether we are to be a conscript nation, whether private property and savings will be secured or confiscated, whether we are to be imprisoned without trial, whether we are again to enjoy the right of buying and selling where and how we please—in short whether we are to be ruled as slaves by the bureaucracy of a Police State or as free men by our chosen representatives. This conflict will be symbolized and personified by Richard Cobden and Karl Marx.

The calamities predicted by Cobden's opponents did not come to pass, and from 1849 to World War I, Britain's growth was unprecedented. It might well be argued that this was due more to Cobden's accurate analysis of Britain's comparative advantages in the world marketplace throughout that period (during which time it was the world's most influential and prosperous nation) than to the universal applicability of his underlying theories about the appropriate roles for government and nation. That is surely to be debated by those who are his intellectual lineal descendants today and by those who represent the rising chorus who argue that more open global trade periodically produces episodes of dislocation or moments in which competitors emerge who are unwilling to embrace truly free markets and thus distort them intolerably. What is undeniable is that as a result of this Manchester calico manufacturer's efforts, Great Britain, the world's undisputed superpower of the nineteenth century, unilaterally signaled a move to free-trade economics with the repeal of the Corn Laws. Other states followed suit in Europe and then in North America and worldwide, especially as they saw Britain prosper. Further, it is also clear that, through efforts like those of Cobden, the era of the primacy of agriculture and by extension of the aristocracy had come to an end in England and the era of the ascendancy of the industrial class had begun.

The Multinational Impulse: Playing the Field
at Home and Abroad

If one way that business leaders could usher in the current era and its explosion of global commerce was through directly influencing public policymaking, another, naturally, was through devising the management structures and techniques that would in many ways make companies better suited to operating internationally than states, territory-bound as they are.

With the passing of the torch for global economic leadership from England to the United States at roughly the same time as the Corn Laws were repealed, American businessmen were readily accepting responsibility for driving the next waves of economic and political change. One of these was a flamboyant, philandering, reckless itinerant actor and sometime inventor named Isaac Singer. Singer, the son of German immigrants, had made a small fortune as the inventor of a rock-drilling technology and then squandered it supporting an acting company that spent five years touring with him and his mistress in leading roles. (He would ultimately father eighteen children by four women and become involved in a sordid public scandal featuring apparently accurate accusations of bigamy.)

When his time on the road performing theatrical favorites had taken too much of a toll on his bank account, Singer went to New York in an attempt to take a crack at marketing a new machine he had developed to produce signs. There he met George B. Zieber, who provided him with modest backing that initially amounted to $40 and an office space. It was Zieber and an explosion that destroyed Singer's prototype sign-making machine that later persuaded Singer to move the business to Boston, where the backer felt the ambitious almost-forty-year-old designer might have a better chance of success.

The reception for this sign-making machine was not what he hoped for, but in the shop out of which Singer had been working, there had been a pretty robust trade in manufacturing the complex and unreliable sewing machines of the day. Singer saw an opportunity here and set to work trying to develop a more dependable alternative. Singer later recalled:

> I worked on it day and night, sleeping but three or four hours out of twenty-four . . . The machine was complete in eleven days. About nine o'clock in the evening we got the parts together and tried it; it did not

sew . . . Sick at heart, about midnight we started for our hotel. On the way, we sat down on a pile of boards and Zieber mentioned that the loose loops of thread were on the upper side of the cloth. It flashed upon me that we had forgotten to adjust the tension on the needle thread. We went back, adjusted the tension, tried the machine, sewed five stitches perfectly, and the thread snapped. But that was enough.

Given the importance of the textile trade worldwide, Singer was not alone in trying to solve the problem of producing a reliable sewing machine. But Singer's design was sound, and, thanks to some clever lawyering that brought together a number of competing design patents into an ownership pool under the auspices of the Singer Company, the company soon became a dominant player.

One of Singer's early ambitions was to explore international markets. Just four years after he founded his company in 1851, he made his first foray abroad, selling a patent to a French partner named Charles Callebaut. Singer's relationship with his French partner was no more successful than his multiple romantic entanglements (and considerably less productive). Callebaut proved unreliable and uncooperative when Singer pressed him to adhere to business practices that were in the interests of the American company. His poor experience with Callebaut ultimately convinced Singer that the right way to conduct business was not through informal relationships but by a more direct approach—although not before his international aspirations had, by 1858, resulted in the establishment of independent franchise relationships responsible for growing sales in Europe and throughout the Americas. While within a few years of its establishment the company could be called a multinational, it lacked the systematic organization and operating procedures that could ensure its growth. It was suffering a problem common to other companies trying to test international markets in this era of burgeoning international trade.

The organizational model Singer used was becoming increasingly popular in the United States as transport and communications technologies enabled central control over national operations in a way that would have been difficult in the past. Within just over a decade of operations, Singer had fourteen branches operating across the United States, and he saw this as a system that he could also apply to his international operations. He sought to systematize foreign operations by establishing sales offices abroad. His approach may well have been an even bigger contribution than his sewing machine, even though his basic technological design is still widely employed today. He blazed a trail that would ultimately lead to the centralized, self-contained structure adopted by many modern multinationals.

Singer's British operations were especially important to the company because two of his chief rivals were already active in Britain (William Thomas, an English company, and the American firm of Wheeler and Wilson). But his business was hamstrung because of its system of shipping fully assembled machines to Great Britain. Shipments often did not keep up with demand, and delays meant failures of cash flow. Nonetheless, his representatives in Britain, Germany, and Sweden were reporting great appetite for the product and lamenting their inability to depend on the company they were representing for timely delivery of sewing machines.

With this as a backdrop, Singer recalled his British manager, George B. Woodruff, and announced that he intended to help solve his problems by opening a plant in Britain. This was a bold stroke, unprecedented among U.S. manufacturers and carefully conceived to put pressure on local competitors and reduce manufacturing costs, which had skyrocketed in the United States after the end of the Civil War. Singer and his company's directors had concluded that if they could move their production offshore, it would drastically cut shipping, storage, and related expenses. Singer recognized that in the industrial age, it was possible to successfully manage multiple business operations with perhaps even greater ease than he oversaw his "uptown" and "downtown" families in New York.

Singer also recognized that the multinational strategy would produce significant tax advantages, a fact that also motivated the company to expand further around the world. Between his overseas factories and closer company management of its international business networks, the company's worldwide operations grew to the point that by 1874, more than half of its total sales came from outside the United States. Woodruff, Singer's manager, understood the value of the company's approach, writing in one of his letters to the home office, "We can never make our business solid except by branches at all great centres—and wherever we must work by local agents we must bind and tie up the affair within our own control and constant direction."

By the 1880s, Singer's name was recognized around the world. His company was the number-one manufacturer of sewing machines. Branches spread across Europe, Asia, Africa, and Latin America. Soon vice presidents were installed in each branch to ensure that "neither sickness, death, nor any other circumstances may interfere with the smooth workings of the business to any great extent." The Singer Sewing Company grew in search of new markets and also to achieve economies of scale; this made Singer a first mover among modern multinationals. Within a few decades, other big U.S. companies such as Ford, Eastman Kodak, General Electric, and Gillette were emulating Singer's management approaches as well as the company's strategy of using international expansion to seek favorable tax treatment and lower material and labor costs while using their clout as direct investors to win political influence with governments far from their "home" market.

The Trusts Retrace Their Steps on a Bigger Stage

As was the case for Singer, for many multinationals, what is learned at home can be applied overseas. If this was true for the man whose company would be the harbinger of the modern multinational, it was even more true for the man whose brainchild would later become the archetype of the breed: John D. Rockefeller, founder of the Standard Oil Company.

It was said of Cobden that he had been a good businessman who could have been great if he had not been so interested in getting involved with politics and the great issues of his time. He was an idealist first and a businessman second. John D. Rockefeller, son of a snake oil salesman from upstate New York, was all business. But that did not mean he was not deeply involved in the politics of his day. Indeed, Rockefeller recognized that managing politicians was as important as his attentive, even obsessive, management of his refineries. Others saw the connection as well. In 1881, Henry Demarest Lloyd said, speaking of the way Rockefeller manipulated public policy to suit the interests of his firm: "Standard has done everything with the Pennsylvania legislature, except refine it." Rockefeller's articulated mantra was "competition is a sin," a business view that could not contrast more clearly with the views of either Smith or Ricardo, economists who saw competition as a fundamental strength of the capitalist system. Rockefeller sought every possible advantage, including domination of the North American market for petroleum products that was so complete that to say it was not a monopoly is mere pedantry. Thus we see among emerging competing views of capitalism the divergence of perspectives between the theorists of the marketplace and those who seek to make their fortunes in it.

Standard Oil of Ohio was established in 1870. By 1878, one of Standard's executives noted that Standard would account for 33 million barrels of America's 36-million-barrel refining capacity. In 1895, Standard's buying arm declared that from then on, it would unilaterally decide the price of American crude. By the end of the nineteenth century, Standard oversaw more than 80 percent of all U.S. oil refining and one-quarter of petroleum production.

Standard had achieved this status because Rockefeller took advantage of two parallel trends in post–Civil War America, trends that echo those of the current global era. He noted that state economies were being rapidly integrated, thanks to technologies such as railroads and the telegraph. And he recognized that there was a legal void in the regulation of interstate commerce in this new environment, an opportunity to play state laws against one another for his own corporate advantage and to act with impunity when federal laws were not strong enough to push back at his anticompetitive practices. Cobden had preached the ideal of free markets; Rockefeller was illustrating what happens when those markets are too free, when government's role is too small or ineffective.

Admittedly, some state governments had tried to take on Standard. But time after time, Rockefeller demonstrated that a state's "coercive power" can be offset by the "persuasive power" of good lawyers or campaign contributions, or the distribution of other emoluments, or the ability to "venue-shop," playing legislatures and courts against one another until he found the deal he wanted or avoided a legal outcome he sought to skirt. In so doing, he blazed the trail not only for U.S. corporations but for the approaches used today by global companies vying with national governments.

Part of Rockefeller's strategy involved his and his colleagues' essentially putting the lie to the whole idea of "coercive power" by refusing to be coerced. They would avoid court appearances and testimony whenever they could. When they had to testify, they said nothing (JOHN D. ROCKEFELLER IMITATES A CLAM, read one headline) or they lied ("The art of forgetting is possessed by Mr. Rockefeller in its highest degree," wrote another observer.) When an Ohio court found against Rockefeller, he simply dissolved operations in that state and reorganized as a combination of twenty companies known as the Standard Oil Interests, theoretically separate but all operated out of the same location at 26 Broadway in New York, then subsequently run as a holding company organized in New Jersey after state legislators there were persuaded to pass legislation allowing one corporation to hold stock in another. The American system of government and law did not control Standard Oil. It sometimes inconvenienced it, but typically, the law was bent to the needs of the company.

The success of Rockefeller and other early trusts, including Andrew Carnegie's U.S. Steel and the National Biscuit Company, bred imitators seeking the organizational formula that would enable them to reap the greatest profits and operate with the fewest constraints. After the Standard Trust was established in 1882, hundreds of trusts were created, reaching a total of three hundred with capitalization exceeding $7 billion by the early years of the twentieth century—a number over a dozen times greater than U.S. federal spending in 1900. The size and influence of the trusts had grown so great that by that year's presidential elections, the issue of how to control them had become one of the top campaign concerns.

What is said during a campaign and what is actually done are often two different things, and that was true in this instance as well. The newly elected president, McKinley, had talked tough about dealing with the trusts but brought only three antitrust suits. When McKinley was assassinated by a self-professed anarchist, he was replaced by his vice president, the former New York governor and war hero Theodore Roosevelt. Even before Roosevelt took office, the business community worried about how he might deal with the trusts and reached out to him with a message of concern: "there is a feeling in financial circles here that in case you become President you may change matters so as to upset the confidence . . . of the business world."

Roosevelt was pro-business at heart and believed that big corporations were a vital engine of economic progress. He was especially at ease with those of his class and background who were discreet in their exercise of power. Rockefeller was an outsider of dubious breeding and odious methods (his obvious contempt for the efforts to contain him bred considerable ill will). To Roosevelt, he was an example of capitalism gone wrong.

Because Standard had reportedly bought federal officials in the past, Roosevelt signaled that he was going to play by different rules by returning $100,000 in campaign donations made to him by Standard executives. Roosevelt also pushed for congressional reform and new laws that gave him more power to rein in the most abusive trusts, but the grip of the business titans on the members of the House and Senate was sufficient to block legislation, even though it would likely have been very popular with the public.

Roosevelt was therefore forced to use an 1890 piece of legislation called the Sherman Antitrust Act as a hammer with which to beat back the trust leaders. Roosevelt began by going after J. P. Morgan (for more on him, see the next chapter) and winning. This energized the president, and as soon as he won reelection he used the same tools to go after Standard.

Among the reasons public opinion had turned even more strongly in the young president's favor were the tireless efforts of journalists to reveal the excesses of companies such as Standard. The signature work of these efforts was *The History of the Standard Oil Company*, which was published in book form the same month that Roosevelt won reelection. In the book, the author, Ida Tarbell, pointedly attacked Rockefeller for co-opting the legal system within which he was supposed to be operating: "Mr. Rockefeller has systematically played with loaded dice, and it is doubtful if there has been a time since 1872 when he has run a race with a competitor and started fair."

Bristling at Standard's success in systematically and effectively undermining all federal legislation targeting it or impinging on the freedoms from which it so richly profited, Roosevelt was outraged but unsurprised when, as he undertook his case against Standard, the company sent its chief director, John Archbold, to Washington to try to persuade the president that further action was unnecessary, that in fact Standard was openly complying with all the government requests that had come its way. Roosevelt was unimpressed, and he directed his Justice Department to forge ahead with its action against the oil behemoth. The legal proceedings were as gargantuan as their target, involving 444 witnesses, 1,371 exhibits, and almost 15,000 pages of transcripts. At issue was whether Standard was a monopoly, and the government argued:

> We believe that the defendants have acquired a monopoly by means of a
> combination of the principal manufacturing concerns through a holding

company; that they have, by reason of the very size of the combination, been able to maintain this monopoly through unfair methods of competition, discriminatory freight rates, and other means set forth in the proofs. If this act did not mean this kind of monopoly, we doubt if there is such a thing in this country.

Finally, in May 1911, the Chief Justice of the Supreme Court, Edward Douglass White, slowly and almost inaudibly read out the decision that temporarily rocked the business world. The decision turned on what would come to be known as the "rule of reason," which held that an individual's or a corporation's actions in restraint of trade would be considered a violation of the Sherman Act if such actions were unreasonable and against the public interest. Wrote White:

> The main cause which led to the legislation was the thought that it was required by economic conditions of the times, that is, the vast accumulation of wealth in the hands of corporations and individuals, the enormous development of corporate organization, the facility for combination which such organizations afforded, the fact that the facility was being used, and that the combinations known as trusts were being multiplied, and the widespread impression that their power had been and would be exerted to oppress individuals and injure the public generally.

It seemed the state had gained the upper hand. Standard was dissolved. Rockefeller's empire appeared to be dead and defeated. The parent company was broken into seven new companies: Standard Oil of New Jersey, Standard Oil of New York, Standard Oil of California, Standard Oil of Ohio, Standard Oil of Indiana, Continental Oil, and Atlantic. However, suffice it to say that if the goals were to contain the influence of these organizations, or to dissuade companies from seeking the advantages associated with awesome size, or to persuade them not to seek to pressure government officials, not a single one of those goals was met. In this respect, the episode presages other subsequent "victories" of government over private power such as the reforms introduced in the wake of the financial crisis of 2008–2009 to reduce the influence of banks that were "too big to fail"—reforms that were so ineffective that within just two years there were more such megabanks than there had been at the time of the crisis.

Standard Oil of New Jersey became Exxon. Standard Oil of New York became Mobil, which later merged again with Exxon to become what was and has since been at or near the top of the list of the world's largest corporations. The California company became Chevron, the ninth-largest company in the world in 2010. Standard Oil of Ohio became an important part of BP, the fourth-largest company in the world in 2010. The Indiana company became Amoco, also now part of BP. Continental is now ConocoPhillips, today the third-largest energy company in the United States and the fifth-largest refiner in the world. Atlantic became ARCO, now part of Sunoco, the seventy-eighth-largest company in America. The total sales of the successor companies was, in 2010, over $615 billion. To put this in perspective, the GDP of the world's seventeenth-largest country, according to the World Bank, was roughly the same. While it is important to note that such illustrations are meant purely to give a sense of size and are fraught with problems (notably the fact that GDP and annual sales are apples and oranges as statistical indicators go), it is also worth noting that ExxonMobil alone has sales roughly equivalent to the GDP of Sweden.

More important from the point of view of this chapter, in breaking up Standard Oil, the U.S. government set in motion forces that would dramatically alter the global economic landscape and would do so using tactics to influence public policy worldwide that would hark back to the techniques employed by Rockefeller in America's state legislatures of the nineteenth century, and in some cases would make them look positively quaint by comparison.

The Myth of National Allegiance: Krueger, IG Farben, IBM, and GM

As private companies grew globally, they behaved in ways that were dramatically different from early state-sponsored enterprises whose existence was clearly predicated on advancing the needs of the state. While this issue has come into focus with ever greater clarity in the first years of the twenty-first century, it is not a new one. From the earliest days of the modern multinational companies like Singer, these companies were acting not in the interest of their home nation—whether that be job creation or generating tax revenue or stimulating investment—but in the narrow nationality-free interests of their shareholders. Indeed, the fulsome rhetoric of politicians, union chiefs, and pundits aside, that is the legal obligation of every corporation, and it should come as no surprise that the easier it has become for companies to seek new markets and more favorable economics around the world, the more rapidly they have done so.

In fact, early in the twenty-first century the move toward globalization had become so pronounced that the majority of the revenues of the Standard and Poor's 500, America's top companies, came from overseas. Their interests and prospects had begun to lie outside the United States. When it suited them to pose as U.S. companies, they would. They would even go to comic extremes to do so. When I was a senior official in the U.S. Commerce Department during the 1990s, I recall perverse displays of "patriotism" by international companies seeking the support of the U.S. administration to help them win international contracts, U.S. government advocacy, or financing for their deals. In one such case, two airplane manufacturers—Gulfstream and Bombardier—were eager for U.S. help. Gulfstream, based in Georgia, argued that it deserved the support of the U.S. government because it was headquartered domestically and Bombardier was headquartered in Montreal. Bombardier responded that a greater percentage of its components were manufactured in the United States than was the case for the nominally U.S. firm.

These issues posed, and continue to pose, a real dilemma for U.S. policymakers. For example, both Siemens and Toyota employ tens of thousands of U.S. citizens. Are they U.S. companies? Their profits are repatriated to Germany and Japan, but they are helping Americans in many cases much more than U.S. competitors based here. Further, their shareholders often include large U.S. institutional and individual investors. Lines are blurred, but the vocabulary and outlook have not changed much from the mid-to-early twentieth century, when it was still possible for a man like the General Motors chief executive and future U.S. defense secretary Charles "Engine Charlie" Wilson to say: "What's good for GM is good for America." Even before Wilson had uttered those words, the lie was being put to the concept underlying it. Not only did global companies have interests that lay outside the countries in which they were born, they often pursued those interests in ways that were either in conflict with the official national policies of their homelands or otherwise directly contrary to their national interests.

For example, General Motors has throughout its history periodically sought favor in the United States by emphasizing that it was part of the war machine that helped America to victory in the two world wars. But GM played an important role in supporting the German war effort as well. In 1929, GM bought Adam Opel AG, a German auto manufacturer well known at the time for its reliable cars and modern production techniques and facilities. By the late 1930s, it had transformed much of the business into an armaments producer for the German military, currying favor and seeking every possible means of winning significant contracts. From producing trucks to building bombers, GM's Opel was clearly not good for America.

GM was not alone in seeking a cozy relationship with even the most odious foreign leaders such as Hitler. IBM provided direct assistance to the German government in supporting the operations of the Nazi's extermination and slave labor programs. In his *IBM and the Holocaust*, Edwin Black writes: "The head office in New York had a complete understanding of everything that was going on in the Third Reich with its machines . . . that their machines were in concentration camps generally, and they knew that Jews were being exterminated." IBM was not merely providing technology, either. It was manning the equipment, and it continued to do so until the United States declared war in 1941.

In his blunt and thought-provoking book *The Corporation: The Pathological Pursuit of Profit and Power*, Canadian law professor and unabashed corporate critic Joel Bakan discusses the IBM case in depth. Echoing Black, who asserted that IBM was not supporting evil but was rather operating in a completely values-free, allegiance-free way, Bakan writes: "Corporations have no capacity to value political systems, fascist or democratic, for reasons of principle or ideology. The only legitimate question for a corporation is whether or not a political system serves or impedes its self-interested purposes."

Bakan concludes that companies are "singularly self-interested and unable to feel genuine concern for others in any context." He bases his assertion that they are pathological on this observation. But another way to look at it is to note that these are, after all, only "artificial persons." Corporations are simply what society requires and enables them to be. The real problem is not in the nature of corporations, it is in the nature of the relationship between those who can redefine corporate roles— that is, governments—and the companies themselves. If the public increasingly finds it difficult to impose its will on companies grown ever more independent by virtue of changes in the law, by virtue of operating globally and beyond the reach of national powers, and by virtue of their size and influence, then it is in the public-private relationship that the problem lies.

Sometimes, however, the pathologies within the public-private relationship result not from its breakdown but from ugly collaborations, particularly when governments with dark objectives work together with companies without scruples, without the ability to refuse unsavory requests. One of the most notorious cases of this also occurred during the World War II era when I. G. Farben, the pharmaceutical giant, compromised decades of work providing the world with lifesaving health innovations when it agreed to work with the Nazi regime to make the chemicals used for the mass extermination of concentration camp prisoners. This is not an isolated instance, though. Regularly in this global era, self-interested companies cross borders, and when it is combined with the need to co-opt or bend state power to their needs, the pursuit of enhancing shareholder value leads them to enter into troubling alliances and relationships that are difficult to defend. To choose but one recent example, a report from New Economy Information Services found that

> The democratic countries in the developing world are losing ground to more authoritarian countries when it comes to competing for U.S. trade and investment dollars . . . This finding raises the question whether foreign purchasing and investment decisions by U.S. corporations may be inadvertently undermining the chances of survival of fragile democracies.

Despite the revealing misuse of the term "U.S. trade and investment dollars" to refer to stateless corporate resources, the report that includes this statement accurately cites many reasons why U.S.-based corporations often prefer to invest in nondemocracies: lower worker wages, looser environmental regulations, bans on labor unions, and the fact that dictators often are strong leaders who make rapid decisions in a very value-free environment. Dictators are easy to cut deals with, even if doing so regularly runs afoul of U.S. foreign policy goals.

Even if corporations are not themselves pathological, it sometimes happens that their leaders may be. This phenomenon too has intersected with the evolution of globalization in troubling ways. Ivan Kreuger was the heir to a small, struggling Swedish match factory. But Ivan was ambitious and an adherent of the Rockefeller view that competition of any kind is not the soul of capitalism but the enemy of business. So Kreuger set about seeking every possible advantage for his enterprise. He began by merging his United Swedish Match Factories with the Vulcan Group, another Swedish match maker, thereby creating a monopoly in his home country. He then followed the model followed by aspiring multinationals pioneered by Singer, "pushing exports, building factories abroad [and] forming alliances with competitors." He had a special appetite for monopolies and he found a path to forging them that broke new, if unsavory, ground for companies seeking to turn economic leverage into special favors from governments.

In the wake of World War I, many European nations were under heavy financial burdens. Kreuger saw this as an opportunity. In exchange for providing loans, he could secure monopoly status for his company in individual nations. He started with a loan to Poland for $6 million and followed with one to France for $75 million. He would issue bonds in his company and use the capital to buy market domination in country after country, culminating in a 1929 loan to Germany for $125 million.

On its face, the strategy was just multinational business as usual. The problem was that Kreuger was raising money by promising rich returns to investors of as high as 25 percent, but the countries were paying him a fraction of that. To stay ahead of the game, he issued new bonds and shares internationally in such countries as the United States. Eventually he branched out of monopolies in matches and grew to be the third-richest man in the world by using his access to capital to purchase monopolies in a wide variety of basic industries, often abetted by the know-how he gained from banks in which he bought shares or to whom he directed significant business.

He became the number-one private lender to the countries of Europe during the twenties and stayed ahead of the game by riding that decade's investment boom, translating a huge appetite for securities into cash to cover his operations. He was also very discreet. This was not because of some old-school sensibility about business appearances. It was better described by the economist John Kenneth Galbraith, who recalled that Kreuger's "great aversion to divulging information, especially if accurate, had kept even his most intimate acquaintances in ignorance of the greatest fraud in history."

Kreuger was not focused on profits, nor was he just illustrating the ease with which corporations could use the power of persuasion to trump national governments' powers of coercion. He was a criminal. But he was so successful that even U.S. president Herbert Hoover sought his advice on international trade. A BBC story written decades later illustrates how he operated (and laid the groundwork for future fraudsters such as Bernard Madoff):

> Kreuger's financial methods were becoming increasingly devious. He had always sailed close to the edge of legitimacy; keeping liabilities "off balance sheet," establishing a network of more than 200 firms that bamboozled auditors and bankers, and inventing non-voting shares. He also conjured up "options," derivatives, and stashed cash away in secret subsidiaries in Liechtenstein and Switzerland.

As was the case for Madoff, when the depression came, Kreuger's Ponzi scheme came undone. He had floated $200 million in loans that were coming due, but the markets were no longer eager to provide him with new cash. Pressure grew from creditors. Then, on a chilly day in Paris in the early spring of 1932, the fifty-two-year-old Kreuger got up, got dressed, wrote three letters, lay down on his bed, undid his waistcoat, and shot himself through the heart.

Thirty-six years later, his story—the greatest scandal of an era fraught with them—intersected with the story at the heart of our book when Stora bought Swedish Match. It was not a marriage made in heaven, and within just a couple of years the conservative businessmen at Stora discovered that they could not digest the businesses that survived Kreuger's misdeeds. Just as hard to digest is the fact that Kreuger's multinational misdeeds remain shocking while the support of IBM, GM, and I. G. Farben plus many other still-familiar corporations for Hitler's genocidal conquest of Europe is shrugged off as "business as usual"—which in fact it was.

Free Trade Redux: Kodak, NAFTA, and the WTO

The years after World War II saw "history's most sweeping reorganization of the international order" as the victorious United States, along with its European allies and now-defeated and occupied former enemies, built a constellation of new global institutions, most of which still exist today. U.S. president Franklin Roosevelt, Teddy Roosevelt's fifth cousin, sought to lock the formerly warring countries of Europe into "an open multilateral economic order managed through new institutional mechanisms." Europeans, in need of American financial and security support, readily agreed.

The reluctance to embrace the creation of international institutions that had produced such a chilly welcome for Woodrow Wilson's League of Nations after World War I was replaced with a recognition that the world required supranational mechanisms as never before in order to address global threats and broadly shared needs. A new layer of governance was seen as necessary, but it was deliberately built to be weak, not to pose a threat to national sovereignty. The Allies built protections into it to ensure the consolidation of their victory—from ensuring American and European domination of international financial institutions to granting veto powers to the five great allied powers in the UN Security Council. Elsewhere, institutions required consensus or complex ratification procedures to take any meaningful action. Nonetheless, the recognition that the new era required new structures further challenged the traditional role of the state. Signing international treaties and joining international organizations, from the UN to the World Bank to the International Criminal Court to the GATT (and later the WTO) to the International Labor Organization to regional development and security organizations, had the effect of constraining national governments. The complications extend to corporations as well, but the implications are not what they might seem at first glance.

When Standard Oil of New Jersey made agreements to do business in Iraq after World War I, the company had to worry about two sources of law: the United States and British-controlled Iraq. Now when Exxon does business in a foreign country such as Malaysia, it not only has to worry about making sure its activities comply with American and Malaysian law, it also has to consider international human rights treaties for which it can be found liable in American courts under the Alien Tort Claims Act, relevant WTO provisions under which any country whose trade privileges are being infringed can bring a complaint and seek binding enforcement, regulations on global public health, the law of the sea, international labor agreements, or violations of any investment treaties signed by the United States or Malaysia.

A logical assumption might be that such a web of interlocking and overlapping legal obligations would be a great burden to international corporations and a real constraint. While the regulations are a burden and require hiring armies of lawyers and compliance officers, the reality is rather different than it was during, say, the era of trust-busters and tough enforcement of national laws. International law is a patchwork quilt of disaggregated institutions and legal regimes that do not and cannot coordinate their attempted regulation of corporations. This situation enables companies to systematically analyze the legal playing field and use their resources to devise strategies by which they regularly score victories that make them considerably freer to operate on the global stage than they were when they were limited to activity within the ambit of a single sovereign.

Furthermore, there is a host of areas in which the need for international laws or regulations has been stifled or has undermined the concerted efforts of organizations. The failure of international efforts to create a binding international agreement on climate change resulted from many factors including, notably, differences between developed and developing countries over how to share the costs associated with producing cleaner energy. But another important force to impede, dilute, or direct climate policies was an effective alliance between private actors who did not wish to undertake the additional expenses associated with the more efficient, cleaner production of energy. This group was actively led by oil and gas companies, as well as the coal industry, spending more than $1 billion on lobbying during the last decade to impede approval of component steps of the agreement including the Kyoto Protocol, which, although ratified by 192 countries worldwide, was never ratified in the United States thanks to the power of corporate special interests in Congress.

Another area in which strong regulation has been regularly and effectively blocked, again by an alliance of corporations and states that have sought to maintain their own sovereign autonomy (often with the cajoling support of very powerful corporate interests), is the global financial services sector. But in areas such as the environment or financial services, the result has been that corporate actors have taken advantage of a more relaxed global regulatory and legal environment than they would find in many advanced economies, and the advanced economies in turn have been compromised because they face the choice of enforcing their laws and seeing investment flows directed to less demanding regions of the world, or not enforcing them and seeing their prerogatives as sovereigns diluted.

Similarly, the existence of international regulatory regimes is also regularly used by corporations to pressure countries into creating an atmosphere more favorable to their businesses. As we have seen, this atmosphere can alternatively be more open or more protectionist depending on the companies' narrow corporate interests, as is the case with Chevron to General Motors to raw materials producers everywhere. Likewise, countries use these international regulatory regimes to pry open foreign markets or defend their own markets based on political factors, which typically means economic pressure back home. In this way, the organizations created to advance the free trade ideals of Smith, Ricardo, and Cobden have become party to the creation of an international trading system that is both driving globalization and at the same time is now so convoluted and compromised by players seeking to manipulate it that it may be facing its greatest challenges in the years ahead.

The modern global trading system was born in 1947 as part of that era's blossoming of weak international institutions. It was known at the time as the General Agreement on Tariffs and Trade (GATT), the name itself an illustration of the fact that in area after area, global governance ambitions had to be compromised to produce progress. The original idea had been to create an International Trade Organization, but when that entity did not get off the ground, the treaty that had been created to lay the foundations for it took its place. Periodically, the signatories to the GATT would meet with the purpose of reducing barriers to trade. While creating such a system has clear economic merits, it must also be acknowledged that by negotiating away the ability to impose tariffs at their borders, states are giving up an important element of sovereign control. That's not just a philosophical issue, either. When, as is increasingly happening today, important states choose to trade unfairly by subsidizing national players or creating nontariff barriers to trade and others are legally obligated to remain open, it can create imbalances and tension.

In the "Uruguay Round" of GATT negotiations, which took place from 1986 to 1994, the 123 signatory nations reflected on the importance of being able to address such tensions by finally agreeing, half a century after the idea was proposed, to create a World Trade Organization. The

WTO enables countries who feel their trading rights have been violated or "nullified or impaired" by another country's actions to seek redress, first through confidential consultations, then before a panel of experts that can make binding rulings in favor of one or the other of the parties, then before a larger appellate body that has the final say in such matters— unless states choose to simply ignore the rulings, an option that, for example, the United States has retained since the WTO's founding.

Theoretically, this is a process among sovereign states. However, in practice, corporations and corporate lawyers drive the process in most cases. To choose but one example from hundreds, on December 5, 1997, the WTO announced the resolution of a case between the United States and Japan regarding American accusations of Japanese protectionism in the photographic film industry. The headline in the next day's *New York Times* was KODAK IS LOSER IN TRADE RULING ON FUJI DISPUTE. Despite the theory underlying the WTO and its rules that even prohibit private actors like NGOs or corporations from filing amicus curiae briefs to support particular sides in a case—it has increasingly become a forum for private special interests pleading their cases behind the veil of nation-states' sovereignty (even though, as we have seen, multinational companies tend to have national allegiance only when it suits them).

The Kodak-Fuji case had its origins in the fact that when Kodak hired George Fisher as its chairman in 1993, he had come from Motorola, where he had effectively lobbied the U.S. government to pressure Japan to liberalize their phone markets. As someone who worked on trade issues in the U.S. government at the time, I well remember Fisher as a smart, affable, and understated but effective chief executive who was as comfortable in Washington as any senator or cabinet member. Frustrated that Kodak had only a 10-percent market share in the Japanese film market, much lower than it enjoyed in similar markets elsewhere in the world, Fisher lobbied the U.S. government to step in and act on his behalf. When that did not produce the desired results, Fisher did what any corporate CEO would do: he hired a very big, high-priced law firm full of former senior U.S. government officials—in this case, Dewey Ballantine, whose trade practice led by former deputy U.S. trade representative Alan Wolf—to develop a petition under Section 301 of U.S. trade law requesting that Wolf's old agency, the trade representative's office, pursue a case against the Japanese.

Fuji responded with its own lawyers and a 585-page brief it presented to the USTR defending its position titled "Rewriting U.S. History." Despite the fact that any international case would ultimately be between governments, it was Fuji that lobbied USTR Mickey Kantor in its ultimately unsuccessful attempts to forestall a confrontation in the WTO. When the case did go to the WTO, both companies stayed actively involved, providing their governments with thousands of pages of legal documents at a cost of millions and millions of dollars to each. At every stage of the legal process, from the initial filing through the consultations, panelist selection, submissions to the panel, and response to the panel's questions, Kodak's and Fuji's teams were effectively driving and subsidizing their "national" efforts. Ultimately, after the WTO found for the Japanese, Kodak kept up the heat by pushing the Commerce Department, where I had worked, to monitor the Japanese film market and make periodic reports pushing for their interests. Fuji continued its work on the other side of the Pacific, seeking to "defend" its home market.

The fact that virtually simultaneously with the announcement of the WTO decision, Kodak announced it was cutting fourteen thousand jobs in the United States and moving many to lower-cost labor environments such as its factory in Guadalajara, Mexico, was not seen as an impediment to the U.S. government's support of Kodak in the WTO case. The company was using the country but felt no obligation in return, nor did the officials of the U.S. government carefully weigh the theoretical economic merits of free trade with the clearly painful dislocations associated with globalization and the opening of vast new cheap labor markets to corporations, many of which were once seen as "U.S." enterprises. Kodak's industry has seen great upheaval as a consequence of the burgeoning of digital photography. But whereas the company once supported eighty thousand jobs, the vast majority of them in the United States, today it employs only about twenty thousand people, of whom half are located outside the United States. Once part of the bedrock of its headquarters city, Rochester, New York, Kodak is now yet another global actor without any true national identity, that nonetheless continues to seek to use the U.S. government wherever possible to advance its interests.

The behavior is common. We used to see it in government regularly. I remember, for example, being actively lobbied for U.S. government support by the Caterpillar tractor company to help it win access to the Three Gorges Dam, a major project in China. When the U.S. government declined to provide it with the support it sought, Caterpillar simply slipped off the U.S. flag in which it had draped itself and sought preferential export treatment from European countries where it had operations. I remember visiting a Caterpillar factory in Indonesia, getting the big welcome, being offered bowls of local cashews, taking a tour of the plant, and then asking how much of the equipment they were assembling and selling in Indonesia came from the United States. The plant official with whom I was walking smiled and said, "Only the stencils for the Caterpillar logos. Most everything else is made right here in Asia."

Gaming the system is what companies do. They shape it through lobbying, influence it through their lawyers, and use it in much the same way that sailors passing through a port treat the local girls they will never see again. They even dress themselves up prettily in national uniforms, but their motives are purely personal in nature. In addition to the WTO, thousands of bilateral investment treaties exist that have been created in abundance, despite the degree to which they clearly cut away even more of the sovereign prerogatives once enjoyed by states. Companies with clever lawyers can use the WTO or these agreements to structure their approaches so that if they don't get the judgments or support they want from one government or multilateral entity, they can press forward in multiple forums in the hopes of getting the desired outcome.

Out of the Ashes of Europe: The EU and Stora

After 1945, Stora Kopparberg integrated itself into the world economy. Forestry had continued to become one of its most important lines of business for the same reason it was so important to Sweden: forests cover 60 percent of the country. But the industry is heavily dependent on foreign markets. It is also fiercely competitive worldwide, a fact that only grew more pronounced as more and more forest products from distant corners of the globe were made available and affected international pricing and demand. To cope with the competition, the company purchased one of Sweden's leading cardboard producers, and in 1962, it made a bold venture overseas, literally retracing the initial international route of the Vikings to establish a forest products plant in Nova Scotia.

The company would later receive criticism from Canadians who sued because they objected to Stora's spraying of local forests with dioxin, a poisonous herbicide. For Stora, this raised for the first but not the last time the important issue of what social obligations international companies have to local populations and to what degree they assume responsibility for meeting the terms of the social contract from governments whose rights they have assumed or whose influence they have superseded.

Gradually during the 1970s, Stora reduced its increasingly uncompetitive exposure to the steel business and focused more and more on forests. The result was that the company grew steadily throughout the next decade. By 1988, a journalist noted that Stora, this ancient enterprise about which so few people have heard a thing or given a thought, "owns forests half the size of Belgium, produces enough liquid-packaging board to make two milk cartons for every person in the world and makes newsprint for Sweden's newspapers and some of Europe's other largest dailies." To offer another such analogy, today Stora either owns, manages, or leases land in Europe, Asia, and South America that is equivalent in acreage to Qatar.

In the late 1980s, by the time of the Swedish Match deal, Stora had clearly embarked on another chapter in its long, twisting story. Its acquisition of Kreuger's old firm, although ultimately not the game changer it was thought it might become, was at the time the largest cash and securities deal in Sweden's history. The country, sensing the importance of international markets to its business, was also working like other Swedish firms to position itself to be competitive in the unifying markets of the European Union.

Bo Beggren, Stora's president at the time of the Swedish Match deal, stated: "We have been a fairly quiet, silent company over the years but [recently] we have embarked on an aggressive expansion. We were searching for something new to develop, and Swedish Match, with its international organization, was an obvious partner." Beggren further underscored the company's new course during a "coming-out" party in 1988, hosted to celebrate the seven hundredth anniversary of Bishop Peter of Vasteras's deal for his shares in the old mining company. The event was held at the bottom of the mine's Great Pit.

Beggren used the occasion both to celebrate and to lobby Swedish officials who attended the bash to set aside protectionism and embrace the changes that entering the European Union would bring—a ceding of national sovereignty that would have been virtually impossible for Gustav

Vasa to comprehend. "The ability of the old mine to survive continues to amaze," stated Beggren to the 6,500 guests gathered below the cliffs that were once so rich with copper. He celebrated the company's long life in his remarks, then turned to the issue of the moment. "Our future lies in European integration," he asserted. "We should be open for new changes and new worlds."

Typically neutral, Sweden's political leadership had long attempted to steer clear of Europe's Common Market, steadfastly maintaining its ability to compete as an independent actor. But with the creation of the European Union looming just four years away, Sweden's business leaders argued that remaining outside the world's largest market would put them at too great a disadvantage. Arguing that the new Stora was now "too big to be ignored" in Europe, Beggren went on to say that, for the well-being of the Swedish nation, the country would have to join the European Union to avoid isolation.

The moment was symbolic of the several larger global trends driving the latest and most transformative era of globalization. Within six years, Sweden would join the European Union. At the same time, the country began to relax economic regulations that had been in place since the most interventionist era that had made the country notorious as a resolute capital of the Eurosocialist welfare state ethos. There was a sense that in the era of Reagan, Thatcher, Greenspan, and globalization, Anglo-American capitalist values were transforming the world, business was permanently and irreversibly claiming "the commanding heights" from government, and global competition demanded that nations cede sovereignty, dial back regulations, give up control of their borders, and do so for the competitive good of their people (and of course "their" corporations).

It should be noted, though, that even as Sweden was swept up in the regionalization-globalization tsunami that seemed to be leading all nations to harmonization around a free-market ideal that had its roots in Anglo-U.S. capitalism, there were still key differences. A former Swedish finance minister described these to me in a Stockholm restaurant not far from the offices of the Swedish government. Par Nuder, a Social Democrat who is not only a seasoned participant in the Swedish political scene but also a sharp-eyed and thoughtful analyst of international economic trends, cited one seemingly paradoxical way in which a country with a tradition that is a classic example of what might be described in the

United States as "big government" attitudes had a competitive edge in the global era.

"We have," said Nuder, "at the center of everything we do here a very strong social compact. Government and labor and business have always seen it as essential to collaborate. That means that when there are the kind of competitive dislocations that globalization causes, there are programs to support and retrain those who might lose their jobs. And everyone in the country knows this. So we have never feared globalization the way so many in America do because in the United States there is really no social safety net. Here, there is confidence that the system will take care of people long enough to adapt to change."

Nuder illustrated his point by citing the case of the crises that impacted auto manufacturers worldwide. He noted that "free-market" America had to step in and temporarily nationalize General Motors in order to avoid catastrophic job losses but that "socialist" Sweden did not intervene with Saab in the same way because it knew the workers were already taken care of. "We have," he said, "a greater freedom to embrace globalization without fear"—something he noted as ironic given Sweden's small size and the fact that America, which so many around the world saw as the primary driver and beneficiary of globalization, was experiencing a serious antiglobalization backlash in the wake of the financial crises and high unemployment of 2008–2009.

When asked about this phenomenon, the former United States trade representative Charlene Barshefsky nodded, paused for a moment, then said, "I think that's an interesting point. I think we have underestimated the dislocations associated with globalization and have yet to do enough to compensate for them among the members of our workforce. And until we do, there will remain great political pushback on trade issues."

Ten years after the great shareholder party in the old copper pit in Falun that was once the heart of a fiercely independent region, Stora took the natural next step in its evolution, once again keeping it in step with the changing times. It merged with the Finnish forest products and packaging giant Enso to form Stora Enso Oyj.

Immediately, the new company became a global force to be reckoned with in its industry. At the same time, the company whose history was so inextricably bound up with that of Sweden moved its headquarters to Finland. Today, it runs its international operations out of London. The

Swedish government that gave life to the company and was also sustained by it at the time of the nation's greatest triumphs and struggles had acceded to its pressure to join the European Union to maintain national competitiveness, and then it could only watch as the onetime proprietors of the Great Copper Mountain pulled up stakes and moved their headquarters abroad, assuming their role as the latest entry into the ranks of the Global Era's stateless supercitizens.

8 ■ The Coin of Whose Realm?

Give me control of a nation's money and I care not who makes
her laws.

—Mayer Amschel Rothschild

So you think money is the root of all evil. Have you ever asked
what is the root of all money?

—Ayn Rand

One day, in the waning months of the worst of the financial crisis of
2008 and 2009, I had lunch with the U.S. National Economic Council
director, Larry Summers, in his office in the White House. Our conversation turned to the crisis, its consequences, and how it might have
changed his thinking since our years in the Clinton administration.

"Do you ever think," I asked, "that we went too far with reforms, went
too far in the direction of 'leaving it to the markets,' and that now the
pendulum is going to swing the other way?"

He paused for a second, then said, "Do you mean do I think we're going
to go backwards to what it was before? That somehow we're going to
have government much more involved in the marketplace? Play a much
bigger role as a regulator?"

I nodded.

"No," he said without hesitation. "I don't think we can or want to turn
back the clock. I don't think you should worry about the Obama administration undoing everything we did like some critics are suggesting we
will. Frankly, I'm not sure we could even if we wanted to. It's a different
time."

I think he thought this would comfort me, that I would think he was
saying that despite the crisis, President Obama was not going to be the
cryptosocialist he was accused of being by some of his more over-the-top
critics. But to be honest, I wasn't sure I found the response comforting.

In the years since the Clinton administration, even before the crisis, my sense was that the needle had swung too far in favor of what were called market freedoms but were really opportunities for members of the financial community to act recklessly, to profit grotesquely from trading in risks they shouldn't be taking, and to lead the development of an international financial system that had usurped control of everything from monetary policies to market stability from representatives of the public.

I was under no illusions that those representatives of the public were terribly well equipped to add value at the moment, given their generally stunning ignorance of much of what was going on in financial markets and their repeated (and I believe not accidental) inattentiveness to worrisome developments in those markets and among leading financial institutions. The fact was that Obama himself rode into office on the largest wave of donations from the financial community in history; he brought with him many with a firmly Wall Street frame of mind and related biases, and if anything, the U.S. Congress had been even more corrupted by a campaign finance process that made it totally dependent on donations from the companies it was supposed to regulate. It all smacked of the days of the British Parliament when 10 percent of all members were in some way direct beneficiaries of, or related to beneficiaries of, the British East India Company. In systems like that, skewed outcomes are inevitable.

The broader question, however, was whether the financial upheavals that had taken place were actually in part due to something larger, a historical trend in which yet another pillar of traditional government control over a society—monetary and financial control—had been undermined thanks to the systematic and very long-term efforts of the business community's acting in its narrow self-interest—abetted, as ever, by philosophers and opinion makers who had for one inducement or another come to share their views. The evidence, consistent with Summers's conclusion, was that the profound changes that have occurred were, at least to some degree, irreversible. This implies not, however, that government's role must continue to shrink, but that it must adapt to new market realities in which the balance of power lies with big private players and the scope and sophistication of instruments is vastly beyond the grasp of most government regulators and policymakers.

Clearly, we had come a great long way from that first document commemorating the stock transaction of Bishop Peter of Vasteras, or, for that matter, from the days when in an effort to fund its empire, Sweden went on the copper standard and forged coins made from the metal found in the depths of the mines at Falun. Copper, of course, was not seen as being as valuable as gold or silver, and to be worth enough to be useful in most transactions, many of the coins, imprinted with royal likenesses certifying their officially sanctioned status, ended up being 9.5 inches in diameter, so they were not really an efficient form of pocket change. And even though the royal seal was affixed to the stock transfer agreement, there was no organized open market on which shares could trade, so its value was hard to determine. But these were not the only reasons these links to the distant past seem deeply outmoded. Much had transpired, including events that drew on the rise of corporations like Stora Kopparberg, the British East India Company, and the other ancient antecedents of modern enterprises such as the Goldman Sachses and Morgan Stanleys of this world, companies that seem to have, if anything, even more clout than their giant, state-sponsored forebears.

The Philosophies of Money and the Uneasy Reality of Financial Sovereignty

In their excellent book *Money, Markets and Sovereignty*, Benn Steil and Manuel Hinds note that monetary sovereignty—the ability of states to set the value of and manage their national currency and by extension many important dimensions of their state's fiscal life—"is incompatible with globalization, understood as integration into the global marketplace for goods and capital. It has always been thus, but it has become blindingly apparent over the past three decades of human history."

The middle part of that statement—that "it has always been thus"—may seem odd to the casual observer. To undertake a study of money, however, is to embark on what often seems like an examination of unfounded beliefs wrapped in perceptions shrouded in mythologies. That any nation ever truly could control its money supply is one of those myths. This is because the underpinnings of the idea of money are dependent on public perception of what is valuable, and thus on a wide range of external variables ranging from the value of commodities to factors that affect that value such as the weather and wars and other conditions influencing the health of national economies.

Monetary sovereignty was therefore a kind of aspiration. It is the idea that states could exert meaningful influence over the value of the monies exchanged within their societies, which was important to the states because it meant tax revenues would have value, wars could be paid for, and economic activity could take place that would ensure more tax revenues to pay for more wars. Even so, a quick look at history shows that even this more qualified view of states' control over their financial destinies has seen the public sector's influence compromised from the start and waning ever since, until, as Steil and Hinds suggest, it has shriveled to a nubbin of its former self during the last thirty years.

Perhaps perversely, the less the means of exchange in a society is actually worth, the more perceived influence on its value a government has. Most early societies started out with "commodity" money, units of exchange that were seen to have intrinsic value—gold pieces, shells, a predetermined amount of grain. For example, the word "shekel" refers to a unit of weight that in its monetary sense referred to a specified amount of barley. But over time, states switched to "representative" currencies, types of money that were deemed to have value based on the word of the government that they would be backed up or redeemable in some way by the state. Later, they would switch to "fiat" currencies, which do not imply convertibility to the commodity in question but are seen to have a value primarily because either the state or the market asserts they do (we shall soon see how the balance of power shifted in this instance very recently).

Because banks emerged as repositories of precious commodity-based currencies and often it was more convenient to conduct transactions with some portable, easily transferred representative currency, paper money came into use. It first appeared in China during the Song dynasty around the year 1100. This was a very economically advanced society that, among other things, saw the widespread creation of joint-stock companies and used copper coins—minting as many as six billion in the year 1085. Given the weight of copper, a large industry grew up in the printing of *jiaozi*, or paper banknotes.

Sweden had, as noted, during the period of its greatest expansion in the early seventeenth century, turned to a currency system that was based on *dalers* minted from silver or copper. The silver *dalers* were, because of the perceived intrinsic value of silver, much smaller, and as a consequence they tended to be hoarded. The copper coins were the size of dinner plates. The problems associated with this system were further compounded by the fact that banks were taking short-term deposits in these coins but making long-term loans. Demand for the coins was high and only grew higher as Falun's copper became in such high demand by 1660 that the copper content of the coins was reduced by almost a fifth, creating a greater desire on the part of depositors to get their old coins back.

The solution was arrived at by the predecessor of Sweden's national bank, which was founded in 1656 by two royal charters from King Karl Gustav. The bank was called Stockholms Banco, and it was operated by an entrepreneurial character named Johan Palmstruch. Palmstruch solved the problem of the heavy coins and the uneven demand flows by creating Europe's first paper money. The notes, backed by a promise of redemption from the bank, were called *kreditivsedlar*, and they were an immediate hit. Transactions that once required a wagonload of coins could be handled with a few notes in standard quantities. The denominations of Europe's first paper money were therefore 5, 25, 100, and 1,000 copper *dalers* (*koppermynt*).

Unfortunately, Palmstruch's innovations didn't stop with introducing the first paper banknotes in Europe. Demand for the notes was so high that Palmstruch gave in to the temptation to print more than he had hard currency to cover. By late 1663, the value of the banknotes was falling; by the next year, the bank failed and, setting another precedent, the Swedish government had to take over its operations.

Palmstruch was in jail by 1667. A successor bank, operated by the parliament, called Riksens Standers Bank, was established. The bank, which later changed its named to the Sveriges Riksbank, became Sweden's central bank and remains so to this day.

The experience was so traumatic for the Swedes, however, that despite the fact that they led the West into the world of banknotes, they did not resume their use of them until well into the next century. As noted, states have always required money to support their functions, and in fact it was the concentration of reserves in a treasury that was one of the founding sources of a state's power, because those funds could be applied to build fortifications, hire armies, and create the coercive power needed to enforce the law, including the collection of taxes, which completed the circle of power, feeding into treasuries.

As military expenditures grew, the amounts of money needed grew commensurately. The Swedish experiments with copper and paper currencies came in the midst of a larger trend in this area. The nature of conflict in Europe before, during, and after the Thirty Years' War demanded large standing armies for the first time. The tiny Dutch Republic, for example, already had an army of 60,000 by 1606. The Spanish army grew to 300,000 by the 1630s, fifteen times as large as it had been two hundred years earlier when Columbus led the first explorations in search of gold in the New World. The French army grew threefold in a century, reaching over 150,000 by 1630. Changes in military technologies, the move to firearms, the cost of lengthy sieges, and other factors also made the cost of maintaining each soldier or military unit increase significantly. According to one calculation, during the reign of Elizabeth I, the cost of outfitting an infantry company rose 150 percent. These costs were such that commercial or financial failure meant defeat, as illustrated by the case of Spain during the Thirty Years' War. The situation grew so extreme that by the late seventeenth century, almost three-quarters of French government revenue was being spent on land warfare, with an additional 16 percent being spent on France's navy.

Of course, part of this buildup of military capabilities and expenses was due to the reality that maintaining and expanding control over land or sea lanes was the only way nations could enhance or protect their economic well-being. Armies were economic tools that demanded economic strategies, and the period of the sixteenth and seventeenth centuries saw European states develop much more organized approaches to budgeting, taxation, borrowing, and money policies. The Bank of England, for example, was established in 1694 to help manage finances associated with the latest round of fighting with France.

States had always had to borrow in a pinch, but when a sovereign borrowed and thereby became beholden to another party, sovereignty suffered. If capital grew more concentrated in cities, as it did in the sixteenth and seventeenth centuries, urban elites became more influential. If monarchs depended on the mines of Falun or the fleets of the British East India Company to finance their operations, the operators of those enterprises gained influence. If they borrowed, lenders gained influence. Part of the battle between church and state had been about competing claims for financial resources from the people and the land. In fact, it has been argued that the shifting economics of war and the concurrent requirements for more evolved commercial and banking systems of this period are what drove the creation of the nation-state, organized as it was to support and manage such activities.

This focus on finance and the need for the organized underpinnings to help fuel required wealth creation accelerated the development of capitalism, which actually started during the twelfth and thirteenth centuries as an alternative to the comparatively disorganized, intensively rural, inefficient economics of feudalism. Initial theories about economics during this period were, not surprisingly, rooted in the views of the church, which was still the dominant pan-European power of the era. Thomas Aquinas was the principal author of many of the most influential economic views associated with that period, offering theories on a "just price" and a "just wage" that guided merchants toward deriving what was needed to support their families and the church and nothing more. View this as being spiritually motivated or as a self-serving argument advancing the church's economic interest; an ethos developed in which material wealth was disdained and commerce and trade were distrusted, seen as evidence of sinful impulses such as greed, selfishness, and covetousness.

With movement to the cities accelerating during the Renaissance and then the onset of the Reformation, and with the diminution of the influence of the church, not only did manufacturing expand and a market system take hold, but philosophies also began to change. Part of the change was associated with what Max Weber later addressed in his essay "The Protestant Ethic and the Spirit of Capitalism," in which he argued that the Calvinist approach to life, which emphasized both hard work and doing well as a way of pleasing God, meant that prosperity could be more acceptable if sought for the right motives and by the right kind of people. Or, to draw from another source close to the momentous changes that were taking place, Christopher Columbus observed, "one who has the gold does as he wills in the world, and it even sends souls to Paradise." This is a view that helped underpin the mercantilist economies that would emerge in the sixteenth and seventeenth centuries and would lead to the establishment of many of the great trading companies of the era.

Competing economic views are associated with this period, including those of the "bullionists" of sixteenth-century England, whose thinking focused on how best to ensure that the precious metals were efficiently collected into the coffers of the state. Their views, echoing Machiavelli's admonition that "in a well-organized government, the state should be rich and the citizens poor," supported policies that would promote a healthy tax base, such as having a wide circulation of money within a country's borders, as well as those that would keep precious metals for the use of the sovereign, such as discouraging export of gold and silver. (In Spain, the punishment for illegally exporting gold and silver was death.) Policies of the time also included deliberately seeking to increase the purchasing power of foreign currencies so as to encourage their flow into the borders of a nation.

Although bullionism began to fade during the sixteenth century, it was not until the birth of the big trading companies that an alternative, more trade-based set of theories emerged—largely because companies such as the East India Company needed to export gold and silver in order to purchase the goods in which they were trading. A political debate emerged around whether this was actually good for England, and one of the directors of the Company produced a series of influential writings including a 1621 pamphlet called "A Discourse of Trade from England unto the East Indies" and, more important, a treatise published after his death called "England's Treasure by Foreign Trade," which enumerated the benefits that trade brought to England, from sales of locally produced goods to savings on goods made overseas. The author of these works, Thomas Mun, argued that the problems England faced could better be addressed by a policy of promoting exports and limiting foreign imports to the country— except for those brought in by English charter companies, naturally.

While Mun's work was resisted at first, it ultimately became a basis for England's expansion during the period in which England was indisputably the world's greatest power. Adam Smith, referring to "England's Treasure," would write, "the title of Mun's book became a fundamental maxim in the political economy, not of England only, but of all other commercial economies."

The era during which Smith began to write—the Enlightenment—also saw a broader desire to strip religious pieties out of economic theory once and for all. A leader in this effort was Smith's French contemporary, Voltaire. Reacting against what he saw as too strong a lingering Christian ideological influence on commercial behavior, Voltaire made the case— later echoed by Smith—that the pursuit of wealth through market activity and the consumption of wealth were both politically and morally desirable. In words that would be echoed through the centuries that followed, in the writings of those from Hayek to Friedman, he wrote that "the individual's self-regarding propensities were the basis of social order, rather than the threat to it that Christian and civic moralists have imagined."

In his *Philosophical Letters*, Voltaire argued that market activity should be valued not because it made society wealthier but because it was a more reliable motivator than religious zeal. For Voltaire, intent was paramount. "The whole difference," he wrote in his essay "On the Pensées of Pascal" (Blaise Pascal advanced opposing moralist views), "lies in the occupations being gentle or fierce, dangerous or useful." Seeking personal gain was a rational motivator in the eyes of this ultimate rationalist, whereas the real danger lay with religion.

Voltaire also did much to promote the standing of the financial community, which was viewed with much skepticism at the time (not entirely surprising in the wake of the South Sea Bubble and related perturbations that resonated across the European marketplace). In his *Philosophical Letters*, he describes the Royal Exchange in London, the forebear of the London Stock Exchange, and sketches out the broader benefits of the exchange as a social as well as a financial engine producing considerable and diverse benefits:

> Go into the Exchange in London, that place more venerable than many a court, and you will see representatives of all the nations assembled there for the profit of mankind. There the Jew, the Mahometan, and the Christian deal with one another as if they were of the same religion, and reserve the name of infidel for those who go bankrupt. There the Presbyterian trusts the Anabaptist, and the Church of England man accepts the promise of the Quaker. On leaving these peaceable and free assemblies, some go to the synagogue, others in search of a drink, this man is on the way to be baptized in a great tub in the name of the Father, by the Son, to the Holy Ghost; that man is having the foreskin of his son cut off, and a Hebraic formula mumbled over the child that he himself can make nothing of; these others are going to their church to await the inspiration of God with their hats on; and all are satisfied.

Rueful contempt for religious posturing and ritual aside, Voltaire saw commerce as a natural antidote for much of what ailed contemporary society. He went so far as to suggest that material consumption by the rich is what drove the employment of the poor, which in turn enabled them to consume. He also noted that the pursuit of wealth had driven intercontinental exploration and commerce, thus knitting the world more closely together.

Smith's views, discussed earlier, certainly echo Voltaire's spirit. It is important to note, however, that many of Smith's and Voltaire's views were based on an idealized view of commerce among small enterprises, none of which had the power to distort pricing or market dynamics as giant corporations might. In Smith's eye, the potential distorter was the state. That is the reason he focused on encouraging the state not to meddle in the marketplace (a view that has since been often taken out of context). As Dowd writes in *Capitalism and Economics: A Critical History*: "He did not anticipate the baronial power that would be sought and gained by the enormous companies industrialization facilitated—and that a compliant state allowed."

As Smith himself acknowledged, he was heavily influenced by David Hume, a contemporary and fellow Scotsman, who wrote that "commerce itself . . . gives rise to the notions of justice between peoples." Hume also offered a view of trade that suggested it could trigger a virtuous cycle of growth among participating nations—an argument contrary to zero-sum notions of trade and, as such, a foundational notion behind the ideal of free trade. He also shaped views on postmercantile monetary policy that not only embraced the self-correcting consequences of inflows of foreign gold and silver but would suggest ideas like "beneficial inflation," monetary policies that would lead to some of the thinking of John Maynard Keynes a century and a half later.

This chorus of Enlightenment voices set the stage for a new view of industry and finance that could not have been timelier, given that it helped set the stage and provide the intellectual framework to embrace and rationalize the developments associated with the Industrial Revolution just stirring. As was noted earlier, 1776 not only produced Smith's *Wealth of Nations* and the American Revolution, it also saw the first commercial introduction of the steam engine designs of yet another influential Scotsman of the period, James Watt.

The First Movers of Globalization: The Rise of the Banking Elite

The nature of early banking was based in part on the weight and value of gold, silver, and other treasures that needed to be stored safely and were risky to transport (although not as burdensome perhaps as wagonloads of pie-sized copper coins). To facilitate commerce, banks would establish branches that allowed deposits in one place to be withdrawn in another or that allowed those with deposits to issue checks (the first of which are reported to have been used among Arab merchants) that were essentially IOUs for the treasure that was safely stored in the banks' vaults.

Because of the branch structure, early banks became important globalizing forces. The Medici Bank, for example, the most important of Europe's banks throughout the fifteenth century, had branches stretching up and down the Italian peninsula and across France, Switzerland, and what today would be Belgium all the way to London. Through its accumulation of riches it became a vitally important lender to popes and kings. This was a double-edged sword. The Medici became rich and powerful, and ultimately they produced two popes. They also won important trading concessions that added to their wealth. However, because everyone loves their banker when they are lending but no one loves them when they come collecting, the relationship was precarious. Periodically the Medici would be put in the position of seeking repayment from monarchs and other nobles at just the time that the monarchs were least able to pay and, not surprisingly, not in the best of spirits.

In good times, the Medici played an essential role in supporting rulers from Charles the Bold to Edward IV of England. But when these rulers fell on rough times, they would play rough, resisting repayment, threatening to withdraw special concessions on which the Medici depended, coercing them into not lending to their enemies, and, as a consequence of all such measures, undoing the banks in London and Bruges and ultimately the Medici banking empire.

But, as history has also shown, where one banking empire leaves off, another picks up, because the demand for lending and facilitating commerce is essential to the functioning of both states and economies as a whole. So where the Medici banking story ends, the Fugger story begins.

The Fuggers were a German banking family that, like the Medici, became the richest in the world during the period of their greatest dominance, the sixteenth century. They opened bank branches throughout Europe and financed the rise of kings, notably Charles V, who owed his election as Holy Roman Emperor to their collection of over 850,000 florins (almost 100,000 ounces of gold). Their lending enabled Charles and countless nobles to rule, and in exchange they were granted not only religious but commercial indulgences, including a series of silver and copper mines in central Europe. In fact, they sought to compound their power by actually mining the precious metals that states could mint into the coins that would be stored in their vault, and this led them into competition with and deals linked to the mining ventures in Falun. The Fuggers' vision and ambitions were great, and through their linkages with Charles and the Spanish they also underwrote and profited from mining ventures in the Americas.

Of the banking figures who did the most to shape the rise of the modern era, perhaps the most influential was Mayer Amschel Rothschild. Rothschild was born in a Jewish ghetto in Frankfurt, Germany. His father had been a money changer, and Mayer built upon his family's business by installing each of his five sons at the head of a branch of the family banking business in different capitals of Europe, thereby creating an independent, confidential, resilient, and fully family-controlled network.

While the influence and business of the family grew during the eighteenth century through the support of many ventures taking part in the expansion of the early industrial economy, the most striking example of how a private financial enterprise could influence a state is illustrated in the events surrounding the Napoleonic Wars, which fueled the rise of the Rothschild family to the point that its members ultimately ended up holding aristocratic titles from England to the Austro-Hungarian empire. Again, the leverage of the bankers was linked to the ambitions of the state. To assert public power required money beyond that controlled by public authorities. Thus, they had to reach out to and thereby grant enormous leverage to private lenders. Thanks to the legal and political developments of the seventeenth and eighteenth centuries that made it more difficult for monarchs to simply rebuff bankers as they might have done in the past, the power of the lenders was further amplified. Techniques and markets developed by the Rothschilds, notably those associated with the issuance of government debt instruments, amplified that power even further.

The trigger for this escalation of private influence was the most audacious grab for public-sector power Europe had seen since Charlemagne: that of Napoleon Bonaparte. Napoleon was bringing an industrial-era efficiency to conquest, pioneering the art of "total war." His onslaught, with reverberations from Spain to the frontiers of Russia, remade Europe and set his neighbors on edge as they desperately sought ways to contain him. While the strategies considered were numerous, the prerequisite for all of them was money.

On England's behalf, Lieutenant General Sir Arthur Wellesley, later known as the Duke of Wellington, pursued Napoleon on a campaign so costly that it resulted in a ballooning of the national debt to £745 million, twice the country's GDP. (By comparison, America's debt in 2011 raised alarms because it reached 100 percent of GDP.) The problem was that the government needed not only money but hard currency as well, since merchants on the Iberian Peninsula where Wellesley was fighting refused to accept British bills of exchange.

Knowing of the Rothschilds' reputed abilities, the English chancellor of the exchequer instructed his representatives to "employ that gentleman [Nathan Rothschild, head of the British branch of the clan] in the most secret and confidential manner to collect in Germany, France and Holland the largest quantity of French gold and silver coins, not exceeding in value 600,000 pounds, which he may be able to procure within two months of the present time." The objective was to get the coins to Wellesley to support his efforts.

Using the network to gain advantage—selling gold for bills of exchange in countries where its price was high and using the proceeds to purchase even more gold in countries where the price was lower—by May 1814, the Rothschilds had raised twice the amount the British government required. According to the excellent account of this period in Niall Ferguson's *The Ascent of Money*, the response of a grateful British government in the wake of Napoleon's subsequent exile to Elba was encapsulated by the comment of Lord Liverpool, then the prime minister, who said, "Mr. Rothschild [has become] a very useful friend . . . I do not know what we should have done without him." Metternich's secretary called Rothschild the *Finanzbonaparten*, the Bonaparte of finance. His competitors, such as the Baring family of bankers, used a similar analogy to refer to him. Others were less charitable and resorted to predictable anti-Semitic slurs. (One of the reasons leaders had, through the ages, chosen to use Jewish banking networks was that, merits aside, the low regard in which Jews were held helped keep the bankers in check.)

Nathan and his family continued to profit from the war when Napoleon resumed his quest for empire. They concluded that another war would push up the price for gold, and they bought it up in large quantities, making significant sums available to the British for shipment to Wellington. And while they made significant profits on these transactions, the short war caused the demand for their gold to be more limited than they expected, and they ended up with a substantial quantity of the precious metal on their hands.

Cannily, Nathan estimated that with the war over, despite Britain's enormous debts, the country's bonds would soon rise in price. He and his family were developing a great expertise in bond markets—one that would in some respects help to permanently remake the relationship between private finance and governments—and he showed it here, reaping a profit of 40 percent by buying up the bonds when they were still cheap and selling them two years later when they peaked in price.

As Ferguson lucidly explains, the Rothschilds were early masters of networks, blending their capital-raising connections with superior information-gathering capabilities to make markets and stay a step ahead of other players within those markets. In this way, they became the architects and the masters of European bond markets, working from London, the region's leading center of debt trading. They would charge governments significant commissions for distributing bonds throughout the Continent, and they were careful never to remit the bonds until payment for them had cleared. They made markets not only in British bonds but also in French, Prussian, Russian, Austrian, Neapolitan, and even Brazilian debt instruments. They monopolized bond insurance markets. They pioneered innovations such as promoting the denomination of most bonds in a single currency, sterling, to eliminate transactional inefficiencies. They also developed the then unique capability of issuing bonds from one country in branches across Europe. This gave them a competitive advantage, as did their track record. They dealt only in investment-grade securities, and even during periods when defaults were common, such as some of the early Latin American debt crises of the era, none of their bonds issued during the period (the 1820s) defaulted.

A sense of the Rothschilds' power over governments as well as an indication of the impunity with which modern bankers could now act was illustrated by a letter from Nathan to the director of the Prussian treasury pertaining to a recently negotiated sale of Prussian debt:

Dearest friend, I have now done my duty by God, your king, and the Finance Minister von Rother, my money has all gone to you in Berlin . . . now it is your turn and duty to yours to keep your word and not to come up with new things, and everything must remain as it was agreed between men like us, and that is what I expected, as you can see from my deliveries of my money. The cabal there can do nothing against N. M. Rothschild, he has the money, the strength and the power, the cabal has only impotence and the king of Prussia, my Prince Hardebenberg and the Minister Rother should be well pleased and thank Rothschild, who is sending you so much money raising Prussia's credit.

By dominating the market that countries had to depend on for funds, Rothschild had gained leverage over the courts of Europe that endured long after Bonaparte's similar but less successful efforts had failed. In part this was due to the skill of the Rothschild family bank; in part it was due to the ambitions and follies of states that locked them into this dependent relationship; in part it was due to the spread of capitalism and its enablement by new communications and transport technologies that were linking markets together in ways that required practiced global intermediaries (a role states could not play). And in part it was due to the fact that the idea underlying the rule of law had evolved to the point that heads of state were increasingly less likely to be seen as above the law but rather as servants to it.

J. P. Morgan Bails Out America

When Nathan Rothschild died in 1836, his net worth was equivalent to 1 percent of Britain's GDP. When America's richest man died twelve years later—in that eventful year of 1848—John Jacob Astor, the son of a village butcher from Waldorf, Germany, was worth $20 million, also approaching 1 percent of the GDP of his new country. Astor's wealth, built from an adventurous fur trading business, was very much of the pre-industrial variety. His company employed only a few people and engaged in material commerce. He used his influence to push initiatives that banned foreigners from participation in the fur trade and eliminated government trading posts. Both had the direct effect of reducing government influence over the U.S. economy.

But Astor was a vestige of the eighteenth century. The great fortunes of the nineteenth and twentieth centuries in the United States would be made by harnessing the leveraging power and scale of the new industries and markets of the industrial era. We have considered briefly one example. Another illustrates the massive power that can be wielded by a private actor who has the foresight to harness several of these transformational forces at once.

While we have noted the role that railroads played in breaking down the "island communities" of early America, a parallel and related development was the explosion of interest and activity in American stock markets. When Astor was at his pinnacle, a day of trading on the New York Stock Exchange might involve the transfer of ownership of a few hundred shares, a tiny subset of the value of the rapidly growing European debt markets in which the Rothschilds plied their trade. By the 1850s, hundreds of thousands of shares would trade each day. In 1886, the number hit one million. Many of the enterprises that garnered the greatest interest by investors were railroads, or companies whose fortunes were tied to the expansion of the railroads. Building the infrastructure for a rail-linked national economy demanded constant inflows of capital, and given the small size of the U.S. government at the time, there was no alternative to do the heaviest lifting than private securities markets.

During this period, insider trading was rampant, and robber barons like Jay Gould freely used the markets to advance predatory commercial interests and to influence officeholders whose support they needed for favorable treatment on rights of way, declarations of eminent domain, taxes, and other regulatory matters. Referring to these executives, Charles Francis Adams and Henry Adams wrote:

> Pirates are not extinct; they have only transferred their operations to the land, and conducted them in more or less accordance with the law; until, at last, so great a proficiency have they attained, that the commerce of the world is more equally but far more heavily taxed in their behalf; than would ever have entered into their wildest hopes while, outside the law, they simply made all comers stand and deliver.

Such periods of boom are inevitably followed by consolidation, and John Pierpont Morgan was one actor who stepped up to use the postboom troubles of the railroad business to his advantage by acquiring shares in failing firms and rolling them together to create great economies of scale. Morgan, who came to banking naturally through working for his father's firm, eventually established a firm of his own, J. P. Morgan & Co. The firm was prosperous from the outset, but its power and reach truly began to grow as Morgan used his stock-market skills to accumulate shares in a series of railroad companies. Through reorganization and consolidation, he built these—including what were to become the New York Central Railroad, the Chesapeake and Ohio Railroad, and the Great Northern Railroad—into dominant forces that, even after the passage of the Interstate Commerce Act of 1887, led the remaking of the industry into a prosperous national enterprise that was to remain the backbone of U.S. commerce for three-quarters of a century.

Morgan's first collaboration with the U.S. government in which he revealed the kind of influence that led his colleagues to call him the Jupiter of the markets came during the Gold Crisis of 1893–95. Fresh from his railroad triumphs, helping to oversee the cleanup and consolidation that brought bankruptcy to almost two hundred railroads and from having bailed out the Rothschilds' rivals, the Baring Brothers bank in Britain, he was a natural choice for the government to reach out to. The crisis came through a series of spiraling problems—a Wall Street panic in 1893 led European investors to start selling gold-based U.S. bonds, which led to the hoarding of gold and the dwindling of U.S. gold reserves to minimal levels ($100 million). Government efforts—which amounted to selling gold bonds to itself with the Treasury acting as the purchaser—not only didn't work but made matters worse, and gold reserves spiraled downward, signaling a crisis.

Realizing the problem, Morgan offered a proposal to the Treasury. He would team up with the Rothschilds to lend the United States $100 million, a loan that would certainly end the crisis if half of it were placed abroad as intended, and as the clout of the Rothschild name promised. No other institutions could pull off a deal of such scale. But initially the Grover Cleveland administration balked. It was not until a year after the offer was made that Cleveland realized his policies were in shambles and he turned to Morgan and the Rothschilds for help. Morgan hammered out his terms and cabled London that he had made the deal. Almost immediately, the U.S. Treasury backtracked and said it would manage the deal on its own. Morgan was furious and stormed back to Washington to take matters into his own hands. Despite the president's refusal to see him, Morgan cajoled his way into the president's office at the White House. As a meeting on the crisis progressed, it became apparent that the United States was on its last legs. Only $9 million in reserves remained. Morgan then observed that he had a $10 million gold draft coming due that day. In short, he had the ability to pull the trigger on the ultimate calamity: the emptying of the government's coffers. Cleveland recognized he had no choice, and the deal was done.

Morgan walked out of the meeting with government powers. He would essentially perform the tasks that were usually the purview of a central bank, such as managing the dollar-sterling exchange rate. Since the British currency was the world reserve currency at the time, this meant that Morgan was given responsibility for setting the value of the dollar, and thus for many dimensions of the entire U.S. economy. Manage the problem he did, and by 1896, the U.S. Treasury had been saved from bankruptcy—and his bank was commanding astronomical premiums on gold securities.

Ironically, his call to recap his remarkable feat came after Morgan had been targeted by the Roosevelt administration as the operator of one of the trusts the president sought to "bust." In that case, it was the Great Northern Railroad trust—although it should also be noted that, in the intervening years, Morgan engineered the creation of enterprises that would later become among the most important multinationals of their era, General Electric and U.S. Steel. Nonetheless, Roosevelt had enough admiration for Morgan that when Wall Street suffered yet another crash, on March 25, 1907, it was the aging banker who was seen as the natural savior of the system he sat at the middle of. Panicked selling—a hallmark of markets throughout time, though not one that is regularly cited by the "leave it to the markets" champions—resulted in many financial houses teetering on the brink of collapse. Trusts, once the enemy but still a bulwark of the economy, also lurched toward bankruptcy. The stock market ceased to be able to make markets in even widely held securities.

By October, the situation had grown so dire that Morgan finally gave in to the entreaties that had been coming to him since the beginning of the downturn and convened an impromptu, informal committee of bankers. On the twenty-second of that month, Morgan and the bankers met with the Treasury secretary, George Cortelyou, an experienced public servant who was rapidly coming to the conclusion that the U.S. government lacked the tools it needed to protect the U.S. economy from crashes such as the one then being experienced. Cortelyou made $25 million available to the Morgan group, and the next day Morgan led an intervention that helped put a stop to the run on the trusts.

However, the next morning, trading on the New York Stock Exchange halted. The president of the exchange, Ransom Thomas, made his way to Morgan's 23 Wall Street offices to plead for a cash infusion. Ron Chernow describes the scene in his biography of Morgan:

> Thomas wanted to shut the Exchange. "At what time do you usually close it?" Morgan asked—though the Stock Exchange was twenty paces from his office, Pierpont didn't know its hours; stock trading was vulgar. "Why, at three o'clock," said Thomas. Pierpont wagged an admonitory finger, "It must not close one minute before that hour today." At two o'clock, Morgan summoned the bank presidents and warned that dozens of brokerage houses might fail unless they mustered $25 million within ten or twelve minutes. By 2:16 the money was pledged. Morgan then dispatched a team to the Stock Exchange floor to announce that call money would be available as low as 10 percent. One team member, Anthony Hodges, had his waistcoat torn off in the violent tumult. Then a blessed moment occurred in Morgan annals: as news of the rescue circulated through the Exchange, Pierpont heard a mighty roar across the street. Looking up, he asked the cause: he was being given an ovation by the jubilant stock traders.

Later the same week, Morgan put together $30 million to bail out the City of New York, extracting from the mayor a promise to allow a banking committee to monitor the city's bookkeeping practices.

Morgan was able to extract some benefit from the crisis when he purchased the Tennessee Coal and Iron Company from a faltering brokerage house. Such a purchase would require the president to agree not to invoke the Sherman Antitrust Act, which a grateful Roosevelt did. But Morgan was seventy, and it was clear to all who witnessed the crash of 1907 that a country as increasingly dependent as the United States was on its burgeoning financial markets could not rely on a single individual to preserve the health of the nation's economy. Finally, a century and a half after Alexander Hamilton had made the initial case for a U.S. central bank and after several politically controversial false starts, the crash triggered moves that resulted six years later in the creation of the United States Federal Reserve Bank. Its first president was Benjamin Strong, one of the young bankers who had been on Morgan's rescue committee.

While the creation of the Federal Reserve was seen as a significant strengthening of federal power and was part of an undeniable broadening of federal authority that spanned the first half of the twentieth century—including everything from the creation of a federal income tax to the economic restoration measures (after yet another crash) that came to be known as the New Deal—the question that hung in the air was: Could government authority and resources grow fast enough to keep up with financial markets? Or would other factors ultimately compromise the influence of government authorities and enhance that of private actors so that future committees of bankers might wield great influence over their government again, albeit under different circumstances?

Efficient Markets and the End for All but a Few Currencies

As we have seen, stock market crashes are regular drivers of political reform and adaptation by financial players that lead to even greater market growth. The stock market crash of 1929 was no exception. Despite every new measure created to increase government scrutiny over market activity, including the Securities and Exchange Commission, within a couple of decades there was a major expansion in U.S. and international securities markets that corresponded with the demand to finance post–World War II expansion. The fact that in this postwar era there loomed a threat from a Communist rival that was employing an all-government ideology to build a global bloc challenging that of the United States made such expansion practically a patriotic duty. In the 1950s and 1960s, Wall Street returned to great favor and prominence and drove a series of changes that would ultimately negate the temporary gains in influence the government may have acquired in the first half of the twentieth century relative to private actors.

One by one, from the 1970s onward, an evolving series of policy decisions and related market innovations fueled a profound shift away from the comparatively simple "old world" of money and finance that had existed for four centuries. Several factors drove these changes: the practical realities of competing in an ever more integrated global economy; ideological frustrations with the inefficiencies and missteps of New Deal–era big government in the United States; welfare-state government in Europe and even Communist government elsewhere in the world; the increasing starkness and political salience of the ideological gap between Western bloc market policies and Eastern bloc socialist policies; and new technologies that linked markets, accelerated them, amplified their volatility, and enabled the creation of new instruments, strategies, and scale.

The effect of these changes on the relative role of public and private influence over global financial flows was so profound that it led many to signal that government was on the verge of being permanently marginalized, forced into the role (for which advocates of the change felt it was especially well suited) of part-time referee, part-time coach, and part-time helper of markets, and little else. One of the first moves hinting at the scale, impact, and radical nature of the changes to come took place in the early 1970s, a decade whose influence on international economic policy was so profound that it ranks with the other pivot points in history. This first change was foreshadowed when, on an August Friday the thirteenth in 1971, U.S. president Nixon and his top advisers slipped out of Washington for a secret retreat at Camp David, the presidential mountaintop escape in nearby Maryland. Joining the president were his secretary of the Treasury, John Connally; his budget director, George Shultz; his Federal Reserve chairman, Arthur Burns; and his top economic adviser, Paul McCracken, plus a coterie of political aides and his speechwriter.

At issue was whether the United States should step away from a hard linkage between the U.S. dollar and gold, the promise that had existed since the end of the Second World War that the government would offer to redeem dollars for gold at the rate of $35 an ounce. This promise, the latest manifestation of the idea of representative currency, was the foundation of the international financial system of which the dollar was now the anchor. The problem was that in the several years preceding, the U.S. balance-of-payments deficit had ballooned, foreign countries were holding vastly increased dollar reserves, and the pressure to revalue the greenback downward was growing to potential crisis levels. Early in 1971, the German Central Bank said it would no longer support the dollar, speculators anticipated a revaluing upward of the deutschmark, and in May of that year, foreign exchange market pressures became so great on the dollar that the Germans, the Swiss, the Dutch, the Belgians, and the Austrians all shut their markets in unison. In one week, billions of dollars had flowed into these European currencies, and several nations—the Germans, the Swiss, and the Dutch—felt they had no choice but to let their currencies float, which is to say the markets had sent them a signal that they had to revalue upward versus the dollar. The Europeans saw this as a dollar crisis. The United States denied it.

The Europeans, feeling the U.S. leadership had their heads in the sand, began to seek their conversion rights, asking for gold to stabilize exchange rates. In the months before the Camp David retreat, France asked the United States to convert $282 million into gold, Belgium asked for $80 million, Switzerland for $75 million, the Netherlands for $55 million, and then the British came in with a request for $3 billion. By early August, the U.S. Treasury had only $10 billion in gold left, the lowest amount since 1936. The problem, as in bygone crises, was that more than $18 billion was held by foreign banks. A few more big requests for gold and the United States would be unable to meet demand, a run on gold could start, and the international monetary system would be undermined.

Nixon asked his team to forget their old positions on the issue of the dollar and think in terms of the new reality. According to William Safire, the speechwriter who was present, Nixon "was not about to stick his thumb in the dike and wait for another hole to appear elsewhere. He wanted a whole new dike." Connally led the charge in this direction by proposing to close the gold window. Fed chairman Burns resisted. But the tide turned as other senior officials went along with Connally's arguments that they had no choice but to get out of the gold business, including future Fed chairman Paul Volcker, a man Safire described as "schooled in the international monetary system, almost bred to defend it; the Bretton Woods Agreement [the 1947 deal that pegged the dollar to gold at $35 an ounce and set up the postwar monetary system] was sacrosanct to him."

On the night of Sunday, August 15, 1971, Nixon made an address to the American people that preempted an episode of one of the country's most popular television shows, *Bonanza*. In it, the president explained his moves as being responses to "crises" that had been created by "international money speculators":

> We must protect the position of the American dollar as the pillar of monetary stability around the world. In the past seven years, there has been an average of one international monetary crisis every year. Now, who gains from these crises? Not the working man, not the investor, not the producers of real wealth. The gainers are the international money speculators. Because they thrive on crises, they help to create them.

In recent weeks, the speculators have been waging an all-out war on the American dollar. The strength of a nation's currency is based on the strength of that nation's economy—and the American economy is by far the strongest in the world. Accordingly, I have directed the Secretary of the Treasury to take the action necessary to defend the dollar against the speculators. I have directed Secretary Connally to suspend temporarily the convertibility of the American dollar except in amounts and conditions to be in the interest of monetary stability and in the best interests of the United States.

The argument ignored the fact that it was foreign governments who were putting the pressure on gold and that it was the U.S. government's management of its own affairs that had helped put it into the account hole in which it found itself and which had so unsettled foreign-exchange markets. It also neglected to note that by delinking the dollar from gold, the president had effectively although unintentionally amplified the power of speculators, who would henceforth play an even greater role in setting the price of any currency. In so doing, he would set in motion the creation of modern foreign exchange markets that would have little room for any but a handful of large currencies and would therefore essentially strip all but a few countries of what had once been a fundamental sovereign right—the right to print their own currencies or mint their own money. In a world where ever fewer underlying factors influence the price of money, more power accrues to the markets, and the greatest power goes to those who move the greatest sums of money.

The "Nixon shocks" that killed the Bretton Woods Agreement, while they effectively triggered the move of most of the world to fiat currencies in which the illusory value of money was more illusory than ever, did enable the United States to push through deals with its international economic partners that let the value of the dollar slip and its debt decrease. At a meeting of the Group of Ten in London in September, Connally explained what America expected of the world in trying to turn its deficit around: "We had a problem and we're sharing it with the world—just like we shared our prosperity. That's what friends are for." The deficit at the time was $13 billion. Today it is more than a thousand times that.

Plans to manage the float of the dollar were not long-lived. In 1972, the British followed suit and let the pound float. A year later, the Europeans let the Americans know that they would all let their currencies float together.

What this meant was that markets now ruled, as never before, the setting of the value of money. Today, global foreign exchange volumes are approximately $4 trillion a day. While governments may attempt to influence currency values through market interventions, they have only the reserves in their central banks, and whatever loans they seek to draw against those reserves, to work with. Currently, the country with the world's largest reserves is China, with reserves in the range of $2.85 trillion. However, of this amount, it is estimated that China applies perhaps only $2 billion a day to market trading, one two-thousandth of the total trading volume on a given day. Japan, with the next highest reserves, is the only other country exceeding $1 trillion, which it does by just about $100 billion. Only twenty of the world's countries have more than $100 billion in reserves, with the United States weighing in near the bottom of that list with only $129 billion. Thus, governments' power to intervene in these markets is smaller than at any time in history.

Furthermore, the amount of trading that is actually conducted by speculators, hedge funds, and other investment companies that specialize in foreign exchange trading is estimated to be three-quarters of all volume or more. In addition, of the volumes being traded, only about $1.5 trillion a day is in actual foreign exchange "spot" transactions, with the remainder in various derivative instruments that are often highly complex and whose risk factors are very difficult to assess because they are neither well regulated nor well understood by any but those who specialize in them—and, as we have learned, even the specialists often do not fully understand the scope or consequences of what they are doing. The top ten companies trading currency range from Deutsche Bank, which is responsible for almost one-fifth of market share, through UBS, Barclays, Citi, Royal Bank of Scotland, J.P. Morgan, HSBC, Credit Suisse, Goldman Sachs, and Morgan Stanley.

Nonetheless, as Joseph Stiglitz has suggested, largely for reasons of ideology, economists from Milton Friedman onward have argued that letting market speculation play the kind of dominant role it does in setting modern monetary values is actually healthy. This despite the unprecedented size, complexity, volatility, opacity, and unknown risks associated with such markets. The influence of governments over the pricing of currency was further diminished by the consolidation of many of the world's leading currencies, those of Europe, into the euro at the turn of this century. Governments gave up their control over historic currencies in order to facilitate easier trade within a single European market (as of this writing, the Eurozone is embroiled in a crisis that has raised questions about the future of the euro and how it may be managed in years to come). Just ten currencies account for virtually all of foreign exchange trading today. The dollar is involved in 85 percent of all trades, the euro in 39 percent, the yen in 19 percent, and the pound in 12.9 percent. The remainder of the ten biggest currencies are all in the single digits. For all intents and purposes there are really only four meaningful currencies traded in the world today, with the possibility looming that sometime soon the Chinese renminbi may join the list.

While the economic merits of monetary union in Europe are undeniable, they create new risks and delimit government prerogatives further. The risks have become apparent in the context of the Eurozone crisis of 2010 and 2011, in which fiscally weak countries like Greece, Spain, and Portugal have had to depend on their stronger neighboring countries to maintain their responsibilities within the European Union. Indeed, at the time of this writing, it is uncertain whether the euro experiment will succeed or whether the unwillingness of the German and other more prosperous peoples of Northern Europe to pay for the excesses of their southern neighbors may set back not only monetary union but the seemingly irreversible move toward regionalization, an important corollary to globalization and a critical driver in determining the future role of the state. Alternatively, the crisis may have the opposite effect, should European nations conclude that the costs of breaking up the Eurozone are too high. In that circumstance, the crisis may lead to the embrace of ideas such as that proposed by European Central Bank president Jean-Claude Trichet, that to achieve successful monetary union, fiscal union is also necessary, and that the European Union's power over individual states should be strengthened through the creation of a single pan-European finance ministry to work alongside the European Central Bank.

The fact that there are only a few different currencies of note left in the world suggests that monetary policy is in the hands of just a few central bank officials, principally those in the United States, the European Union, Japan, and the United Kingdom. But we know even this to be misleading, because those central bank governors have comparatively limited resources at their disposal. Given the enormous trading volumes, it is now market forces, dominated by a handful of major private foreign exchange traders and hedge funds, that really set prices for the world's money.

Of course, physical money itself is a very nearly an obsolete concept. Not only is there virtually no currency in circulation today that is backed by real assets, but currency itself holds a diminishing place among the tangible and virtual instruments that are swirling around the world and serving as repositories for value. Today, there are 1,655 billion physical dollars in existence, with some rough estimates of the world's total physical currencies at over eight trillion dollars. On the other hand, the total value of the world's derivatives is estimated at approximately $791 trillion. That's not only almost a hundred times the currencies, it is also about fourteen times the global GDP. Derivative instruments are by far the world's largest pool of instruments of value. Few people understand them, they are not regulated in any meaningful way, and it is impossible to know what they are truly worth, not only because their value is contingent on future conditions but also because factors such as the risks associated with the counterparties of each instrument are utterly opaque.

Other than derivatives, the total value of securities in the world today includes approximately $82.2 trillion in worldwide debt securities and $36.6 trillion in equity value (the total value of all the world's stock markets combined). Not only does the total value of these securities dwarf all the currencies of the world, but all these securities have something in common. They were conceived, issued, and valued by the market, and they will be settled, or undone, by the market. The lifeblood of the world's markets, the repositories of all the world's value, are financial instruments— often complex, certainly stateless, constantly swirling above and beyond the reach and comprehension of virtually all government officials, all created, controlled, and influenced by a comparatively small group of private actors.

First Church versus State, Then State versus Market; Next . . . the Church of the Marketplace

In *The Commanding Heights*, Dan Yergin and Joe Stanislaw describe the pivotal moment during the 1970s when pro-market forces started to gain the philosophical upper hand over prior ideologies that had espoused a bigger role for government, from Marx to Keynes. "The message of the

1970s," they write, "was that government could fail, too. Perhaps markets were not so dumb after all." They quote the former Nixon economic adviser Herb Stein as saying:

> We were at the end of two decades in which government spending, government taxes, government deficits, government regulation, and government expansion of the money supply had all increased rapidly, and at the end of those two decades the inflation rate was high, real economic growth was slow and our "normal" unemployment rate was probably higher than ever. Nothing was more natural than the conclusion that the problems were caused by all these government increases and would be cured by reversing or stopping them.

A contemporary reader can't help but be struck by the fact that in the United States today, many of the same conditions apply after a period of protracted government disengagement from the market. In the United States and in England, the disaffection with old policies grew and ushered in a new ideological bent. Martin Feldstein, one of the most influential economists of the era, described several dimensions of it:

> The intellectual roots of tax reform went beyond the technical concepts of public finance specialists. They reflect a very fundamental retreat from the general Keynesian economic philosophy that had shaped economic policy throughout the post-War period. There were four interrelated aspects of this shift in thinking: attention to the effects of incentives on behavior; a concern with capital formation; an emphasis on the efficiency of resource use; and a negative attitude about budget deficits. None of these represented new ideas in economics; they were in fact a return to the earlier views that had dominated economics from the time of Adam Smith until the Depression of the 1930s ushered in the Keynesian revolution.

As Feldstein observed in his own reflections on the period, the elections of Ronald Reagan and Margaret Thatcher in the United States and the United Kingdom respectively reflected this shift and led to a focus on policies that were intended to shrink the role of government through deregulation, cutting taxes, privatization (in Britain), and eliminating government activities wherever possible. The results were uneven. In the

United States, taxes were cut dramatically, with the top rate falling by half, but government spending went up and consequently so did deficits, making government both less inclined to regulate markets and more dependent on them at the same time. During the 1980s, the number of lawyers in the Justice Department's antitrust division was cut in half and its appropriations were slashed by a third. The Federal Trade Commission was also slashed. More business-friendly judges were appointed. An "extreme position against antitrust enforcement" not only prevailed, but the indoctrination of Justice Department lawyers went so far as to include a requirement that they take an economics course.

In Britain the coal industry was privatized. In the United States, the airline industry gained more autonomy and the private sector gained true control. British Gas and British Steel were restructured to enhance profitability and reduce government influence. The British government's share in its North Sea oil and gas reserves was privatized—so too were airports and ports, and the country's share in British Petroleum was similarly passed along to the people. In the United States, the telecom sector was also deregulated, and other tightly controlled industries such as the energy sector saw significant deregulation.

The former Reagan official turned Wall Street banker David Stockman asserted that "the Reagan administration believed that economic regulation was wrong as a matter of first principles." The view was closely supported by the business establishment for obviously self-interested as well as ideological reasons. Because Reagan and Thatcher were both politically successful and their countries enjoyed periods of economic growth during their terms of office, their views and those of their philosophical guides like Milton Friedman and Feldstein were more broadly embraced. In the United States, centrist Democratic Party politicians such as Bill Clinton led this movement, later to be followed by "third way" candidates such as Labor's Tony Blair in the United Kingdom. This not only closed the ideological gap between them and their opponents, it also made fund-raising much easier.

Too Small to Succeed: Governments in an Era of Crisis

Among the most important fund-raisers for Bill Clinton was the CEO of the company that had assumed the role Morgan once played as the clear leader of the financial community. That company was Goldman Sachs, and the fund-raiser was Bob Rubin, who would later become both the first director of Clinton's National Economic Council and later the Treasury secretary. Rubin was one of a significant number of former Goldman officials who made his way into the U.S. government during the period. Indeed, each of his three successors at Goldman also had senior roles— Steve Friedman ran the National Economic Council for President George W. Bush, Hank Paulson served as Bush's Treasury secretary, and Jon Corzine was both a senator and the governor of New Jersey. Others with Goldman ties took top jobs in the State Department, in the Treasury Department, at the Export-Import Bank, and in the White House. But Goldman was not alone: senior Wall Street executives became the indispensable men and women in modern American government and in governments worldwide. Goldman alone produced dozens of ministers, central bank governors, and subcabinet officials in countries around the world. Citigroup, JPMorgan Chase, and other leading financial institutions added more. But other industries, including aerospace and defense, with companies such as Lockheed Martin and Boeing, also have strong government ties. In all these cases, the revolving doors tend to swing both ways: not only do Wall Street execs snatch up White House positions, but many government employees move on to lucrative private sector jobs (a great reward for those who promote corporate-friendly policies). As a result, there is frequent movement in both directions. For instance, prior to becoming White House chief of staff in 2011, William Daley served on the board of directors of Boeing, Abbott Laboratories, Merck & Co., and JPMorgan Chase. It was not the first time he had made the transition between the public and private sectors, having previously served as secretary of commerce under Clinton. Nor was he the only such example in the Obama administration, with former Goldman employees and contractors found in top jobs from the White House to the Treasury to the State Department.

Selling themselves as the best and the brightest, top financial executives offered to political leaders from both American political parties and to governments around the world not only financial support during campaign seasons but also the ability to understand and communicate with markets that were increasingly seen as vital to the economic success or failure of governments. The more that markets usurped the governments' traditional roles within the economy, and the more entirely new economic mechanisms and markets they created impacted global and national economies, the more vital it became for governments to work with market players who could decipher trends and serve as interlocutors to the financial power brokers. Even foreign leaders would have one campaign at home and another on Wall Street to ensure that markets would not send a signal that might damage them politically.

Furthermore, of course, the increasing dependence of governments on financing their deficits put them in precisely the same position that everyone from Charles the Bold to Lord Liverpool to Grover Cleveland had been in. Except that by the time governments came to deal with financiers in the 1990s and the first years of the twenty-first century, the deregulation, technological revolutions, and globalizations of the preceding decades had made financial actors far, far more influential, put much more money at their disposal, and let them operate, especially in global markets, with far less scrutiny or government regulation than at any time in the preceding century.

Robert Rubin led the Clinton administration to promote an aggressively pro-market agenda, ranging from the free-trade advancement on which I worked while at the Commerce Department to a systematic effort, conducted in conjunction with Larry Summers and a team that included the likes of Timothy Geithner, Gene Sperling, and others who went on to senior positions in the Obama administration, to continue the process of deregulating the American financial community. As the market in financial instruments such as derivatives exploded, Rubin resisted efforts to tighten their oversight, battling even other top Clinton appointees such as Commodity and Futures Trading Commission chief Brooksley Born. Born had urged greater bank disclosure regarding derivatives exposure, but Rubin, Summers, Fed chairman Alan Greenspan, and SEC chairman Arthur Levitt all pushed back, suggesting it was best if markets could "regulate themselves." In June 1998, Rubin publicly denounced Born's regulatory policies and positions and even recommended that Congress strip the CFTC of its regulatory authority. The ultimate result of his effort was an act passed by Congress on the last day of Clinton's last year in office, 2000, called the Commodity Futures Modernization Act, which enabled banks to trade derivatives like default swaps without any government interference to speak of.

At the same time, for all the impetus toward reduced government intervention in the markets, in one area that intervention was embraced.

The federal government was actually encouraged by Wall Street broadly to continue supporting low-rate lending for housing. Turning Americans into homeowners not only had the benefit of creating a big market in mortgages and mortgage-backed securities, but the more home buyers there were, the more homes were thought to be worth, and the more people felt they could borrow or invest—a boon to finance at every turn. In 1997, the total value of real estate owned by U.S. households was $8.8 trillion; by 2006, the figure was almost $22 trillion. During most of the 1980s and 1990s, the ratio of the average American home price to the median household income had hovered around 3 to 1. By 2006 it was almost 5 to 1. In San Francisco's Bay Area and in Los Angeles it was around 10 to 1. While this should have looked like a bubble to anyone familiar with bubbles, government observers like the Fed chairman Alan Greenspan argued that it couldn't be one because houses were illiquid and thus unlikely to attract speculators. Quite aside from the fact that this probably meant Greenspan didn't get out enough to have the experience I did of having waiters touting their condo-flipping strategies to my family while we were on vacation, it ignored the fact that the Clinton administration's liberalizations had fueled the explosive growth of the mortgage-backed securities market, and those securities were quite liquid enough to attract reckless investment.

Knowing Bob Rubin and his colleagues in the Clinton administration and many of their successors during the Bush years, I know that in a very sincere way they felt that they were promoting growth by promoting market efficiency. I don't believe that they were acting in a calculated protection of their interests as former or future bankers or investors. They had internalized predominant contemporary views. But clearly, a miscalculation was made. The Commodity Futures Modernization Act, like the pushback on Born's initiatives and the repeal of the Glass-Steagall Act—a Depression-era regulation designed to keep commercial banks and investment banks separate—all helped enable and thus fuel conditions that led to the housing bubble and to the crash that was precipitated by its bursting.

What is interesting about this latest crisis, however, is the subtle twists in the usual script that actually demonstrate the even greater power and impunity financial giants have in today's world. (These in turn triggered the international backlash against many of the ideologies that led both to the crash and to the erroneous 1990s- and 2000-vintage assumption that

American cowboy capitalism was the inevitable future for markets everywhere.) The crisis had the usual elements—the bubble, the government incompetence, the cadres of government officials co-opted by too-close relationships with those they were supposed to regulate, the lack of understanding of the nature of changing market dynamics, and the panic selling that led observers to fear catastrophe. It even included the meetings of committees of senior bankers with government officials to work through the crisis, officials who recognized (as Tim Geithner acknowledged) that they had to rely on such informal groups—as Roosevelt had done—because they lacked the proper tools to control the markets.

Whereas some might observe that today's banks must be less powerful because they are not the ones bailing out government as Morgan did, the reality is the reverse. These institutions—by virtue of lobbying, of the influence bought by donations, of the influence bought by having their people in senior positions—pushed through a series of regulatory reforms that promoted an idea that would be laughable in any other industry: that they could self-regulate. (Imagine one of those same bankers getting into a self-regulating taxicab or brushing his or her teeth with toothpaste produced by a self-regulated pharmaceutical company.) Then, when that consequence of their exercised power put them in a tough position, they were able to go back to the government and argue that they—champions of free markets and reduced government intervention—were "too big to fail" and that the government had to bail them out. And when the crisis began to pass and they no longer needed the government's funds, they returned them and demanded that the government get out of their hair again. When the government sought to tighten regulations on them, they pushed back hard and managed to influence reform efforts so that the core issues on which the crisis turned—such as the opacity of derivatives markets—were not addressed. The fact that global finance put many of those markets beyond the reach of national regulators was even raised by some heads of state and top government officials, notably France's president Nicolas Sarkozy and Germany's chancellor and finance minister, but reform was blocked by the United States under the argument that we had to protect our sovereignty. That not having any international regulatory mechanisms at all actually ensures zero sovereign influence rather than having at least some through an effective multilateral mechanism was an argument that fell on deaf administration ears.

Companies like Goldman Sachs profited in the run-up to the crisis, were bailed out during the crisis, and have returned to great profitability and rich executive bonuses sooner after the crisis than any other businesses. Goldman may be the most prominent example of a financial firm that distinguished itself before, during, and after the 2008–2009 financial crisis by its apparent excess and its seeming sense of entitlement to a government that served its needs but did not cramp its style. But it is clearly not the only such company. Among other financial firms, Morgan Stanley, Citigroup, Bank of America, and dozens of European firms were all prime beneficiaries of the cozy relationship between big business and government at the time of the crisis; all those companies each received billions of dollars in emergency loans from the Federal Reserve in order to continue operating throughout the crisis. Those loans were not only received on favorable terms but they were dispensed in a fashion that was so far from transparent that their details were not even fully revealed until years afterward.

That said, the roots of contemporary America's discontent with a business culture of excess, abuse, and taking advantage of prolonged periods of lax oversight extends back at least a decade before 2008 (every generation, in fact, has examples of such cases). The Enron and WorldCom scandals are two prominent cases that came to symbolize the apex of a long trend of accounting fraud that shook Americans' faith in the corporate and financial worlds years ago. Both Enron and WorldCom had fraudulently booked millions of dollars in profit over the course of several years, which fooled investors into thinking the companies were performing better than they actually were. Both spiraled into bankruptcy when the extent of their fraud was revealed, doing damage to the public in the form of investors' empty wallets and the thousands of innocent employees who lost their jobs.

Another way in which big corporations have, in recent years, stoked public resentment is through their ability to largely avoid taxes and their ongoing lobbying of the financially strapped U.S. federal government for favorable tax breaks. For example, one of America's oldest and most successful companies, General Electric, has a decades-long history of paying shockingly small percentages of its earnings to the U.S. Treasury through creative tax-avoidance strategies. In a *New York Times* article titled "G.E.'s Strategies Let It Avoid Taxes Altogether," David Kocieniewski describes how the company has systematically slashed the percentage of

U.S. profits it pays to the federal government through the use of "innovative accounting techniques" and aggressive lobbying for lower tax rates. In 2010, G.E.'s total tax burden was 7 percent of its profits—less than a third of what even the average multinational corporation pays in total taxes. The article notes that G.E.'s tax department is known as the "world's best tax law firm," and over the course of the last decade the company spent $200 million lobbying to push for changes in U.S. tax law. This approach—as well as G.E.'s track record of years of relocating major manufacturing facilities overseas—has proved an embarrassment to the Obama administration after it appointed G.E.'s chairman, Jeffrey Immelt, as the chairman of its efforts to stimulate U.S. competitiveness and job creation.

It is therefore not any one of these stories but rather the seemingly endless parade of them—of instances of the (often overly) aggressive pursuit of profits and lax standards or the lack of shared interests with the communities within which certain companies operate—that has contributed to the gradual but steady erosion of public support for the relaxed regulatory regimes and special treatment to which many companies have grown accustomed. In the wake of the crisis, we have also discovered that Goldman and other Wall Street firms had extraordinary influence over even government decisions pertaining to Goldman. In one instance, they argued to the CFTC that their commodities trading division J. Aron should be able to place big bets on oil price fluctuations without government intervention because they had every incentive to be careful enough, since they stood to lose a lot of money if they were wrong. When a congressional staffer later learned of the letter from Goldman to the CFTC and requested a copy, the CFTC didn't release it to Congress until Goldman had given it the okay to do so. On another occasion, I sat in the office of the former AIG CEO Maurice "Hank" Greenberg listening as he described how, as AIG and Lehman Brothers were allowed to fail, the former Goldman CEO and Treasury secretary Hank Paulson was in close consultation throughout with the current Goldman CEO, Lloyd Blankfein. Greenberg was practically spluttering when he described how Paulson determined to direct AIG to accept billions from the government only to pass the funds along to counterparties in order to preserve the counterparties rather than AIG—with the largest of those counterparties and fund recipients being Goldman, and the only financial institution represented in the room with Paulson at the time being Goldman (represented by Blankfein). During that AIG bailout, Paulson called Blankfein twenty-four times.

This last transaction was essentially a direct cash payment from the taxpayers of the United States to the shareholders of Goldman Sachs, formerly prominent champions of small government and leaving it to the markets. Whom did the government put in charge of the TARP program to provide bailout funds to Wall Street? Neel Kashkari, a thirty-five-year-old Goldman man.

The *Rolling Stone* reporter Matt Taibbi, who did groundbreaking work covering this crisis, wrote in his searing article "The Great American Bubble Machine" that

> The collective message of all this—the AIG bailout, the swift approval for its bankholding conversion, the TARP funds—is that when it comes to Goldman Sachs, there isn't a free market at all. The government might let other players on the market die, but it simply will not allow Goldman to fail under any circumstances. Its edge in the market has suddenly become an open declaration of supreme privilege.

That sense of privilege was on display to the world when Goldman executives rudely shrugged off the questions of Congress during hearings and again when soon after the crisis they resumed awarding themselves enormous bonuses, bonuses they could not have enjoyed without the intervention of taxpayers. During 2008, however, the company paid only $14 million in taxes on $1.4 billion in earnings, a 1-percent rate. Part of the reason for this was its "geographic earnings mix," a tool many multinationals use to move earnings offshore where taxes are low. In other words, Goldman was a U.S. company when it needed U.S. funds but less so when it came to paying taxes.

The experience has not been chastening for Goldman. Blankfein argues that the company did not need the bailout—a claim that even the former Goldmanite Kashkari finds absurd. Further, Blankfein asserts, "We're very important. We help companies grow by helping them to raise capital. Companies that grow create wealth. This in turn, allows people to have jobs that create more growth and more wealth. It's a virtuous cycle." As Mae West might have said, "Virtue had nothing to do with it."

Still, there is a certain practical reality that does come into play when considering whether to rein in these giant financial organizations. Perhaps not surprisingly, it comes up in conversation with men like Robert Rubin.

I sat with him in his office at the Council on Foreign Relations in New York, a modest room filled with half-packed crates, before he headed off to his next venture. He is a quiet, very thoughtful man to begin with, and when the conversation turned to whether he had any regrets about the liberalizations of the 1990s, he came out in roughly the same place as had his protégé Summers. He felt that they had advocated the right policies and that he would argue the same things today. He wondered aloud whether we had not taken enough account of the dislocations associated with free trade. And he certainly recognized that more could have been done to anticipate the upheaval in the housing market. But when asked about whether the biggest and most influential financial organizations ought to be broken up, whether being "too big to fail" really was a problem to be addressed, he immediately shook his head.

"No," he said, "don't you see? Too big to fail isn't a problem with the system. It *is* the system. You can't be a competitive global financial institution serving global corporations of scale without having a certain scale yourself. The bigger multinationals get, the bigger financial institutions will have to get."

Another Euro-Anomaly: A Banking Crisis in Sweden

There is logic to what Rubin says. Moreover, there is a certain inevitability to it if the scales of power continue to tip in the direction of the markets and their biggest players. But the crisis of 2008 and 2009 was also a turning point, a wake-up call. In other parts of the world, the American capitalist system, while it was still widely regarded as the world's most effective engine of growth, was seen to be flawed in substantial ways. Those offering other models saw their systems as having a revitalized appeal, from European governments that had long held that the public sector must partner with business, to those in Asia to whom that partnership was something even closer, more symbiotic, and who still saw companies as serving a national as well as a narrow shareholder-focused purpose.

One senior Asian government official with whom I met said that throughout his life, whatever his colleagues from throughout the region may have thought of America, after a meeting with Americans at which differences might be aired he always had the sense that everyone in the room felt that in order to succeed, his country must become more like America. In the wake of the crisis, he argued, "That's no longer the case. Irreparable damage has been done to American capitalism."

Even in little Sweden, Par Nuder made the case that not only did Sweden handle the threat to their automakers and the challenges of globalization better because of the centrality of the social contract to their vision of how markets should work, but when they faced their own banking crisis in the early 1990s, also caused by a burst real estate bubble, "We stepped in and where a bank needed help, we gave it. But if the people of Sweden bailed out the bank, the government made sure the people of Sweden got something in return and not just the token repayments you got in America. We realize that our country and our companies are in a kind of partnership, but unlike what you have developed in America, we don't see that partnership as a one-way street."

9 ■ The Decline of Force

> A state is a human community that successfully claims the monopoly of the legitimate use of physical force within a given territory.
>
> —Max Weber, *Politics as a Vocation*

> Frankly, I'd like to see the government get out of war altogether and leave the whole field to private individuals.
>
> —Joseph Heller, *Catch-22*

Of all forms of power, perhaps the greatest is arbitrary power, because it asserts the will of an actor independent of any other influence; it is the ability to set oneself above a system that allows a ruler to be the defining force within that system. Similarly, for great states, the ability to impose their will without regard for the views of those on whom it is imposed is the ultimate standard of power. Throughout history, the linchpin of such power has been force—the ability to either personally or on behalf of a tribe, a city, or a state, bend others to one's will. Ultimately, for this reason, the ability to amass and project force became the defining prerogative of the state, as expressed by the quotation from Weber above. Whether it was the destructive force of an army or the more limited tools required to enforce the law and preserve the peace, in the interests of "order" and the "public good" the state claimed the sole right to apply and carry out threats to the life, well-being, or freedom of others.

As it has other important pillars of sovereign authority, progress has altered the role that force plays in the modern life of the state. On the one hand, conflict has become so costly that few states can reflexively revert to war as an acceptable choice for the resolution of international differences. On the other, international and domestic systems of law have become so evolved that they have in large degree eliminated the arbitrary power of those to whom the enforcement of the laws is entrusted. Law has reined in the lawmaker and war has largely pacified the warmaker.

This has been to the unquestionable benefit of society as a whole. But it has also indisputably altered the role of the state, and in some areas reduced it to a status in which it today possesses few characteristics that can distinguish it from other actors with similar resources and prerogatives who also operate peacefully within a system of laws—such as multinational corporations. It also raises questions about the evolving role of nonstate actors, who are freer to use force than state actors might be, and about how their influence might grow in a world in which the strongest are "too strong" to freely apply the forces they have at their disposal.

Every Man Against Every Man

According to the tradition of Hobbes, Locke, and Rousseau, man began in a state of nature that was also permanently a state of war, which, for Hobbes, was one of "every many against every man." As Hobbes described it, "the right of nature" was every man's right to do whatever he needed to preserve himself "even to one another's body." So long as this condition was maintained, security was impossible, and since that was intolerable, men were willing to give up the right of nature in order to ensure their own well-being. Each thereby agreed to concede "so much liberty against other men as he would allow other men against himself." This "social contract" required an enforcer, some "coercive power to compel men equally to the performance of their covenants . . . and to make good that propriety which by mutual contract men acquire in recompense of the universal right they abandon: and such power there is none before the erection of a commonwealth."

Similarly, Locke agreed that avoidance of the state of war was "one of the great reason of men's putting themselves into society and quitting the state of nature." Locke's man transferred to the community the right to judge or punish others "even with death itself," thus creating civil society. For Locke, one of the principal goals was to preserve not just the well-being but the property of members of this society, a task to which all members collectively apply themselves. In the conception of both Hobbes and Locke, the right to the use of force is in most instances transferred to the state, which in turn may apply it as it serves the public interest. Of course, this was just political theory. In reality, it was the brute application of force that created the first tribal leaders, whether among the clans of primitive Scandinavia, the horsemen of Mongolia, or the Franks of Central Europe. From prehistory through Charlemagne to totalitarian regimes today from Myanmar to Zimbabwe, fear has been a tool of leaders because they were seen to be willing and able to claim life or property with impunity.

For us, the core question is whether something has changed in the comparatively recent past with regard to the application of force that has permanently altered the nature of the state, or most states, and changed its relationship with other independent actors in the world. Or, to put it more directly: in a world in which the state is limited by its own laws as well as emerging international ones, in which multinational private actors can influence the formation of those laws or dodge their application altogether through global operations, in which global threats and challenges are increasingly beyond the ability of national actors to manage, and in which states and corporations are actors on equal footing whether before courts or in terms of the resources or tactics they can bring to bear to achieve a desired outcome, has something changed so fundamentally that it affects even the nature of the social contract and irreversibly alters the way global civil society is likely to work?

To answer this question, we need to consider the changes that might be characterized as the decline of force as an option most states can realistically or successfully employ, and at the same time ask whether in this area too, private or nonstate actors are actually gaining a new and different role through which they assume some of the prerogatives that were once exclusively the domain of sovereigns.

Mercenaries 1.0: Setting the Record Straight on the State's "Monopoly" on Power

Readers of this book need only think back to the stories of the army of the British East India Company to realize that the idea of states having a monopoly on power is a comparatively recent one. Indeed, for much of history, armies were largely made up of mercenaries, or they were groups with an affiliation not to any political entity but to an individual, a family, a region, a church, or even a guild. As we have seen, the story of the miners of the Great Copper Mountain illustrates this phenomenon well. Prior to the unification of Sweden, the men of Dalecarlia resolved disputes and kept the peace with swords and battle-axes. They protected the mines in the same way, and when they saw a threat to their autonomy from Gustav Vasa as he attempted to unify Sweden, they rebelled three times. Among their other privileges, the master miners of the late Middle Ages were granted the right to carry "sword, shield, iron hat and mailed gloves"— not mining tools exactly, but a sign of both their status and their role in a Europe in which men of standing were periodically called upon to bear arms to resolve the issues of the day.

When the miners followed the Continental trend and formed their own guild, named after their patron saint, Saint George, or in the Swedish transliteration, Saint Orjen, the rules were strict, but the powers were also clear. The group had its own independent judicial functions and required members to support one another in times of sickness or in the face of physical threats. In fact, the bonds were so strong that they were actually expected to help one another out even if one of them turned out to be a criminal, by helping him along the first twenty miles of his escape or by providing a boat. Loyalty to the guild transcended that to local law, "and the word of the Master of the Guild weighed heavier than that of a judge."

During the Thirty Years' War, the men of the mine took their forceful independence to its next step, albeit one that went considerably further than the vast majority of other private enterprises of the era. They organized their own military unit. It consisted of seven infantry companies and a squadron of cavalry. Workaday hierarchies were maintained: miners were the foot soldiers, and shareholders were the officers and presided over their own military court. Among its other responsibilities, the unit policed and defended the mine, which, throughout the period of the war, was considered a national-security priority. But for all the innovations associated with the mines, the development of a private mercenary force was not one of them. Mercenaries had been common throughout Europe since the decline of feudal armies in the thirteenth century. As towns and cities increased in importance, their rulers and elites would hire privately organized military units. These units, called "free companies," would travel around the Continent offering their services to those with a battle to fight and a treasury to finance it. They reached their heyday during the Hundred Years' War between England and France. In 1362, France's king John II the Good tried to wipe out the free companies by raising a feudal army, but the companies banded together and defeated the king's soldiers. They were considered such a threat by subsequent rulers that the next few French kings launched wars against neighboring kingdoms just to get the mercenaries out of France.

Italy too, with its welter of constantly battling cities and principalities, became a mercenary magnet. In *The Prince*, Machiavelli offers an opinion of them that one can imagine captures the view of the aristocratic leaders he advised:

> Mercenaries and auxiliaries are at once useless and dangerous, and he who holds his State by means of mercenary troops can never be solidly or securely seated. For such troops are disunited, ambitious, insubordinate, treacherous, insolent among friends, cowardly before foes and without fear of God or faith in man. Whenever they are attacked defeat follows; so that in peace you are plundered by them, in war by your enemies. And this because they have no tie or motive to keep them in the field beyond their paltry pay, in return for which it would be too much for them to give up their lives.

With the Hundred Years' War over, John the Good's grandson, the new French king Charles VII, came to a similar conclusion. To combat the perceived problem, he created a new tax on the merchants of the kingdom, which he used to hire several of the companies. He then offered these mercenaries regular pay if they would kill off the competing companies. They did, and the survivors became the core of a standing French army.

Mercenaries also took to the seas and played an important role in the battles between the English and the Spanish. Some of them, such as Sir Francis Drake and Sir Walter Raleigh, won the favor of Queen Elizabeth I and made their fortunes thanks to their treasure raids against Spanish convoys; Drake became one of the wealthiest commoners in England.

Similarly, when Sweden's king Gustavus Adolphus led the country to its considerable victories in the Thirty Years' War, he did so not just with the assistance of the miners and the copper they mined for weapons or trade, but also with the benefit of a navy partially provided by Louis de Geer, the Dutchman who was managing the mines at the time. Of the seventy-three thousand men with whom Gustavus attacked the empire in 1630, thirty thousand were paid German mercenaries. The Dutch East and West India companies also provided private armies to help expand the Dutch empire, and the Imperial and Catholic League armies employed thousands of mercenaries during the war.

A century later, half the Prussian army was of foreign birth. Four out of every ten members of the British army were not British. A quarter of the members of the Spanish and French armies were also not native to the countries for which they fought. This centuries-old dependence on swords and guns for hire ultimately began to change in ways that would have the direst consequences in the one country that had gone to perhaps the greatest lengths to be rid of the mercenaries: France.

Mass Armies, Mass Destruction: From the Storming of the Bastille to Nagasaki

The beheading of Louis XIV and his wife, Austria's Marie Antoinette, in January 1793 understandably made Europe's other monarchs uneasy. In an effort to contain the radical republicanism that had brought France's people to a boil, these monarchs, who were eager to maintain heads on which to rest their crowns, assembled the so-called First Coalition against France. The alliance included Austria (which was at war with France from the time of Marie Antoinette's arrest), Prussia, Russia, Britain, Spain, Portugal, the Dutch Republic, and several of Italy's many principalities.

Confronted with the daunting task of defending France against what seemed to be the rest of the Continent, the Committee on Public Safety made a decision that may have been more revolutionary than anything else they had undertaken. Rather than relying on France's Bourbon army, which they saw as a vestige of old and discredited aristocratic ways and raised serious questions about the allegiance of many in its leadership, the Committee determined that what they needed was a true people's army. In August 1793, they declared the *levée en masse*, requiring the service of the entire population and the conscription of all unmarried males between the ages of eighteen and twenty-five:

> From this moment until such time as its enemies shall have been driven from the soil of the Republic, all Frenchmen are in permanent requisition for the services of the armies. Young men will go forth to battle;

married men will forge weapons and transport munitions; women will make tents and clothing and serve in the hospitals; children will make lint from old linen; and old men will be brought to public squares to arouse the courage of soldiers while preaching the unity of the Republic and hatred against kings.

The French army swelled from 290,000 men to 700,000 within four months of the decree. Thus was born the first truly national army of the modern era, and a precedent was set that would change the face of warfare and politics.

When Napoleon came to power, he used the state's resources to field an army that in 1808 consisted of 300,000 troops in Spain, 100,000 in France, 200,000 in the Rhineland, and another 60,000 in Italy. Four years later, this force had grown to one million men. Thanks to the revolution's having swept the aristocracy out of the leadership of the military, France's national army made broad reforms possible, since changes to military structure were no longer seen as threats to society's overall social or political structure. Napoleon's genius for organization and his ability to make use of the early capabilities of the industrial era to supply and manage such an army led to the creation of a new standard of power in Europe. The only choice for Napoleon's adversaries was to attempt to match him step for step. Using similar approaches to marshaling armies, Britain and its allies were able to call 750,000 men to arms, about a third of whom were on the field at Waterloo when Wellington finally dispatched the French emperor once and for all.

While the United States was happily far away from these conflicts, it wanted to make sure that its citizens were not drawn into these battles, especially in ways that might spill over into North America and put the young country at risk. This led to the passage of the Neutrality Act in 1794 prohibiting "citizens or inhabitants of the United States from accepting commissions or enlisting in the service of a foreign state." In 1817, a follow-up act extended the list of foreign states to which the law applied. These laws did not limit what Americans could do overseas, they only stopped them from joining in activities that might bring problems to America's doorstep. European countries including Britain, France, Germany, Brazil, Italy, Portugal, Spain, Russia, and Sweden passed similar laws, as did Mexico. Then, eight years after the turning-point revolutions of 1848 and a year before the final undoing of the world's largest private army in the Sepoy rebellion in India, the Treaty of Paris saw all of the world's major powers agree to outlaw the practice of privateering.

The consequence was that any nation that was going to project force was going to have to mobilize a state-sponsored national army. Further, given the scope of the battles of the Napoleonic era and the growing ability to harness mass-production techniques, new communications tools, and new forms of transport to support warmaking, those militaries were going to have to be both big and expensive. While Britain's army remained at about 250,000 throughout the century, France's grew from 132,000 after Napoleon's defeat to 544,000 by 1880. Russia's army became the Continent's largest at just under a million men. While Prussia's army had comprised 130,000 men before the wars of German unification, afterward it was consolidated into a national force of 430,000.

The need to maintain such large forces played a role in accelerating the rise of the nation-state as the primary actor on the global stage. Whereas there had once been well over a hundred political entities in Europe at the time of the Thirty Years' War, there were just over twenty by 1900. New approaches to managing national force consolidated the power of the states. Under the leadership of Chancellor Otto von Bismarck, first Prussia and later Germany became a model of the muscular modern nation. All young Prussian men were obligated to spend three years in the regular army and then four in the reserves. Later they served in the Landwehr, which provided support away from the front lines. Education that ensured young recruits were better schooled than some neighboring countries' peasant armies and the organizational skills of the Prussian general staff gave the Prussian army advantages that were only amplified after they drove the Habsburgs from Germany and consolidated the other cities and principalities of the region into a single state. Like Napoleon, Garibaldi, and other national leaders, Bismarck recognized that by identifying with the higher calling of serving the nation's greater good, he and the leadership around him could generate both legitimacy and loyalty.

This ability to harness emerging national identities to support the development of ever greater national power was not exclusive to Europe. In the wake of the Civil War, the United States emerged as a stronger union with a clearer national vision of itself and its destiny. It also emerged from a war that claimed six hundred thousand lives with a much greater understanding of and capacity to meet the technological and organizational requirements of modern militaries, skills it kept developing as it pacified its own frontiers. Similarly, after the Meiji restoration in 1868, Japan actively emulated the European model, developing a constitution that echoed Prussia's, reforming its legal, banking, and education systems and going so far as to hire the best Western experts to help rebuild its military. First with French and later with German advisers guiding their armies and British advisers working with their navy, they instituted a draft in 1873 and began to flex their muscles in a series of conflicts including the first Sino-Japanese war, the Boxer Rebellion, the Russo-Japanese war, and their 1910 conquest of Korea. By the time World War I broke out, they discussed plans (that were never realized) of sending one hundred thousand to five hundred thousand men into combat. By 1920, their standing army consisted of three hundred thousand troops.

By 1910, the Russians had 1.2 million men in their regular army. France and Germany had six hundred thousand each. Austria-Hungary had four hundred thousand and the British and the Italians had approximately a quarter of a million. Despite those numbers, within four years a conflict would unfold that would require an almost unfathomable quantum increase in the scale at which military affairs were conducted. During World War I, the Allied Powers—the United States, Britain, France, Russia, and Italy—mobilized a total of 40.7 million men. The Central Powers—Germany, Austria-Hungary, Bulgaria, and the Ottoman Empire—fielded 25.1 million. Between 9 and 13 million died in combat. Another 10 million or more died of starvation. The flu epidemic that followed the war claimed 50 million more, but other outbreaks of disease during the war also claimed millions. The economic costs have been estimated at approximately $350 billion but are impossible to calculate accurately.

World War II required the mobilization of more than 100 million men and women. It is estimated that between 50 and 70 million people died in the conflict. Globalization and the Industrial Revolution had combined to create the most devastating man-made disaster in human history. What is more, the intensity of the conflict, which involved virtually every major power on the planet, produced massive investments in the technology of warfare that resulted, by war's end, in developments that ensured that any future global conflict would come at unspeakably higher cost. Nuclear, biological, and chemical weapons had been used in battle, and billions were spent on developing the infrastructure to maintain, produce, and deliver such weapons should they be required for future conflicts. The detonation of a single bomb, code-named Fat Man, over the city of Nagasaki at 11:02 a.m. on the morning of August 9, 1945, caused in an instant the utter destruction of the city and led to the deaths of almost seventy-five thousand people and grievous injuries to seventy-five thousand more. It also sent a message that, as incomprehensible as the scope of the first two state-sponsored world wars had been, that incomprehensibility was no longer an obstacle to a world capable of the most unspeakable crimes against itself, particularly since these definitions of "total war" had "progressed" from referring to conflicts between armies to including the destruction of large segments of an enemy's entire society.

What Happens When the Great Powers Make the Laws to Keep the Peace?

War had been a legitimate and accepted means of resolving the differences between states throughout the period of their early development. But by nationalizing the mobilization and management of armies and bringing to bear great national resources to support those armies, the costs of war had been raised to levels that beggared the imagination. The search for alternatives to war has occupied the thoughts and efforts of men and women throughout history, but in the wake of each of the global conflicts of the twentieth century, new efforts unprecedented in their geographic scope and ambition were undertaken. While far from wholly successful, they have had an impact in making war more difficult for some. And, combined with the costs of modern warfare, they may also have had the consequence of changing the nature of what kind of warfare is possible.

The first set of approaches sought to use the fragile, fledgling idea of international law to set guidelines for how states could behave. This was a step beyond individual treaties or agreements regarding norms. In the wake of World War I, when Woodrow Wilson went to Europe on the first foreign mission undertaken by any American president (and only the second trip overseas by any American president, following Theodore Roosevelt's journey to Panama in the prior decade), he had the ambition of forging an agreement unlike any other the world had known. He sought nothing less than a constitutional world order that would not only base the existence of states on the right of self-determination but also ensure standards of treatment and behavior among those states that would forestall future conflict. He imagined a new kind of social contract among states in which they would give up power to preserve security in much the same way that individuals did as they emerged from the Hobbesian state of nature. As important, Wilson's rules envisioned a League of Nations that would protect states from aggression.

As is often the case in human behavior, it takes a crisis to produce real change. Or rather, it typically takes more than one crisis. Because even after the "war to end all wars" the sense remained that gross catastrophes are anomalous. Tens of millions dead and hundreds of billions lost were not sufficient motivation for the leaders of the world's major powers to give up on their traditions of sovereignty in the way that was required by the League. European leaders and Republican opponents of the idea back in the United States dragged their feet, and ultimately the idea ran out of steam.

But in the wake of the Second World War, it became clear that the folly of the League of Nations lay not in Wilson's conception of it but in its rejection. For this reason, on April 25, 1945, representatives of fifty nations gathered in San Francisco to contemplate an international organization that might actually be effective in preventing future conflict and clarifying the rights and roles of nations. The group embraced a term used by U.S. president Franklin Delano Roosevelt, originally to refer to the members of the Atlantic alliance: "united nations." This was a clue that the new organization was going to be organized as much to consolidate the postwar gains of the victors as to advance any egalitarian rights of the states involved, but the initiative nonetheless proved considerably more successful than the one undertaken by Wilson.

In the U.N. Charter, which came into effect in October 1945, the rule of force is outlawed explicitly several times, and, where it is deemed acceptable, the right to use it is limited to the U.N. Security Council. Article 2(4) reads:

> All members shall refrain in their international relations from the threat or the use of force against the national integrity or political independence of any state, or in any other manner inconsistent with the purposes of the United Nations.

Article 39 says that the U.N. Security Council shall "determine the existence of any threat to the peace, breach of the peace or act of aggression and shall make recommendations or decide what measures shall be taken . . . to maintain or restore international peace and security." Article 42 permits the Security Council to "take such action by air, sea, or land forces as may be necessary to maintain or restore international peace and security."

These principles have been further amplified in the intervening years by the International Court of Justice, which was also established by the U.N. Charter. In 1949, it ruled that intervening in the domestic matters of foreign states is forbidden even if international organizations are incapable of addressing the situation. In 1986 the court went further in the case of *The Republic of Nicaragua v. The United States of America*, in which it stated that the "principle of non-use of force . . . may thus be regarded as a principle of international law" outside of any proscriptions of force that are included in the U.N. Charter. Subsequently, legal scholars have asserted that a wide prohibition against the use of force "has the nature of a preemptory norm of international law," which is to say it cannot be modified or excepted.

While these laws would seem to put all states on an equal footing, in practice that has not been the case. One reason for this is the reluctance of the United Nations to use force even when it is clearly warranted. Thus the one institution that is designed to take up arms on behalf of smaller powers and to level the playing field for them does not do so except rhetorically. Meanwhile, because the U.N.'s structure gives special powers to the largest of the post–World War II victors, these larger powers, which can veto any resolutions against them, have acted as though they were less constrained by the United Nations, its rules, and the views of its other members.

For example, in the case of Nicaragua versus the United States cited above, which focused on U.S. support for a Contra army (yes—they never entirely left the picture) that violated Nicaragua's "sovereignty, territorial integrity and political independence," the ICJ ruled against the United States. The Reagan administration shrugged off the decision, first arguing that the court lacked jurisdiction and then simply refusing to pay the required billions in reparations to the Nicaraguans. Later, the United States pressured a new Nicaraguan government to drop the case in exchange for continued aid payments.

Writing about the case, Harvard professor Lawrence Tribe asserted that "at home and abroad, the Reagan Administration has made it clear that it will not be inconvenienced by mere laws; it will do as it likes." In this respect, President Reagan had much in common with the leaders of the world's other major powers in the years since the formation of the United Nations. The Soviets vetoed the Security Council's resolution condemning their invasion of Afghanistan. Britain and France vetoed resolutions calling for their withdrawal from the Suez Canal. NATO bombed Yugoslavia without the fig leaf of U.N. support because Russia had made it clear it would veto any effort to authorize the mission.

Major countries also twist the law to suit their purposes because there is no power able to enforce a contrary opinion. When the United States invoked its "right of self-defense" to preemptively attack Iraq, it was more than a stretch, it was a clear misrepresentation. There was no threat.

While some small countries have been able to use great-power sponsorship to help them dodge pressure from the United Nations, many feel less free to do so. This is due in part to the fact that these smaller entities are more vulnerable to economic pressure, whether in the form of withheld funds from international financial institutions (wherein great powers dominate by the voting terms) through the imposition of sanctions, or by the establishment of a no-fly zone, as in the case of seeking to pressure Libya's Muammar Qaddafi to desist from the wholesale slaughter of opponents of his regime. Similarly, while some smaller states have deftly used the United Nations and its one nation–one vote structure to gain an even larger influence than they might otherwise have—as Sweden and Norway have on environmental issues, for example—this is seldom the case with security-related concerns. International institutions can therefore be said to have been successful in constraining the impulse to use force by nations, but only by some of them—the smaller ones. As it turns out, of course, that didn't actually make smaller nations safer than large ones; quite the contrary.

Two factors fed this paradox. First, large countries cornered the market on the ability to project meaningful force. Secondly, the decline of the vast majority of countries into what might be called "semi-states" unable to project force or, in most instances, even defend themselves, has led to growing instability among some members of their ranks— especially the weakest failing and failed states.

Who Can Bear the Costs of Modern War?

It is estimated that America's interventions in Iraq and Afghanistan will cost, when all is said and done, between $2 trillion and $3 trillion. At the time of this writing, the United States was spending approximately $2 billion a week in Afghanistan to support approximately a hundred thousand troops. Those troops are supported by supply chains that stretch back to the United States and by technologies that employ advanced capabilities from outer space to beneath the surface of the oceans, from unmanned drones to complex information systems. These forces may not ultimately achieve the goal of bringing democracy to Afghanistan or stabilizing the region, but they have capabilities no other armed force has.

In fact, in the first two decades of the twenty-first century, there is only one nation that has the ability to project force anywhere in the world from space, air, land, or sea. That country is the United States, which annually spends on defense as much as all the other countries of the world combined. Its closest rival, China, spends only one-tenth as much as does the United States. In fact, China, France, Great Britain, and Russia—the other members of the top five in defense spending—each accounts only for 4 to 6 percent of total global defense spending. The ten countries after that are responsible for only about one-fifth of global defense spending among them. Those fifteen countries are really the only countries on the planet that can be considered to have a serious military capability, the ability to successfully project force for any period of time. Even among them, the ability for most is extremely limited. The total defense spending of the remaining 175 countries of the world accounts for only 18 percent of all defense spending.

Beyond the issue of overall budgets, there is the fact that modern warfare requires special and difficult-to-acquire technological capabilities. For example, there are only nine nuclear powers in the world, and only five official "nuclear weapons states." Only twenty states are believed to have ballistic missile capabilities, and most of these are very limited and of dubious effectiveness for any prolonged conflict. What is more, the cost of most weapons systems is prohibitive. It is estimated that the real dollar cost of new bomber aircraft has risen approximately 2,000 percent since 1933, an estimated annual growth rate of 13.3 percent, far faster than the growth of all but one or two national economies. Fighter aircraft have increased in cost by 9.9 percent a year. Aircraft carriers, unaffordable by most nations, increase at about 10 percent a year. At the same time, personnel costs have also climbed, leaving less and less for new weapons or replacement parts.

As a consequence, most states have been priced out of the ability to project force. Only forty of almost two hundred countries have active forces that can muster more than a hundred thousand troops. Only twenty-three have more than two hundred thousand. Currently, for example, Sweden's active duty military is down to just over thirteen thousand troops, which, despite reserves of a couple hundred thousand, still leads to halfhearted jokes among insiders that there are more admirals and generals in the Swedish military today than there are ships, tanks, planes, or men for them to command.

Whether the reason that fewer states have the ability or the inclination to either project force or repel aggression lies in the unthinkable nature of modern conflict, its financial costs, or international laws, one thing is certain: each passing century has seen fewer wars involving great powers. The twenty-first seems as if it will continue the trend. According to Charles Tilly, the sixteenth century saw 34 such wars, the seventeenth saw 29, the eighteenth saw 17, the nineteenth saw 20, and the twentieth saw 15. The average duration of the wars has fallen from 1.6 years to 0.4, and the proportion of years of the century during which wars were under way has fallen from 95 percent to 53 percent.

It is clear that by accident or design, for the moment at least, the great powers have made the world safer for themselves. Smaller countries, however, must contend with both a diminished ability to influence affairs and, increasingly, the reappearance of private actors who are taking many forms, some ancient and some quite new.

Wars of Giants, Wars of Pygmies

Winston Churchill said, "When the war of the giants is over the wars of the pygmies will begin." As prophetic as that may sound, the reality is that the wars of pygmies have been going on all along. In an era in which giants do not fight, smaller conflicts gain in profile and relative importance. Of course, after the consolidations of the nineteenth century, the post–World War II era saw the concept of the right of self-determination and the collapse of empire produce a proliferation of states. At the first meeting of the United Nations in 1945, only 51 states were represented. Today, there are more than 190 members. Many of these newer states are clearly among those who are the most limited in exercising the most basic of state powers, from controlling their borders to projecting force to creating a currency. And in many of these places where effective force was lacking and the void was compounded by the ineffectiveness of the United Nations and the inattentiveness of the greater powers, that void was filled by nonstate actors seeking to flex their muscles, gain an advantage, engender change, profit, or simply take refuge. Sometimes the greater powers actually collaborated in exacerbating such situations, encouraging these destabilizing activities because they perceived them as benefiting the bigger states' broader strategies.

From Colombia to the Lakes Region of Africa, rebel groups, narcotics traffickers, and even powerful street gangs have played dominant roles in writing the history of violent conflict in the years since the great wars. One place that exemplifies the modern phenomenon is no stranger to the turmoil caused when the world's most important countries seek to impose global order. This place, Afghanistan, experienced such turmoil in the time of Alexander the Great, and it experienced it in the days when the most important force in its region was the British East India Company. In fact, it was the forces of the British East India Company entering Afghanistan via the Bolan Pass that set in motion the first Anglo-Afghan war in 1839, the opening move in what was called "the Great Game," a competition for regional influence between the British and Russian empires.

From the middle of the twentieth century through the 1970s, Afghanistan was ruled by a king who kept the largely tribal and ethnically fragmented country more or less unified and functional. After a series of coups, however, the country's government allied itself with the Soviet Union and began implementing secular laws. This triggered a backlash by the more religious and culturally conservative members of the country's population. The United States, reflexively trying to contain any extension of Soviet influence, seized this opportunity and backed the country's Islamist opposition.

In 1979, the Soviets invaded Afghanistan. They had an easier time shrugging off the condemnation of the United Nations than they did the tenacious mujahideen on the ground in Afghanistan—especially given the increasingly active support that the United States was smuggling to them from Pakistan. The conflict became the Soviet equivalent of Vietnam, and the hunger for candid talk about it was one of the triggers for glasnost and a tipping point in the series of reforms and upsets that ultimately undid the Communists in Moscow.

America's allies on the ground—the Taliban—took control of the country and began imposing strict fundamentalist rule. They also provided a haven for terrorist groups, such as Al Qaeda, which itself had been a beneficiary of U.S. support during the war with the Soviets. It was, of course, Al Qaeda's attacks on the United States on September 11, 2001, that made the world understand the potential impact of nonstate actors. Al Qaeda's attack also framed in stark relief the difficulties associated with entering into a conflict against an enemy without a border, a capital city, or a formal army. The United States illustrated this by invading not one but two countries to go after Al Qaeda, and in the decade since, Al Qaeda has demonstrated the advantages of its structure by not only evading the United States in the mountains between Afghanistan and Pakistan and forcing the United States to spend great amounts of money, but also developing a network structure with nodes cropping up in weak states from Yemen to the Sudan to North Africa and even cells in the United States and Europe. By June 2010, the United States had been involved longer in its war with Al Qaeda than in any other war in its history. Almost certainly before the war is over, the United States will have spent more on it than on any war in its history. And it is a war with an entity that almost certainly has fewer members and affiliates than, say, the Swedish army, most of whom are impoverished, on the run, underarmed, or all of the above.

Meanwhile, back in Afghanistan, a U.S.-supported government with a massive Western coalition at its side is finding it nearly impossible to exert sufficient force on its own people to bring stability—despite the fact that the U.S. Senate Foreign Relations committee has estimated that coalition spending in Afghanistan provides in 2011 a staggering 97 percent of the country's GDP. Porous borders, an inability to project force, total dependence on aid or illicit trade for the bulk of its economic prosperity, social and political instability—to call Afghanistan a true state is a classic case of the triumph of hope over experience. Indeed, it is something less than even a semi-state, more a failed state that has during extended periods of its recent history ceded control over significant portions of its territory to nonstate actors from tribal warlords to terrorist extremists.

Despite the presence of the world's most advanced military and all its new technologies, the power vacuum created by the weakness of that state has produced the kind of chaotic situation that has occurred throughout history in ungoverned or ineffectively governed regions.

Similarly, Somalia, despite having been colonized by both Britain and later Italy, has never shed its clan-based structure and has thus had a very hard time developing the necessary functions of a nation-state. In 1991, chaos there briefly drew in U.S. troops fresh from their triumph in the first Gulf war who were almost immediately humiliated in the blunder-and heroism-filled "Black Hawk Down" incident and its aftermath. Years later, order was briefly imposed by Islamists who held the local warlords in check for a few months, but then the United States backed an Ethiopian intervention to remove the Islamists and prevent the spread of Al Qaeda to yet another orderless corner of the globe. The Ethiopians attempted to impose the fourteenth new government the "country" had seen since 1991, but the cobbled-together coalition of thugs and gangsters who had been recruited to prop up the regime came apart and once again chaos ensued.

The world turned its back on the situation until groups of pirates— warlords of the African littoral—began to emulate the heroes of Britain's golden age such as Drake: these pirates raided ships that passed through their waters off Somalia's coast. Twenty thousand such vessels make their way to and from the Suez Canal by the Gulf of Aden each year, and the pickings were rich. Though the pirates were lightly armed and few in number, trying to contain them has motivated an effort incorporating support from the navies of the United States, China, India, Italy, Russia, France, Denmark, Saudi Arabia, Malaysia, Greece, Turkey, Britain, and Germany. The results have been disappointing at best, illustrating that while failed states can do little to defend themselves, they can offer excellent cover for nonstate actors, a far more difficult-to-penetrate cloud of disorder that represents one of the most prominent threats in a world of dramatically shifting power relationships.

It is certain that those relationships will change even further the moment one of those nonstate groups gets its hands on a weapon of mass destruction and deploys it against a more powerful foe and then retreats into, say, Waziristan or Somalia to plan its next move. In a series of interviews with leading terrorism experts, virtually all reckoned the possibility of such an event's occurring in the next two decades as between "likely" and, in the words of one who is currently working with the U.S. government, "a certainty. We live in a world in which no one is as strong as us but in which virtually everyone is equally vulnerable."

Mercenaries 2.0: The Reprivatization of Force

The redistribution of military power in the world was also abetted by the forces that led to the redistribution of economic power from the state to the market. Even as the U.S. government was dismantling Glass-Steagall and keeping the CFTC from monitoring the derivative instruments that would ultimately trigger the biggest financial crash in three-quarters of a century, it was also working on privatizing its national security capabilities. A report released in 1996 by the Department of Defense and the Defense Science Board urged consideration for outsourcing noncombat defense functions. It argued that such measures could "reduce the cost and improve the performance of [DoD's] support activities." The next year, the Defense Department's Quadrennial Defense Review announced intentions to "adopt and adapt the lessons of the private sector."

The champion for many of these reforms was an avowed disciple of Milton Friedman, someone who attended Friedman's lectures while he served in the U.S. Congress and who actively supported Friedmanesque ideas such as an all-volunteer army. His name was Donald Rumsfeld. And, as secretary of defense under George W. Bush, he would oversee the accelerated privatization of many American defense capabilities that had historically been purely the responsibility of the state. In this he was, of course, abetted by Vice President Dick Cheney, who, prior to joining the government, was the CEO of one of the biggest beneficiaries of this process—Halliburton.

When the Bush team took office, defense spending was at its lowest level since 1979. Therefore, turning to the private sector for assistance with the rapid ramp-up "required" in the wake of 9/11 was easily defended—to the extent that anyone was even questioning the moves. And few were. Outsourcing, which had previously been used for administrative support, was now being widely and increasingly applied to field operations. In an interview with Middlebury professor Allison Stanger on her definitive study of this phenomenon, called *One Nation Under Contract*, Theresa Whelan, deputy assistant secretary of state for African affairs, argued that "we crossed the Rubicon in 2002 when we allowed Northrop Grumman to do training for peacekeeping in Africa. Before then we had used contractors for training in the classroom and for computer simulation exercises, but never before had they been deployed on the field."

The move was also embraced by many within the military because they recognized that the increasingly technologically sophisticated nature of the modern military required skills that were more readily found within the private workforce. Further, those same technologies make it easier to network together disparate and far-flung public and private groups and have them effectively work as cohesive units. This in turn allows military leaders to focus their attention on core operations that can only be performed by government personnel.

Of course, it is becoming harder to know where such core operations end and "appropriate" activities for contractors begin. According to Stanger, over 80 percent of Department of Defense funds go to contractors, and an even greater amount of State Department funds go to private sector actors. Over 90 percent of U.S. Agency for International Development resources are channeled through private companies. The United States and the international public were generally unaware of these activities until March 31, 2004, when Sunni insurgents killed four contractors in Fallujah, Iraq. The men all worked for a company based in the swamps of North Carolina called Blackwater. Once a low-profile private security company that performed increasingly "mission-critical" assignments in the Iraqi war zone, Blackwater has since been renamed Xe Enterprises in an effort to regain the anonymity that once served it well but was squandered through a series of abuses.

Despite the fact that individual Blackwater foot soldiers were reportedly earning salaries greater than many of the generals who were giving them their orders, the company's work in Fallujah that day in March 2004 was pretty humdrum. In the middle of a very volatile region, it was providing armed escorts for a convoy of trucks that were operated by yet another contractor—Eurest Support Service, a Halliburton company that provided kitchen equipment to the U.S. military. The operation had all the hallmarks of a screwup in waiting. The Blackwater men had never worked together. One had just arrived in the country. The team was undermanned in terms of what their contract required. The vehicles weren't armored, a violation of Blackwater's contract with ESS. And, unknown to all, someone had leaked the details of the convoy to insurgents. Slowed by the aftereffects of a roadside bomb as they entered the city, they were ambushed. A grenade was thrown. Machine gun fire rang out. Two of the Blackwater men were shot while trying to evade the attack in their jeep. They were torn apart. Two others were killed and then dragged to the Euphrates River, where their bodies were hung for ten hours before being cut down, burned, and paraded through the city.

Suddenly the private contractors were in the spotlight, even though the military was actually well along its way to hiring 1.8 million new contract employees between 2002 and 2005. (The United States is not alone in employing such contractors. It has become an increasingly common phenomenon worldwide, with British, South African, Russian, and Israeli companies among those noted for providing services that once were undertaken primarily by direct employees of national governments.) Among these was a new class of "military provider firm" that provided both support and combat services. As the families of the killed Blackwater employees found out, and as did other victims of missteps by contractors in the years since, one of the most serious problems associated with shifting so much of the responsibility for the defense of the world's most powerful nation to such people is their lack of accountability.

After the Fallujah incident, the families of the four Blackwater contractors sued the company, alleging that it mismanaged the entire affair and then tried to cover it up. Blackwater argued it could not be sued because it was part of the U.S. "Total Force," so any lawsuit would violate the president's power as commander-in-chief. KBR, a Halliburton subsidiary, filed an amicus brief supporting this view. Blackwater used the same argument again when sued after an aircraft crash that claimed the lives of three U.S. soldiers. This time the company also made the astonishingly brazen argument that it was not liable for tort claims under the doctrine that grants the government sovereign immunity for tort suits when servicemen are injured in situations that "arise out of or are in the course of activity incident to service." At the same time, the company has also asserted that its employees are not liable as they might be under the Uniform Code of Military Justice (UCMJ) because of their private status. Thus Blackwater has attempted to wedge itself into a space between existing laws in which it is accountable to no one and in fact would be less accountable than the government for which it was working.

Since these developments, Congress has attempted to add language to recent appropriations legislation that would make contractors liable under the UCMJ. Further, one of my former Kissinger Associates colleagues, L. Paul Bremer, the U.S. "viceroy" in Iraq who was famously protected not by the military but by Blackwater contractors, has asserted that his Order 17 giving immunity to all contractors did not make Blackwater and others immune from the law because they could still be subject to Iraqi law—a not wholly satisfactory argument, given the low likelihood that the United States would allow such a trial to take place or that Blackwater would allow its employees to wait in the country long enough to find out what would happen. The U.S. Justice Department avoided wading into these waters until September 2007, when five Blackwater men killed seventeen Iraqi civilians and wounded twenty others at a busy traffic circle in Baghdad. Charges were filed fifteen months later.

Another problem associated with private contractors is that the profit motive will not necessarily lead them in the same direction as the public interests of the United States This kind of conflict of interest came to light when one of the company's cofounders, Al Clark, a former mentor of Blackwater's CEO, quit because of a difference regarding a training assignment. Clark stated that he believed the company should share with the law enforcement officials it was training every bit of knowledge it had, while Prince argued that that was a business loser because it meant the officials would have no incentive to come back for more training. Other instances have seen contractors illegally inflate their invoices to the government, as in the case of the bizarrely named Custer Battles Company that was found to have defrauded the Coalition Provisional Authority in Iraq of millions of dollars. At the time the gouging was discovered, the company had already been awarded $100 million in contracts with the United States.

In Africa, the exploits of another private contractor named Executive Outcomes, which employed former elite soldiers of the South African military and police forces, made its name by offering itself for hire to regimes in West Africa to protect them from uprisings. In 1995, as rebel forces closed in on the capital of Sierra Leone and the governments of the United States and the United Kingdom as well as the United Nations refused to intervene, EO was retained by a Sierra Leonean army captain named Valentine Strasser who had read about it in *Soldier of Fortune* magazine. It had come highly recommended by a former British Special Forces soldier named Anthony Buckingham, an executive at a local diamond mine. Since the regime couldn't afford EO's fees, a deal was struck in which Buckingham offered to pay it for concessions in the diamond mining region.

Within a month, 160 EO personnel arrived with their own helicopter gunships. Within just over a week, the rebels were pushed deep into the jungle. Hundreds of rebels were killed or wounded. Once the battle was won, EO kept going straight to the diamond fields. There it held its ground and protected the operations of the mining company. Periodically, it reengaged on behalf of the government against the rebels, repeatedly defeating them. Strasser was ultimately pushed from office and elections were held. The new government invited the foreign mercenaries to depart. EO warned this would lead to problems for the government, and when the request to leave was not retracted, it departed, followed ninety-five days later by the new government, which was deposed by the rebels that EO had previously kept from the capital.

Finally, another problem cited by Stanger and other experts regarding the privatization of military affairs through the hiring of contractors is that the government has far too few people working on procurement to effectively oversee contracts. Consequently, contracts often call for the contractors themselves to monitor the activities of their subcontractors as the only, or at least the primary, means of ensuring the fulfillment of the government's requirements. Needless to say, this too leads to undeniable conflicts of interest. Wrongdoing often escapes notice until a scandal hits the headlines. For example, twenty-seven of the thirty-seven interrogators at Abu Ghraib prison were contractors. DynCorp, a prominent contractor, was found to operate a sex slavery ring in the former Yugoslavia in which "girls as young as twelve were sold on an hourly, daily, or permanent basis." And in August 2009, two former Blackwater employees testified in federal court that Blackwater's owner, Erik Prince, may have "murdered or facilitated the murder of individuals who were cooperating with federal authorities investigating the companies." They added that Blackwater was illegally smuggling weapons into Iraq, with Prince's knowledge. When these revelations came to light, thanks to a public interest lawsuit, others followed, including one that Blackwater and specifically Prince were involved in a covert assassination program run by the CIA and the U.S. Joint Special Forces Command.

The CIA program became public when the agency's director, Leon Panetta, alerted Congress that he had discovered and canceled the program, which had, among its objectives, the assassination of Osama bin

Laden—one set of CIA-sponsored private operatives in pursuit of an-other from a prior era. It was subsequently revealed that Blackwater had participated in other intelligence-gathering operations run out of Pakistan in cooperation with the military, engaging in "snatch and grabs" and assassinations of Taliban and Al Qaeda operatives. Allegedly, unlike the program initially reported by Panetta, the second program was actually implemented and operated under a classified no-bid contract.

The Next War, Non-War, and Stora's Brazilian Army

Controversy surrounds the use of private contractors by the U.S. national security establishment and major powers around the world. But no one predicts that the practice will be abandoned. This is due in part to the fact that virtually all developed world powers face major budgetary constraints and consequent pressure to reduce permanent government overhead, a condition that typically leads to hiring contractors. Further, the nature of future warfare is likely to grow more complex and to require more public-private collaboration. In fact, that collaboration may take new forms. For example, following the widely reported Stuxnet malware attack on the Iranian nuclear program, Iran accused Siemens, the company that wrote the code that was being penetrated in the targeted Iranian power facility, of helping the United States and Israel to launch the cyeberattack. An informed source who has investigated the matter has told me that he believes but could not prove that the attack would not have been possible without some assistance from Siemens. Siemens denies any involvement in that attack.

As the total war of the past is replaced by the invisible, highly technical "non-war" of tomorrow—constant probing and penetrating via advanced information technologies—what options will governments have when all the best and brightest programmers and technologists are working for the better salaries and benefits offered by the private sector? Similarly, as information technology providers are seen as offering the connective tissue of the electronic polities of tomorrow, how much of intelligence and security work will require similar collaborations—and create real ethical dilemmas for the businesses involved?

At the same time, it is unlikely that most of the states of the world will see a substantial enhancement of their ability to project force or even to protect their own borders from incursions by more powerful or technologically resourceful adversaries or rivals. For the most part, they will use it to maintain the peace at home.

Here again we arrive at another new public-private power equation, in which public power is used to lure global corporations to invest at home. There are countless examples each year of local authorities putting down protests or stabilizing regions in order to enable investors to move in. Take for example the case in rural Brazil in which women of the peasant network Via Capesina occupied lands they believed had been illegally purchased by a foreign shell company in contravention of announced Brazilian land reform policies intended to benefit the poor. The military was called in to suppress the protests. Protesters allege that the reason they were able to do so was a too-cozy relationship between the local Brazilian government and the foreign company seeking to expand its pulp and paper business to that developing part of Brazil's state of Rio Grande do Sul.

The global company that was earning profits for its international shareholder base thanks to the Brazilian government's local monopoly on the legitimate use of force was, of course, Stora Enso. It was no longer in need, it seems, of its own private army if it could influence a host government to use its own on Stora's behalf.

Part 3

The Reckoning: Forging a New Order

10 ▪ Supercitizens and Semi-States

> We can't let little countries screw around with big companies like this—companies that have made big investments in the world.
>
> —anonymous Chevron lobbyist

> We live in a time when people are losing confidence in the ability of government to solve problems. But at Wal-Mart, we don't see the sidelines that politicians see. And we do not wait for someone else to solve problems.
>
> —H. Lee Scott, Jr., Wal-Mart CEO, 2008

The world's largest company, Wal-Mart Stores, Inc., has revenues higher than the GDP of all but twenty-five of the world's countries. Its employees outnumber the populations of almost a hundred nations. The world's largest asset manager, a comparatively low-profile New York company called BlackRock, controls assets greater than the national reserves of any country on the planet. A private philanthropic organization, the Gates Foundation, spends as much worldwide on health care as does the World Health Organization.

There is no disputing the rise of private power. There are literally thousands of striking statements like those in the preceding paragraph that can challenge expectations and the ingrained sense of the world order that is taught in schools. The question is: What does the centuries-long rise of private power mean to the way the world works? The question is accompanied by important ancillary considerations: What does this mean for ordinary people? For the governments that represent them? How are current trends likely to further alter the relationship between those people, countries, and companies? Do we need a new rulebook or a new playbook for leaders that better reflects current and evolving realities? What can or should be done to ensure that the new global power mix serves the needs of all people as justly as possible?

To begin with, we need to acknowledge that the lines between public and private power have become so blurred that old distinctions and frameworks no longer work. Whether or not there was ever a truly Westphalian moment when the system of nation-states defined international relations, certainly the new picture is both messier and more dynamic than the conventional view that the Westphalian order took hold for a time. National, international, and private sector leaders alike need a new framework that goes beyond a world of sovereign states acting as the ultimate arbiters of international issues. Most of the planet's states have had so many of their sovereign prerogatives stripped away and are so impotent to address key global challenges, from climate to fighting disease to combating nuclear proliferation to regulating global financial markets, that they can no longer fulfill the basic terms of the social contract that is the sole justification for their existence. At the same time, most of the new powers on the scene are constituted in such a way that they are precluded by nature and by law from acting in the broad public interest. There are few effective interfaces between the two, and most thoughts of public-private partnerships or networks are vague, aspirational, impractical, and limited in their potential impact.

At the same time, and for the same reasons, in the United States in particular we need to finally move past ideological and political views of business and government that are artifacts of the cold war. The false choice between "big government" and "free markets" is a distraction that echoes the zero-sum Manichean battle between communism and capitalism, left and right. If there is one thing that history conclusively shows, it is that unlike some dimensions of the battle between church and state, which was in fact over ultimate supremacy and could not end in a tie, the public and private sectors are—when properly balanced—complementary halves of a whole. They may often be rivals, but they are also essential to each other and to the well-being of everyone. When public interest is allowed to determine that final balance, promoting cooperation and collaboration between these forces, everyone benefits. The issue then becomes finding the appropriate balance and the best mechanisms to ensure that it serves the greater good.

To develop a framework suited to rapidly evolving contemporary global realities, we need to move beyond the notion of a world of sovereign states and subordinated private actors that is more suited to seventeenth-century sensibilities (and not entirely even to seventeenth-century realities). We must come to understand and accept that the mix of the world's most influential players is one of major countries that can still act largely as countries are expected to act; semi-states that have seen the pillars of their sovereign power undermined and their ability to serve their constituents undercut; supercitizens that are private actors with narrow, self-interested, primarily (but not exclusively) economic agendas; and the rest of us, just citizens, the governed, who at least in theory are to empower those who lead us through our consent and who as signatories to the social contract expect the powers that organize society to provide us with certain basic rights and conditions.

Lies, Damned Lies, and Something like the Truth

The fact that power is abstract, relative, and as changeable as a teenager's moods has not stopped generations of academics and pundits from trying to quantify it, classify it, and work out its recipe. There is a cottage industry among political scientists, for example, in trying to develop power metrics for states. Single-variable metrics are so simple as to be meaningless, but they are regularly bruited about.

Gross domestic product (GDP) is the metric that has been used most frequently to measure the economic health, vitality, and related strength of countries. It is derived from attempting to calculate the market value of the goods and services being produced in a country. It is a fairly recent idea, having been introduced in a report to the U.S. Congress in 1934. Almost as soon as it was developed, its inventor, Simon Kuznets, noted that it is not a good way of measuring the well-being of a nation. It has other deficiencies as well, but that doesn't stop people from using it for the same reason that it is often used throughout this book: it's easy. It roughly tallies up consumption, investment, government spending, and net trade, sometimes swapping out some of these elements and adding in wages or other earnings metrics in order to get an estimate of the economic output of a country. (It differs from gross national product in that, while GDP looks at what is produced within certain borders, GNP looks at what is produced by the people living within those borders, by the enterprises they own.) Also, and not coincidentally, it is a number that guides the attention of political leaders to the issues of greatest importance to business leaders.

Of course, any such number is a gross approximation, full of estimates and inaccuracies. The worth of the currencies by which value is measured shifts all the time. Ownership changes on markets daily. Profits flow in and out of countries in a variety of forms. Some products are ephemeral and hard to track or have values that are hard to calculate. Some portion of every economy is illicit and unrecorded. Tax records are also inaccurate. The whole idea of GDP is further confused greatly by globalization, with all the cross-border intellectual property transfers, complex intracompany trade, and deals going on in the ether of the Internet. But having some number is better than having no number, and over time, methodologies have developed that allow us to make fairly accurate calculations and comparisons between countries with regard to this one crude statistic.

Perhaps the greatest defect associated with GDP is not how it is calculated but how it is interpreted. GDP has come to be seen as perhaps the primary score measuring the performance of countries and governments. If GDP goes up enough, that's a sign of success. If it goes down, it's a problem. It can make or break political careers. If it goes down for two consecutive quarters, a recession is said to occur. A very high rate of growth represents a boom. But of course, as Kuznets noted and most people immediately forgot, GDP is really a kind of a statistical blunt instrument that fails to capture many aspects of a society's condition or progress. GDP does not tell you anything about whether income is distributed equitably within a society. It doesn't measure quality of life. It doesn't measure whether what's being produced is new or duplicative or better or worse than what was produced before. As a consequence, it—like stock market indices or other financial market metrics—is one of those dangerous numbers that is seen to reflect far more than it really measures, that distorts perceptions of the real condition of societies, that distracts from real problems or successes, and that therefore can send leaders off on statistical wild goose chases, pursuing numerical outcomes and ignoring what's really happening or needs to be done.

The flaws of overrelying on GDP as a measure are well illustrated by considering the case of the world's GDP leader, the United States. America outstrips the world by many measures but lags, sometimes shockingly, in many others. Countries that could hardly hope to outperform the world in any category are far ahead of the United States when it comes to things that matter more to average people. Choosing metrics to measure our performance as a society is not a value-free process. As a country, America has consistently relied on indicators that keep us focused on the interests of business, financial institutions, or the defense industry, whereas equity, quality of life, and even social-mobility metrics are played down.

Americans use GDP in discussions about how well we are doing. It's at the heart of discussions of whether we are in a recession or not, ahead, or spiraling into a troubling decline.

Yet, when China "passes" the United States, it will remain for the most part a very poor country racked with social problems. And though the past decade was marked mostly by U.S. "growth," census data shows that since 1999, median American incomes have fallen more than 7 percent while the top 1 percent showed gains. Almost one in four American children live in poverty. The United States has a high level of unemployment compared to many of its peers.

The GDP number is not the only culprit, of course. Listening to the news, you might be forgiven for thinking that stock-market performance was linked to reality. But markets are oceans of teeming emotions that make the average hormone-infused high school look calmly rational, and much of the "data" that moves markets is just bunk. Trade-deficit numbers may be scary, but they are also frighteningly flawed, doing a terrible job of accounting for trade in services, trade via the Internet, and intercompany trade, to pick just three among many problem areas.

Worse than the shortcomings of these statistics are the consequences of our overdependence on them as measures of the success of our society. A country, for example, that overemphasizes GDP growth and market performance is likely to focus its policies on the big drivers of those—corporations and financial institutions—even when, as during the recent past, there has been little correlation between the performance of big businesses or elites and that of most people.

Furthermore, of course, the purpose of a society is not merely the creation of wealth, especially if most of it goes to the few. Even John Locke, who famously enumerated our fundamental rights as being to life, liberty, and property, qualified this by asserting that people should appropriate only what they could use, leaving "enough and as good" for others. As we have noted in chapter 4, Thomas Jefferson later consciously replaced the right to property with a right to "the pursuit of happiness." And happiness has become the watchword for those seeking different measures that might better guide governments.

According to the economist Carol Graham, the author of a recent book called *The Pursuit of Happiness: An Economy of Well-Being*, "happiness is, in the end, a much more complicated concept than income. Yet it is also a laudable and much more ambitious policy objective." While Graham notes distinctions between approaches to happiness—with some societies more focused on such goals as contentment, and others on the creation of equal opportunities—she joins a growing chorus of leading thinkers who suggest that the time has come to rethink how we measure our performance and how we set our goals.

This diverse group has included thinkers and public figures like President Nicolas Sarkozy of France, who established a commission to address the issue in 2008 that was co-led by the Nobel Prize–winning economist Joseph E. Stiglitz; the Columbia economist Jeffrey D. Sachs; the British prime minister, David Cameron; and the trailblazing people of Bhutan, who since 1972 have set a goal of raising their gross national happiness.

Graham admits that it's a challenge to set criteria for measuring happiness. However, in a conversation, she told me she did not see it is an insurmountable one: "It doesn't have to be perfect; after all, it took us decades to agree upon what to include in GDP, and it is still far from a perfect metric."

But for Americans, beyond choosing the right goals, there remains the issue of being No. 1. Many of us have lived our lives in a country that has thought itself the world's most powerful and successful. But with the U.S. economy in a frustrating stall as China rises, it seems that period is coming to an end. America is suffering a national identity crisis, and politicians are competing with one another to win favor by assuring a return to old familiar ways.

This approach, too, is problematic. The United States, as a developed nation, is unlikely to grow at the rapid pace of emerging powers (the United States is currently ranked 127th in real GDP growth rate). Europe and Japan, too, are grappling with the realities of being maturing societies.

But maturing societies can offer many benefits to their citizens that are unavailable to most in the rapidly growing world—the products of rich educational and cultural resources, capable institutions, stability, and prosperity.

As a consequence, countries that at different times in history were among the world's great powers, such as Sweden, the Netherlands, France, Britain, and Germany, have gradually shifted their sights, either in the wake of defeat or after protracted periods of grappling with decline, from winning the great power sweepstakes to topping lists of nations offering the best quality of life.

When *Newsweek* ranked the "world's best countries" based on measures of health, education, and politics, the United States ranked eleventh. In the 2011 Quality of Life Index by Nation Ranking, the United States was thirty-first. Similarly, in recent rankings of the world's most livable cities, the Economist Intelligence Unit has the top American entry at number twenty-nine. Mercer's Quality of Living Survey has the first U.S. entry at number thirty-one, and *Monocle* magazine showed only three U.S. cities in the top twenty-five.

On each of these lists, the top performers were heavily concentrated in Northern Europe, Australia, and Canada, with strong showings in East Asian countries from Japan to Singapore. It is no accident that there is a heavy overlap between the top-performing countries and those that also outperform the United States in terms of educational performance—acknowledging, of course, the mistake it would be to overemphasize any one factor in contributing to something as complex as overall quality of life. Nearly all the world's quality-of-life leaders are also countries that spend more on infrastructure than the United States does. In addition, almost all are more environmentally conscious and offer more comprehensive social safety nets and national health care to their citizens.

That virtually all the top performers place a much greater emphasis on government's role in ensuring social well being is also undeniable. But the politics of such distinctions aside, the focus of those governments on social outcomes—on policies that enhance contentment and security as well as enrich both human capabilities and opportunities—may be seen as yet another sign of maturity.

It is also worth noting that providing the basics to ensure a high quality of life is not a formula for excess or the kind of economic calamities befalling parts of Europe today. For example, many of the countries that top quality-of-life lists, including Sweden, Luxembourg, Denmark, the Netherlands, and Norway, all rank high in lists of fiscally responsible nations—well ahead of the United States, which ranks twenty-eighth on the Sovereign Fiscal Responsibility Index.

What these societies have in common is that rather than striving to be the biggest, they instead aspire to be constantly better. Which, in the end, offers an important antidote to both the rhetoric of decline and mindless boosterism: the recognition that whether a country is falling behind or achieving new heights is greatly determined both by what goals it sets and how it measures its performance.

The search for more useful measures of national performance, strength, or weakness has led to the creation by social scientists of other "big number" metrics. These include gross military capability, total fuel and electric consumption, or territorial size and population. All are useful to the degree to which their defects and limitations are recognized.

The same cannot be said for some of the multivariable approaches that have been cooked up to assess broader definitions of national power. These factor in a specified number of elements perceived to be contributing to or otherwise affecting a nation's power. The problem with them is that in degree of inaccuracy, they are very similar to single-variable approaches in that there are millions of constantly changing factors impacting national power, and choosing to look at one or six or twenty-five is still leaving out millions. Hans Morgenthau, the father of modern international relations theory, developed one approach that looks at eight factors: geography, natural resources, industrial capacity, military preparedness, population, national character, national morale, and quality of diplomacy. He later added a ninth: quality of government. You can see the problem at first glance; small nations with few resources, little industrial capacity, small population, defective national character, low national morale, and no diplomacy at all can be quite powerful if they are willing to blow themselves and their neighbors to kingdom come. North Korea is quite powerful, at least as far as bankrupt, small, failing states run by deranged, out-of-touch leaders go.

Other models include Clifford German's formula for assessing national power, which tried to weigh nuclear capability, land, population, industrial base, and military size to come up with a power number. Or Wilhelm Fuck's approach, which used population, energy production, and steel production. Or the regression analyses of Alcock and Newcombe or the Correlates of War Project, which looks at demographic, urban, and military capabilities. Wayne Ferris and Ray Cline offered approaches that use these variables but include others like trade and the "will to pursue national strategy." And although all these subjective efforts were as distorting as they were illuminating, they go on to this day because people want an answer to who is up and who is down.

In the same way, while assessing a company's sales is a useful way of knowing the volume of its business, it is not so useful when comparing a retail company (whose sales reflect the value of goods others manufacture, bought at a wholesale price and resold) to a manufacturer (selling what it makes). And if one company has big sales but is losing money hand over fist, it may not be as "strong" as a smaller company making big profits. Market capitalization is a helpful guide except that, as we know, markets can make big mistakes in under- or overvaluing stocks, and so you can end up with Internet companies with very limited revenues and perhaps not even a real business model having a higher market cap than companies with real assets and sales histories. Number of employees, value of assets, and other measures make a difference but can be deceiving, given the divergence in structure among companies in different industries.

The point is that coming up with one-size-fits-all or definitive numbers to measure power or relative power is a slippery and deceptive business. For our purposes, we are better off going in with our eyes wide open, taking some rough numbers, knowing that they are rough and sometimes terribly inexact (as noted earlier, comparing a country's GDP and a company's sales is comparing a value-added measure to one that is not) but using a little common sense in weighing them. For example, if a company has annual sales of $400 billion and profits of $80 billion, that is not the same as a country with a GDP of $400 billion and an annual budget with discretionary spending within it of $80 billion, but we know that such a big company probably has resources and clout and global operations that may give it the relative advantages of a "similar-sized" country in a number of key areas (in the courts, including the court of public opinion; in influencing foreign governments; in mobilizing assets quickly, and other areas of influence) and that it certainly has more resources than countries that are much smaller. (The character of the power they have is very different, but you don't really doubt that Exxon has more clout than say, Guatemala, do you? On most issues, internationally?)

Private actors may typically (but not always) possess more "persuasive" tools, while countries' tools are more in the "coercive" vein. Businesses may be more easily able to operate globally and to do so with less concern about public opinion than many governments. But both control financial, human, and natural resources; both have proven mechanisms for advancing their interests, and history shows that when both seek to influence a single issue, either can prevail. And so even as we understand the distinctions between the two kinds of power and the difficulties associated with coming up with finely tuned comparative metrics, we can nonetheless use the inexact tools at our disposal to conclude that there has been a change in the character of the international system associated with the introduction of a large number of big private actors that have at least as many resources and tools available to them as do most countries on many issues, and that it is therefore worth studying the consequences.

Or, to put it another way, as we consider the following section, we will work under the assumption that, for example, supercitizens do not have to be absolutely or definitively more powerful than every state for us to consider them large, influential, and worthy of note. In the same way, semi-states do not have to be inferior to companies in every way to be less powerful than some in some very important ways. And if both things are true, then we need to account for the new players and the new strata of power in the international system and the way that we—as public or private actors—may participate in that system.

Semi-States

Our definition of a semi-state is a state that, while legally sovereign, is not practically sovereign. It may claim control over its territory and assert all the rights and privileges appertaining to statehood, but more than one of its four key pillars of statehood has been so compromised as to be little more than a symbol. Those pillars are the ability to make and enforce its laws; to control its borders; to manage its finances through monetary, tax and fiscal policies; and to project force or at least effectively defend itself. A fifth characteristic of a true state that may be a useful metric is whether its citizens believe that a state can effectively meet the terms of its social contract with them: Can it keep them safe, bring order to their lives, preserve their basic rights to life, liberty, property, and happiness?

In the global era, no state can be said to control all its borders at all times, to control all aspects of its financial destiny in a world of interconnected markets, or to manage or hold at bay all global threats. But some states have seen the pillars of their sovereignty more degraded than others. (There is a school of thought that "sovereignty" is a legal concept and thus not reducible. But it can be compromised in practice, and it is challengeable if it cannot be preserved and asserted, and that's the point here.) As we discussed in the last section, the factors that have undercut the status and powers of many states are diverse and do not always operate in the same way or to the same degree in all countries. In some cases, globalization is the driver of the diminution of traditional powers. In some cases, legal evolution is. In some cases, multiple revolutions in military affairs are what have done the trick. In some cases, new technologies or changing public attitudes have done it. In some cases, it is just circumstances—not enough money, not enough people, not enough institutional infrastructure, not enough critical mass to make it as an independent actor in the community of nations and among the others who are joining them on the global stage. And of course, in many cases, it is the rise of new private actors to become supercitizens, interlopers into the social contract with rights, influence, and opportunities that rival or exceed that of the states that gave them artificial life, that has underscored the diminished nature of these status-challenged public-sector powers.

Because the metrics available to us are so inaccurate or misleading, and because we would like to be as objective as possible in determining which countries are and are not semi-states, we need to come at the problem from several directions. There are 192 member countries in the United Nations. Some of these are indisputably major powers by any definition. They can demonstrate strength in each of the pillars of their sovereign power and exert measurably greater influence than almost any other actors on the planet. The United States, for a brief post–cold war moment considered the world's hyperpower, is foremost in this group. The permanent members of the U.N. Security Council or the members of the G8 or perhaps the G20 or the world's nuclear states might all fall into this group. We will revisit this idea in a moment.

But first, it is also worth noting that there are some states that no one would dispute have had their claims to practical sovereignty deeply and perhaps irreparably compromised. These are the so-called failed states, the countries where anarchy reigns and that often attract bad actors, conflict, and, with unsettling frequency, the United States military. Since 2005, *Foreign Policy* magazine and the Fund for Peace have published the Failed States Index, examining 177 states based on criteria including demographic pressures, delegitimization of the state, and factionalized elites to establish which states can be categorized as "critical" (failed), "in danger," "borderline," "stable," or "most stable." In 2009, fourteen states were listed as critical, including Sudan, Haiti, and Burma. Certainly, these failed states and those that come nearest to that category would qualify as semi-states because of their inability to provide the most basic services expected of a country. They may have the right to self-determination, but they don't have the capacity to serve their people in the minimum way a state should.

To give some idea of the gap between the major powers and the rest, let's go back to the discussion of military muscle in the last chapter. One of the symbols of a world-class navy is the aircraft carrier. But only ten navies in the world have even one aircraft carrier. The United Kingdom and Italy have two each. France, Japan, Spain, Russia, Brazil, India, and Thailand have one. The U.S. Navy has eleven carriers, ten of which are Nimitz-class nuclear-powered giants that each displace nearly a hundred thousand tons of water. The U.S. Navy will, in 2015, launch a new generation of carriers with the planned christening of the USS *Gerald Ford*. The estimated price tag for this new type of seagoing behemoth is $14 billion—larger than the total annual military budget of all but eleven nations worldwide. Or, to put it monetary terms, the U.S. financial stimulus and Troubled Asset Relief Program launched after the financial crisis of 2008 and totaling $1.487 trillion were together larger than the 2008 GDP of all but eleven countries.

To understand where to draw the line between fully empowered, fully functioning states in the global era and those that might be characterized as semi-states, we can build from the bottom up. *Foreign Policy*'s full list of fourteen states considered to have failed due to a combination of demographic, political, social, and economic pressures includes Haiti, Burma, Afghanistan, Pakistan, Iraq, Somalia, Kenya, Sudan, Chad, the Central African Republic, the Democratic Republic of the Congo, Zimbabwe, Ivory Coast, and Guinea. The "in danger" countries that just missed the cut include Nigeria, Ethiopia, North Korea, Yemen, Bangladesh, and East Timor. Nigeria is big. North Korea is noisy. But neither can effectively meet the basic terms of the social contract for most of its people, albeit for completely different reasons (in one case too little government control or power, in the other case too much).

We can also help the selection process by identifying which states are too big to be included on the semi-state list. To begin with, let's take a look at the twenty-three states that have GDPs bigger than the annual revenues of the world's largest corporations, such as Wal-Mart or Royal Dutch Shell ($458 billion in revenue) or Exxon ($442 billion). According to the IMF, a GDP of $458 billion would place a country at twenty-fourth in the world's rankings, right after Saudi Arabia and right before Norway. A few of these twenty-three are obvious candidates that rise above the level of semi-states. That includes the United States and China, the world's number-one and number-two economies, which are also number one and two in military spending and other measures. If the European Union were a state, of course, it would be bigger than these two, but it is just a collection of states and semi-states.

The next ten countries also all clearly make the cut: Japan, Germany, France, the United Kingdom, Italy, Russia, Spain, Brazil, Canada, and India. This group plus the top two contain all the original G7 members, the five permanent voting members of the U.N. Security Council, the four countries most often mentioned as candidates for additional permanent seats (Japan, India, Brazil, and Germany), and the BRICs, the most important of the world's fast-growing emerging economies. (BRICs is the Goldman Sachs–created acronym for Brazil, Russia, India, and China.) All twelve also have significant voting power in the IMF and the World Bank, comparatively strong militaries, functioning economies, orderly borders, and systems of law that the governments clearly control—all the hallmarks expected of a state with all the attributes needed to preserve and act upon sovereignty in the global era, an important and increasingly important criterion.

Once we get into the next eleven, however, we see how difficult it is to maintain the full range of practical dimensions of sovereignty. These eleven include Mexico, Australia, Korea, the Netherlands, Turkey, Poland, Indonesia, Belgium, Switzerland, Sweden, and Saudi Arabia. Of these, four are listed as "borderline" in the Failed States Index, indicating potential problems: Mexico, Turkey, Indonesia, and Saudi Arabia. All no longer really control their own currencies, Indonesia and Mexico are having trouble controlling their borders, and Turkey and Saudi Arabia are facing powerful internal stresses that could test their ability to enforce their laws. Given their size and resources, however, perhaps it is best to describe them as states at risk of becoming semi-states if they cannot reform and strengthen institutions quickly enough. All the top twelve countries are in the top sixteen in military spending, but among the next group, only Australia, Korea, and the Netherlands are. Poland, Belgium, Switzerland,

and Sweden are much more limited in their military capabilities. Does a state have to be bellicose to be a state? No, but ceding any real ability to defend yourself or to influence at least your near neighbors does forfeit one of the traditional prerogatives of being an independent country. (And whereas being part of an active alliance like NATO might help offset this, there is no denying that such alliances are often fitful, sluggish, hostage to the views of reluctant or larger members, and, when relied on as a nation's primary means of projecting force, thus dilutive of traditional state power.) Among the remaining 158 states, some certainly possess the characteristics of functioning states that color our views as to how they should be classified. Stable, high-functioning, prosperous, secure, financially at least fairly independent, these candidates for full-state status include, from the next twenty or so countries on the GDP list, Taiwan, Norway, Austria, South Africa, Denmark, Finland, Singapore, Israel, and Chile. Of the next twenty, who? Almost certainly New Zealand and Vietnam.

A lively debate is possible as to whether there are twenty or thirty or forty states that are *not* semi-states. But it is very difficult to look at the remaining 160 or so countries in the world and say, in an era in which few truly control their currencies, their ability to tax, their ability to regulate their economies and their borders, the ability to enforce laws against major independent economic actors, their ability to defend themselves, project force, or meet the terms of a social contract for the global era, that they qualify as anything but a faded version of what a state used to be or was supposed to be.

To underscore the point, look at a couple of other criteria in just the financial areas we have already discussed:

- 64 percent of all foreign exchange holdings are held in dollars; 4.1 percent are held in British sterling; 3.3 percent are held in yen. Of the remaining 28.6 percent, almost all of it—26.5 percent—is held in euros.
- The euro is, of course an example of how the seventeen members of the Eurozone have given up monetary control to the European Central Bank, as have semi-states such as Montenegro, Kosovo, Andorra, the Vatican, and Monaco. More than two dozen other states have pegged their currency to the euro. And countries such as Ecuador, Panama, El Salvador, East Timor, and a number of Caribbean

and Pacific Island nations use the American dollar, while countries such as Saudi Arabia, the United Arab Emirates, and Oman have currencies pegged to the dollar.

- Not only have most states given up monetary sovereignty, but when they get into trouble, they find themselves at the mercy of institutions effectively controlled by what might be called the Big Fifteen nations. The United States, the European nations, and Japan have historically dominated these institutions, and recent structural changes are likely to primarily benefit those largest emerging powers that are also among the top fifteen countries in GDP.

- The shift of coordinating economic control of the world economy from the G8 to the G20 is encouraging, although the group is still dominated by its largest members and 85 percent of the countries on the planet are not represented within it.

Finally, to put the relative size and influence of these countries in some perspective, consider that of the five hundred largest companies in the world according to *Fortune* magazine's Global 500 list, *all five hundred* would rank with the top one hundred countries according to the World Bank (again, by applying the flawed but nonetheless usefully illustrative annual-sales-to-annual-GDP comparison). Stora Enso, the multinational most readers never heard of before picking up this book, would be seen to have more economic clout than half the countries in the world.

Supercitizens

What makes a supercitizen? To begin with, the characteristics that give corporations their special advantages: their immortality; their ability to operate globally independent of national ties with great flexibility, mobility, and leverage; and their status as artificial persons with special rights and limited liability. In addition, they are made "super" by virtue of their size. On the one hand, size brings them economies of scale, greater competitiveness, and thus the ability to grow further, to raise capital, to make acquisitions, to invest in research and development, and to extend their commercial and political reach. On the other hand, it gives them the ability to weather tough times, to gain leverage over competitors and even public-sector opponents through costly legal or political strategies, and to powerfully impact the lives of all the people in their very considerable spheres of influence: employees, shareholders, customers, suppliers, competitors, and all the family members of each group, plus the communities in which they live and work. In addition, they often control key resources, land, technologies, infrastructure, systems, and other tools that give them special leverage.

It must be acknowledged that many companies, tens of thousands of them worldwide, have a lifespan, political clout, resources, and options unavailable to ordinary people. But for the purposes of this discussion, we want to limit ourselves only to those private actors who don't just exert more influence than average citizens but also rival many states.

As noted above, the metrics for comparison are troublesome. But again, if we use them just as a rough reference point, it is very compelling to note that:

- Using annual sales as a criterion, the one-thousandth-largest company in the world according to *Forbes* magazine would still be larger than a third of all the world's countries. That company, Owens-Illinois, had annual sales in 2010 in excess of $7 billion.
- That company's sales were larger than the GDPs of countries like Malta, the Bahamas, Monaco, Haiti, Chad, Benin, Nicaragua, Bermuda, Laos, Moldova, Niger, Kosovo, Rwanda, Liechtenstein, Tajikistan, Malawi, Kyrgyzstan, Mongolia, and more than fifty others.
- For those who fear that state-owned companies are dominating the ranks of the world's biggest companies, only a small handful of the companies in the top one thousand are state-owned, and only four of the top one hundred.
- Each of the world's ten biggest companies in terms of number of employees has in excess of approximately four hundred thousand employees working for it. If, as is estimated, each of the families dependent on those employees is approximately five people, that would mean the smallest of these has an extended family directly supported by it of two million, a population the size of Namibia, Botswana, Qatar, or Estonia, larger than the fifty smallest countries. Wal-Mart, with more than two million employees, supports an employee/family community of eight to ten million, which is about the size of Austria, Switzerland, or Israel, and larger than a hundred other countries. Add in suppliers, distributors, and other

companies reliant on these companies for support, you get enormous reach and countrylike scale, but spread worldwide in ways that vastly exceed the global personnel reach of all but a tiny handful of public-sector entities.

- To put the previous point in perspective, Wal-Mart serves 200 million people a week, Royal Dutch Shell provides fuel to approximately ten million customers a day at forty-four thousand service stations worldwide, Toyota sells more than seven million cars a year, and AXA has almost 100 million insurance clients.
- Royal Dutch Shell alone produces 2 percent of the world's oil and 3 percent of the world's gas.
- The world's largest asset manager, BlackRock, as noted at the outset of this chapter, controls assets worth almost as much as the total currency reserves of the number-one and number-two countries, China and Japan, combined. BlackRock has $3.3 trillion under management; China and Japan's combined reserves are $3.6 trillion. BlackRock controls twenty-five times the assets that the United States has in its national currency reserves.
- The top twenty countries in the world in terms of currency reserves each hold hard currency worth in excess of $100 billion. The top 125 asset managers each control the same amount.
- Each of the top twenty-seven banks in the world controls over $1 trillion in assets. The largest, BNP Paribas, controls almost $3 trillion. The fiftieth-largest bank controls almost $500 billion.
- While the role of big philanthropies is important—the Gates Foundation puts as much money in the field each year as the World Health Organization—it needs to be put in perspective as a force. Currently, the total annual giving to philanthropy of all Americans is about $300 billion. That's a very large sum of money, but taken together it does not equal the annual revenues of even one of the world's biggest companies. Furthermore, the top four hundred American taxpayers, who had total adjusted income of $138 billion in 2007, donate only about $11 billion, including the big donations of people such as Warren Buffett.
- While the annual budget of World Vision, the world's largest nongovernmental organization (NGO), is $2.1 billion, bigger than the GDP of the world's thirty smallest countries, other "big" NGOs wouldn't even make it near the lists of the top one thousand companies.

The next biggest is Save the Children, with almost $900 million in annual spending. Clearly, many of these organizations are providing vital social services that governments cannot otherwise handle on their own. They also are very influential in terms of disaster relief and development efforts generally. So their influence can, at times, often be greater than their absolute size—a fact that, as we have seen, is true for both public and private actors.

Using statistics such as these, it is easy to conclude that there are among the world's corporations, financial institutions, and private nonprofit organizations well in excess of two thousand supercitizens whose clout rivals that of a substantial number of countries.

One final note is worth inserting here about the GDP-to-sales comparison. Those who do not like it argue that since GDP is a value-added measure, it does not reflect the total "sales" of a country, thus putting the state at a disadvantage in such comparisons; but such an analysis cuts both ways. First, much of what is counted against GDP is private revenue that quickly leaves the country one way or another. Further, the resources available to a state are of course limited to what is in a budget or a treasury or can be borrowed. National budgets typically constitute a fraction of GDP, and even when that is a high fraction, most of what is in a budget is in many cases not discretionary spending. For example, while the U.S. federal budget is estimated to be in excess of 24 percent of U.S. GDP in 2010, less than one-third is discretionary and only about 12 percent of that budget is nondefense discretionary spending. That means that what the government spends that it actually has some control over is the equivalent of about 12 percent of the GDP number, whereas companies have much greater control over the allocation of sales revenues.

Finally, and importantly, GDP represents the aggregated output of disaggregated producers: the people, companies, government, and other actors in a complex national economy. It is not an expression of a *coherent* economic activity. Unlike a company's economic plan, virtually all the activity is unconnected, undirected, and difficult even to nudge in one direction or another except in very small, comparatively homogeneous economies (see the discussion that follows on entrepreneurial states). On the other hand, a company's economic activity is directed and coordinated, and assets are allocated rationally and with a common, consistent purpose. This is an economic force multiplier for corporate economies versus national ones and is another reason it may actually be possible to argue that in terms of economic power, the GDP-to-sales comparison, while undeniably apples and oranges, may actually be understating the clout not of countries but of companies.

Often, however, it is not just financial clout that gives a special edge to these supercitizens. The ability to shift domiciles in order to avoid tax consequences has already been cited. This is often controversial, as when Halliburton, the big U.S. government contractor mentioned earlier, moved its headquarters to Dubai from Houston. In 2008, in response to a spate of relocations of headquarters operations of U.K. companies to Ireland, Vince Cable, treasury spokesperson for the opposition Liberal Democrats, attacked the moves as "blatant tax avoidance." Switzerland, Luxembourg, and the Netherlands have also actively competed for and won corporate relocations by tailoring their tax codes to attract companies. While the countries showed initiative and their sovereign ability to reset their tax rates, it was the mobility of the companies that suddenly made a market out of what was once a situation whose terms could be dictated by a single actor, the sovereign.

Said one prominent chief executive of a leading technology company to me, "I am an American. Our company was founded in the United States. Most of our management is from the United States. But having a national allegiance is a luxury we can't afford. We have to go where the conditions are best, and if that means shifting jobs or triggering a bidding war for financing or tax treatment, all the better. Being global means being competitive . . . and we know we are in the driver's seat when it comes to setting terms."

In their useful book *The Nation-State and Global Order*, Walter Opello and Stephen Rosow offer the following observation:

> The global market has increasingly taken on the role of a regulator of sovereignty, creating institutions and generating norms and discourses that make it appear necessary and inevitable that states both adopt free market economic policies and proffer interpretations of the national interests that conform to the norms of global competitiveness. This is especially true of the poorest states, whose economies are heavily influenced by international regulatory agencies . . .
>
> The growth of the internet and other digital networks will make it increasingly difficult for nation-states to tax global commerce effectively.

These new technologies are undermining the efficiency of the state as a
taxing entity, which may shift authority away from the state and reduce
its capacity to make the financial resources necessary to make war.

This accurate depiction explains the motivations behind many state
reforms, framing them not as acts of national will so much as acts of capitulation to market forces. This assessment can also be used to explain
why, for example, China, in desperate need of capital to fuel growth to
provide social stability, found itself eschewing Maoist and Marxist economics and embracing capitalism. This was the act not of an authoritarian leadership dictating terms to the people, as the Chinese Communist
Party is often depicted as doing. Rather it was that of a "supreme" leadership giving in to the demands of high powers on Wall Street and in the
boardrooms of the corporations on which China knew it would depend
to fuel its future growth. Money talks. The world listens.

To find an example of the clout supercitizens wield versus that of
states, we need look no farther than Sweden. Sweden's GDP in 2009 was
$406 billion. Exxon's annual sales that year were $442 billion. Although
Sweden ranks ninth in the world in per capita GDP, in terms of almost any
fair assessment of clout it cannot keep up with the flagship descendant of
Rockefeller's empire. Sweden has nine million inhabitants. While Exxon
has 83,600 employees, that accounts for directly supporting perhaps half a
million lives. Add in its global network of 175,000 supplier companies
and ten million customers and the reach grows. Exxon has 2.5 million
shareholders, of which two thousand are institutional and represent the
retirement savings of millions who are thereby also linked to the company's fate. With its ownership interest in forty-six refineries, Exxon
has a distillation capacity of six million refined barrels a day. In 2006,
Exxon's budgeted expenditures exceeded $400 billion. Sweden's were less
than one-third of that amount. Further, following on the earlier point,
Sweden's budget is heavily dominated by entitlement spending, over
which its government has little control. Exxon spent $66 billion on oper-
ating costs alone and $20 billion on capital projects—several times what
Sweden could afford.

While Sweden has embassies in about thirty countries, Exxon operates
in almost every country worldwide, with product and marketing offices
in more than eighty countries and more than a hundred exploration and
production sites in thirty countries internationally. In terms of force, Swe-

den's standing army is tiny, and its reserves, while consisting of approximately 290,000 people, represent a neutral nation and are virtually never deployed. ExxonMobil has been known to hire private forces and members of the local military for security missions in countries throughout Asia and Africa, notably in the province of Aceh in Indonesia. In 2000, during a period of heightened conflict between the government and the separatist movement, ExxonMobil spent over half a million dollars a month on security personnel—many of whom were accused of committing human-rights abuses including torture and murder—illustrating the company's willingness to protect its assets with force worldwide.

Finally, to give a head-to-head example of influence related to the climate change debate we cited earlier in this respect, while Sweden was one of the leading nations in engineering the Kyoto Protocol on reducing the emissions of greenhouse gases, it managed to help get only 173 countries to sign up. This was at least one too few, since the world's leading emitter—the United States—opted not to sign, in part due to an orchestrated, well-financed push by a group of corporations, including ExxonMobil, oil and gas industry peers, car companies, and emissions-intensive groups. *The Guardian* later reported that the undersecretary Paula Dobriansky wrote in a pre-briefing note to this group, "POTUS rejected Kyoto in part based on input from you." Sweden had a vote and used its leverage cannily. But ExxonMobil, as it turned out, had a veto.

If there is any consolation in this for the Swedes, it is that companies that at least once had a Swedish identity, like Stora Enso, handily make the supercitizen list. Stora Enso's annual sales of $20 billion would place it squarely in the middle of the country rankings, between Bosnia and Iceland. Stora today has thirty-two thousand employees and eighty-five production facilities in more than thirty-five countries worldwide. It owns land the size of Qatar. Other Swedish companies of comparable or slightly larger size—all of which, unlike Stora, remain headquartered in Sweden—include Volvo, L. M. Ericsson, Vatenfall, Nordska Bank, and Skanska.

Companies More like Countries: The Myth and Reality of Corporate Social Responsibility

We have already seen many instances throughout history in which corporations, evolving supercitizens, acted in ways that mimicked, duplicated, or exceeded those of states. From Stora's providing housing, schooling, its own courts, and even its own military to the miners of Falun and their families, to the British East India Company's governing the Indian subcontinent and managing one of the world's largest armed forces, to the small cities for workers built, supplied, and even suffused with a semblance of cultural life by Andrew Carnegie, Henry Ford, and some of the other great industrialists of America's Gilded Age, the phenomenon is not new. However, over the course of the past century, the statelike roles of companies have grown and changed and become both more common and more complex as multinational corporations themselves have grown bigger.

Today's corporations often conduct something very much like their own foreign policy, and it is not uncommon for former senior diplomats, generals, or naval flag officers to be hired by corporations to interface with governments and to shape international strategies. These companies conduct active political advocacy campaigns. They undertake significant security initiatives. They also provide health care, training, shelter, security, and other functions that states ought to but can't or won't provide. Increasingly, companies are found to be either co-opting the role of governments or seeking to profoundly and sometimes illegally influence their direction. At the same time, there is a rapidly growing set of companies that are identifying and pursuing what they are characterizing as their "corporate social responsibilities."

In fact, some academics, such as Rosabeth Moss Kanter in her book *SuperCorp*, argue that "vanguard companies," by pursuing such high-minded goals, also become better corporate performers. It's a canny if circular argument, because in my experience working with companies, the primary reasons they actively pursue "corporate social responsibilities" is to improve the bottom line—either by satisfying a political need, engendering community support, saving money, getting a tax benefit, winning investor support, or some such goal. It's not that CEOs aren't fine people. The vast majority that I know are, and they truly seek to "give back" to their communities—within very circumscribed limits. According to a 2008 report issued by the Committee Encouraging Corporate Philanthropy that surveyed the CSR (corporate social responsibility) contributions of 155 companies (69 of them Fortune 100 corporations), the median total spending on CSR as a percentage of corporate revenue was only 0.13 percent. Change is unlikely unless it is mandated by investors or by governments that increasingly recognize that they require assistance in fulfilling social-contract obligations. Of course, the precise role in fulfilling the terms of the social contract played by the public and the private sector is different in each variant of capitalism that exists in the world, a fact that we will discuss in the next and final chapter.

However, in other areas, the history of private actors undertaking roles or behaving in ways typically associated with states is extensive and seems to be accelerating with the growth and broadening interests of very large corporations, and the results are not always in the public interest, or for that matter in the interest of liberal society's fundamental values such as democracy or respect for the rule of law. The following brief examples from the past century help illustrate this point.

The United Fruit Company in Central America

The United Fruit Company was a trailblazer, literally and figuratively. It got its start building railways in the midst of the forbidding, sweltering jungles of Central America late in the nineteenth century. Minor C. Keith of Boston and his uncle Henry Meiggs, an experienced railroad man, encountered brutal circumstances on their first project in Costa Rica. Due to the heat and jungle diseases, more than five thousand men died during construction. Among them were Meiggs's and Keith's two brothers. As a way of feeding the workers, Keith planted bananas along the line. Although there wasn't much demand for the railroad, Keith saw an opportunity with the bananas. The fruit wasn't well known in the United States, but it was cheap to grow and easy to ship, and the Costa Ricans were happy to give him the unused jungle land for a pittance in exchange for his railroad building. Soon the principal cargo of the railways was the bananas, and following the merger of his Tropical Trading and Transport Company with the Boston Fruit Company to become United Fruit, Keith was centrally involved not only in building extensive elements of the region's transportation, port, and telegraph infrastructure, but also in building the export industry for which the region would come to be known for decades.

This gave the company both leverage and a deep interest in maintaining stable governments in the region. In the interest of contributing to the well-being of the local population, UFC built a private hospital system that was the largest private health organization in the world. It built trams and put in streetlights. And, in the words of one commentator, "United Fruit . . . possibly launched more exercises in 'regime change' on the banana's behalf than had even been carried [out] in the name of oil."

In 1911, when Honduran president Miguel Dávila, in cooperation with the U.S. government, sought to launch financial reforms that UFC felt might threaten some of its cozy dealings, the company teamed up with another big fruit provider and supported Dávila's overthrow and replacement with a former president who was more willing to deal. Later, the two companies got into a dispute over land on the Honduran-Guatemalan border and both sides enlisted the help of the local army to bring pressure to bear, almost triggering a war over banana rights. As a consequence of repeated incidents of this nature, in which political leaders were lifted up and brought down and national governments operated essentially as a support organization for a big foreign investor (a company that later became known as Chiquita Brands), the companies gave the region something else: a nickname. The countries would henceforth be known as "banana republics."

ITT in Chile

Another Latin American country also witnessed another instance of a corporate kingmaker seeking to obtain favorable working conditions. The place was Chile, and the company was the International Telephone and Telegraph Company. ITT had a healthy little business in Chile covering everything from telecom services to rental cars. But when the socialist Salvador Allende arrived on the scene in 1970 as a presidential candidate, ITT and its CEO, Harold Geneen, worried about deteriorating conditions or, worse, expropriation of their assets via nationalization if Allende were to triumph. ITT had a lot to lose: assets worth over $200 million, the biggest of which was a 70 percent stake in the Chilean national telephone company.

Geneen had close ties to the U.S. government, was a substantial donor to President Nixon, and was one of America's most high-profile CEOs at the time. In order to foil Allende's candidacy, his people began to work with other concerned U.S. companies to tip popular support in the direction of the right wing. Dow Chemical, Pfizer, and Firestone Tire and Rubber formed a secret "Chile Ad Hoc Committee" to advance their political interests. But, as it was later revealed, they didn't stop there. According to explosive reports in *The Washington Post* by the columnist Jack Anderson, what ensued were "regular discussions between ITT and the United States Central Intelligence Agency concerning the role of American transnational corporations in creating economic chaos within Chile to push the country to the right. [Documents found by Anderson] mentioned discussion of the feasibility of an American-backed coup. They even revealed an offer by ITT Chairman Harold Geneen to contribute 'up to seven figures' to the CIA to stop Allende."

ITT didn't stop there. It donated $700,000 to Allende's opponent. When Allende won anyway, Geneen lobbied hard for a U.S. coup. President Nixon and his advisers resisted, and the CIA and ITT agreed to focus on placing economic pressures on Allende. At least that was the stated plan. On September 11, 1973, General Augusto Pinochet assumed power in a bloody coup d'état that resulted not only in Allende's death but also in the ascendancy in Chile of the pro-business, pro-market policies of Milton Friedman and Arnold Harberger of the University of Chicago. The coup thereby marked the culmination of a U.S. State Department–Ford Foundation project dating back to the 1950s designed to introduce protocapitalist U.S. policy frameworks to Chile. It involved the training over a period of just over a dozen years of more than a hundred Chileans in a program that even its funder, the Ford Foundation, criticized because "its ideological narrowness constituted a serious deficiency." Orlando Letelier, Allende's ambassador to Washington, who was later murdered, characterized the coup as "an equal partnership between the army and the economists." (I don't want to give the wrong impression here. Many of these economists instituted important reforms and managed programs that brought great growth and stability to the Chilean economy. Rather, I offer the program and the process within Chile as an example of the not exactly market-driven nature of the spread of key free-market ideas.)

Despite repeated public statements to the contrary, it is clear that the coup was enabled through the support of the U.S. government with blessings at the highest level. Kissinger himself is quoted as saying just days after the coup, in a conversation with Nixon: "In the Eisenhower period we would be heroes."

He then adds, "We didn't do it. I mean we helped them [by making] the conditions as great as possible." Geneen was once quoted as saying, "You read a book from beginning to end. You run a business the opposite way. You start with the end, and then you do everything you must do to reach it."

Royal Dutch Shell in Nigeria

Such freelancing in government affairs is hardly a historical relic, consigned to stories about "old-school" CEOs and corporations far removed from today's business ethos. The Wikileaks scandal, for example, revealed much about the activities of one of the world's largest and most powerful companies, Royal Dutch Shell, in one of the world's largest and most wild and corrupt semi-states, Nigeria. In one confidential document, the chairwoman of Shell Australia, Ann Pickard, is quoted as claiming that Shell Oil had "access to everything that was being done" in the country. In a cable dating from 2009, Robin Sanders, the U.S. ambassador to Nigeria, writes that Pickard had boasted that the Nigerian government had "forgotten" that "Shell had seconded people to all the relevant ministries and Shell consequently had access to everything that was being done in those ministries." At the meeting with Sanders, Pickard claimed Shell had obtained evidence that Nigeria had invited "bids for oil concessions from China." According to Celestine AkpoBari of a local NGO, Social Action Nigeria, "Shell is everywhere. They have an eye and an ear in every ministry in Nigeria. They are more powerful than the Nigerian government."

Whether this is overstatement or not, the fact is that the oil industry in Nigeria has extraordinary clout, having generated over $600 billion since the 1960s. Shell's own estimate is that its venture in the country between the years 2005 and 2009 "contributed about $36 billion to the government," plus $3 billion in offshore operations. About 80 percent of budgetary revenues in the country come from the oil sector. At the same time, Shell also illustrated the "nonaligned" nature of multinational corporations by both cultivating relations that have been accused of being "too close" with Nigeria's corrupt and often brutal military regimes and also having attempted to improve their standing with governments like that of the United States by sharing with them intelligence on politicians it suspected of cooperating with militants in the Niger Delta. The immediate quid for that particular quo was that, according to the Wikileaks information, Shell requested sensitive information about its Russian rival Gazprom from the U.S. consulate.

As for the benefit to the people of Nigeria, take the Niger Delta, from which a large proportion of the country's oil wealth is extracted, a region that is home to more than thirty million people and has been called "one of the ten most important wetland and coastal marine ecosystems in the world." Despite the economic activity generated there, the U.N. Development Program describes the region as suffering from "administrative neglect, crumbling social infrastructure and services, high unemployment, social deprivation, abject poverty, filth and squalor, and endemic conflict." Most residents of the region do not have access to either clean water or health care. While, for example, Transparency International in 2004 ranked Nigeria's then president Sani Abacha as number four on its list of most self-enriching leaders, asserting that he stole $2 billion to $5 billion during his presidency, the people of the region have suffered disproportionately. According to a recent Greenpeace report, "although Shell operates in more than 100 countries, 40 percent of all its oil spills happen in Nigeria." With the government of Nigeria content to look the other way, Shell reported double its 2007 number of oil spills in the country in 2008, and double the 2008 number in 2009. According to one estimate, "some 13 million barrels of oil have been spilt in the Niger Delta since oil exploration began in 1958. This is the equivalent of one *Exxon Valdez* every year for 50 years."

For years, it seemed Shell was embracing the view of economists like Friedman, who said, "a corporation is the property of its stockholders . . . Its interests are the interests of its stockholders. Now, beyond that should it spend the stockholders' money for purposes which it regards as socially responsible but which it cannot connect to its bottom line? The answer I would say is no." In the past, Shell put the blame on the shoulders of the government without acknowledging its influence within that government. But that has recently started to change.

In a 2004 internal ethics study, Shell admitted that "we sometimes feed conflict by the way we award contracts, gain access to land and deal with community representatives." Further, in 2010, Shell announced a plan to clean up 268 oil spills in the Niger Delta. While it remains to be seen to what extent these developments will be successful, they do reflect a broader sense that corporations that blindly seek profit without consideration of social consequences incur hidden costs not only to their standing and influence but in terms of real liabilities and shareholder value. In this respect, the Kanter thesis and the work of groups such as the Clinton Global Initiative and the World Economic Forum to promote social entrepreneurship may have some starkly practical roots that even Friedman would appreciate in the context of his formulation. In particular, the growing focus of major public-sector institutional investors, who have enormous governance clout with big companies on socially responsible practices among their portfolio companies, actually may be an area in which good old-fashioned capitalist self-interest drives companies toward serving the greater good.

Countries More Like Companies: The Promise of the Entrepreneurial State

Just as companies are assuming a wide variety of roles historically played by governments, or, alternatively, are actively collaborating with governments to influence public-policy decisions, openly or otherwise, so too are some governments recognizing that to better compete in the modern global economic environment, they would benefit by embracing practices that are more commonly found in corporate suites. These entrepreneurial states are typically small, but they can be seen as laboratories for best practices and innovation in government that might help larger governments, or regional or metropolitan governments within them, compete more successfully for the private-sector investment dollars that have become essential to the survival of most economies.

Here again we see the recurrent historical paradox: governments gave birth to companies, but today it is the private sector upon which governments must depend for approval and support, whether these come in the form of good credit ratings, demand for debt offerings, or flows of foreign direct or indirect investment that are essential to maintaining growth and political stability. Indeed, it has come to the point that many current and prospective government leaders feel they serve two constituencies. One votes in polling stations in the elections within their countries. The other votes with their money in a global referendum that takes place twenty-four hours a day on every continent.

Candidates for high office in countries worldwide go to New York and

London not only to raise funds for their campaigns but also to raise their stature within the companies that will vote for them. During the Clinton years, one of the reasons for the Treasury secretary Robert Rubin's clout was that Clinton dreaded losing the support of the financial community. He was to Clinton's market campaign what political advisers like James Carville or George Stephanopoulos were to his political efforts. I have sat with senior Latin American government leaders as they planned and opened offices on Wall Street or set up "campaign" lunches with investors (and donors) like George Soros or senior executives from Goldman Sachs, Citigroup, or JPMorgan Chase.

For some, this dependency is a matter of life and death. I recall sitting in the office of a well-known sovereign-debt specialist during the late 1990s. During our conversation, he got a call from the deputy prime minister of Russia, who also served as finance minister. The two talked for about five minutes and then the banker, an old friend, hung up the phone. "It's crazy," he said. "It's short-term debt. They can't get enough of it. It's how they pay their army, how they pay their bills. They're like crack addicts."

"Well, if they are addicts," I said, "what does that make you?" The fact that months later Russia's addiction triggered a crisis throughout the emerging world is yet another illustration of the leverage the markets have over such leaders. My friend the banker continued in his long career of making money even though the fellow he lent it to couldn't repay it and caused an international crisis. The government leader who couldn't repay—well, of course he was fired immediately.

Further, the intelligence and analytical tools that financial firms have at their disposal make even greater demands on countries to manage their information flows to the financial community much like the investor-relations arms of big companies. Just as an illustration of how Wall Street monitors global developments, take BlackRock, the world's biggest asset manager. They have 8,900 employees, at the core of whom are a group of elite high-paid analysts who meticulously assess the state of play in countries and markets in real time all the time. According to a CNN story filed in 2008:

> Currently BlackRock runs tens of millions of risk models a day. On each of these, computers continually run through an ever-changing number of potential risk scenarios, some 200 million of them per week—everything

from what happens if the U.S. starts defaulting on its debt to what happens if China stops buying it. This type of analytical power is [what sets BlackRock apart].

They are not alone. But that power not only to make millions of judgments a day but to translate those judgments into the allocation of trillions of dollars of capital is, in a real sense, what amounts to the life force of the global economy in the twenty-first century. And clearly it is not controlled within governments. At best they can only influence it.

Some of those who have been most effective at doing so are the entrepreneurial states. They share many characteristics with business entrepreneurs. They are often small, scrappy, pugnacious, sometimes even arrogant, and cognizant that they are battling long odds. These factors play into a sense of urgency and a recognition that they will require innovation and energy and special commitment in order to succeed. They also demonstrate that being small does not mean being limited by semi-statehood. You can either look at smallish states as being too little and too stripped of traditional state powers to play with the biggest public actors, or, alternatively, you can look at them as being very big economic actors compared even to most very big corporations. This comparison is only apposite to the extent that they make themselves companylike creatures of the global marketplace.

Singapore, Israel, and the United Arab Emirates have done that. By rights, none has any right to survive, much less thrive. They are small. Singapore has essentially no resources; Israel's are limited. The UAE has oil and gas but is not willing to succumb to the pitfalls of complacency that destroy many petro-states. They all face challenging local geopolitical environments. And they all have made the decision that to succeed they must aggressively cultivate the international business and financial communities, attract technology, and train world-class students. In addition, all have embraced approaches that are right out of best management practices from international corporations, whether that means aggressive recruiting of top people into the government, implementation of systematic strategic planning processes, embrace of meaningful metrics, strong outreach to investor communities, or a focus on innovation as a part of a national "corporate culture."

Singapore

When you land at Singapore's Changi Airport from the United States, Europe, or even Tokyo's Narita, you cannot help but be struck by its modernity, cleanliness, and efficiency. Frankly, if you are stepping off a Singapore Airlines flight, it is hardly a shock, because no airline in the world compares to it for quality of service. And then you drive into downtown Singapore along wide, well-lit, immaculate highways, past glistening office towers nestled among carefully manicured gardens, tropical flowers, and palm trees. And, like many other visitors, you wonder whether this tiny island that did not even exist as a truly independent nation until 1965 is perhaps the best-run city in the world, whether maybe the ancient Greeks and Singapore's founder, Lee Kwan Yew, were on to something when they settled on the idea of city-states.

Once a Sumatran outpost and then a British trading post run in conjunction with the British East India Company, Singapore was the site of a catastrophic British defeat during World War II. Winston Churchill called the defeat in the Battle of Singapore "the worst disaster and largest capitulation in British history." When the bits and pieces of the British empire came undone in the years after the war, Singapore was among them, assuming the right of self-government in 1959. When the island gained sovereignty on August 9, 1963, it had a special advantage working in its favor. Its new prime minister was a forty-one-year-old politician who led the most important political party on the island: the People's Action Party. He was a Cambridge-educated lawyer named Lee Kwan Yew, and during the course of the half century in which he has led Singapore, he has emerged as one of the world's most effective if sometimes controversial leaders.

The controversy surrounding Lee is often associated with the strong control he and his party have maintained over the state and the strong controls the Singaporean state has maintained over its people. From strict rules about public behavior (don't spit out your chewing gum in the street) to caning as a form of punishment, Singapore does not conform to Western standards of a free society in key respects. What has made these issues more noisome to Western critics, however, is that Singapore has been so successful at creating a superior quality of life for its people by an active and creative embrace of the power of the marketplace that it seems a contradiction. To Lee, who now holds the title of Minister

Mentor, there is no contradiction. They have created what leading Singaporean diplomat Kishore Mahubani once described to me as "a very Asian model, a Singaporean capitalism that blends our ideas about the importance of and respect for community with our appreciation of free markets and competition."

Over a dinner, Singapore's finance minister, Tharman Shanmugarantnam, placed the idea in a broader perspective. An economist educated at the London School of Economics, Cambridge, and Harvard—regarded by other finance ministers as among the world's very smartest and most capable—Tharman spoke in the wake of the 2008 2009 financial crisis, saying, "We have seen the defects in Anglo-American capitalism. We have seen some of the challenges associated with Eurosocialism. We certainly know that communism has failed. There is a place now for a different view, a different balance . . . and it is one we have cultivated for a long time here in Singapore."

When pressed as to his meaning, Tharman said: "Our view is [that] the role of government is to empower people to be able to seize their own opportunities. We must provide the education, the infrastructure, and the climate in which they can then succeed for themselves."

Lee has himself said the goal is to "offer what every citizen wants—a good life, security, good education and a future for their children. That is good governance." While this means a more paternalistic state in the Singaporean view and more controls on the press and public discourse than many Americans or Europeans would be comfortable with, it also means a systematic national effort to develop and update a national competitiveness strategy every two years, an effort that starts with public-private-academic discussions of how the world is changing and where Singapore's comparative advantages lie and that ends with reallocation of assets to support new priorities. These have not been mere exercises, and as a result Singapore has shifted from building up traditional manufacturing sectors to becoming a world leader in areas such as biotech and water.

To reduce corruption in the government and to continue to attract the best and the brightest, Lee determined that Singaporean ministers should get salaries comparable to those of CEOs in the country's leading industries. A compensation system was devised that calculated a rate based on what top executives in several important sectors make. The country's prime minister makes over $3 million a year; other ministers make over $1 million. To critics who say the officials get too much, Lee has responded, "the cure to all this talk is really a good dose of incompetent government. You get that alternative, and you'll never put Singapore together again."

Similar ideas are seen throughout the system, such as the utilization of an interdepartmental charging system that "makes use of the market concept to impose incentives and discipline on both the providers and consumers of internal [government] services." More efficient ministries are rewarded with more resources. Health care, housing, and education services are all provided via user-pay market mechanisms with prices determined by demand. This doesn't mean the government doesn't provide for people; during the economic crisis, its bailout and protections for displaced workers were among the most extensive in the world. The stimulus was $15 billion, 6 percent of GDP, and included "skills upgrading, the lowering of the corporate income tax to 17 percent, loan assistance to small and medium enterprises, helping low-income households through fee waivers and cash payouts, as well as increased public expenditures for infrastructure, health care, and education."

To an American or a British citizen accustomed to polarizing ideological debates on these issues, the Singaporean approach is turning market thinking on its head—combining innovation and belief in competition with a recognition of the importance of an active role for the state and values that place community ahead of the individual. It is hard to argue with the results. Singapore has the second-highest per capita income in Asia, one of the highest in the world. Its GDP per capita is $62,200, fifth in the world. It has one of the lowest unemployment rates in the world and is among the lowest in infant mortality. It offers the thirteenth-highest life expectancy and is ranked sixth in health system performance while spending only 1 percent of its GDP on health care (the United States is currently heading toward spending at twenty times that rate).

Singapore is rated number one among the world's easiest places to do business and the second-freest economy in the world (after Hong Kong, an interesting development given that both are part of systems with very different roles for the state than found in the West). At the same time, it is seen as the Asian country with the most business-conducive labor relations. All these things taken together are why Global Business Network founder and chairman Peter Schwartz has said of the city-state, "Singapore is the best-managed company in the world." They are also the reasons that the night that I was having dinner with Tharman in 2010, he was concerned about having to go back and explain to his parliament why the country would record growth for the year of "only" approximately 14 percent.

While Singapore is "just" a city-state, and while many of its policies are difficult to replicate across much larger, more diverse economies and societies, the relevance of its case is enhanced for several reasons. First, it is one of Asia's most important entrepots and is thus connected to the economies of the region not only economically but intellectually as well. Singapore has not only attracted the attention and inspired the emulation that any other success story would, but the government has actively sought to share its approaches to building and managing modern urban societies throughout the region, in particular with the Chinese. After observing China's "new city" projects like Suzhou, Singapore has taken a cutting from China's stem and replanted it in a much larger field. Further, because the city-state has prominent Chinese and other Asian populations, Singaporeans find it easy to communicate with leaders throughout Asia, and, given their English colonial heritage, around the world. So although Singapore is small, its impact has been amplified and continues to grow.

The United Arab Emirates

If the contrast between Changi airport and airports in America is striking, so too is the comparison between the modern highway stretching from Dubai Airport to Abu Dhabi and the pothole-riddled routes you might find in the American heartland. In the United Arab Emirates, the modern skyscrapers look like something out of a futuristic movie. In America, you often creep along congested roads and look out at rusting industrial wastelands. It reminds one just how far the United Arab Emirates has come since oil was discovered there in the 1960s. These are world-class places that, even after the UAE was rocked by the global financial crisis, are still hatch-marked with construction cranes and scaffolding, major projects, giant skyscrapers, and entertainment complexes rising everywhere. But the real story is what is happening in these cities: the Emiratis are not doing like so many of their neighbors and simply spending the money from their oil. They are actively diversifying, spending money on new industries, educating their people, importing talent from around the world. They are, in fact, so aggressively turning their country into a business incubator that one westerner at an Aspen Institute conference on innovation I attended in Abu Dhabi in October 2010 said, "This is not a country, it's a venture capital fund."

Today only 25 percent of the UAE's revenues are derived from oil and gas. Within Dubai, this number is even lower, only about 5 percent. From construction to engineering, from information technologies to the experimental "green city" of Masdar, where next-generation energy technologies are being developed, the UAE is seeking to turn the fact that it holds 9 percent of the world's proven oil reserves and almost 5 percent of the world's natural gas reserves into a legacy of growth that can benefit the country's approximately one million people for decades to come, long after the reserves run out.

One way the Emiratis have done this follows the Singaporean model of developing major sovereign wealth funds that redirect national wealth into global investment projects that produce both return and know-how about important sectors. They are also affording semi-states new sources of power and leverage associated with their active market engagement. The Abu Dhabi Investment Authority is the largest sovereign wealth fund in the world, with an estimated $627 billion worth of assets under management.

The Singapore-like spirit of development in the UAE is not an accident. The Emiratis have studied Singapore's story carefully. And the results they have achieved in a short time are Singaporean as well. The World Bank currently lists the UAE in third place in terms of its ease of trading across borders. The World Economic Forum ranks it third in countries of the world in investments in infrastructure, fourteenth in penetration rates of new technologies, and sixth in terms of having highly efficient goods markets. The country's per capita income is eighteenth in the world at $40,000 a year.

While Dubai in particular was buffeted by the financial crisis because of its dependency on tourism, it is clear that the country is being prudent and creative in terms of diversifying its long-term assets. Again, this is not by any means a democracy, and the state has serious potential tensions brewing between the empowered local elites and the workers from elsewhere in the greater Middle East who have been imported and live in cramped communities and with comparatively less opportunity for advancement. (It is estimated that the per capita income of UAE nationals ranges from $275,000 a year in Abu Dhabi to $120,000 in Dubai, which gives an idea of the gap between them and the workers who bring the average "down" to the $40,000 level.) But the country's leader, Khalifa bin Zayed Al Nahyan, has aggressively worked to promote education and entrepreneurship in ways that are unheard of elsewhere in the Middle East (outside of Israel). During the group discussions at the Aspen event I attended, among the most outspoken, compelling, and challenging of the participants were young, very well educated professional women—clad in traditional garb but offering far from traditional views and suggesting a very bright promise for the country.

Israel

Elsewhere in the Middle East, Israel has long been famous for turning the desert green, for building a thriving economy that has recently enabled Israel to become an Organization for Economic Co-operation and Development (OECD) member despite not having the oil and gas on which its neighbors are largely dependent. While Israel differs from Singapore and the UAE in that it has a thriving and contentious democracy, it also differs from the Anglo-U.S. model of capitalism in that it has managed to combine the "big government" traditions of a welfare state with a culture of innovation. Israel is currently ranked sixth in the world in capacity for innovation and twenty-fourth in overall competitiveness.

Israel's early political and economic approaches were heavily influenced by the fact that the country's founding was led in large part by the labor Zionist movement, a group with strong far-left positions and an ideology that held that a powerful Jewish state, to be successful, must originate from working-class settlers through cooperative agricultural labor. This philosophy has been characterized as "a hybrid socialist-nationalist ideology of Marxist dogma mixed with utopian agrarianism." This is the thinking that gave the world the kibbutz and a range of public policies that included central controls and ownership so extensive that it was labeled "the most socialist economy outside the Soviet bloc."

At one point during the first forty years of the country's life, the public sector's role got so large that it accounted for as much as 80 percent of the total economy. However, by the 1970s, other factors were putting pressure on the system, including a large inflow of Jewish immigrants (many from the Soviet Union), spiraling inflation, a growing deficit, and a big public debt. The economy was stalled, and it became increasingly clear that something needed to be fixed in the overall policies of the government.

Inflation hit 500 percent in 1984, and by 1985 a major reform, called the Economic Stabilization Plan, was under way. It called for a major reduction in government spending, a deal with labor unions to put wage controls in place, a devaluation of the shekel, and a flat exchange rate. Inflation was brought under control, but the socialist structure of the economy had not been addressed. At this point, Israel received a contingent of University of Chicago–educated young leaders who advocated an Israeli version of a "Thatcherite revolution." Among this group of neoliberals was a young Israeli-born former commando, brother of a war hero, son of a leading historian, named Benjamin Netanyahu. Like others in the group, he decried the failures of the socialist model and worried that Israel would not be able to keep up with the IT revolution or the other trends reshaping the world economy.

While little progress on reform was made in the 1990s, from 2001 to 2003 Israel suffered the worst recession in its history. In 2003, Netanyahu took over as finance minister and launched an initiative called the Program for the Resuscitation of Israel's Economy. Its four main elements included "shrinking the public sector," "privatization and tax reform," "reforming monopolies and cartels," and "restructuring the Israeli capital market." By 2008, the Israeli public sector was down to being "just" 45 percent of GDP. And a period of unprecedented economic growth and stability followed.

While there is much debate about what worked, one area in which there is consensus is that Israel's ability to innovate played a central role. Today, Israel "has the highest number of start-ups in the world per capita, 3,850, or 1 for every 1,844 Israelis." Israel has more tech companies listed on the NASDAQ stock exchange than does all of Europe combined. Limited by its lack of raw materials, Israel has focused instead on its strong comparative advantages in the high-tech sector, becoming an important exporter of high-tech and IT goods and services. More than 40 percent of industrial output is now directed at exports, with about one-quarter of that being electronics and about one-half services exports pertaining to technology-intensive offerings.

Again, Israel, like Singapore and the UAE, was responding to world markets in a way a successful company might: adjusting its strategy, playing to its strengths, innovating. As an illustration, in the area of IT, in 2008,

Israel attracted VC (venture capital) investments thirty times greater than did Europe, and eighty times greater than China, on a per capita basis.

What's a Semi-State (or Ordinary Citizen) to Do?
or, Coping with the Post-Sovereign Reality

The example offered by the entrepreneurial states offers only a partial answer to the question of how semi-states must adapt in order to adjust to the new realities of the radically repopulated and still rapidly changing international system. In the same way, the stories of a few big companies flexing their muscles around the world and pushing around weakened nation-states in the process only partially describes the reality of a world in which the majority of countries are now smaller or less capable than perhaps two thousand very significant independent economic and political powerhouses. Furthermore, what has changed is still changing. Globalization, the proliferation of multinationals, continuing growth, and the redefinition of the whole idea of sufficient scale for companies, new technological breakthroughs, and the inevitable strengthening of international institutions will all serve as potent solvents for sovereignty.

In this "post-sovereign" environment, in which what sovereignty remains is more concentrated among a few big actors and less meaningful for most nations, in which nations and companies will be forced to collaborate and compete in a variety of ways in a broad number of different systems to achieve the goals of constituents and shareholders alike, we can expect, however, that some of the problems hinted at in this chapter will continue to dog the system and new ones will arise.

Among the pervasive challenges most likely to arise in this emerging international environment of states, semi-states, supercitizens, and the rest of us are:

- *Inequality*
  This will take various forms. The spread of free-market ideologies over the past several decades has seen both rising incomes for the poorest and worsening income inequality almost everywhere. Further, the inequalities in influence between major powers and semi-states is likely to grow, producing tensions and inequalities in markets between global megacorporations and smaller regional

competitors are also likely to result in consolidations and anticompetitive pressures.

- *Corruption and abuse*
  The combination of weak states, many impoverished and falling further behind, and large corporations that have the ability to evade legal consequences of their actions due to their resources or transnational status is likely to worsen corruption problems, particularly in the weakest of the semi-states.

- *Nationalism and backlash against globalization*
  We are already seeing it. If the system appears to promote inequality and provide unfair benefits to foreigners, backlash is inevitable. Not only will political nationalism be embraced by populists, but in a world of growing demand for scarce commodities, resource nationalism is likely to produce further tension and possible further reversals for liberalization of global markets.

- *Alienation of multinational corporations*
  If they are seen as entities without allegiance, they will increasingly be targets of populists, nationalists, and political opportunists.

- *Growing frustration with impotent national leaders*
  The uprisings in the Middle East in 2011 illustrate the shape this might take, as they were, at their core, uprisings of young, economically disenfranchised people seeking opportunities that they felt their governments were keeping from them.

- *Trade conflict*
  A weak trading system overburdened with cases, combined with divergent philosophies, backlash against globalization, and resource nationalism, could make the next decade one of the worst in modern memory in terms of trade conflict.

- *A continuing race to the bottom on taxes and labor costs before any hope of a rising tide*
  Supercitizens will continue to play states and semi-states against one another to gain economic advantage. They will succeed, and

states will see tax revenues squeezed and wages grow more slowly than expected.

- *More widespread embrace of national industrial policies and unfair competitive practices*
  This goes with the trade-conflict issue. A study my company conducted for the Business Roundtable on energy and climate competition worldwide showed twenty-three of twenty-five governments actively trying to partner with corporations to produce jobs and investment flows. The United States was the outlier, rejecting too big a role for governments in the marketplace.

- *Rogueism*
  Nuclear weapons were once called by Bill Clinton "North Korea's only cash crop." Pakistan too has gained U.S. support and attention due to a desire to support leaders who could control its nuclear stockpiles. Iran has gained international status and leverage by its mere pursuit of nuclear weapons. For marginalized semi-states with disaffected leaders, extreme bad behavior may be the only way to get attention or leverage. The easy and rapid spread of new technologies contributes to this problem, making formerly hard-to-manufacture weapons of mass destruction easier to fabricate, terrorist and black-market networks easier to support, and new tools for potential rogues, such as cyber-terrorism or warfare, increasingly available.

At the same time, states will need to constructively explore other options to enable them to better cope with this new reality, including:

- *New coalitions and alliances (including state-state and public-private)*
  For weaker states, the only strength will come from numbers. Regional alliances, alliances between like-minded countries, regional groupings, ad hoc collaborations around developing threats or opportunities: all will play a key role in this regard.

- *Strengthening international organizations and international law*
  Typically, political systems and systems of law arise to remedy perceived inequalities and to level the playing field. If the biggest states and companies are perceived as bending international systems to

serve them at the expense of others, strengthening the weak systems that currently exist may become a more popular option. This will require a change of outlook toward global governance. It must be recognized that empowering multilateral organizations to help, as only they can, in meeting the core demands of the social contract is not "ceding sovereignty upward." Rather, it is pooling sovereignty, sharing it in order to preserve it at the national level. Stronger global governance and government mechanisms are actually not the enemy of traditional national sovereignty on most transnational issues; they are its only hope.

- *Altering their strategic outlook, revising their worldview, adjusting structures accordingly*
  Acknowledging what has changed will, of course, be an especially good first step. Most states are not organized terribly well to collaborate effectively with other states, much less with private actors. Diplomacy has in the past been seen primarily as a form of communication, and periodically of cooperation, around pressing issues. But a new era of multilateralism will require multiple layers of government—supranational, national, and local—to work seamlessly together on a daily basis. At a moment in history when many developed powers are cutting back their international resources due to fiscal burdens, careful assessments of the difference between perceived and real savings must be undertaken. International burden sharing in all its forms will be an increasingly central way to leverage limited state resources in addressing shared problems. It may also play a role in next-generation government revenue generation—global governance will require resources, some of which may demand taxes or fees that are paid on a supranational basis. Beyond this, of course, new interfaces and strategies will be needed for states to interact with private actors as they must—whether it is to effectively regulate them in the global marketplace or to collaborate with them in combating new threats or seizing new opportunities.

The Reckoning That Lies Ahead

According to the *Oxford English Dictionary*, the word "international" only entered common usage in English in the late eighteenth century. Originally intended to refer to the law of nations, it emerged a century and a half after Westphalia had cemented the idea of nation-states as the primary political building blocks of global society.

As the term gained popularity, it gradually came to describe the full sweep of world affairs. Most of life's activity was contained within nations, and that which happened between them was seen primarily as the responsibility of those nations. The most significant interactions on the world stage were thus defined by the relationships among the governments representing individual countries.

Today, the term still describes a location where interactions take place—between nations—suggesting activities that cross borders on a map. But it no longer effectively describes the key players in such affairs. Even as the role of states is changing, they are being joined on the stage by new actors who will be as important as states to solving or exacerbating the problems of the century ahead.

Future developments, from how we manage the international economy to how we manage our environment, will turn on whether or not we are able to strike an appropriate balance between public and private centers of power, not just between states and businesses, but between companies that increasingly find they must meet responsibilities and address challenges once faced only by countries, and countries increasingly finding they must be as flexible and entrepreneurial as companies.

To strike such a balance will require not only new mechanisms but new attitudes and ideas—both at the supranational level and within nations. Whereas not too long ago it was thought that the answers had been found to the age-old debate about how to manage the rivalry between public and private actors—that in the wake of the cold war, the proto-capitalism of late-twentieth-century and early-twenty-first-century American market fundamentalists would prevail—crisis and change now suggest a different outcome.

A reckoning is on the horizon. Alternative approaches are gaining adherents and even a degree of coherence. While virtually all nations are offering variations on the capitalist theme, important distinctions between approaches remain, and those providing a more active role for government and private actors from outside the business world seem to be gaining the upper hand in both popularity and performance over the now doubted and discredited American model.

The final chapter of this book will briefly consider just how that reckoning is likely to come to pass.

11 ▪ Competing Capitalisms

Let me be frank: If we did not have the good points of the West
to guide us, we wouldn't have got out of our backwardness. We
would have been a backward economy with a backward society.
But we do not want all of the West.

—Lee Kwan Yew, Minister Mentor of Singapore, 1994

The widely held perception that excesses in U.S. financial markets and inadequate regulation were responsible [for the 2008
financial crisis] has increased criticism about free market policies,
which may make it difficult to achieve long-time U.S. objectives . . .
It already has increased questioning of U.S. stewardship of the
global economy and international financial structure.

—Admiral Dennis C. Blair, U.S. Director
of National Intelligence, 2009

There is a runestone in the fields near Vasteras in Sweden that tells of
Grimmundr, son of Viofastr. The characters etched into the stone are
colored red with the iron oxide that according to local legend also once
stained the horns of Kare the goat. The stone dates to roughly the time
mining began on the copper mountain. The inscription tells of a bridge
being constructed linking the area of Vasteras, later home of Stora Kopparberg shareholder Bishop Peter, to Dalarna.

Grimmundr, however, was part of Sweden's other great enterprise of
that era, one commemorated not only on hundreds of runestones that
dot the Swedish countryside, but via similar carvings that stretch from
Central Asia to North America. Grimmundr was a Viking warrior, and
according to the stone, he traveled, like most Swedish Vikings, to the
East. But take the totality of all Viking journeys around the world and
you have the greatest global enterprise undertaken in the world until that
date. Centuries before Genghis Khan, before the transpacific explorations

of China's great eunuch admiral Zheng He, before the West's "Age of Exploration" or today's global era, Viking ambition and courage were linking seemingly impossibly distant corners of the planet.

Nearby stones, such as the one near what remains of the church of Stora Rytterne, tell of destinations as far away as Khwarezm in what is today Uzbekistan. The Vikings were also known as "Rus," and they founded Kievan Rus, which later became Russia. They traded with the Khazars. They led raids into Baghdad. One Viking leader, Ingvar the Far-Travelled, was famous for his ill-fated expedition to the Caspian region, the last of its kind, that took place in the middle of the eleventh century. And they made a strong impression. An Arabic traveler described them by saying he had "never seen more perfect physical specimens, tall as date palms, blond and ruddy."

Their far-flung global enterprise was, in terms of the ideas to which this book has been devoted, both public and private. It was both entrepreneurial and as officially sanctioned as things got back then, around the turn of the first millennium, carefully planned yet necessarily largely improvised. It depended on the best seagoing transportation technologies of the time and large amounts of brute force. It required vision and was driven by a desperate instinct for survival. It won for most of its participants temporary victories in short, bloody lives. Glory came in the form of the songs of the skalds or the runes scratched into rough-hewn stones left scattered about the countryside.

For a Viking, or a goat farmer, or a miner to live to the age of forty in the year 1000 was a major triumph. It is thought that Ingvar's expedition was ravaged by disease to the point that there were no survivors. Hygiene was not a strong suit; baths were rare, shelters were crude and afforded little comfort from the extremes of the weather. Teens were effectively adults, and adulthood typically lasted just a decade or two. While Swedes enjoyed more independence than many in feudal Europe and did not really experience slavery or other ills common to the era, famine, ignorance, and hardship were daily companions.

In the knitting together of the world via the trade routes pioneered by those Vikings and in the creation of enterprises like the copper mine not far from the bridge referred to on the Vasteras runestone, seeds were planted, however, that have borne fruit we are enjoying to this day. In the thousand intervening years, the story of the rivalry between public and private power and how each has shaped the world and each other has been as far-fetched, hair-raising, and compelling as any sagas of the Vikings. But for all the great questions that story has raised and all the injustices that may be associated with it, one thing is certain: we are far better off today because of the rise of private enterprise and the evolution of government that—although it is a global phenomenon stretching back to the beginning of recorded history—also has such important roots in the rolling hills northwest of Stockholm.

In other words, while much of this book is devoted to exploring the tensions between public and private power, and in particular how we have come to a time when the balance between the two has clearly been lost in many parts of the world, we must be sure to frame any conclusions we draw in the context of the great benefits we continue to derive from the thriving markets and the advancing notions of modern government that distinguish our era from times past.

Virtually all the aspects of your daily life that place you at an advantage over poor Grimmundr, who almost certainly died a very unpleasant death somewhere in "the East," owe some credit to products, processes, or champions of the marketplace. Virtually every major new technology, the breakthroughs in agriculture that have largely defeated famine, the rise of incomes, rising levels of education and understanding, and the diffusion of culture have roots in the rise of modern business.

Similarly, we need to note that most of the innovations that business helped spur were enabled by the actions of governments, beyond laws and regulations, via underwriting highways, canals, railways, and airports, via providing schools and hospitals and security.

More broadly speaking, the greatest mistake we could make in our interpretation of the history briefly covered by this book would be to fall prey to oversimplifications. Businesses are, for the most part, more powerful than ever, larger than ever, with greater global reach than ever. Supercitizens have emerged as a new class of significant players on the international stage. But they are not all-powerful, and the character of the power they possess is much different from that of states. States have lost some of the traditional powers they had; but all of them, even the weakest of semi-states, maintain some prerogatives, some ability to enforce the law, some ability to apply force, some control over their borders or their economy. And sometimes, as in the case of rogue states mentioned in the last chapter, some are using new technologies and strategies to remain relevant actors—much as weak states and political players have done throughout history.

Our study of the history of the relationship between business and government should leave us certain that we would not want to turn back the hands of time, that the evolution of the mechanisms of both government and business has been essential to the story of the progress we rightly celebrate, that the issues we face today have deep roots, and that fairness requires a subtler eye than the knee-jerk reflexes of contemporary litmus-test politics often allow for.

Nonetheless, as we look for patterns among the developments of the past thousand years, clear conclusions of immediate relevance do emerge. Perhaps foremost among these is that time and time again, when either public or private actors gain too much influence over the other or over society as a whole, the public at large suffers, sometimes grievously. What the past two decades have shown with striking clarity is that government overreach as embodied in Soviet communism crushed the economic life and spirit out of a great nation, while market overreach as embodied in America's recent reign of unchecked financial and corporate greed can send even the world's richest nation hurtling toward fiscal crisis, social division, and diminishing influence on the global stage.

The question we should consider is not, as some modern politicians implicitly or explicitly frame it, whether business or government is good or whether one is relatively better than the other. The more salient and constructive question is what roles we want business and government to play in society, and this in turn forces us to ask what goals we have for society in the first place.

Once nation-states exclusively possessed the right and responsibility to answer these questions for themselves, and undoubtedly today they maintain central roles in that regard. But even as nations seek to address such core issues, they must do so with the awareness that historical forces such as those manifested under the broad rubric of globalization are changing the ground rules that define the options available to states. Some issues require regional or global efforts. Some issues are beyond the reach of most states. While the available options are different for major powers and for semi-states, the arrival on the scene of supercitizens, powerful stateless global private actors, alters further the possible coalitions that may seek to influence each outcome.

So, for this era, we also need to consider what has changed and what has not. What choices are being made by peoples and governments, and how do they impact the choices made by private actors? How are these different choices likely to impact one another? And finally, we need to ask what we ought to hope and work for, what our era ought to contribute to this vital, unending debate.

A Shining but Isolated Moment

Other than students of political science or philosophy, few people today spend much time thinking about how societies ought to be organized. Fewer still ask why we even organize them in the first place. But clearly, with or without public debate or even much thought, citizens of every country of the world, leaders in every kind of enterprise, take steps that provide de facto answers. Actions are taken. Results occur. Institutions and laws and regulations and budgets and consequently economies and societies are made and remade. The problem is that too often, too few people have any say in those decisions, and of those, too few have given much thought to the consequences of their actions for average people.

And while the role of countries is changing, it is still the political and economic decisions made within the largest and most influential of those countries that lead global opinions and drive global actions. In each case, based on the system in place within those countries, the way in which the public, their representatives, and private actors influence outcomes is different. But each case also produces outcomes that drive, inspire, and provoke opinion leaders in other nations.

In other words, in the global marketplace of ideas, the stock of some systems is always rising and the stock of other systems is falling. We have seen this throughout history as ideas cross borders and are embraced or rejected, as some countries blaze trails and others follow. The Reformation and the Enlightenment and the Industrial Revolution and the Information Age are all names we give to periods in which a few key ideas, often spurred by geopolitical and economic swings of fortune and often triggered by the advent of new technologies, catch on and set the tone for an era. Throughout history other waves, smaller, also momentous—from the adoption of paper money to the embrace of the idea of limited liability corporations—also begin in one corner of the world or another and then catch on, both changing the planet and indicating to observers which innovators are setting the course for their times.

For the past century, certainly from the First World War onward but likely for several decades before that, given the importance of the rise of American industrialists like Rockefeller and Morgan, the United States has been the undisputed leader in terms of advancing one vision of how societies ought to be organized. Free-market capitalism plus democracy was the simplified formula, with the recipe differing from generation to generation. For most of that century an alternative view, that of communism, primarily of the Soviet type, was promoted as an option in which equity came not from the free choice of individuals but from the actions of a state entrusted with responsibility for planning a future that would be best for most of the people.

First the Soviet version collapsed from its own weight and the profound flaws in its approaches—from the failure of central planning to the inability of closed societies to compete effectively in a world in which the free flow of information was the oxygen on which economies depended in order to grow.

America was triumphant, and then, as often happens, it misinterpreted its victory. It assumed that its triumphs were primarily due to its own virtues rather than to the weaknesses of its enemy. And it then misidentified those virtues to the point that American capitalism became almost a parody of itself—at the same time that professional American athletes were using steroids to pump themselves up to cartoonish dimensions, American businesspeople were blazing new trails in excess and using their unprecedented wealth to gain new license to behave ever more excessively. America was not alone in this—financial capitals and corporate suites around the world saw similar displays. But it was the American example they were following, and, as indicated in the epigraph from Admiral Dennis Blair at the outset of this chapter, the America example is what they were discrediting.

In history it is impossible to tell for decades whether any particular period, regardless of how fraught or momentous it may seem at the time, is a true turning point, whether its spirit or its ideas will endure. Clearly, the years 1648, 1776, and 1848 were, in retrospect, such watersheds. Were the 1970s, when we saw currencies delinked from gold, a backlash against the New Deal, the accelerated rise of both multinational corporations and income inequality, and the forces that triggered the beginning of the end of communism, such a watershed? Perhaps.

In retrospect, it also seems possible that the 1990s and the first decade of the twenty-first century mark one of those turning points. It was a period that began with the end of Soviet communism and what was then perceived as "the end of history," and ended approximately seventeen years later with a financial earthquake that ended all that "end of history" talk as well as the notion of ever-ascendant America, hyperpower and ideological beacon.

In the early days of the period, a time of comparative economic euphoria in the United States, we didn't see the ways in which destructive forces within U.S. markets were being unleashed, inequalities exacerbated, and new powers like China, India, and Brazil unleashed to rise to relative importance they hadn't enjoyed for a century and three-quarters. The market triumphalism of that period, while capturing an important dimension of what America's cold war victory had meant, paid too little heed to the challenges that were coming next, assumed that too much of what seemed true in the moment would endure.

Clarity would come with the economic and political upheavals of the early twenty-first century: America bogged down in wars in the Middle East it could not afford and battered by economic crises it should have foreseen and forestalled but did not, the BRICs rising, Europe and Japan struggling to reinvent themselves. September 11, 2001, suggested that non-state actors could pose a destabilizing challenge even in the era of a seemingly unassailable sole superpower. But from an ideological perspective, from the point of view of how the world viewed itself and the question of how it should organize itself, the shocks associated with the financial crises of 2008 and 2009 were far more important than that devastating September day in which seventeen acres of Lower Manhattan were laid to waste.

After the financial crises, observers raised on a bipolar ideological diet pitting capitalism against communism saw no less than a turning point in public opinion on the purpose of the state and the role of markets. Both the "too much state" of Soviet communism and the "too much market" of American capitalism had been revealed to be deeply flawed (although the flaws of Soviet communism proved to be fatal, while American capitalism contains the means to identify and remedy its own weaknesses).

"We had grown so cynical of Marxist talk of the contradictions of capitalism," Peter Jay commented to the BBC in September 2008, "because

Marxism itself had, by the 1970s, so conspicuously failed—while capitalism thrived—that its acolytes were discredited." "The post–Cold War period," wrote one columnist for London's *Guardian* newspaper, gave rise to "another utopian ideology . . . a type of market fundamentalism became the guiding philosophy." Thus, he wrote, also in a statement shot through with post-traumatic-stress-induced overstatement, "in a change as far-reaching in its implications as the fall of the Soviet Union, an entire model of government and the economy has collapsed." *The New York Times* wrote during the crisis that it is "certainly not too soon to look beyond the current crisis to the flaws and fallacies of the anti-regulatory ideology that has held Washington in its grip since the Reagan years . . . The nation needs a new perspective on the markets, one that acknowledges the self-destructive bent of unfettered capitalism." Two days later, across the ocean, Tony Benn wrote that "there will be a big demand for a major policy change. This is a failure of a system where we relied on the markets and excluded government. And the markets failed."

America's European allies and the spokespeople for rising powers from China to India questioned aloud, and in stark and inflammatory terms, whether the American model had been undone. In 2008, the German finance minister Peter Steinbruck predicted, "The U.S. will lose its status as the superpower of the world financial system. This world will become multipolar . . . The world will never be the same again . . . When we look back 10 years from now, we will see 2008 as a fundamental rupture." French president Nicolas Sarkozy in April 2009 stated at a G20 summit that "the all-powerful market that is always right is finished" and argued that "the page has been turned" on Anglo-American capitalism. Perhaps more surprisingly, the British Conservative shadow chancellor of the exchequer George Osbourne joined the chorus of doubters when he repudiated the foundational premise of the Anglo-American model that free markets are always efficient and therefore government should just get out of the way. Even Alan Greenspan admitted that his "belief in deregulation had been shaken," undermining his lifelong view that "government regulators were no better than markets at imposing discipline."

In the search for solutions, all manner of ideas were floated and embraced. It seemed clear that a new era of international collaboration and perhaps new institutions was called for. The G8 morphed into the G20 and stepped to the center of the crisis. *The Economist* noted that central-bank policies "would be more powerful if coordinated. But it is not only central banks [that] need to combine." National governments would have to work together too: "Even if, as the Europeans claim, the crisis was made in America it now belongs to everyone." The BBC saw the changes as a watershed, stating that a "new world order emerges from the chaos" and noting that "slowly the shape of the world after financial flood is beginning to emerge. The first thing to be said is that everyone is in the same boat. And they have to bail together." The article announced a "new superpower diplomacy—not East versus West, nor a return to the disastrous maneuvering of the late nineteenth century of the 1930s, but the management of relationships within better agreed rules."

The obvious question then was what those rules would be. Would the old rules be tossed aside? For a moment, it looked as if they might. Massive government stimulus programs amounting to hundreds of billions or trillions of dollars of intervention were announced in the United States, the European Union, Japan, and China. Smaller countries offered smaller programs. New coordinating mechanisms were bruited. Market reforms were debated. Where seemingly needed, in the United States for example, the government stepped in and bailed out automakers and financial institutions.

Within short order a predictable backlash occurred. The world and the president of the United States had embraced "socialism," and "statism" was on the rise. Everything from a U.S. debate about how to provide health care more efficiently, to a population that was both overburdened with costs and had major segments who were without care altogether, to the rise of China, was interpreted as a sign that more than reform was afoot, that an ideological swing back to the ideas of the 1930s was taking place. Whether those ideas were the ideas of Franklin Roosevelt, John Maynard Keynes, or Leon Trotsky depended on how hysterical the backlash critic was. With the passage of months, the voices calling for reform and those warning against it still hang in the air, shifting shapes as the arguments bounce from U.S. Tea Party spokespeople on the right to anti-establishment protesters from Cairo to Athens to London to cities across the United States. Pundits and more thoughtful observers alike are seeking to make sense of the swirling forces buffeting world leaders, trying to understand which are meaningful and will have lasting consequences and which will prove evanescent and spin off into the air like the whirlwinds of an afternoon dust storm.

Clearly, it is my view that a look to history provides better answers to what the long-term trends are, the forces that are in play, and the questions that need to be addressed than does listening to campaign rhetoric, scrolling through blogs, or reading opinion columns. It lets us better see many sides of key issues—the technological, social, and economic benefits introduced by the rise of markets and their limitations. We can talk about who is commanding the economic heights, but when we study how they got there, we find we must ask: Have they also taken the commanding heights of the polity? Is that a good thing? We can see the great benefits of the spread of democracy worldwide at ground level and the equivalent value of the spread of entrepreneurship and the opportunities created by the capitalist system, but we also see that democracy is being forsaken at several strata above ground level by the concentration of enormous power in the hands of a few supercitizens who increasingly have zero allegiance to any nation-state.

There has been a decoupling of the interests of supercitizens and those of the ordinary people around them, between those who represent the views of people who must necessarily live within borders and those for whom borders no longer have meaning, between those who require jobs and capital flows and those who view people, villages, cities, and states as economic options, part of a constantly changing calculus in which efficiencies and profits rule. At the same time, those supercitizens and their ideological and political allies and champions (often the beneficiaries of their largesse) have falsely conflated economic growth with economic well-being. Metrics that aggregate and hide inequality, such as GDP, are embraced over those that reflect better the real and variant conditions within a society. Meanwhile increasingly as state power has been eroded and transnational challenges have grown, the question arises of how public interests are served and private ones are effectively and appropriately channeled and counterbalanced. Institutions are changing more slowly than the environment in which they operate. Both national and international mechanisms for translating the public will into action are inadequate to the moment.

The Marketplace of Ideas Works Slowly

If there is a lesson to the historical study of these issues, it is that even as financial marketplaces accelerate to such a pace that major actors make hundreds of millions of assessments and decisions a day and commercial marketplaces are rapidly evolving to suit a complex global reality, the marketplace of ideas moves much more slowly. Even revolutions as they arise—whether in 1776, 1789, 1848, or 2011—while seeming to produce swift and dramatic upheaval, can mislead. The French Revolution produced a stunningly different world overnight, yet within little more than a decade France was coping with a new kind of monarch. Eighteen forty-eight touched many of the most important capitals of Europe, blowing through like a violent summer storm, leaving scars and disorder, but the ideological shifts it promised were slow to take root.

Thus, the upheavals of the past two decades—the fall of communism, the stunning blow of 9/11, the shock of financial crises from the emerging world in the late 1990s to the bursting of the tech bubble to the collapse of Bear Sterns, Lehman Brothers, and AIG to the Eurozone's debt troubles—hint at changes that may be afoot but do not answer long-term questions about where we are headed in the way that newspaper headlines may have suggested they did.

That is going to be worked out in the marketplace of ideas, and the process that will resolve it will be, as it has been in the past, a struggle among competing systems. The past two decades have not only seen the fall of communism and a blow to the appeal of market fundamentalism, they have also seen a worldwide embrace of the idea that markets play an important role in all societies. While American capitalism did not triumph per se, capitalism did. But that clearly did not mean the end of ideological tensions in the world. With the crises of the past decade in the United States, Japan, and parts of Europe and the rise of emerging powers around the world, with some of the fastest-growing states—like China—involving considerable state control and some of the most resilient in the developed world—as in Germany and other countries in Northern Europe—featuring very different ideas about how government, business, and labor should collaborate, it is clear that this competition will not just turn on the issue of how to balance the roles of public and private power, but will determine just what that balance is and how it is to be achieved for decades to come.

The upheaval of the immediate post–cold war era behind us, we are now entering an era of competing capitalisms. Political scientists who were early observers of this phenomenon include Peter Hall and David Soskice, who, in 2001, published *Varieties of Capitalism: The Institutional*

Foundations of Comparative Advantage. Since the idea first emerged, though, the nature of that competition and the view of America's place within it have changed markedly.

Five Capitalisms: If Not America's Model, Then Whose?

One of the models to compete, of course, will be the American model, bloodied but unbowed. Judging from the debates prevailing in Washington in the first years of the second decade of the new century, old ideologies die hard. One political party in the United States, the Republicans, have as a central tenet of their philosophy the idea that government should be rolled back wherever possible. "Big government" means regulations, taxes, numbers of federal employees, the federal budget as a percentage of GDP. The other party, the Democrats, while more comfortable with government programs, are nonetheless reluctant to offer an opposing view to that of the Republicans. They tend to compromise, in part because they too are heavily dependent on the financing provided by large corporate and financial interests, much as the Republicans are. There are no moves presently afoot to reform campaign finance in the United States to help address this problem. In the run-up to the 2012 presidential elections, the incumbent U.S. president's advisers have told him that he will have to raise $750 million to $1 billion to hold on to the office he already has. That kind of money can only be achieved through close ties with centers of private power that in turn advocate for the U.S. "government-lite" approach to capitalism. A fault line in the current U.S. debate can nonetheless be seen in the disagreement over whether America's recovery will best be triggered—as Republicans argue—by cutting back government to reduce the bloated U.S. federal deficit or whether, as some Democrats assert, the answer is more government spending and involvement in major infrastructure and other job-creating programs. It is, however, all a matter of nuance within the traditional American "Lockean liberal" ideal that government should stay out of people's affairs whenever possible. Neither side advocates government-controlled industrial policies or broadly expanded social safety nets or greater government involvement in the day-to-day affairs of business and markets, as might be found in other countries.

While virtually every nation offers its own variation on capitalism, several are associated with countries that are so big or influential that their approaches are likely to be the prime contenders when it comes to vying with the United States to produce the ideas that will shape twenty-first century political and economic philosophies and practices. One of these is the world's most populous country, its fastest-growing major economy, an economy that is likely to pass that of the United States in size in purchasing-power-parity terms by 2016 and in real terms by 2030. That country is China, and in many respects its system, because of its roots in communism and central planning, is the most radically different among the leading versions of capitalism. In fact, in China, it has been referred to as "socialism with Chinese characteristics," which translates in the eyes of many others as "capitalism with Chinese characteristics." Called everything from "bamboo capitalism" (by *The Economist*) to "authoritarian capitalism" by its critics, it is a rapidly and somewhat chaotically evolving hybrid encompassing everything from wildly underregulated, intensively competitive and entrepreneurial "cowboy capitalist" enclaves to five-year plans and the heavy hand of government direction and ownership of major enterprises that recalls traditional socialism.

Other developing economies come at the issue of public-private balance from a different perspective, although many of the most important, including the other three BRICs, Brazil, India, and Russia, are all much more comfortable with a major role for the state in their economies than are traditional developed economies. Setting aside the Russian example as being too idiosyncratic, corrupt, and authoritarian to win broad support, you are left with the Indian and Brazilian models, which share some important similarities. Called by the Indians "democratic development capitalism" and referred to by Lawrence Summers as forming the core of an emerging Delhi consensus to rival the Washington consensus of the 1980s, 1990s, and early 2000s, this approach recognizes the special needs of developing societies for an active government role in addressing the social, economic, and political requirements of massive populations of historically disenfranchised citizens while seeking to harness the energizing qualities of the marketplace. The third major alternative is what once was called Eurosocialism, best exemplified among large states by the German example. Germany has outperformed not only all the other major countries of Europe but all the world's leading developed economies in the swiftness of its recovery from the economic crisis of 2008–2009. In fact, so robust was its recovery that as the Eurozone faced a crisis due to the fiscal failings of several countries in its southern tier (Greece, Portugal, and Spain), Germany was seen as the indispensable economy of the entire European Union, the locomotive all were looking to for power. But Germany is not the only example of an approach to capitalism that involves a strong social safety net, an active role for government in promoting business, and a unique collaborative relationship between business, government, and labor. Sweden is another fine example, demonstrating that reports of the death of the European model were, to paraphrase Mark Twain, greatly exaggerated. Finally, there is a fourth important non-U.S. variation on capitalism from states that are not large but are nonetheless influential because of the success they have achieved. These states were dealt with in the "countries behaving like companies" section in the last chapter. They are the entrepreneurial states, small countries with vibrant economies responding to an active government role—although with varying degrees of government intervention in markets. In addition to Singapore, the United Arab Emirates, and Israel, countries as diverse as Chile and Lithuania might also be included in this group.

Other models are also influential to varying degrees. The size of Japan's economy gives it prominence, but unfortunately, since the mid-1990s, so does its dysfunctionality. South Korea's success has led it to grow to be one of the few strong examples of a developing country that "graduated" to first-world status. But it is small, and it is likely soon to face unique challenges associated with absorbing the remnants of a failed north. South Africa is especially influential in Africa. Turkey is influential but anomalous in the Middle East due to its size, proximity to Europe, and trade- rather than resource-based economy. Other important states such as Nigeria, Egypt, and Mexico are far too troubled to set examples for anyone.

So it seems most likely at this point that much as approaches to the Reformation that came from England, France, Germany, Holland, and Scandinavia vied with one another to shape the standards of the era, so too will it be that ideas on how to balance public and private power in the twenty-first century are likely to come from one of these four schools of thinking if they do not come from the United States.

To determine which ideas may prevail, rather than viewing this as a zero-sum contest in which one will win and the others will lose, we should instead ask how these approaches are the same, how they are different, and how their similarities and differences are likely to be reflected in action. This is particularly necessary given that, as we have already established, the limitations of national power in terms of addressing global challenges will require in the next several decades ever greater collaboration among nations and the creation of stronger global governance mechanisms. The rules and values of those institutions are likely to be shaped by these groups as well, and thus how this competition plays out is likely to end up determining the shape and mandates of those new entities (or the evolving shape of existing entities from the G20 to the international financial institutions or the World Trade Organization and others).

"Capitalism with Chinese Characteristics"

It is easy to understand the escalating interest in and influence of the Chinese model. Since China began economic reforms in the late 1970s, perhaps 400 million Chinese have been lifted out of poverty. The country has averaged double-digit annual growth rates for almost two decades. In 2010 it passed Japan to become the world's second-largest economy. It may become the world's largest in nominal terms by 2020. It holds the world's largest reserves of foreign capital, with the total now exceeding $3 trillion.

China is home to the most dynamic economy in the world. Yet beyond descriptions of the scope and speed of its growth, the Chinese economy defies easy description. On the one hand, China is still nominally communist, working from five-year plan to five-year plan with the government playing an active and sometimes heavy-handed role in the affairs not only of state-owned companies but of foreign companies seeking a share of its burgeoning market. Plans passed by the National People's Congress are implemented by economic authorities coordinated by the State Council.

The state is the architect and chief funder of major initiatives in areas as diverse as new energy technologies (in which China has outspent the rest of the world together over the past three years) to building a new transportation infrastructure to acquiring critical natural resources through neomercantilist deals around the world. The state is also the entity that demands and typically wins major investments and technology transfers from would-be foreign entrants into the economy. Yet since the reforms initiated by Deng Xiaoping, the role of the state in the economy has shrunk dramatically. While the state still plays a larger role in the Chinese economy than in any other major economy by far, companies that are not majority owned by the state account for two-thirds of output. These companies are also responsible for the lion's share of profits in the economy, and according to one South Korean estimate, they contribute almost three-quarters of Chinese GDP.

State-owned enterprises have steadily seen their share of assets, profits, and sales in the economy decline over the past several decades, to the point that in each category they represent a minority share. Further, while the Chinese government can be heavy-handed in negotiations and brutal in enforcing its laws, it is also extremely haphazard in enforcing those laws. While this approach has a name suggesting it is part of a plan, "one eye open, one eye shut," observers suggest that this approach not only exacerbates some of the greatest weaknesses in the Chinese economy, such as financial mismanagement and lack of transparency, it also is indicative of one part of the "system" that is not very systematic. China is just growing too fast for the government to keep up. This "riding the tiger" element of China's government involvement in the private sector is complemented by another contradiction: social programs that are so limited in their benefits to citizens that the country is constantly facing the potential of massive unrest—with more than 180,000 demonstrations reported in the last year alone. While such problems and challenges associated with rapid growth and a constantly evolving rule book have led observers like the editors of *The Economist* to conclude that "'capitalism with Chinese characteristics' works because of the capitalism, not the characteristics," this assessment deliberately downplays the further contradiction that China's leaders have, for three decades, defied the predictions of their critics by making central planning work in very effective way, driving the most profound economic transformation ever seen by such a large population over such a short period of time.

Indian and Brazilian "Democratic Development Capitalism"
One clear way that China's economic values and policies are gaining influence is through the integration of China into the core discussions of leading global economies. This began in November 2008 when President George W. Bush in mid–economic crisis convened not a meeting of the traditional powers of the G8 but of a new, more broadly inclusive group that included China: the G20. While getting China to the table was clearly the primary reason for this approach, the rising economic weight of other emerging powers like Brazil and India was also a factor in the decision.

The subsequent intensification of coordination of the policies and activities of the four BRICs has added to this group's influence on the global stage as have related efforts to collaborate with additional mid-level emerging powers such as South Africa and Turkey. Both countries have also, beginning notably with their collaboration at the World Trade Organization ministerial in Cancún in 2003, played a much more active role in international diplomacy, seeking to advance their national interest and to anchor developing world coalitions on issues as diverse as climate change talks, reforms at international institutions, nuclear non-proliferation, and even key elements of Mideast diplomacy. That said, the differences among the BRICs are as significant as their similarities. Most notably, India and Brazil are, unlike China, democracies, thus giving their citizenry a much more direct say in how they balance public and private interests. India is a regional rival of China's with a long history of border tensions, and Brazil, while much more closely engaged with China via trade and investment (China is Brazil's number-one trading partner, surpassing the United States), has had significant disagreements with the Chinese over monetary policies.

At the same time, differences with U.S. capitalism are also deep, with both India and Brazil possessing strong socialist and socially activist political parties and with both, like China, necessarily heavily focused on their great development challenges. Four hundred million Indians, for example, still live without regular access to electricity. Fifty million Brazilians, almost a third of the population, live below the poverty line. While Brazil is now the world's eighth-largest economy and will be fifth within a decade, it ranks 73rd on the Human Development Index. While India is currently the world's tenth-largest economy and fourth in purchasing power parity terms and may be nominally the third largest by 2030, it ranks 121st. (China ranks 89th, the United States 4th, Norway first, Sweden ninth, Germany tenth, Israel 15th, Singapore 27th.)

An illustration of the engagement of the Brazilian government in social issues is the Bolsa Familia program introduced under the administration of Luiz Inácio Lula da Silva. The program is the world's largest conditional cash transfer program and involves aid to poor Brazilian families to ensure proper health care, education, and the development of human capital. The program is credited with playing a central role in helping to reduce Brazilian poverty, which fell from 22 percent to 7 percent during the Lula administration. Lula, a socialist, saw fighting poverty at home and abroad as one of his principal missions, but in a break with Brazilian political dogma of decades past, he also actively maintained liberal market policies that helped ensure continued foreign investment in Brazil that reached record levels by the time he left office. Again, as in China, what is seen is a mix between activist government and a respect for the power of markets. Certain key enterprises, notably the oil company Petrobras, are still owned and controlled by the state. However, the complexity of such "mixed" systems was illustrated to me in a conversation with a former Lula cabinet minister who told me he once complained to Lula that when he went to Petrobras to seek aid for an important national priority, management argued that because they had private shareholders they could not comply, but that on other occasions they would argue, if it suited them, they were limited in their ability to cooperate due to the constraints on them as a state-owned company.

In a speech in Mumbai in 2010, Larry Summers argued that India's approach to balancing its public and private interests would actually be a more attractive model to the world than the view promulgated in Washington or Beijing. Summers cited India's "peoplecentric" policies and its focus on stimulating consumption rather than exports, saying that within decades, "the discussion will be less about the Washington consensus and the Beijing consensus than the Mumbai consensus." In part, his views were linked to an Obama administration effort to draw closer to India and to offer its democratic model as a counterweight to China in Asia. But in part they were linked to a broader sense that thanks to its democratic heritage, and in part thanks to systems and cultural attitudes that date to the years of the British East India Company and have prepared India for an active, outward-looking role in the global economy, many feel that it will not be long before India's approach places it ahead of China both in growth rate and in the appeal of its system to the world.

In several important elements of the Indian economy, from nuclear power to other energy resources to manufacturing enterprises like Hindustan Aeronautics or Hindustan Machine Tools, India also still has a shrinking but notable group of "public sector undertakings," state-owned companies that are indicative of the fact that the Indian government continues to feel that for both security and development reasons it is sometimes necessary for the public sector (either at the national, state, or territorial level) to play an active role in the management of business activities.

The roots of this approach are in the almost four and a half decades of social democratic policies that guided India immediately upon gaining independence. But the evolution of the approach since 1991 to one with greater market freedoms has made India the world's second-fastest-growing major economy after China. A failed experiment in Fabian socialism (which at one point produced the world's highest income taxes) was replaced by a system that saw widespread regulatory reforms and much greater financial liberalization. The economy has opened to the world after having spent much of its first half century as a closed economy (no doubt in some respects reeling from the injuries associated with its exploitation at the hands of the BEIC). It also has taken the lead not only in striking its own public-private balance but in developing its own approaches to the development of industries. This includes what one leading Indian businessman has referred to as "Gandhian engineering"—which he characterizes as basing pricing and product development models on the needs of the population of poor average Indians. This has produced cell phones that are available for pennies per month and the world's cheapest car, the Nano, and thus has imbued the public-private climate in India with a very different ethos and set of metrics.

German, French, and Scandinavian "Eurocapitalism"
In earlier sections of this book, we have considered briefly examples of how modern Swedish economics has evolved to encompass social programs that ensure workers of a safe haven when confronted with the volatility of international markets and at the same time create a consequently greater willingness to embrace the risks associated with freer trade and entrepreneurship. Similarly, during Sweden's financial crisis of the 1990s, the government did not just bail out banks as in the United States, but because it was more comfortable with a public sector role, it demanded bank equity in exchange for its investment, thus ensuring a return for the Swedish people for putting tax dollars at risk and an incentive for banks to pay down their obligations as quickly as possible. (In the United States no such guarantees were made for returns, and although most Wall Street bailout funds have been recouped, massive U.S. government guarantees remain in place, thus putting taxpayers at risk in the event of another sudden market downturn.) Said the former Swedish deputy finance minister Bo Lundgren, "If I go into a bank, I'd rather get equity so that there is some upside for the taxpayer." And the Swedish

government went into banking with a vengeance at the time, at one point dedicating about 4 percent of Swedish GDP to its banking rescue and controlling over 20 percent of the entire banking system.

Through such approaches, the Eurosocialist impulses Americans once derided as a backward drag on Europe's economies have actually propelled a number of them to considerable growth and ensured their stability. In fact, as such approaches indicate, more active government policies may actually be better suited to dealing with the dislocations and pressures associated with active exposure to the global marketplace. And even as Europe has been buffeted by crisis, many European states have prospered, showing economic resilience while balancing both notable fiscal prudence and achieving a high enough quality of life that they top world rankings of this attribute.

No country is a more prominent or influential example of the renewed relevance and appreciation for the European model than Germany. This is not just because it is Europe's largest economy. It is also because, in the words of David Leonhardt of *The New York Times*, "despite its reputation for austerity, Germany has been far more willing than the United States to use the power of government to help its economy. Yet, it also has been more ruthless about cutting wasteful parts of government." Had Germany not outstripped the United States in growth since 2005, these observations would have less impact. But they also have resonance because not only did Germany outperform the United States in its top-line numbers, but average Germans benefited more from the growth than their U.S. counterparts. While income inequality in the United States has been hitting new highs, average German wages have grown five times as fast as those in America over the past quarter century.

Part of the reason for Germany's success with its workforce, at a time when the number of Americans working has actually contracted over a decade for the first time in our history, was that the German government got actively involved, revamped unemployment practices, and went to work finding ways to better place German workers in suitable jobs. German education programs were also beefed up so that as America plummeted on international math and science skills, German performance rose. Also, German regulators have been much tougher with German financial institutions, requiring greater capital reserves. Finally, Germany has worked to maintain a strong voice for labor in its economy, both by including labor unions on corporate boards (which has worked well for the companies and the unions) and by ensuring that workers themselves remain competitive and well paid. Nothing has undercut the influence of American unions like the collapse of American manufacturing. And while some might say that it was the unreasonable demands of unions that brought about that collapse, it could just as easily be argued that efforts to roll back the government's ability to keep America's education system, infrastructure, and other competitive factors up to global standards played as great or a greater role in that respect.

The German government has also been unhesitating, like the governments in virtually all the other examples cited here, to promote its businesses internationally. Here American business interests have suffered from their own success (or believing their own press releases). American businesses wanted government out of markets, and American capitalist theoreticians wanted America to avoid "industrial policy" like the plague. But the rest of the world didn't get the memo. So Germany spends roughly thirty times as much as the United States promoting exports and similar amounts seeking foreign direct investment. As Jacob Kirkegaard of the Peterson Institute in Washington said in an interview with *The Washington Post*, "There's a pervasive sense in the United States that government and the economy are supposed to be completely distinct and separate realms. During a deep recession, the fact that you have a more activist government has some advantages." Of course, as we have noted, even prior to the recession, Germany—now home to the world's number-four economy—was outperforming the United States in wage growth, education, and training and providing a strong social safety net for workers. Said the former Obama official Jared Bernstein, also to the *Post*, "It is true that other countries are more comfortable with this thing called 'industrial policy.' If you accuse Germans of practicing industrial policy, I'm not sure [Chancellor Merkel] would automatically take it as an insult. Over here . . . we just don't like the words."

The German model is also worthy of note because, unlike any of the other models, it is actually part of a regional model that has involved ceding significant national sovereignty to a supranational power, the European Union. The boldness of what Germany did should not be underestimated. It controlled one of the world's most respected currencies and gave up that control to participate in the Eurozone. While the Eurozone experiment has undergone deep stresses as a result of the fiscal crises of Greece, Portugal, and other countries, as of this writing it seems likely that it will not only survive but that in order to avoid similar problems in the future, Europe's monetary union will have to be complemented by a true fiscal union. If that is the case, and the countries of the region commit to living within common fiscal guidelines and to bearing responsibility for one another's missteps, it will only be because Europe's largest economy has decided that the costs of allowing the euro experiment to fail are too great. This vision that the role of the state is actually enhanced through ceding some sovereignty to supranational entities could have major implications in a world in which so many semi-states will be looking for collaborative mechanisms to enhance their influence and regain some control over their destiny that their current status is less likely to provide.

Singaporean "Entrepreneurial Small-Market Capitalism"

We have described what sets apart countries like Singapore, Israel, and the UAE in the previous chapter. It is true that these economies have the advantage of being small. It is also true, as many note, that their small size may mean that the lessons drawn from their successes—particularly those associated with their nimbleness, the role of government officials in managing aspects of the state very much as though they were managing a large corporation—are not broadly applicable. But first, there are many small economies that could benefit from applying their lessons (much as the economies of the Baltic countries have done in the years since the fall of communism and much as a Palestinian state might once it is established). And next, as Singapore has shown, the skills of the city-state in managing city-sized development issues in places like Suzhou in China, where Singapore has effectively exported its urban planning know-how, can work successfully within larger national economies and thus play the kind of influential role that warrants the inclusion of these entrepreneurial small-market capitalists on this list.

While this competition among capitalisms will produce relative winners and losers, it is unlikely to produce the absolute triumph of one view over another. As noted, what may work for small entrepreneurial states like the UAE, Israel, or Singapore almost certainly will not work for the mega-states of the emerging world like the BRICs. What will work in a China fixated for five thousand years on maintaining internal stability and founded on Confucian values regarding family and community will not work in nearby India, with its democratic and multicultural traditions. What may work on the southern fringes of the Eurozone will surely differ from what may work in Germany or Scandinavia. For some parts of the world, regional integration may help offset the weakness of semi-states. On some issues such as trade or the environment or regulation of global financial markets to a common standard, stronger international institutions are the only possible way to preserve national interests. They don't pose a threat to sovereignty, but rather offer the only option for sovereigns seeking to maintain influence over what ultimately does happen within their borders.

For most of the world, the balance between public and private power will be struck in a way in which the state plays the crucial role that only it can play as the institutional power center charged with serving the public interest. That role is virtually certain to be larger and more activist than it has been in the touted U.S. ideal for the past three decades. In fact, it is likely to be more like the role the U.S. government has historically played, whether it was through the interventions that helped create the railroads or those that led to the national highway system or the birth of the Internet.

The fact that virtually every other form of capitalism "on the market" has significantly greater roles for the state than advocated in and by the United States suggests that not only is the U.S. view unlikely to prevail, but indeed the momentum is actually with the alternatives. They are growing faster, they are combating inequality more effectively, they are competing more tenaciously, and they are protecting their people against the volatility of the modern marketplace more competently.

The Mines of Falun Revisited

Not much could have seemed more passé than the Swedish model of social welfare back in the 1990s when American capitalism was humming along. Sweden was buffeted by banking crises, seemingly being absorbed by the European Union, and pieces of its national heritage like Stora were spirited away by the forces of globalization to foreign homes and futures. Even before Stora's merger and relocation, the signs were ominous. Just a few years after the shareholders meeting in the great pit of the mine, just a few years before the company gave up its Swedish identity for good, after a thousand years of mining, the soil of Falun had finally given up its last bit of ore and the company closed the mines.

But if we dig further and see what that goat's accidental discovery led to, in terms of the development not just of a corporation but of an idea that made a nation and helped change the world, then rather than a loss, we are left with what is in Falun now, something well preserved that is resonant with echoes and lessons of meaningful past lives. It had hints of Hoffmann's fictional story:

> Nobody in Falun remembered them. More than fifty years had gone by since Forebom's luckless wedding day, when it chanced that some miners who were making a connection passage between the two shafts found, at a depth of three hundred yards, buried in vitriolated water, the body of a young miner, which seemed when they brought it to the daylight to be turned to stone.
>
> The young man looked as if he were lying in a deep sleep, so perfectly preserved were the features of his face, so wholly without trace of decay his new suit of miner's clothes, and even the flowers in his breast. The people of the neighborhood all collected round the young man, but no one recognized him or could say who he had been and none of the workmen missed any comrade.
>
> The body was going to be taken to Falun, when out of the distance an old, old woman came creeping slowly and painfully up on crutches . . . The moment she saw the body, she threw away her crutches, lifted her arms to Heaven and cried in the most heart-rending way.

But the final quieting of the racket of the mines and the snuffing of the smelters and the long-ago clearing away of the hellish black smoke and constant flames had left, much like the smelting process itself, a residue considerably more valuable and even precious in appearance than the rock that had been hewn out of the earth.

From that rock had come an idea, a company that trailblazed for other companies, a changing view of the relationship between such companies and the state, the wealth to raise a nation, new ideas about the nature of money and about private property and power. It laid the groundwork for a society that, as the former Swedish finance minister Par Nuder noted, "felt like it had a kind of equilbrium, a better balance than others between caring for its people and remaining competitive, between growth and quality of life, between public and private power, between the interests of a nation and the requirements of globalization." It was a view and a goal that resonated with other conversations I had with leaders from Singapore, Brazil, India, and other states seeking a better balance between public and private power.

At the same time, the story of Mats resonated with me in another way—as the poor miner remained largely unchanged while the world evolved around him.

In this, he was in some respects like the world's governments today, which have been trapped by their inability to adapt and by the unceasing and frequently successful efforts of private interests to contain or alter those dimensions of public power that might restrict their growth and freedoms. They have been largely calcified, still very much in the national, centralized, hierarchic forms that first took shape centuries ago. What experiments there have been, such as those in global and regional transnational institutions, have been deliberately kept weak, often by public officials at the nation-state level reflexively defending sovereignty without sufficient awareness of how their stance might actually limit their ability to effectively serve the interests of their constituents in the global era.

And as many traditional components of government power have atrophied or been contained (even as governments themselves have sometimes grown more bloated and dysfunctional), the world has kept changing, much as did life in Falun high above the collapsed tunnel that entombed the young miner.

Global private actors have evolved so that, while lacking many of the legally enshrined powers of governments, they nonetheless can rival, challenge, defeat, or sidestep public power or, alternatively, they can simply manipulate it to serve their needs. Those actors, great corporations and financial institutions, operate far more nimbly on the global stage than governments still trapped within their own borders. In fact, they have learned to flourish in the voids where national governmental power has yet to reach effectively, as in the regulation of global financial markets, or by using their enhanced mobility to play governments against one another to win beneficial treatment. Throughout, these adaptable, creative private enterprises have taken advantage of progress itself, as well as official incompetence or greed, to influence the development of the laws and regulations that once contained them, in ways that ultimately have enabled them to profit and grow far beyond the imaginings of any who first conceived of the idea of "artificial persons." Their growth and the innovations they have cultivated have undoubtedly benefited the world at large to the degree that they have stimulated economic activity, technological and social development, and progress. But at times their development has just as undeniably had negative consequences, spoiling the environment, distorting good governance, propping up cronies, and rapaciously capturing wealth and resources for the benefit of the few.

The challenge for governments and for the constituents they serve is determining whether the institutions of public power can adapt and evolve to effectively and appropriately counterbalance the super-empowered private actors when they threaten the public interest, and to enable them and work effectively with them when they serve it. Global regulatory and supervisory mechanisms will be needed, as will global laws and global representative-governance institutions. So too stronger national institutions and enhanced cooperation between nation-states. So too new forms of public-private partnerships—the best way for these organizations to serve society's momentary and longer-term needs.

While it is undeniable that poor Mats was prematurely entombed, it need not be the case that governments meet the same fate. They need not be consigned as in that crude evolutionary chart I imagined to be simply a withering branch on the evolutionary tree of human social organization. Indeed, part of the crudeness of the imaginary chart is in the mistaken implication that somehow public and private power are actually separate. They are part of an ecosystem that, like any other, seeks and requires balance. The competition between capitalisms we see today is a manifestation of a major rebalancing that is taking place within that greater ecosystem, an effort to harness markets as engines of growth without having to simultaneously consume as their fuel the lives or dignity of billions, the environment around us, or the ideals of social justice.

The near- and longer-term outcomes of that rebalancing are unclear. What seems certain is that in America, and in other parts of the world, the balance has been lost and basic greater goods like equity of opportunity and of outcome have been compromised. It also seems certain that the final balance will exist among a new mix of states, semi-states, super-citizens, and the rest of us, within a system of global, regional, and national public and private mechanisms that will look quite different from what we have had in the past. Large corporations will have to revisit the ancient notion that they serve not just their shareholders but also society at large, and that the simple fact of their growth is insufficient fulfillment of their obligations to society—especially if through that growth they distort or impede the achievement of important social goals. Governments will have to recognize that they must cede sovereignty upward if they are to preserve it at the national level, and that ultimately their purpose is not to enable wealth creation alone but to ensure the best possible quality of life for all citizens. Companies must, as noted earlier, become in some ways more like countries, and countries more like companies. In both cases, we will need to maintain the discipline to regularly and constantly ask why we have such institutions in the first place, recognizing that neither has any right to exist unless they serve our collective as well as our individual needs and aspirations. For in the end, the twist in our story is that all power in that social, political, and economic ecosystem mentioned a moment ago ultimately flows from the people, the ordinary, fragile, mortal citizens, who grant it to the great enduring organizations that they create and allow to be created to serve them. They are not the bottom of the pyramid but its foundation, the only actors within it who are actually initially endowed with any power or rights at all, and thus the sole grantors of power to that changing mix of public and private organizations that have been or ever will be conceived and allowed to exist.

Notes

Introduction: Bodies but No Souls

3 "Where possessions be private, where money bearethe all the stroke": Thomas More, *Utopia*, Raphe Robynson, ed. (Cambridge: Cambridge University Press, 1908), 61.

3 "Corporations have been enthroned and an era of corruption": Stephen R. Barley, "Corporations, Democracy, and the Public Good," *Journal of Management Inquiry* XVI, no. 201 (September 2007): 203.

5 Goldman Sachs's CEO, Lloyd Blankfein, and several other top officials: Dan Farber, "Goldman CEO Blankfein Uses Don't Ask, Don't Tell Defense," CBS News, April 27, 2010, www.cbsnews.com/8301-503983_162-20003586-503983.html.

6 Congress attacked and the Goldman executives squirmed: Louise Story, "Panel's Blunt Questions Put Goldman on Defensive," *New York Times*, April 27, 2010.

6 Senator Carl Levin, who chaired the hearing: U. S. Senate Committee on Homeland Security and Governmental Affairs, *Wall Street and the Financial Crisis: The Role of Investment Banks; Hearing Before the Permanent Subcommittee on Investigations*, 111th Cong., 2nd sess., 2010, pp. 1–7. http://frwebgate.access.gpo.gov/cgi-bin/getdoc.cgi?dbname=111_senate_hearings&docid= f:57322.wais.

6 Goldman Sachs doled out $15.3 billion in pay and bonuses to its staff: Jill Treanor, "Goldman Sachs Bankers to Receive $15.3bn in Pay and Bonuses," *Guardian*, January 19, 2011; Colin Barr, "Trading Shortfall Smacks Goldman Sachs," CNN Money, January 19, 2011, http://finance.fortune.cnn.com/2011/01/19/trading-shortfall-smacks-goldman-sachs/.

6 new financial reforms that had been passed in the middle of the year hung in limbo: "Dodd-Frank in Limbo," *New York Times*, May 27, 2011.

7 In the United Kingdom and across Europe, anger also welled up: Jill Treanor and James Robinson, "Anger over £6.4bn Bonus Bonanza at Four City Banks," *Guardian*, December 21, 2008.

7 were squeezed by harsh austerity programs from their governments: "European Cities Hit by Anti-austerity Protests," BBC News, September 29, 2010, www.bbc.co.uk/news/world-europe-11432579.

8 the top four hundred Americans have, according to *The Wall Street Journal* in March 2011: Robert Frank, "Billionaires Own as Much as the Bottom Half of Americans?" *Wall Street Journal*, March 7, 2011, http://blogs.wsj.com/wealth/2011/03/07/billionaires-own-as-much-as-the-bottom-half-of-americans/.

8 protests had spread to more than nine hundred cities worldwide: Karla Adam, "Occupy Wall Street Protests Continue Worldwide," *Washington Post*, October 16, 2011, www.washingtonpost.com/world/europe/occupy-wall-street-protests-continue -world-wide/2011/10/16/gIQAcJ1roL_story.html.

10 were assailing the "American model": Philip Augar, "It Is Time to Put Finance Back in Its Box," *Financial Times*, April 13, 2009.

10 "People around the world once admired us for our economy": Quoted in "The End of American Capitalism?" *Washington Post*, October 10, 2008.

11 pitting the dangers of "big government" versus those of "big business": See, for example, Arthur C. Brooks, *The Battle: How the Fight Between Free Enterprise and Big Government Will Shape America's Future* (New York: Basic Books, 2010).

11 the status China held as the world's largest economy: Simon Cox, *Economics: Making Sense of the Modern Economy* (New York: Bloomberg Press, 2006), 94.

11 India was second after China: Eugene P. Trani and Robert D. Holsworth, *The Indispensable University: Higher Education, Economic Development, and the Knowledge Economy* (Lanham, MD: R&L Education, 2010), 199.

12 "a great vampire squid wrapped around the face of humanity": Matt Taibbi, "The Great American Bubble Machine," *Rolling Stone*, July 13, 2009, www.rollingstone .com/politics/story/29127316/the_great_american_bubble_machine.

12 Ida Tarbell's landmark muckraking history of the Standard Oil Company: Ida M. Tarbell, *The History of Standard Oil Company* (New York: McClure, Philips and Co., 1904).

12 Upton Sinclair's *The Jungle*: Upton Sinclair, *The Jungle* (New York: Doubleday, Page and Company, 1906).

12 Frank Norris's novel: Frank Norris, *The Octopus: A Story of California* (Garden City, NY: Doubleday and Company, Inc., 1901).

12 Norris, basing his book on a real bloody land war: Ibid., 48.

12 John Trenchard and Thomas Gordon, wrote a series of 140 essays: John Trenchard and Thomas Gordon, *Cato's Letters*, vol. I (4th ed., 1737). Accessed via GoogleBooks.

13 Trenchard and Gordon continued the theme: Ibid., vol. III, 177, 184.

13 three hundred years ago they asserted: Ibid., 189.

13 *The Guardian* published a column: Prem Sikka, "The Best Democracy Money Can Buy," *Guardian*, June 25, 2009.

13 Trenchard and Gordon observed that "Companies": Trenchard and Gordon, vol. III, 177.

13 "The influence of finance over political life": Augar, "It Is Time to Put Finance Back in Its Box."

13 "Merchants have no country": Thomas Jefferson, in a letter to Horatio G. Spafford (March 17, 1814).

14 "In effect, U.S. multinationals have been decoupling from the U.S. economy": Michael Mandel, "Multinationals: Are They Good for America?" *BusinessWeek*, February 28, 2008.

14 "I hope we shall crush in its birth the aristocracy of our moneyed corporations": Thomas Jefferson, 1816, quoted in Lawrence Goodwyn, *The Populist Moment: A*

Short History of the Agrarian Revolt in America (Oxford: Oxford University Press, 1978), xxix.

14 "We are in the presence of a new organization of society": Woodrow Wilson, *Woodrow Wilson: The Essential Political Writings*, Ronald J. Pestritto, ed. (Oxford: Lexington Books, 2005), 107.

14 "Through size, corporations . . . have become an institution": Quoted in *Louis K. Liggett Co. v. Lee*, 288 U.S. 517 (1933), available online at http://caselaw.lp.findlaw .com/cgi-bin/getcase.pl?court=us&vol=288&invol=517.

15 "The liberty of a democracy is not safe": Franklin D. Roosevelt, in a message to Congress (April 20, 1939).

15 threaten America's ability to lead both economically and politically: See, for example, U.S. Admiral Dennis Blair's comments about the difficulty of achieving American objectives now that free-market policies have been increasingly criticized in the wake of the 2008 financial crisis. Dennis C. Blair, "Annual Threat Assessment of the Intelligence Community," *Testimony to the Senate Select Committee on Intelligence*, Washington, D.C., February 12, 2009, 2.

18 As I noted in my last book, *Superclass*: David Rothkopf, *Superclass: The Global Power Elite and the World They Are Making* (New York: Farrar, Straus and Giroux, 2009), 72.

20 "corporations are far from the 'engines of development' that they claim to be": Quoted in Robert O. Keohane, "Not 'Innocents Abroad': American Multinational Corporations and the United States Government," *Comparative Politics* 8, no. 2 (January 1976), 307–20.

20 "power of the nation-state to maintain economic and political stability": Richard J. Barnet and Ronald E. Muller, *Global Reach: The Power of the Multinational Corporations* (New York: Simon and Schuster, 1974), 302.

20 Vernon believed that the relationship between multinational companies and national governments: Raymond Vernon, *Sovereignty at Bay: The Multinational Spread of U.S. Enterprises* (New York: Basic Books, 1971).

20 notably Daniel Yergin and Joseph Stanislaw's *The Commanding Heights*: Daniel Yergin and Joseph Stanislaw, *The Commanding Heights: The Battle for the World Economy* (New York: Simon and Schuster, 2002).

20 equally influential books such as John Micklethwait and Adrian Wooldridge's *The Company*: John Micklethwait and Adrian Wooldridge, *The Company: A Short History of a Revolutionary Idea* (New York: Modern Library, 2003).

20 Even Vernon, writing his last book: Raymond Vernon, *In the Hurricane's Eye: The Troubled Prospects of Multinational Enterprises* (Cambridge, MA: Harvard University Press, 1998).

21 the recent profusion of books: Ian Bremer, *The End of the Free Market: Who Wins the War Between States and Corporations?* (New York: Portfolio, 2010); John Kampfner, *Freedom for Sale: Why the World Is Trading Democracy for Security* (New York: Basic Books, 2010).

21 a host of other books on the lasting impact of globalization: Thomas L. Friedman, *The World Is Flat: A Brief History of the Twenty-first Century* (New York: Farrar,

Straus and Giroux, 2005); Thomas L. Friedman, *Hot, Flat, and Crowded: Why We Need a Green Revolution—and How It Can Renew America* (New York: Farrar, Straus and Giroux, 2008); Anne-Marie Slaughter, *A New World Order* (Princeton, NJ, and Oxford: Princeton University Press, 2004).

21 "I think that's why I would have made a terrible journalist": Lawrence Summers, interview with the author, 2009.

1 ▪ The Goat with the Red Horns

28 much like the giant interconnected families of *Armillaria ostoyae*: "Armillaria Root Rot, Shoestring Root Rot, Honey Mushroom (*Armillaria Ostoyae*)," Washington State University Department of Natural Sciences Extension, 2011, http://ext.nrs.wsu.edu/forestryext/foresthealth/notes/armillariarootrot.htm.

31 observant students of the world have noted important aspects of these problems: Jessica T. Mathews, "Power Shift," *Foreign Affairs* 76, 1, January/February 1997; Anne-Marie Slaughter, *A New World Order* (Princeton, NJ: Princeton University Press, 2004); Joseph S. Nye, Jr., *The Future of Power* (New York: PublicAffairs, 2011).

32 according to local lore, the goat was named Kare: Sven Rydberg, *Stora Kopparberg: 1000 Years of Industrial Activity* (Stockholm: Gullers International, 1979), 9, 58.

33 Because now, the previously perfectly ordinary goat's: Aline Sullivan, "Stora's Story: A Company as Old as the Millennium Puts On a New Face," *New York Times*, November 27, 1999.

33 For most of the past thousand years, Stora Kopparberg was also the name: "The Oldest Corporation in the World," *Time*, March 15, 1963.

33 Today, the company, renamed Stora Enso: "Stora Enso in Brief," Storaenso.com, www.storaenso.com/ABOUT-US/STORA-ENSO-IN-BRIEF/Pages/stora-enso-in-brief.aspx.

34 You could hardly pick a place that would seem less likely: Gunnar Olsson and Burnett Anderson, *Stora Kopparberg: Six Hundred Years of Industrial Enterprise* (Falun, Sweden: Stora Kopparbergs Bergslags Aktiebolag, 1951), 24.

34 residents of Dalecarlia have continued to be known as an independent breed: Michael Roberts, *The Early Vasas: A History of Sweden 1523–1611* (Cambridge: Cambridge University Press, 1968), 32.

34 under the region's typically cold and often forbidding landscape: Eli F. Heckscher, *An Economic History of Sweden* (Cambridge, MA: Harvard University Press, 1963), 86.

34 producing at one point in the seventeenth century 70 percent: Olsson and Anderson, *Stora Kopparberg*, 19.

34 The Japanese construction company Kongo Gumi: James Olan Hutcheson, "The End of a 1,400-Year-Old Business," *BusinessWeek*, Special Report, April 16, 2007.

35 What makes Stora so relevant: Henrietta M. Larson, "A Medieval Swedish Mining Company," *Journal of Economic and Business History*, vol. II (Cambridge, MA: Harvard University Press, 1930), 554–55.

35 The idea of incorporation: Jonathan Baskin and Paul J. Miranti, Jr., *A History of Corporate Finance* (Cambridge: Cambridge University Press, 1997), 29, 38.

35 Initially, the corporation was seen as something endowed with its status: Nick Robins, *The Corporation That Changed the World: How the East India Company Shaped the Modern Multinational* (London and Ann Arbor, MI: Pluto Press, 2006), 7.

35 That document is a Deed of Exchange dated June 16, 1288: "And Still Going Great," *Economist*, June 18, 1988; Olsson and Anderson, *Stora Kopparberg*, 5–6.

35 Living on a large estate featuring its own little subeconomy: Arthur Max, "Sweden's Stora Celebrates Its First 700 Years of Success," *Los Angeles Times*, July 5, 1988.

36 the Catholic Church was really the world's first global "private" enterprise: Franklin D. Scott, *Sweden: The Nation's History* (Carbondale and Edwardsville: Southern Illinois University Press, 1998), 126, 188.

36 One journalist has cited this first recorded corporate transaction: Max, "Sweden's Stora Celebrates."

36 "We, Peter, by the grace of God bishop in Vasteras": Larson, "A Medieval Swedish Mining Company," 554–55.

38 He had also married a member of the French aristocracy: Erik Opsahl, "Magnus 7 Eriksson-Utdypning (NBL_artikkel)" (Swedish), *Store Norske Leksikon* (no date).

38 What Magnus found when he got to Falun in 1347: Sullivan, "Stora's Story."

38 not seen to resemble the 'peaceful communities filled': Olsson and Anderson, *Stora Kopparberg*, 24.

38 "The traveler on his way here is seized by terror": Quoted in Rydberg, *Stora Kopparberg*, 58.

39 "Sweden's greatest wonder, but as terrible as Hell itself": "The Falun Copper Mine," EU 2001 Falun website, www.falun.se/eu2001/eu2001uk.nsf/dokument/DA9D010272570FC5C12569FA005948B3?OpenDocument.

39 "No *theologus* has ever been able to describe Hell": Olsson and Anderson, *Stora Kopparberg*, 26.

39 Linne wrote, "A cave-in, in which": Rydberg, *Stora Kopparberg*, 63, 44.

39 that E.T.A. Hoffmann, the famed German: E.T.A Hoffmann and R. J. Hollingdale, *Tales of Hoffmann: The Mines of Falun* (New York: Penguin Group, 1982).

40 The story is based loosely on the sad tale: "Work in the Mine and Outside," Storaenso.com: http://81.209.16.116/History/Organisational_history/Stora_Kopparbergs_Bergslags/Stora_Kopparbergs_Bergslags/Work_in_the_mine_and_outside.

40 "In the abyss itself lie in wild confusion": Hoffmann and Hollingdale, *Tales of Hoffmann*, 193.

41 Linne observed, "In these dark chambers": Olsson and Anderson, *Stora Kopparberg*, 26.

41 "We, Magnus, by the grace of God King of Sweden": Larson, "A Medieval Swedish Mining Company," 555–59.

42 During those centuries, royally chartered enterprises: Karl Moore and David Lewis, *Foundations of Corporate Empire: Is History Repeating Itself?* (London: Pearson Education, 2000), 184.

42 For example, as the Reformation arrived: Both kings and the medieval bourgeois desired a centralized, territorially bounded state. See Hendrick Spruyt's *The Sovereign Nation State and Its Competitors: An Analysis of Systems Change* (Princeton: Princeton University Press, 1994).

43 "men of Dalarna . . . men who are independent and unafraid": Olsson and Anderson, *Stora Kopparberg*, 72.

43 "an almost pathological greed for power": Vilhelm Moberg, *A History of the Swedish People*, vol. II, *From Renaissance to Revolution* (Minneapolis: University of Minnesota Press, 2005), 155.

43 He asserted his will in other ways: Scott, *Sweden: The Nation's History*, 111–19.

44 the Dalesmen revolted, not once but three times: Moberg, *History of the Swedish People*, 175–80.

45 Quickly following this with strong measures: Scott, *Sweden: The Nation's History*, 158, 188.

45 In 1613, Gustavus Adolphus, a successor to Vasa: Eli Heckscher, "The Place of Sweden in Modern Economic History," *Economic History Review* 4, no. 1: 8.

45 a ransom that was 80 percent funded by proceeds from the mine: Heckscher, *Economic History of Sweden*, 85–87.

45 Indeed, in 1625, five years before Sweden entered the Thirty Years' War: Ibid., 88; Olsson and Anderson, *Stora Kopparberg*, 19.

46 "The greatness of the realm": Quoted in "And Still Going Great."

46 Further, it established secular state sovereignty: Kimon Valaskakis, "Long-term Trends in Global Governance: From 'Westphalia' to 'Seattle,'" in *Global Governance in the 21st Century* (OECD, 2000), 47–48.

47 Overseas trade built economies and also helped fuel a prosperity: Nathan Rosenberg and L. E. Birdzell, Jr., *How the West Grew Rich: The Economic Transformation of the Industrial World* (New York: Basic Books, 1987), 75.

2 ▦ 1288: The Battles That Gave Birth to Modernity

51 Even as Rome was in decline and emperors seldom spent much time: R. Gerberding and J. H. Moran Cruz, *Medieval Worlds* (New York: Houghton Mifflin, 2004), 55–56.

51 Indeed, among the early popes of the era: F. Homes Dudden, *Gregory the Great: His Place in History and Thought*, vol. I (London: Longmans, Green and Co., 1905), 4.

51 For example, the prohibition against clerical marriage: *Canons of Gregory the Illuminator*, c. 2. A. Mai, *Scriptorum veterum nova collectio*, X, 2 (Rome 1838), p. 269.

51 The "Dark Ages" that followed the fall of Rome: H.W.C. Davis, *Medieval Europe* (Fairfield, IA: 1st World Library Literary Society, 2004), 68–84, www.1stworld publishing.com/ebooks/e1-4218-0940-0.pdf.

52 His nickname was "the Hammer," which tells you: Barbara H. Rosenwein, *A Short History of the Middle Ages* (Peterborough, Ontario: Broadview Press, 2004), 72–73.

52 the Merovingians, established in the middle of the fifth century: "Merovingian Dynasty," Encyclopaedia Britannica Online, 2011, www.britannica.com/EB checked/topic/376284/ Merovingian-dynasty.

52 So when, in 751, Pope Zachary needed help: Rosenwein, *Short History of the Middle Ages*, 72–73.

53 This "Donation of Pepin" was seen as a foundation: Hendrik Spruyt, *The Sovereign State and Its Competitors: An Analysis of Systems Change* (Princeton: Princeton University Press, 1994), 97.

53 The son, known today as Charlemagne: Alessandro Barbero, *Charlemagne: Father of a Continent* (Berkeley: University of California Press, 2004), 116.

53 (It's worth noting that the Lombards: Sir Robert Buckley Comyn, *The History of the Western Empire: From Its Restoration by Charlemagne to the Accession of Charles V* (London: W. H. Allen & Co., 1851), 12.

53 While Charlemagne had sent his hopes: Rosenwein, *Short History of the Middle Ages*, 74.

54 Charlemagne listened as Leo enumerated the injustices: John Bagnell Bury and Zachary Nugent Brooke, *The Cambridge Medieval History*, vol. II (New York: Macmillan Company, 1913), 619–20.

54 The symbolism worked its magic: Ibid.

55 "Despite all the benefits that cooperation between church and king yielded": Spruyt, *Sovereign State and Its Competitors*, 97.

55 The challenges associated with this tension: Mark Kishlansky, Patrick Geary, and Patricia O'Brien, *Civilization in the West*, 3rd ed. (New York: Longman, 1998), 289–91.

55 He "conceived of Christendom as an undivided state": Davis, *Medieval Europe*, 86.

56 Gregory did this through a papal bull: Spruyt, *Sovereign State and Its Competitors*, 49.

56 "Henry, King not by usurpation but by pious ordination of God": Quoted in ibid.

57 while en route to Germany: Uta Renate Blumenthal, *The Investiture Controversy: Church and Monarchy from the Ninth to the Twelfth Century* (Philadelphia: University of Pennsylvania Press, 1988), 122–23.

57 "I have loved justice and hated iniquity": Quoted in ibid., 126.

57 In the near term, it was resolved in 1122: Kishlansky, Geary, and O'Brien, *Civilization in the West*, 292.

58 For example, in Sweden, it was only in the twelfth century: Vilhelm Moberg, *A History of the Swedish People*, vol. I, *From Prehistory to the Renaissance* (Minneapolis: University of Minnesota Press, 2005), 73–87.

58 King Sverker the Elder was a major proponent of the church: Ragnar Svanstrom, *A Short History of Sweden* (Sweden: Stubbe Press, 2008), 25–27.

58 Importantly, through the charter, "a privileged clerical class came into being": Ibid., 27.

59 He did brilliantly, and as a young man: Frank Barlow, *Thomas Becket* (Berkeley and Los Angeles: University of California Press, 1990), 10–17, 30–39.

60 Henry was canny in legal matters: Charles Tilly, *Coercion, Capital, and European States: AD 900–1992* (Cambridge, MA: Blackwell, 1992), 154.

60 He sent royal justices on regular trips: Rosenwein, *Short History of the Middle Ages*, 140–42.

61 Weeks later, fuming, Henry, infirm and in his sickbed: Barlow, *Thomas Becket*, 235.

62 "The wicked knight leapt suddenly upon [Becket]": Quoted in Christopher Lee, *The Sceptred Isle: 55 BC–1901* (London: Penguin Group, 1997), 71.

64 Although this was not unheard of: Spruyt, *Sovereign State and Its Competitors*, 96–97.

64 In his *Clericis Laicos* he asserted that kings could only tax the clergy: Rosenwein, *Short History of the Middle Ages*, 171.

65 The document was called *Unam Sanctum*: Christopher T. Carlson, "Church and State Consistency of the Catholic Church's Social Teaching," *Catholic Lawyer*, vol. 35 (1992): 342.

65 In 1302, he convened the First Estates Assembly: Ephraim Emerton, *The Beginnings of Modern Europe (1250–1450)* (Boston: Ginn and Company, 1917), 120.

67 In England, for example, at the turn of the millennium: Karl Moore and David Lewis, *Foundations of Corporate Empire: Is History Repeating Itself?* (London: Pearson Education, 2000), 137–43.

67 While the owners of the companies still bore complete liability: Jonathan Baskin and Paul J. Miranti, *A History of Corporate Finance* (Cambridge: Cambridge University Press, 1997), 29–42.

67 The Peruzzi family lent money to the king of Naples: Edwin S. Hunt, *The Medieval Super-Companies: A Study of the Peruzzi Company of Florence* (Cambridge: Cambridge University Press, 1997), 134.

68 In one instance, reported by the chronicler Joceline of Brakelond: Sir Ernest Clarke, *The Chronicle of Jocelin of Brakelond* (London: Bury St. Edmunds Pageant Edition, 1907), 75–76.

69 as is expressed in *The Canterbury Tales*: Geoffrey Chaucer, "The Reeve's Tale" from *Canterbury Tales* (Garden City, NY: International Collections Library, 1913), p. 109, 112, quoted in Moore and Lewis, *Foundations of Corporate Empire*, 147.

69 But in the end, the result was a flowering of free enterprise: Moore and Lewis, *Foundations of Corporate Empire*, 146–48.

69 They moved away from traditional strongholds of feudalism: Spruyt, *Sovereign State and Its Competitors*, 62.

70 In fact, in the biggest battle of the era: J. F. Verbruggen, *The Art of Warfare in Western Europe During the Middle Ages* (Woodbridge, UK: Boydell Press, 2002), 261.

70 That battle, four thousand to a side: Jan Mahler, *The Battle of Worringen, 1288: The History and Mythology of a Notable Event*, 1993, Master's Thesis, University of Alberta, 83.

70 Much like the rest of Europe, Sweden had been grappling: Svanstrom, *Short History of Sweden*, 27.

71 To counterbalance the power of the church, in 1280 Magnus also issued the Alsno Decree: Franklin D. Scott, *Sweden: The Nation's History* (Carbondale and Edwardsville: Southern Illinois University Press, 1998), 57, 68–69.

72 In 1319, after Birger's ouster: Thomas Lindkvist, "The Making of a European Society: The Example of Sweden," *Medieval Encounters* 10, no. 1–3: 178.

72 This led to Sweden's involvement in the Kalmar Union: Byron J. Nordstrom, *The History of Sweden* (Westport, CT: Greenwood Press, 2002), 38–39.

73 "The peasants balked at paying taxes for the war": Scott, *Sweden*, 123.

3 ■ 1648: The Beginning of the Great Leveling

75 Dark, cool and still, the first few hours: Michel Roberts, *The Early Vasas: A History of Sweden, 1523–1611* (Cambridge: Cambridge University Press, 1968), 197.

76 That trend reflected the decline of the Catholic Church: Hendrik Spruyt, *The Sovereign State and Its Competitors: An Analysis of Systems Change* (Princeton: Princeton University Press, 1994), 61.

76 Sweden was a state because he had pushed out the Catholic Church: Franklin D. Scott, *Sweden: The Nation's History* (Carbondale; Edwardsville: Southern Illinois University Press, 1998), 121–25.

77 His funeral, carefully planned prior to his demise: Joseph Gonzalez, "Rewriting History: Humanist Oration at the Funeral of Gustav Vasa, 1560," *Journal of the Society for the Advancement of Scandinavian Study* 78, no. 1 (2006): 21–42.

79 In 1609, a forty-two-year-old nobleman: Tryntje Helfferich, *The Thirty Years War: A Documentary History* (Indianapolis, IN: Hackett Publishing), 19.

79 As part of the deal, in order to cement the support of Thurn: Peter H. Wilson, *The Thirty Years War: Europe's Tragedy* (Cambridge: Harvard University Press, 2009), 112–115, 270.

80 He arranged to have a captain of the castle guard let his men in: Helfferich, *Thirty Years War*, 15.

83 Advances in the design of seagoing vessels: Kimon Valaskakis, "Long-term Trends in Global Governance: From 'Westphalia' to 'Seattle,'" *Global Governance in the 21st Century* (OECD, 2000), 50.

83 As a consequence, some of the earliest companies: Karl Moore and David Lewis, *Foundations of Corporate Empire: Is History Repeating Itself?* (London: Pearson Education, 2000), 197–99.

83 Among the first of these ventures was the British East India Company: Sir Courtenay Ilbert, *The Government of India: A Brief Historical Survey of Parliamentary Legislation Relating to India* (Oxford: Clarendon Press, 1922), 4.

83 The anticipated duration of the company's existence: Nick Robins, *The Corporation that Changed the World: How the East India Company Shaped the Modern Multinational* (London and Ann Arbor, MI: Pluto Press, 2006), 7, 27.

83 (The company was actually modeled in part on an earlier venture: Ann M. Carlos and Stephen Nicholas, "Giants of an Earlier Capitalism: The Chartered Trading Companies as Modern Multinationals," *Business History Review* 62, no. 3 (1988): 403, 411.

84 holdings of the Dutch company become what we now know as: J. H. Elliott, *Imperial Spain: 1469–1716* (New York: St. Martin's Press, 1964), 44.

84 the Habsburgs for whom Martinitz worked were fighting a two-front war: Philip Bobbitt, *The Shield of Achilles: War, Peace, and the Course of History* (New York:

Alfred A. Knopf, 2002), 116; Myron P. Gutmann, "The Origins of the Thirty Years' War," *Journal of Interdisciplinary History* 18, no. 4 (Spring 1988): 767.

84 Those holdings had reached their zenith: H. G. Koenigsberger, *The Habsburgs and Europe: 1516–1600* (Ithaca, NY: Cornell University Press, 1971), 1–10.

85 Not long into Philip II's reign, just such a test came: Geoffrey Parker, *The Dutch Revolt* (Ithaca, NY: Cornell University Press, 1977), 68–71.

85 Protestant nobles in the northern provinces: Wilson, *Thirty Years War*, 130.

85 This overreach led Phillip's treasury to declare bankruptcy: Elliot, *Imperial Spain*, 191, 257, 280–81.

85 No money in the treasury meant no money for troops: Parker, *Dutch Revolt*, 231.

86 Of the Dutch Republic's gross national product: Wilson, *Thirty Years War*, 138.

87 This enterprise, modeled on the early success of its Asian-oriented cousin: Elliot, *Imperial Spain*, 174–77, 262–71.

88 Hein returned to the Netherlands with almost two hundred thousand pounds of gold: E. H. Carter, G. W. Digby, and R. N. Murray, *From Earliest Times to the 17th Century (History of the West Indian Peoples)*, new ed. (Nelson Caribbean, 1997), 116.

89 In the early years of the conflict, Denmark's king Christian made a move: William P. Guthrie, *The Later Thirty Years War: From the Battle of Wittstock to the Treaty of Westphalia* (Westport, CT: Greenwood Press, 2003), 6–7.

90 Their defeat in turn emboldened the emperor Ferdinand: Wilson, *Thirty Years War*, 448–49.

90 They sought a champion and got one: Vladimir Brnardic, *Imperial Armies of the Thirty Years' War (1): Infantry and Artillery* (Oxford: Osprey Publishing, 2009), 7.

90 he recognized a need to counter the Spanish *tercio* system: Elliot, *Imperial Spain*, 124.

90 He sought a more flexible, versatile approach: Scott, *Sweden*, 177.

91 Initially just an investor at Falun, De Geer: D. G. Kirby, *Northern Europe in the Early Modern Period: The Baltic World, 1492–1772* (New York: Longman, 1990), 149.

91 "For those of you who wish to create a picture of the Mine": Sven Rydberg, *The Great Copper Mountain: The Stora Story* (Hedmora, Sweden: Stora Kopparbergs Bergslags Aktiebolag in Collaboration with Gidlunds Publishers, 1998), 85–87.

92 Johann had tried to remain neutral: Geoffrey Parker, *The Thirty Years' War* (New York: Routledge, 1997), 113–14.

93 Oxenstierna wrote of her when she was fourteen that: Oskar Garstein, *Rome and the Counter-Reformation in Scandinavia: The Age of Gustavus Adolphus and Queen Christina of Sweden, 1622–1656* (Boston: Brill, 1992), 553–54.

93 Speaking to the gathered miners, she said: "And Still Going Great," *Economist*, June 18, 1988.

93 agreed in 1635 to the Peace of Prague, which dissolved the Catholic League: Parker, *Thirty Years' War*, 136.

94 Then, in 1643, the French won a striking victory over the Army of Flanders: Wilson, *Thirty Years War*, 667.

95 The simple act of convening so many different actors: Leo Gross, "The Peace of Westphalia, 1648–1948," *American Journal of International Law* 42, no. 1 (1948): 20.

95 For centuries, hierarchy had been a central organizing principle of European society: Mark Kishlansky, Patrick Geary, and Patricia O'Brien, *Civilization in the West Since 1300*, 3rd ed. (New York: Longman, 1998), 481; Wilson, *Thirty Years War*, 672–73.

95 the Swedes arrived with a delegation of 165 including: Wilson, *Thirty Years War*, 673.

95 Leo Gross, the noted international legal scholar, has described the outcomes of Westphalia: Gross, "The Peace of Westphalia, 1648–1948," 28–29.

96 "autonomous, unified, rational actors": Stephen D. Krasner, "Compromising Westphalia," *International Security* 20, no. 3 (1995–1996): 115.

96 Sweden received five million *dalers*: Scott, *Sweden*, 200.

96 the Swedes, the Dutch, and the French emerged particularly strengthened: Bobbit, *The Shield of Achilles*, 507.

97 The pope's representative to Westphalia, the nuncio Fabio Chigi: Koenigsberger, *The Hapsburgs and Europe*, 673.

97 The official response of the Vatican to the treaty: Bobbitt, *Shield of Achilles*, 116.

97 It was a massive, gorgeous, unprecedented, excessive celebration: Rydberg, *Great Copper Mountain*, 94.

98 The queen herself was a contradiction: Garstein, *Rome and the Counter-Reformation in Scandinavia*, 505, 707–38.

98 a patron of knowledge and of the arts: Susanna Akerman, *Queen Christina of Sweden and Her Circle: The Transformation of a Seventeenth-Century Philosophical Libertine* (Leiden and New York: E. J. Brill, 1991), 289.

99 a new record for the mine: Maria Munk, "Världsarvstaden Falun—Ett världsarvs påverkan på marknadsföringen av en destination," Baltic Business School (Tourism Program), 2008, 21, http://74.125.155.132/scholar?q=cache:4WbnkzvHPg8J:scholar.google.com/+stora+kopparberg+december+1650+3,000+tons+of+copper&hl=en&as_sdt=0,9.

99 her secret Catholicism: Francis W. Bain, *Christina, Queen of Sweden* (London: H. Allen & Co., 1890), 322.

99 she had created so many new nobles: Veronica Buckley, *Christina, Queen of Sweden: The Restless Life of a European Eccentric* (New York: Fourth Estate, 2004), 78.

99 a master miner from Germany named Hans Filip Lybecker: Rydberg, *Great Copper Mountain*, 118–20.

4 ▪ 1776: Two Revolutions

101 As noted in the introduction, Thomas Jefferson was a great admirer: Joseph J. Ellis, *American Sphinx: The Character of Thomas Jefferson* (New York: Alfred A. Knopf, 1997), 49, 64, 335.

101 "Neither aiming at originality of principle or sentiment": John P. Foley, *The Jeffersonian Cyclopedia: A Comprehensive Collection of the Views of Thomas Jefferson* (New York: Funk, 1900), 43.

102 A notable countervailing voice: Ron Chernow, *Alexander Hamilton* (New York: Penguin, 2005), 302–47.

103 Smith's *An Inquiry into the Nature and Causes of the Wealth of Nations:* James Buchan, *The Authentic Adam Smith: His Life and Ideas* (New York: W. W. Norton, 2006), 88–90. See also Ian Simpson Ross, *The Life of Adam Smith* (Oxford: Clarendon Press, 1995), 248, 269.

103 It would be years before the book assumed the stature: Richard F. Teichgraeber III, "'Less Abused Than I Had Reason to Expect': The Reception of *The Wealth of Nations* in Britain, 1776–90," *Historical Journal* 30, no. 2 (June 1987): 339.

103 Smith's book was also written in large part as a reaction: Adam Smith, *The Wealth of Nations*, R. H. Campbell, A. S. Skinner, and W. B. Todd, eds. (Oxford: Clarendon Press, 1976), IV.vii.b.50, V.i.e.30.

104 From the councils of elders or of those who were of an age: Thorkild Jacobsen, "Primitive Democracy in Ancient Mesopotamia," *Journal of Near Eastern Studies* 2, no. 3 (July 1943): 166.

104 to the *ganas* of ancient India: U. B. Singh, *Administrative System in India: Vedic Age to 1947* (New Delhi: APH Publishing Corporation, 1998), 49.

104 Even in oligarchies like Sparta: Charles D. Hamilton, "Spartan Politics and Policy, 405–401 B.C.," *American Journal of Philology* 91, no. 3 (July 1970): 295.

104 Sometimes, of course, the institutions were more clearly the ancestors: James V. Cunningham, "Citizen Participation in Public Affairs," *Public Administration Review* 32, Special Issue: Curriculum Essays on Citizens, Politics, and Administration in Urban Neighborhoods, October 1972, 590.

105 "Its administration favors the many instead of the few": Quoted in Robert A. Dahl, *Democracy and Its Critics* (New Haven: Yale University Press, 1989), 17.

105 The oldest of the world's parliaments that is still in existence: Henry Chu, "Iceland Seeks to Become Sanctuary for Free Speech," *Los Angeles Times*, April 2, 2011, www.latimes.com/news/nationworld/world/la-fg-iceland-free-speech-20110403 ,0,5332545.story.

105 It was first convened in A.D. 930: Christopher J. Moore, *In Other Words* (New York: Walker, 2004), 65.

106 The chairman of the gathering was called the Lawspeaker: Jon Johannesson, *Islendinga Saga: A History of the Old Icelandic Commonwealth* (Ann Arbor, MI: University of Michigan Press, 2007), 47.

106 The concept of the "thing" was common throughout Scandinavia: "Thing," Online Etymology Dictionary, Douglas Harper, 2010, http://dictionary.reference.com /browse/thing.

106 the parliament of Norway, which is called the Storting: "Storting," Dictionary.com Unabridged, 2011, http://dictionary.reference.com/browse/storting.

106 the Danish parliament, which is called the Folketing: "Folketing," *Collins English Dictionary: Complete & Unabridged*, 10th ed. (HarperCollins, 2011), http://dictionary.reference.com/browse/folketing.

106 In Sweden, the word was used to refer to provincial gatherings: Kathleen N. Daly, *Norse Mythology A to Z*, revised by Marian Rengel, 3rd ed. (New York: Infobase Publishing, 2009), 20.

106 This fact—that political participation was limited: As per Max Weber's definition of a state: "a human community that (successfully) claims the *monopoly of the legitimate use of force* within a given territory." Max Weber, "Politics As a Vocation," in *From Max Weber*, translated and edited by H. H. Gerth and C. Wright Mills (New York: Oxford University Press, 1946), 78.

107 The surrounding armed throngs cheered so enthusiastically: Carl Ernst Sigfried Swansson, *Social Wrongs and a Practical Remedy* (New York: Shakespeare Press, 1913), 45–46.

107 Similarly, two centuries later: William Stubbs, *The Constitutional History of England in Its Origin and Development*, vol. I, 6th ed. (Oxford: Clarendon Press, 1903), 563–69.

108 Oliver Cromwell, in fact, was so dismissive of lawyers: Roy Edward Sherwood, *Oliver Cromwell: King in All but Name, 1653–1658* (New York: St. Martin's Press, 1997), 129.

108 It was a conflict that would bring down Charles I: Ann Lyon, *Constitutional History of the United Kingdom* (London: Cavendish, 2003), 206–26.

108 one of the target groups he quashed within his own forces: "Oliver Cromwell (English statesman): First chairman of the Council," Encyclopaedia Britannica Online, www.britannica.com/EBchecked/topic/143822/Oliver-Cromwell.

109 one who would grow to become a good friend, Isaac Newton: Roger Woolhouse, *Locke: A Biography* (Cambridge: Cambridge University Press, 2007), 70–71, 314.

110 He was appointed secretary of the Board of Trade and Plantations: Neal Wood, *John Locke and Agrarian Capitalism* (Berkeley, Los Angeles, and London: University of California Press, 1984), 22.

110 *An Essay Concerning Human Understanding*, which explored the limits: John Locke, *An Essay Concerning Human Understanding*, available at Project Gutenberg, www.gutenberg.org/browse/authors/l#a2447.

110 and *Letters Concerning Toleration*, drawn in part: John Locke, *An Essay Concerning Toleration*, full text online at www.earlymoderntexts.com/t_locke.html.

111 Central to the assumption of the throne by William and Mary: William and Mary signed the English Bill of Rights in 1689. The text is available at the Yale Law School website, http://avalon.law.yale.edu/17th_century/england.asp.

111 "*Political power*, then, I take to be a *right* of making laws": John Locke, *Two Treatises on Government* (London, Printed for R. Butler, 1821), 46–47, 189, 191, 289–29.

112 This document not only described limits on the power of the monarch: English Bill of Rights, available at the Yale Law School website, http://avalon.law.yale.edu/17th_century/england.asp.

113 This led to Locke's *Some Consideration of the Consequences*: John Locke, "Some Considerations of the Consequences of the Lowering of Interest and the Raising the Value of Money," in Antoin E. Murphy, ed., *Monetary Theory, 1601–1758* (New York: Routledge, 1997), 1–99.

113 He served for four years, during which time: Adam Kuper and Jessica Kuper, eds., *The Social Science Encyclopedia*, 2nd ed. (New York: Routledge, 2003), 827.

113 It also ventured as far as the Straits of Malacca and China: Nick Robins, *The*

Corporation That Changed the World: How the East India Company Shaped the Modern Multinational (London and Ann Arbor, MI: Pluto Press, 2006), 58–78.

115 Bengal, the richest province: Ibid., 61.

115 "it is not inferior in anything to Egypt": Quoted in Sunsil K. Munsi, *Calcutta Metropolitan Explosion: Its Nature and Roots* (New Delhi: Peoples Publishing House, 1975), 11, 54, 66.

115 The company had already been involved in the Bengal textile market: John Keay, *The Honourable Company: A History of the English East India Company* (New York: Macmillan, 1991), 221–41.

117 Yet in retrospect he said, "When I think, of the marvelous riches": P. Kanagasabapathi, *Indian Models of Economy, Business and Management* (New Delhi: Prentice-Hall of India, 2008), 51.

117 "the industrial revolution could not have happened in Britain": Quoted in Rajeev Srinivasan, "The uncouth reality of the present is not the only possibility for India: In our many pasts lie the seeds of our future," www.rediff.com/news/aug/04rajee1.htm.

118 One member of Burgoyne's committee observed: "Never did . . .": Robins, *The Corporation That Changed the World*, 106.

118 With Stora on the ropes due to declining copper output: Eli F. Heckscher, *An Economic History of Sweden* (Cambridge, MA: Harvard University Press, 1963), 8; Sven Rydberg, *The Great Copper Mountain: The Stora Story* (Hedmora, Sweden: Stora Kopparbergs Bergslags AB in Collaboration with Gidlunds Publishers, 1998), 143.

119 Charles had many opportunities to settle the war on favorable terms: Stewart P. Oakley, *War and Peace in the Baltic, 1560–1790* (London: Routledge, 1993), 111–16.

120 Critics rose up among the aristocracy and, led by: Robert Nisbet Bain, *Gustavus III and His Contemporaries, 1742–1792: An Overlooked Chapter of Eighteenth Century History* (London: Kegan Paul, Trench, Trubner, & Co., 1894), 8.

120 The Hats sought to restore ties with France and to advance an international policy: Michael Roberts, *The Age of Liberty: Sweden 1719–1772* (Cambridge: Cambridge University Press, 1986), 1–15.

120 "the Age of Freedom had discovered or reinterpreted certain democratic fundamentals": Franklin D. Scott, *Sweden: The Nation's History* (Carbondale and Edwardsville: Southern Illinois University Press, 1998), 251.

121 "war is not merely a political act": Quoted in Troy S. Thomas, Stephen D. Kiser, and William D. Casebeer, *Warlords Rising: Confronting Violent Non-State Actors* (Oxford: Lexington Books, 2005), 164.

121 some of the key battles in the war took place around the world: Tom Pocock, *Battle for Empire: The Very First World War, 1756–1763* (London: Michael O'Mara Books, 1991).

122 Boston colonists organized by Samuel Adams disguised themselves as Mohawk Indians: Garry Wills, *Inventing America: Jefferson's Declaration of Independence* (New York: Vintage Books, 1979), 26–27.

123 Further, the governor was granted the power to try royal officials: Gordon S. Wood, *The American Revolution* (New York: Modern Library, 2003), 37–38.

123 While it is no doubt true that the stripes on the American flag: It is unclear

whether the East India Company's flag directly influenced the design of the American flag; Sir Charles Fawcett, a British historian who served in the India Civil Service, suggested that it did in a famous article written in 1937 and reproduced at www.crwflags.com/FOTW/flags/gb-eic2.html. Even if no direct influence was involved, the likeness is still remarkable.

123 In 2005, U.S. Federal Reserve Bank chairman Alan Greenspan: Remarks by Alan Greenspan, Chairman of the Federal Reserve Board, at the Adam Smith Memorial Lecture, Kirkcaldy, Scotland, February 6, 2005, available at the Federal Reserve Board website, www.federalreserve.gov/boarddocs/speeches/2005/20050206/default.htm.

124 While today *The Wealth of Nations* is seen as a landmark work: Ian Simpson Ross, *The Life of Adam Smith* (Oxford: Clarendon Press, 1995), 248, 269.

124 "if you wait till the fate of America be decided": Edinbury, February 8, 1776, in *Correspondence of Adam Smith*, quoted in Buchan, 90.

124 Although he argued that Britain was more liberal: Adam Smith, *The Wealth of Nations*, R. H. Campbell, A. S. Skinner, and W. B. Todd, eds. (Oxford: Clarendon Press, 1976), IV.viii.b.50; subsequent Smith quotes from IV.vii.b.44, IV.vii.b.49, IV.vii.c.77, IV.vii.c.79, V.i.e.30, IV.vii.b.11, V.i.e.26, V.i.e.32.

126 Smith's ideas did provoke some unease among the landed gentry: Teichgraeber, "Less Abused Than I Had Reason to Expect," 351.

127 He made three motions to Congress: Wills, *Inventing America*, 336–44.

127 So America had to assert independence not primarily out of a need: David Armitage, *The Declaration of Independence: A Global History* (Cambridge, MA: Harvard University Press, 2007), 33–36.

128 He also drew upon George Mason's Virginia Declaration of Rights: Dumas Malone, *Thomas Jefferson: A Brief Biography* (Chapel Hill: UNC Press Books, 2002), 15–17.

128 "Nations being composed of people naturally free and independent": Quoted in Armitage, *Declaration of Independence*, 39.

129 "When in the course of human events": The Declaration of Independence: In Congress, July 4, 1776, "A Declaration by the Representatives of the United States of America, in General Congress Assembled," in Armitage, *Declaration of Independence*, 165, 170–71.

130 Crossing the Delaware River in the dark of night: David Hackett Fischer, *Washington's Crossing* (Oxford: Oxford University Press, 2004), 193–200.

131 Massachusetts, for example, granted only five charters: Oscar Handlin and Mary Flug Handlin, *Commonwealth: A Study of the Role of Government in the American Economy; Massachusetts, 1774–1861* (Cambridge, MA: Belknap Press, 1969), 99, 160.

132 Within two decades the cases of *The Trustees of Dartmouth College*: Ibid., 160.

132 they did not produce the final chapter for the copper mountain: Sven Rydberg, *The Great Copper Mountain* (Stora Kopparbergs Bergslags AB in Collaboration with Gidlunds Publishers, 1988), 129–41.

134 Factors driving those changes ranged from the Industrial Revolution to famines in Europe: Ralph W. Hidy and Muriel E. Hidy, "Anglo-American Merchant Bankers and the Railroads of the Old Northwest, 1848–1860," *Business History Review* 34, no. 2 (Summer 1960): 153.

134 the year a fourteen-year-old Irish immigrant to America named Andrew Carnegie: Andrew Carnegie, *Autobiography of Andrew Carnegie* (Boston and New York: Houghton Mifflin Company, 1920), 34.

135 "It is not worthwhile to try to keep history from repeating itself": Mark Twain, *Eruption: Hitherto Unpublished Pages About Men and Events*, Bernard DeVoto, ed. (New York: Harper & Brothers, 1940), 66.

135 the Congress of Vienna, where the treaty was hammered out: David King, *Vienna 1814: How the Conquerors of Napoleon Made Love, War, and Peace at the Congress of Vienna* (New York: Crown Publishing Group, 2008), 2.

136 The maestro of the Vienna negotiations was the Austrian nobleman Prince Klemens Wenzel von Metternich: Mike Rapport, *1848: Year of Revolution* (New York: Basic Books, 2008), 4.

136 Kissinger made his first notable headlines on the public stage: Henry Kissinger, *A World Restored: Metternich, Castlereagh and the Problems of Peace, 1812–1822* (New Haven, CT: Phoenix Press, 2000).

136 Kissinger was seen to have emulated Metternich's strategies and values: Robert D. Kaplan, "Kissinger, Metternich, and Realism," Atlantic Online, June 1999, www.theatlantic.com/past/docs/issues/99jun/ 9906kissinger.htm.

136 messy French emulation of the American experiment in democracy: Peter Jones, *The 1848 Revolutions* (Burnt Mill: Longman Group Limited, 1981), 21.

136 industrial revolution was undoing and reshaping economies: Jonathan Sperber, *The European Revolutions, 1848–1851* (Cambridge: Cambridge University Press, 1994), 18; Jones, *1848 Revolutions*, 6.

136–37 many felt that the return to stability in France that came in the person of Napoleon: Arnold Whitridge, "1848: The Year of Revolution," *Foreign Affairs* 26, no. 2, January 1948, 272.

137 he turned to nationalism to give his people a sense of purpose: Philip G. Dwyer, "Napoleon and the Foundation of the Empire," *Historical Journal* 53, no. 2, 2010, http://newcastleau.academia.edu/PhilipDwyer/Papers/167092/Napoleon_and_the _Foundation_of_the_Empire.

137 Metternich and his sponsors sought to do so in a way that would restore the monarchy: Rapport, *1848: Year of Revolution*, 4–5.

137 "It is in times of crisis that monarchs are principally called upon": Quoted in Rapport, *1848: Year of Revolution*, 5.

138 put a final end to feudalism and ultimately aristocracy, monarchy, and the "old way": Jones, *1848 Revolutions*, 28, 45.

138 Alexis de Tocqueville, who recognized on his visit to the United States: Richard

Swedberg, *Tocqueville's Political Economy* (Princeton, NJ: Princeton University Press, 2009), 17, 58. 65.

138 "depraved taste for equality": Alexis de Toqueville, *Democracy in America*, vol. 1 (Charleston, SC: CreateSpace, April 27, 2011), 50, 419.

138 a redistribution of power that elevated commoners and civil centers of power: Alexis de Tocqueville, *Democracy in America*, vol. 2, unabridged ed., translated by Henry Reeve (Lawrence, KS: Digireads.com, January 1, 2007), 11, 148.

139 Tocqueville decried America's obsession with money: Tocqueville, *Democracy in America*, vol. 2, 261.

139 Old ways dating back to the guild structures: Sperber, *European Revolutions*, 18; Jones, *1848 Revolutions*, 6.

139 "Artisans and craft workers": Rapport, *1848: Year of Revolution*, 31.

140 "In their obscure cellars, in their rooms": Quoted in Rapport, *1848: Year of Revolution*, 35.

140 Advances in farming promoted a shift: Niek Koning, *The Failure of Agrarian Capitalism: Agrarian Politics in the UK, Germany, the Netherlands, and the USA, 1846–1919* (London: Routledge, 1994), 14–16.

140 "Iron and leather manufacture": Sperber, *European Revolutions*, 40.

140 Stora had become both one of Europe's pig iron producers: Sven Rydberg, *The Great Copper Mountain: The Stora Story* (Hedmora, Sweden: Stora Kopparbergs Bergslags AB in Collaboration with Gidlunds Publishers, 1998), 170, 176.

140–41 Sperber suggests the ramifications of these conflicts: Sperber, *European Revolutions*, 42.

141 *Phytophthora infestans* was known commonly as potato blight: Arline Tartus Golkin, *Famine, a Heritage of Hunger: A Guide to Issues and References* (Claremont, CA: Regina Books, 1987), 52.

141 the disease took a devastating toll on the potato crops: Terry Glavin, *The Sixth Extinction: Journeys Among the Lost and Left Behind* (New York: Thomas Dunne, 2007), 220.

141 with agonizing consequences for poor workers: Helge Berger and Mark Spoerer, "Economic Crises and the European Revolutions of 1848," *Journal of Economic History* 61, no. 2 (June 2001): 296–303.

141 falling demand for manufactured goods and businesses failing throughout Europe: Berger and Spoerer, "Economic Crises and the European Revolutions of 1848," 303–304.

141 Hundreds of major mills closed: Ibid., 306; Arthur L. Dunham, "Unrest in France in 1848," *Journal of Economic History*, vol. 8 (1948): 75.

142 there was little money to help import food: Dunham, "Unrest in France in 1848," 77, 81.

142 Metternich, Guizot, and their confreres were children of the upheavals: Rapport, *1848: Year of Revolution*, x, 2, 4, 37.

142 "I believe that right now we are sleeping on a volcano": Quoted in Rapport, *1848: Year of Revolution*, 42.

142 the Enlightenment's attacks on all forms of arbitrary power: Jones, *1848 Revolutions*, 21, 23.

143 The first person to use the term *socialisme*: Aruther John Booth, *Saint-Simon and Saint-Simonism: A Chapter in the History of Socialism in France* (Charleston, SC: Nabu Press, 2010), 4–5, 56–57.

143 Louis Blanc was another early socialist: Branko Horvat and Mihailo Markovic, *Self-governing Socialism: A Reader* (Armonk, NY: M. E. Shape, 1976), 9.

144 Guizot's opponents had intended to hold a dinner: Rapport, *1848: Year of Revolution*, 50–56.

145 given the uncreative pseudonyms "Mr. and Mrs. Smith": Arnold Whitridge, "1848: The Year of Revolution," *Foreign Affairs* 26, no. 2 (January 1948): 265.

145 "France into the family of republics": Ibid., 264.

146 conceived by Blanc to use railway income to fund a program for workers: Jones, *1848 Revolutions*, 36.

146 "After 1848 . . . the workers acquired a new status in the community": Whitridge, "1848: The Year of Revolution," 275.

146 Metternich was seventy-four when the news of Louis Philippe's downfall reached Vienna: Rapport, *1848: Year of Revolution*, 4.

146–47 there were concerns the old man had already been in office for too long: Jones, *1848 Revolutions*, 42.

148 the dilemma of how to reconcile social justice with individual liberties: Rapport, *1848: Year of Revolution*, 255, 407.

149 This was why Marx was so troubled by what he saw as a journalist: Karl Marx and Friedrich Engels, *The Communist Manifesto* (New York: Tribeca Books, 2011); Eduard Heimann, "Marxism: 1848 and 1948," *Journal of Politics* 11, no. 3 (August 1949): 530.

150 "We see then: the means of production and of exchange": Marx and Engels, *Communist Manifesto*, 5.

150 He sought to reverse or forestall the rampant inequality: Marx and Engels, *Communist Manifesto*, 81; Heimann, "Marxism: 1848 and 1948," 523.

150 "These laborers, who must sell themselves piece-meal": Marx and Engels, *Communist Manifesto*, 479.

151 "Not only are [the workers] the slaves of the bourgeois class": Ibid.

151 With words like these, accompanied by his call for the socialization of private goods: Heimann, "Marxism: 1848 and 1948," 524.

151 "Let the ruling classes tremble at a communistic revolution": Marx and Engels, *Communist Manifesto*, 500.

152 the United Kingdom enjoyed comparative stability: Miles Taylor, "The 1848 Revolutions and the British Empire," *Past and Present Society*, no. 166 (February 2000): 146–58.

153 From British Guiana to Canada there were peasant uprisings: Ibid., 171.

153 the East India Company was at a turning point in its existence: Nick Robins, *The Corporation That Changed the World* (London and Ann Arbor, MI: Pluto Press, 2006), 6.

153 Tensions had run high between the British and the Indians: Ibid., 162–63.

155 one Indian soldier named Mangal Pandey protested and announced he would rebel: Lion M. G. Agrawal, *Freedom Fighters of India* (McMinnville, TN: Isha Books, 2008), 145.

156 "With all my love for the army, I must confess": Quoted in ibid., 74.

156 with Dickens coauthoring a call for destruction: Priti Joshi, "Mutiny Echoes: India, Britons, and Charles Dickens's *A Tale of Two Cities*," *Nineteenth-Century Literature* 62, no. 1 (June 2007): 49.

156 Under the Government of India Act of 1858: Robins, *Corporation That Changed the World*, 163–64.

156 "Mill first of all argued that the Company had": Quoted in ibid., 164.

156 "no civilized government ever existed on the face of this earth": Quoted in ibid.

157 On March 10, 1848, the U.S. Congress ratified the Treaty of Guadalupe Hidalgo: John S. D. Eisenhower, *So Far from God: The U.S. War with Mexico 1846–1848* (New York: Random House, 1989), 383.

157 two men made a discovery on a riverbank in Coloma, California, that changed the world: H. W. Brands, *The Age of Gold: The California Gold Rush and the New American Dream* (New York: Doubleday, 2002), 15, 23–24.

158 made large-scale enterprises possible: Glenn Porter, *The Rise of Big Business, 1860–1820* (Wheeling, IL: Harlan Davidson, 2006), 34–35.

158 English and Dutch investors, among others, who sought to invest: Hidy and Hidy, "Anglo-American Merchant Bankers," 153–55.

158 railway tracks tripling in length between 1850 and 1860: Porter, *Rise of Big Business*, 35, 37–38.

159 he needed the railroads to get oil from those fields to market: Daniel Yergin, *The Prize: The Epic Quest for Oil, Money, and Power* (New York: Simon and Schuster, 1991), 29–30.

159 Because his company, Standard Oil, became the largest refinery in the United States: Peter Collier and David Horowitz, *The Rockefellers: An American Dynasty* (Austin, TX: Holt, Rinehart and Winson, 1976), 22; ibid., 40. At the time, refineries that bought crude from the producers and then transported it using the railroad companies, acting as middlemen, were well positioned to organize crude production and stabilize freight traffic.

159 enabling Rockefeller to negotiate excellent rates: Porter, *Rise of Big Business*, 72–73.

159 "One capitalist always kills many": Marx, *Capital*, vol. 1, part vii: Primitive Accumulation, chapter 32: Historical Tendency of Capitalist Accumulation, http://marxists .org/archive/marx/works/1867-c1.ch32.htm.

160 the immigrant bobbin boy who got his first job in 1848: Carnegie, *Autobiography*, 34.

160 Erik Johan Ljungberg, the general manager of Stora Kopparberg: Sven Rydberg, *The Great Copper Mountain: The Stora Story* (Hedmora, Sweden: Stora Kopparbergs Bergslags Aktiebolag in Collaboration with Gidlunds Publishers, 1998), 171–191.

160 Ljungberg's father squandered his savings: Gunnar Olsson and Burnett Anderson, *Stora Kopparberg: Six Hundred Years of Industrial Enterprise* (Falun, Sweden: Stora Kopparbergs Bergslags Aktiebolag, 1951), 37.

161 "prevent speculators from ruthlessly exploiting these resources": Rydberg, *Great Copper Mountain*, 179.

162 Ljungberg too promoted education, the welfare of his workers: Ibid., 188.

162 "The old nations of the Earth crawl forward": Quoted in Rydberg, *Great Copper Mountain*, 191.

6 ▮ How the Rule of Law Backfired

167 he proposed a variety of reforms: Goran B. Nilsson, "Sweden 1848: On the Road to the 'Middle Way,'" in Dieter Dowe et al., eds., *Europe in 1848: Revolution and Reform* (New York: Berghahn Books, 2001), 326.

167 Sweden passed limited liability laws for the first time: John Micklethwait and Adrian Wooldridge, *The Company: A Short History of a Revolutionary Idea* (New York: Modern Library, 2003), 24; Oskar Broberg, "The Emergence of Joint-Stock Companies During the Industrial Breakthrough in Sweden," in Gerald D. Feldman and Peter Hertner, eds., *Finance and Modernization: A Transnational and Transcontinental Perspective for the Nineteenth and Twentieth Centuries* (Burlington: Ashgate Publishing, 2008), 165–86.

168 In 1840, he published a book titled *What Is Property?*: Pierre-Joseph Proudon, *What Is Property? An Inquiry into the Principle of Right and Government* (Middlesex: Echo Library, 2008).

168 He wrote, "The economic idea of capitalism": Quoted in Iain Mckay, ed., *Property Is Theft! A Pierre-Joseph Proudon Anthology* (Edinburgh, Oakland, and Baltimore: AK Press, 2011), 4.

169 the socialist movement gradually gained momentum in Europe: Michael Rapport, *1848: Year of Revolution* (New York: Basic Books, 2008), 260–62.

169 A young tailor named August Palme: Franklin D. Scott, *Sweden: The Nation's History*, enl. ed. (Carbondale: Southern Illinois University Press, 1998), 429.

169 and toward a view of "social reform as a way to socialism": Ibid.

169 abetted by the parallel rise of labor unions: Jae-Hung Ahn, "Ideology and Interest: The Case of Swedish Social Democracy, 1886–1911," *Politics & Society* 24, no. 2 (June 1996): 175.

169 as Stora's Ljungberg had appreciated: Sven Rydberg, *The Great Copper Mountain* (Stora Kopparbergs Bergslags AB in Collaboration with Gidlunds Publishers, 1988), 188.

171 The change in those rights has come by marrying the legal concept: Brian Lane, "The Abuses of Corporate Personhood," *USA Today Magazine*, May 2004.

171 medieval Europeans inherited from Rome the idea: Karl Moore and David Lewis, *Foundations of Corporate Empire* (London: Pearson Education, 2000), 100–106, 114–16; Janet McLean, "The Transnational Corporation in History: Lessons for Today?" *Indiana Law Journal* 79, no. 363 (April, 2003): 364–65.

171 Just before the South Sea bubble burst: John Carswell, *The South Sea Bubble* (Stroud, Gloucestershire: Alan Sutton Publishing, 1993), 129.

172 in the eyes of legal scholars like Douglas Arner: Douglas Arner, "Development of the American Law of Corporations to 1832," HeinOnline, 55 SMU L. Rev. 23, 2002, 33, http://heinonline.org/HOL/Page?collection=journals&handle=hein.journals /smulr55&type=Text&id=35.

172 something of a surge in the formation of companies: Gregory A. Mark, "The Court and the Corporation: Jurisprudence, Localism, and Federalism," *Supreme Court Review,* vol. 1997, no. 403, 410–12.

172 James Madison proposed an amendment: Ibid., 412 n. 27, citing Charles C. Tansill, ed., *Documents Illustrative of the Formation of the United States* (Washington, D.C.: Government Printing Office, 1927), Madison's notes, 724.

173 Hamilton was an advocate for a U.S. version of the Bank of England: Ibid., 344.

173 "to attach full confidence to an institution of this nature": *Report on a National Bank* (1790), in Papers *on Public Credit, Commerce, and Finance by Alexander Hamilton,* Samuel McKee, ed. (New York: Columbia University Press, 1934), 53–83.

173 Congress chartered the Bank of the United States early in 1791: Ron Chernow, *Alexander Hamilton* (New York: Penguin, 2005), 349–51.

173 He argued that Hamilton was playing fast and loose: Thomas Jefferson, "Opinion on the Constitutionality of Establishing a National Bank," in Noble E. Cunningham, Jr., *Jefferson vs. Hamilton: Confrontations That Shaped a Nation* (New York: Palgrave Macmillan, 2000), 53.

174 Hamilton, who responded vehemently: Alexander Hamilton, "Opinion on the Constitutionality of Establishing a National Bank," in Cunningham, *Jefferson vs. Hamilton,* 56.

174 "[Hamilton] made your bank": Quoted in Broadus Mitchell, "Alexander Hamilton, Vol. II," 99, cited in Chernow, *Alexander Hamilton,* 353.

175 the Court decided the case of *Head & Amory: Head & Amory v. Providence Insurance Co.,* 6 U.S. 127 (1804), 167.

175 in 1809, in his opinion in the case *Bank of the United States v. Deveaux:* Mark, "The Court and the Corporation," 421.

175 one of the Marshall era's most famous decisions, *McCulloch v. Maryland*: Ibid., 422.

175 later in 1819, Marshall participated in a decision that would dramatically alter: *The Trustees of Dartmouth College v. Woodward,* 17 U.S. 518 (1804), Preface, 2–7. See also Albert J. Beveridge, *The Life of John Marshall,* vol. iv (Orlando, FL: Houghton Mifflin Company, 1919), 223–25.

176 When Wheelock died a decade later: Beveridge, *Life of John Marshall,* 226–36.

176–77 Daniel Webster . . . presented arguments on behalf of the college: *Trustees of Dartmouth College v. Woodward,* Preface, 68–73.

177 Webster then made a connection as remarkable: Ibid., 76.

178 Webster closed his case by arguing: Ibid., 95–96, 115.

178 According to witnesses, when Webster finished his arguments: Rufus Choate, "A Discourse Commemorative of Daniel Webster," in Samuel Gilman Brown, *The Works of Rufus Choate: With a Memoir of His Life,* vol. I (Boston: Little, Brown, & Co. 1862), 516–17.

386 ■ Notes

179 When the Court announced its decision: *The Trustees of Dartmouth College v. Woodward*, 625–57.

179 "A corporation is an artificial being": Ibid., 636.

180 When King James II had decided in 1686: George Louis Beer, *The Old Colonial System: 1660–1754* (Charleston, SC: BiblioLife 2008 ed., 1913), 324.

180 Parliament was also able to cancel the East India Company's charter: Nick Robins, *The Corporation That Changed the World: How the East India Company Shaped the Modern Multinational* (London and Ann Arbor: Pluto Press, 2006), 164.

180 Seven years later Connecticut created what would be a popular model: John Mickelthwait and Adrian Wooldridge, *The Company: A Short History of a Revolutionary Idea* (New York: Modern Library, 2005), 46.

180 more than 50 percent of publicly traded corporations are incorporated in that state: Delaware Department of State, Division of Corporations, official website of the State of Delaware, January 19, 2011, www.corp.delaware.gov/aboutagency.shtml.

181 in the case of *Santa Clara County v. Southern Pacific Railroad*, the Court declared without argument: *Santa Clara County v. Southern Pacific Railroad*, 118 U.S. 394 (1886), 396.

181 In 1890, it used this principle to start a series of rulings: Carl. J. Mayer, "Personalizing the Impersonal: Corporations and the Bill of Rights," *Hastings Law Journal* 41, no. 3, March 1990, 588–93.

181 U.S. Supreme Court justice Hugo Black lamented: *Connecticut General Life Ins. Co. v. Johnson*, 303 U.S. 77 (1938), 90 (dissent by Justice Black).

181 The language of the amendment speaks of protections: U.S. Constitution, Amendment XIV.

182 they were seen as quasipublic extensions of the state: Mayer, "Personalizing the Impersonal," 580.

182 the theory of corporations evolved: Ibid., 581.

182 presided over by Chief Justice Morrison "Mott" Waite: Andrew Glass, "House Funeral for U.S. Chief Justice, March 29, 1888," Politico, Life section, www.politico.com/news/stories/0311/52015.html.

182 Chief Justice Waite informed the participants: *Santa Clara County v. Southern Pacific Railroad Company*, 118 U.S. 394 (1886).

183 Justice Louis Brandeis would later write: Mayer, "Personalizing the Impersonal," 585.

183 The Court thereby essentially identified a "substantive economic doctrine": Ibid., 588–89.

184 corporations have successfully asserted the applicability of five: Stephen G. Wood and Brett G. Scharffs, "Applicability of Human Rights Standards to Private Corporations: An American Perspective," *American Journal of Comparative Law*, vol. 50, Supplement: "American Law in a Time of Global Interdependence: U.S. National Reports to the 16th International Congress of Comparative Law" (Autumn 2002): 548–51.

184 For example, in a 1977 case, the Court held: Mayer, "Personalizing the Impersonal," 606.

185 Dow Chemical was upheld when it objected to Environmental Protection Agency overflights: Ibid., 610–611.

185 The Fifth Amendment protects against double jeopardy: U.S. Constitution, Amendment V.

186 "All contributions by corporations to any political committee": *United States v. Automobile Workers*, 352 U.S. 567 (1957), 572 (quoting 40 Cong. Rec. 96).

186 Justice John Paul Stevens cited "the enormous power corporations had come to wild": *Citizens United v. Federal Election Commission*, 08 U.S. 205 (2009), 42–43.

187 That ban was made permanent by the Taft-Hartley Act of 1947: *Federal Election Commission v. Wisconsin Right to Life*, 551 U.S. 06-969 (2007), 7–9 (dissent by Justice Souter).

188 a campaign finance case called *Buckley v. Valeo*: *Buckley v. Valeo*, 424 U.S. 1 (1976).

188 this case was silent on the specific issue of corporate political free speech "rights": Wood and Scharffs, "Applicability of Human Rights Standard to Private Corporation," footnote 91.

188 the Supreme Court found in *First National Bank of Boston v. Bellotti*: *First National Bank of Boston v. Bellotti*, 435 U.S. 765 (1977), footnote 26.

188 "corrosive and distorting efforts": *Austin v. Michigan Chamber of Commerce*, 494 U.S. 652 (1990).

189 A later case allowed a not-for-profit organization to use its treasury: *Federal Election Commission v. Beaumont et al.*, 539 U.S. 146 (2003).

189 Obama, a former professor of constitutional law, argued that the case: "2010 Barack Obama," transcript, 2010 State of the Union address, January 27, 2010, http://stateoftheunionaddress.org/2010-barack-obama.

190 "the showstopper moment": Benjamin F. Carlson, "Seeking a Second Joe Wilson, Press Pounces on Alito," Atlantic Wire, January 28, 2010, http://atlanticwire.theatlantic.com/opinions/view/opinion/Seeking-a-Second-Joe-Wilson-Press-Pounces-on-Alito-2334.

190 It asserted it had no other choice "without chilling political speech": *Citizens United v. Federal Election Commission*, majority opinion by Justice Kennedy, 12.

191 Further, they argue that even if PACs were construed: Ibid., 21–22.

192 a statement arguing that favoritism and influence are unavoidable in politics: Ibid., 45.

193 "The Court's opinion is thus a rejection of the common sense": *Citizens United v. Federal Election Commission*, dissent by Justice Stevens, 90.

7 ▪ **Beyond Borders**

196 We cannot wait for governments to do it all: Kofi Annan, "A New Coalition for Universal Values," *International Herald Tribune*, July 26, 2000, www.un.org/News/ossg/sg/stories/articleFull.asp?TID=31&Type=Article.

196 economist Joseph Stiglitz calls it "the removal of barriers to free trade": Joseph Stiglitz, *Globalization and Its Discontents* (New York: W. W. Norton, 2002), ix.

196 Left-wing social scientists who clearly have an ax to grind dub it: Alex MacGillivray, *A Brief History of Globalization* (New York: Carrol and Graf, 2006), "The International Forum on Globalization," 5.

196 T. N. Harper . . . called it a "recolonization": T. N. Harper, "Empire, Diaspora, and Languages of Globalism 1850–1914," in A. G. Hopkins ed., *Globalization in World History* (London: Pimlico, 2002), 141.

197 "The obligations of subjects to the sovereign": Thomas Hobbes, *Leviathan*, quoted in Larry May, *Crimes Against Humanity: A Normative Account* (Cambridge: Cambridge University Press, 2005), 74.

197 multinational actors can take advantage of the absence of regulations: Brian Roach, "A Primer on Multinational Corporations," in Alfred D. Chandler, Jr., and Bruce Mazlish, eds., *Leviathans: Multinational Corporations and the New Global Industry* (Cambridge: Cambridge University Press, 2005), 38.

198 the number of connected countries reached a hundred: "Intellectual Property on the Internet: A Survey of Issues," World Intellectual Property Organization, 2002, ii, www.wipo.int/copyright/en/ecommerce/ip_survey/.

198 when the Egyptian government cut off Internet access: Daily Mail Reporter, "How the Internet Refused to Abandon Egypt: Authorities Take Entire Country Offline . . . but Hackers Rally to Get the Message Out," Daily Mail Online, January 30, 2011, www.dailymail.co.uk/news/article-1351904/Egypt-protests-Internet-shut-hackers-message-out.html.

198 Thomas L. Friedman, passing through Tahrir Square, noted: Thomas Friedman, "Egyptians Finally Find Their Voice in Tahrir Square," *New York Times*, February 8, 2011.

199 According to the United Nations, it is now nearly five billion: Donald Melanson, "UN: Worldwide Internet Users Hit Two Billion, Cellphone Subscriptions Top Five Billion," engadget website, January 28, 2011, www.engadget.com/2011/01/28/un-worldwide-internet-users-hit-two-billion-cellphone-subscript/.

199 Advances in nautical technologies enabled a new era in global trade: Kevin H. O'Rourke and Jeffrey G. Williamson, *Globalization and History: The Evolution of a Nineteenth-Century Atlantic Economy* (Cambridge: MIT Press, 1999), 93.

199 Ice from frozen ponds in New England was shipped: Debra Cottrell, "Ice Harvesting," Heart of New England online magazine, www.theheartofnewengland.com/LifeInNewEngland-Ice-Harvesting.html.

199 Steamships replaced clippers and enhanced the safety of transoceanic voyages: Karl Moore and David Lewis, *Foundations of Corporate Empire: Is History Repeating Itself?* (London: Pearson Education, 2000), 270.

199 Alexander Graham Bell spoke the words "Mr. Watson, come here": "Mr. Watson—Come here!" American Treasures of the Library of Congress, Reason Gallery A, July 27, 2010, www.loc.gov/exhibits/treasures/trr002.html.

199 the SS *Great Western* became the first steamship to ply the Atlantic: Ewan Corlett, *The Iron Ship: The Story of Brunel's S.S. Great Britain*, (London: Conway Maritime, 1990).

200 called by Friedman "Globalization 1.0.": Thomas L. Friedman, *The World Is Flat: A Brief History of the Twenty-first Century* (New York: Farrar, Straus and Giroux, 2006), 9.

200 we can go back to the Assyrians, the Romans, and the early caravan leaders: Moore and Lewis, *Foundations of Corporate Empire*, 1–5.

200 the Hanseatic League of traders that linked: Philippe Dollinger, *The Emergence of International Business 1200–1800*, vol. I, *The German Hansa* (London: Routledge/ Thoemmes Press, 1999).

201 there were perhaps 1,500 to 2,500 enterprises that could be called "multinational": Medard Gabel and Henry Bruner, *Global Inc: An Atlas of the Multinational Corporation* (New York: W. W. Norton, 2003), 3.

201 Current estimates for the number of multinationals are over eighty thousand: "The Number of Transnational Companies Grows by 2,500 a Year," PPI Trade Fact of the Week, December 3, 2008, www.dlc.org/ndol_ci.cfm?contentid=254841&kaid= 108&subid=900003.

201 global exports equaled less than 5 percent of global economic output: Gabel and Bruner, *Global Inc.*, 18.

203 divisions arose in the early eighteenth century: O'Rourke and Williamson, *Globalization and History*, 77.

203 Reformers argued that the Corn Laws benefited agriculture: Betty Kemp, "Reflections on the Repeal of the Corn Laws," *Victorian Studies*, 5.3 (March 1962): 194.

204 he concluded that if he gave in to them on this one issue: Michael Lusztig, "Solving Peel's Puzzle: Repeal of the Corn Laws and Institutional Reservation," *Comparative Politics* 27.4 (July 1995): 393–408, 393.

204 Ironically, this came from a man who in 1841 made the famous proclamation: H. L. Wesseling, *Certain Ideas of France: Essays on French History and Civilization* (Westport, CT: Greenwood Publishing Group, 2002), 12.

204 and who expelled Karl Marx from Paris in 1845: François Furet, *Revolutionary France, 1770–1880* (Indianapolis, IN: Wiley-Blackwell, 1995), 377.

204 Cobden's first work, *England, Ireland and America*: Richard Cobden, *The Political Writings of Richard Cobden*, vol. I (1835), with a Preface by Lord Welby, Introductions by Sir Louis Mallet, C.B., and William Cullen Bryant, Notes by F. W. Chesson and a Bibliography (London: T. Fisher Unwin, 1903), http://oll.libertyfund.org /title/82/39682.

204 Cobden became a member of Parliament: John Morley, *The Life of Richard Cobden* (London: T. Fisher Unwin, 1905).

205 Reading Cobden's arguments, one is struck by the parallels: Richard Cobden, *Speeches on Questions of Public Policy*, vol. I, John Bright and James E. Thorold Rogers, eds. (London: Macmillan and Co., 1870), 385.

205 "Peace will come to earth when people have more to do with each other": Quoted in Toby Baxendale, "David Miliband's Rejection of State-Directed Socialism," The Cobden Center (Economics), September 23, 2010, www.cobdencentre.org/2010/09 /david-milibands-rejection-of-state-directed-socialism/.

205 "The great rule of conduct for us": Quoted in Ralph Raico, "The Case for an America First Foreign Policy," in *The Failure of America's Foreign Wars*, Richard M. Ebeling and Jacob G. Hornberger, eds. (Fairfax, VA: Future of Freedom Foundation, 1996), 22.

205 Hirst wrote of Cobden that he "believed in individual liberty": Francis W. Hirst, *Richard Cobden and John Morley. Being the Richard Cobden Lecture for 1941* (The Cobden Club, 1941), 37–38.

206 the aristocracy had come to an end in England: O'Rourke and Williamson, *Globalization and History*, 92.

207 itinerant actor and sometime inventor named Isaac Singer: Lin Van Buren, "Isaac Merritt Singer," The USGenWeb Project, www.rootsweb.ancestry.com/~nyrensse /bio206.htm.

207 supporting an acting company that spent five years touring with him: Nicholas Fox Weber, *The Clarks of Cooperstown: Their Sewing Machine Fortune, Their Great and Influential Art Collections, Their Forty-Year Feud* (New York: Alfred A. Knopf, 2007), 19.

207 Singer went to New York in an attempt to take a crack at marketing a new machine: Mira Wilkens, *The Emergence of Multinational Enterprise: American Business Abroad from the Colonial Era to 1914* (Cambridge, MA: Harvard University Press, 1970), 37–38.

207 "I worked on it day and night": Quoted in ibid.

208 Callebaut proved unreliable and uncooperative: Fred V. Carstensen, *American Enterprise in Foreign Markets: Studies of Singer and International Harvester in Imperial Russia* (Chapel Hill: University of North Carolina Press, 1984), 17.

209 Singer recalled his British manager, George B. Woodruff: Wilkens, *Emergence of Multinational Enterprise*, 41–44.

209 "We can never make our business": Ibid.

210 Within a few decades, other big U.S. companies such as Ford: Mira Wilkens, "Multinational Enterprise to 1930: Discontinuities and Continuities," in Alfred D. Chandler, Jr., and Bruce Mazlish, eds., *Leviathans: Multinational Corporations and the New Global Industry* (Cambridge, MA: Harvard University Press, 2005), 75.

210 John D. Rockefeller, son of a snake oil salesman: Ron Chernow, *Titan: The Life of John D. Rockefeller, Sr.* (New York: Random House, 1998), 63–64.

210 "Standard has done everything with the Pennsylvania legislature": Quoted in Kevin Phillips, *American Theocracy: The Peril and Politics of Radical Religion, Oil, and Borrowed Money in the 21st Century* (New York: Viking, 2006), 34.

210 Rockefeller's articulated mantra was "competition is a sin": Chernow, *Titan*, 149.

211 Rockefeller sought every possible advantage including domination: Elizabeth Granitz and Benjamin Klein, "Monopolization by 'Raising Rivals' Costs': The Standard Oil Case," *Journal of Law and Economics* 39, no. 1 (April 1996): 26–27.

211 Standard would account for 33 million barrels of America's 36-million-barrel refining capacity: Peter Collier, and David Horowitz, *The Rockefellers: An American Dynasty* (Austin, TX: Holt, Rinehart and Winston, 1976), 28–29.

211 it would unilaterally decide the price of American crude: Daniel Yergin, *The Prize: The Epic Quest for Oil, Money, and Power* (New York: Simon and Schuster, 1991), 53–54.

211 (JOHN D. ROCKEFELLER IMITATES A CLAM, read one headline): Ibid., 97.

211–12 ("The art of forgetting is possessed by Mr. Rockefeller in its highest degree"): Quoted in Collier and Horowitz, *Rockefellers*, 43.

212 the business community worried about how he might deal with the trusts: James MacGregor and Susan Dunn, *The Three Roosevelts: Partician Leaders Who Transformed America* (New York: Grove Press, 2001), 69.

213 by returning $100,000 in campaign donations made to him: Yergin, *The Prize*, 107; MacGregor and Dunn, *Three Roosevelts*, 96–97.

213 the author, Ida Tarbell, pointedly attacked Rockefeller: Quoted in Yergin, *The Prize*, 105.

213 The legal proceedings were as gargantuan as their target: Ibid., 108.

213 "We believe that the defendants have acquired a monopoly": *The Standard Oil Company of New Jersey et al. v. the United States*, 221 U.S. 1 (May 1911), 504, http://biotech.law.lsu.edu/cases/antitrust/ Standard_Oil_case.htm.

214 Edward Douglass White, slowly and almost inaudibly read out the decision: Ibid., 512.

215 The total sales of the successor companies: See their sales on the Fortune 500, http://money.cnn.com/magazines/fortune/fortune500/2010/full_list/index.html.

217 GM played an important role in supporting the German war effort: Joel Bakan, *The Corporation: The Pathological Pursuit of Profit and Power* (New York: Free Press, 2004), 87–88.

217 "The head office in New York had a complete understanding": Edwin Black, *IBM and the Holocaust*, quoted in Bakan, *The Corporation*, 88.

217 "Corporations have no capacity to value political systems": Bakan, *The Corporation*, 88.

218 it agreed to work with the Nazi regime to make the chemicals: Peter Hayes, *Industry and Ideology: IG Farben in the Nazi Era* (Cambridge: Cambridge University Press, 2001).

218 "The democratic countries in the developing world are losing ground": "Globalization Survey Reveals U.S. Corporations Prefer Dictatorships," by R. C. Longworth, *Global Exchange*, November 19, 1999, www.globalexchange.org/campaigns/econ101/survey.html.

218–19 Ivan Kreuger was the heir to a small, struggling Swedish match factory: Archibald MacLeish, "The Grand Scheme of the Swedish Match King," CNN Money, April 28, 2009, http://money.cnn.com/2009/04/24/news/companies/swedish_match_king.fortune/index.htm.

219 merging his United Swedish Match Factories with the Vulcan Group: "Business: Poor Kreuger," *Time*, March 21, 1932, www.time.com/time/magazine/article/0,9171,743409-2,00.html.

219 He would issue bonds in his company and use the capital to buy market domination: Ibid.

219 "great aversion to divulging information": Quoted in Bill Wilson, "Kreuger: The original Bernie Madoff?" BBC News, March 13, 2009, http://news.bbc.co.uk/2/hi/7939403.stm.

220 "Kreuger's financial methods were becoming increasingly devious": Ibid.

220 undid his waistcoat, and shot himself through the heart: "Business: Poor Kreuger."

220 Stora bought Swedish Match: Arthur Max, "Sweden's Stora Celebrates Its First 700 Years of Success," *Los Angeles Times*, July 5, 1988, http://articles.latimes.com/1988 -07-05/business/fi-5265_1_swedish-match-ab.

220 "history's most sweeping reorganization of the international order": G. John Ikenberry, *After Victory: Institutions, Strategic Restraint, and the Rebuilding of Order After Major Wars* (Princeton, NJ: Princeton University Press, 2001), 163.

221 to lock the formerly warring countries of Europe into "an open multilateral economic order": Ibid., 165.

222 to impede approval of component steps of the agreement like the Kyoto Protocol: Bob Ward, "Why ExxonMobil Must Be Taken to Task over Climate Denial Funding," *Guardian*, Guardian.co.uk, July 1, 2009, www.guardian.co.uk/environment/cif -green/2009/jul/01/bob-ward-exxon-mobil-climate.

223 In the "Uruguay Round" of GATT negotiations: Uruguay Round Agreement, Annex 2, "Understanding and Procedures Governing the Settlement of Disputes," World Trade Organization, www.wto.org/english/ docs_e/legal_e/28-dsu_e.htm.

224 The headline in the next day's *New York Times*: Keith Bradsher, "Kodak Is Loser in Trade Ruling on Fuji Dispute," *New York Times*, December 6, 1997.

224 when Kodak hired George Fisher as its chairman in 1993: Jeffrey L. Dunoff, "The Misguided Debate over NGO Participation at the WTO," *Journal of International Economic Law* 1, issue 3 (1998): 433, 442.

224 Fisher lobbied the U.S. government to step in and act on his behalf: Bradsher, "Kodak Is Loser in Trade Ruling on Fuji Dispute"; Dunoff, "The Misguided Debate over NGO Participation at the WTO," 442.

224 he hired a very big, high-priced law firm: Dunoff, "Misguided Debate," 443 (note 43).

225 Kodak announced it was cutting fourteen thousand jobs: "Can George Fisher Fix Kodak?" *BusinessWeek*, October 20, 1997, www.businessweek.com/1997/42/b3549001 .htm.

226 thousands of bilateral investment treaties exist: Susan D. Franck, "The Legitimacy Crisis in Investment Treaty Arbitration: Privatizing Public International Law Through Inconsistent Decisions," *Fordham Law Review* 73 (March 2005): 1522–23.

226 Forestry had continued to become one of its most important lines of business: "Report on Sweden: Stora Celebrations Will Cap Turnaround in Forest Products Industry," *Globe and Mail* (Canada), March 14, 1988.

226 in 1962, it made a bold venture overseas: Rydberg, *Stora Kopparberg*, 89.

226 Stora's spraying of local forests with dioxin: Douglas Martin, "Fearing Illness, 15 Sue to Bar Spraying of Dioxin," *New York Times*, May 2, 1983.

227 Stora reduced its increasingly uncompetitive exposure to the steel business: "Stora Enso History," Storaenso.com, http://81.209.16.116/History/History_timeline.

227 "owns forests half the size of Belgium": Max, "Sweden's Stora Celebrates Its First 700 Years of Success."

227 Stora either owns, manages, or leases land in Europe, Asia, and South America:

"Stora Enso Oyj," Stora Enso website, Storaenso.com, http://81.209.16.116/History/Stora_Enso.

227 the largest cash and securities deal in Sweden's history: Max, "Sweden's Stora Celebrates Its First 700 Years of Success."

227 "We have been a fairly quiet, silent company over the years": Quoted in Joanne Mason, "700-Year-Old Swedish Timber Company Is Still Going Strong by Branching Out," *Los Angeles Times*, June 7, 1988, http://articles.latimes.com/1988-06-07/business/fi-3731_1_swedish-match.

227 hosted to celebrate the seven hundredth anniversary of Bishop Peter of Vasteras's deal: Ibid.; Max, "Sweden's Stora Celebrates Its First 700 Years of Success"; "After 700 Years, Stora Throws a Party," *Globe and Mail* (Canada), June 17, 1988.

228 "Our future lies in European integration": Quoted in "After 700 years, Stora Throws a Party."

228 Arguing that the new Stora was now "too big to be ignored: Max, "Sweden's Stora Celebrates Its First 700 Years of Success."

228 Par Nuder, a Social Democrat: Par Nuder, interview with the author, 2010.

229 "I think that's an interesting point": Charlene Barshefsky, interview with the author, 2010.

229 It merged with the Finnish forest products and packaging giant Enso: "History," Stora Enso website, http://81.209.16.116/WebRoot/503425/Taso2_content_siivottu.aspx?id=515562.

8 The Coin of Whose Realm?

231 I had lunch with the U.S. National Economic Council director, Larry Summers: Larry Summers, interview with the author, 2009.

232 the days of the British Parliament when 10 percent of all members were in some way direct beneficiaries: Arnold A. Sherman, "Pressure from Leadenhall: The East India Company Lobby, 1600–1678," *Business History Review* 50.3 (Autumn 1976): 329–55, 344.

233 to be worth enough to be useful in most transactions, many of the coins: Eli F. Heckscher, *An Economic History of Sweden* (Cambridge, MA: Harvard University Press, 1954), 88–89.

233 monetary sovereignty . . . "is incompatible with globalization": Benn Steil and Manuel Hinds, *Money, Markets and Sovereignty* (New Haven: Yale University Press, 2009), 10.

234 It first appeared in China during the Song dynasty: Valerie Hansen and Kenneth R. Curtis, *Voyages in World History* (Boston: Wadsworth Cengage Learning: 2010), 336.

235 The bank was called Stockholms Banco, and it was operated by an entrepreneurial character named Johan Palmstruch: "Stockholms Banco, Sveriges Riksbank," Riksbank website, www.riksbank.com/templates/Page.aspx?id=30894.

236 The tiny Dutch Republic, for example, already had an army of 60,000: Maarten Roy Prak and Diane Webb, *The Dutch Republic in the Seventeenth Century: The Golden Age* (Cambridge: Cambridge University Press, 2005), 69.

236 The Spanish army grew to 300,000 by the 1630s: Olaf Van Nimwegen, *The Dutch Army and the Military Revolutions, 1588–1688* (Rochester, NY: Boydell Press, 2010), 11.

236 French army grew threefold in a century: Stephane Thion, *French Armies of the Thirty Years War* (Auzielle: Little Round Top Editions, 2008), 79.

236 the cost of outfitting an infantry company rose 150 percent: M. S. Anderson, *War and Society in Europe of the Old Regime 1618–1789* (Buffalo: McGill–Queen's University Press, 1998), 17.

236 commercial or financial failure meant defeat: Mark Kishlansky, Patrick Geary, and Patricia O'Brien, *Civilization in the West*, vol. II, *Since 1355*, 5th ed. (New York: Pearson, 2002), 464.

236 almost three-quarters of French government revenue was being spent on land warfare: Anderson, *War and Society in Europe*, 87.

236 The Bank of England, for example, was established in 1694: Charles Tilly, *Coercion, Capital, and European States, AD 990–1992* (Malden, MA: Wiley-Blackwell, 1992), 157.

237 accelerated the development of capitalism: Ernesto Screpanti and Stefano Zamagni, *An Outline of the History of Economic Thought* (Oxford: Clarendon Press, 1993), 16.

237 seen as evidence of sinful impulses like greed: E. K. Hunt, *Property and Prophets: The Rise of Economic Institutions and Ideologies* (New York: M. E. Sharpe, 2003), 10–12.

237 what Max Weber later addressed in his essay "The Protestant Ethic and the Spirit of Capitalism": Hunt, *Property and Prophets*, 35–37; Luciano Pellicani, *The Genesis of Capitalism and the Origins of Modernity* (New York: Telos Press, 1994), 31–32.

237 "one who has the gold does as he wills": Quoted in Michel Beaud, *History of Capitalism: 1500–2000* (New York: Monthly Review Press, 2000), 15.

237 "in a well-organized government": Quoted in Beaud, *History of Capitalism*, 17.

238 one of the directors of the Company produced a series of influential writings: Lynn Muchmore, "A Note on Thomas Mun's 'England Treasure by Forraign Trade,'" *Economic History Review*, 23.3 (December 1970): 498–503, 498; Henry William Spiegel, *The Growth of Economic Thought* (Durham: Duke University Press, 1991), 107–8.

238 "the title of Mun's Book became a fundamental maxim": Quoted in Spiegel, *Growth of Economic Thought*, 107.

238 "the individual's self-regarding propensities": Jerry Z. Muller, *The Mind and the Market: Capitalism in Modern European Thought* (New York: Alfred A. Knopf, 2002), 35.

238 In his *Philosophical Letters*, Voltaire argued that market activity: Quoted in Muller, *The Mind and the Market*, 27, 29.

239 Go into the Exchange in London: Voltaire, *Philosophical Letters (Letters Concerning the English Nation)*, trans. Ernest Dilworth (Mineola, NY: Dover Publications, 2003), 26.

240 "He did not anticipate the baronial power": Douglas Dowd, *Capitalism and Economics: A Critical History* (London: Pluto Press, 2000), 30.

240 As Smith himself acknowledged, he was heavily influenced by David Hume: Cited in Steil and Hinds, *Money, Markets, and Sovereignty*, 6.

241 became the richest in the world during the period of greatest dominance: Jacob Strieder, Norman Scott Brien Gras, and Mildred L. Hartsough, *Jacob Fugger the Rich: Merchant and Banker of Augsburg, 1459–1525* (Washington, D.C.: Bearbooks, 2001).

242 Rothschild was born in a Jewish ghetto in Frankfurt: Niall Ferguson, *The Ascent of Money: A Financial History of the World* (New York: Penguin Press, 2008), 79–82.

242 the Napoleonic wars, which fueled the rise of the Rothschild family: Liaquat Ahamed, *Lords of Finance: The Bankers Who Broke the World* (New York: Penguin Press, 2009), 210.

243 a ballooning of the national debt to £745 million, twice the country's GDP: Ferguson, *Ascent of Money*, 82.

243 the English chancellor of the exchequer instructed his representatives: Ibid., 82.

243 the response of a grateful British government: Ibid., 83.

243 they made significant profits on these transactions: Herbert H. Kaplan, *Nathan Meyer Rothschild and the Creation of a Dynasty: The Critical Years, 1806–1816* (Stanford: Stanford University Press, 2006), 137; Ferguson, *Ascent of Money*, 84–89.

244 "Dearest friend, I have now done my duty": Quoted in Ferguson, *Ascent of Money*, 87.

245 John Jacob Astor, the son of a village butcher from Waldorf: John N. Ingham, *Biographical Dictionary of American Business Leaders*, vol. I (Westport, CT: Greenwood Press, 1983), 26–27.

246 In 1886, the number hit one million: Micklethwait and Wooldridge, *The Company*, 61.

246 "Pirates are not extinct": Glenn Porter, *The Rise of Big Business 1860–1920* (Wheeling, IL: Harlan Davidson, 2006), 41.

247 Through reorganization and consolidation, he built these: Charles Morris, *The Tycoons: How Andrew Carnegie, John D. Rockefeller, Jay Gould, and J. P. Morgan Invented the American Supereconomy* (New York: Henry Holt, 2005), 235–36.

248 Morgan engineered the creation of enterprises: Micklethwait and Wooldridge, *The Company*, 62.

248 the aging banker who was seen as the natural savior of the system: Morris, *The Tycoons*, 249–50.

248 Cortelyou made $25 million available to the Morgan group: Ron Chernow, *The House of Morgan: An American Banking Dynasty and the Rise of Modern Finance* (New York: Atlantic Monthly Press, 1990), 123.

249 "Thomas wanted to shut the Exchange": Quoted in ibid., 125.

251 Joining the president were: William Safire, *Before the Fall: An Inside View of the Pre-Watergate White House* (New York: Doubleday, 1975), 509.

251 the Germans, the Swiss, the Dutch, the Belgians, and the Austrians all shut their markets: Susan Strange, "The Dollar Crisis 1971," *International Affairs* 48, no. 2 (April 1972): 191, 199.

252 In the months before the Camp David retreat: Ibid., 202; Yergin and Stanislaw, *Commanding Heights*, 44.

252 Nixon "was not about to stick his thumb in the dike": Safire, *Before the Fall*, 512, 518.

252 "We must protect the position of the American dollar": Richard Nixon, speech made August 15, 1971, www.ena.lu/speech_richard_nixon_15_august_1971-2-5019.

253 In 1972, the British followed suit: Robert Solomon, *The International Monetary System, 1945–1981* (New York: Harper and Row, 1982), 209, 233.

254 Today, global foreign exchange volumes are approximately $4 trillion a day: "Global Forex Reserves Exceeding 4 Trillion USD for the First Time," People's Daily Online, December 23, 2005, http://english.peopledaily.com.cn/200512/23/eng20051223_230380.html.

254 Currently, the country with the world's largest reserves is China: "Country Comparison: Reserves of Foreign Exchange and Gold," CIA World Factbook, www.cia.gov/library/publications/the-world-factbook/rankorder/2188rank.html.

254 China applies perhaps only $2 billion a day to market trading: Mike Mish Shedlock, "China's Foreign Exchange Reserves Jump by Record $199 Billion," Minyanville, January 12, 2011, www.minyanville.com/businessmarkets/articles/china-china-economy-exchange-reserves-inflation/1/12/2011/id/32145.

254 as Joseph Stiglitz has suggested: Joseph Stiglitz, "What I Learned at the World Economic Crisis," *New Republic*, April 17, 2000, www.globalpolicy.org/component/content/article/209/42760.html.

255 Just ten currencies account for virtually all of foreign exchange trading today: "Triennial Central Bank Survey of Foreign Exchange and Derivatives Market Activity in 2007," *Bank for International Settlements*, December 19, 2007, www.bis.org/publ/rpfxf07t.pdf.

256 with some rough estimates of the world's total physical currencies at over eight trillion dollars: Josh Clark, "How Much Actual Money Is There in the World?" http://money.howstuffworks.com/how-much-money-is-in-the-world.htm.

256 the total value of the world's derivatives is estimated at approximately $791 trillion: "International Banking and Financial Market Developments," BIS Quarterly Review, December 2008, www.bis.org/publ/qtrpdf/r_qa0812.pdf.

256 about fourteen times global GDP: According to Google public data, global GDP was $58.26 trillion in 2009, www.google.com/publicdata?ds=wb-wdi&met=ny_gdp_mktp_cd&tdim=true&dl=en&hl=en&q=global+gdpm.

256 $82.2 trillion in worldwide debt securities: World Stock and Bond Markets and Portfolio Diversity," Asset Allocation Advisor, November 2009, www.aametrics.com/pdfs/world_stock_and_bond_markets_nov2009.pdf.

256 $36.6 trillion in equity value: "World Equity Market Declines: –$25.9 Trillion," *Seeking Alpha*, October 8, 2008, http://seekingalpha.com/article/99256-world-equity-market-declines-25-9-trillion.

256 In *The Commanding Heights*, Dan Yergin and Joe Stanislaw describe: Yergin and Stanislaw, *Commanding Heights*, 47, 48.

257 "The intellectual roots of tax reform": Martin Feldstein, "American Economic Policy in the 1980s: A Personal View," in *American Economic Policy of the 1980s*, Martin Feldstein, ed. (Chicago: University of Chicago Press, 1995), 13.

258 More business-friendly judges were appointed: Martin Feldstein, "Antitrust Policy:

Summary of Discussion," in Feldstein, ed., *American Economic Policy in the 1980s*, 620–21.

258 "the Reagan administration believed that economic regulation was wrong": Martin Feldstein, "Economic Regulation: Summary of Discussion," in Feldstein, ed., *American Economic Policy in the 1980s*, 452.

259 each of his three successors at Goldman also had senior roles: John Arlidge, "I'm Doing 'God's Work.' Meet Mr Goldman Sachs," *Sunday Times*, November 8, 2009, www.timesonline.co.uk/tol/news/world/ us_and_americas/article6907681 .ece.

259 there is frequent movement in both directions: "Revolving Door: Top Agencies," OpenSecrets.org, www.opensecrets.org/revolving/top.php?display=G.

259 prior to becoming White House chief of staff in 2011, William Daley served: Biographical data available at OpenSecrets.org, www.opensecrets.org/revolving/rev _summary.php?id=70872.

260 battling even other top Clinton appointees: Matt Taibbi, "The Great American Bubble Machine," *Rolling Stone*, July 13, 2009, www.rollingstone.com/politics /story/29127316/the_great_american_ bubble_machine.

261 the ratio of the average American home price to the median household income: John Cassidy, *How Markets Fail: The Logic of Economic Calamities* (New York: Farrar, Straus and Giroux, 2009), 238–39.

262 even raised by some heads of state and top government officials: Philip Augar, "It Is Time to Put Finance Back in Its Box," *Financial Times*, April 13, 2009, http://delong .typepad.com/egregious_moderation/2009/04/philip-augar-it-is-time-to-put -finance-back-in-its-box.html; Bertrand Benoit, "US 'will lose financial super-power status," *Financial Times*, September 25, 2008, www.stwr.org/global-financial -crisis/us-will-lose-financial-superpower-status.html.

263 Among other financial firms, Morgan Stanley: Bradley Keoun and Phil Kuntz, "Wall Street Aristocracy Got $1.2 Trillion in Secret Loans," *Bloomberg*, August 22, 2011, www.bloomberg.com/news/2011-08-21/wall-street-aristocracy-got-1-2-trillion -in-fed-s-secret-loans.html.

263 The Enron and WorldCom scandals: Alexei Barrionuevo, "Enron Chiefs Guilty of Fraud and Conspiracy," *New York Times*, May 26, 2006; "WorldCom Company Timeline," Reuters and *Washington Post*, March 15, 2005, www.washingtonpost .com/wp-dyn/articles/A49156-2002Jun26.html.

263 In a *New York Times* article titled: David Kocieniewski, "G.E. Strategies Let It Avoid Taxes All Together," *New York Times*, May 24, 2011.

264 When a congressional staffer later learned of the letter: Taibbi, "The Great American Bubble Machine."

265 Paulson called Blankfein twenty-four times: Arlidge, "I'm Doing 'God's Work.' Meet Mr. Goldman Sachs"; Bethany Mclean, "The Bank Job," *Vanity Fair*, January 2010, www.vanityfair.com/business/features/2010/01/goldman-sachs-200101.

265 "The collective message of all this": Taibbi, "The Great American Bubble Machine."

265 a claim that even the former Goldmanite Kashakari believes is absurd: Mclean, "The Bank Job."

265 "We're very important. We help companies grow": Quoted in Arlidge, "I'm Doing 'God's Work.' Meet Mr. Goldman Sachs."

267 Even in little Sweden, Par Nuder made the case: Par Nuder, interview with the author, 2010.

9 ▪ The Decline of Force

268 conflict has become so costly: Bernard Loo, ed., *Military Transformation and Strategy: Revolutions in Military Affairs and Small States* (New York: Routledge, 2009), 50.

269 a state of war, which, for Hobbes, was one of "every many against every man": Thomas Hobbes, *Leviathan*, chapter XIII, http://oregonstate.edu/instruct/phl302 /texts/hobbes/leviathanc.html.

269 Similarly, Locke agreed that avoidance of the state of war: John Locke, "Second Treatise of Government," in Michael J. Sandel, ed., *Justice: A Reader* (Oxford: Oxford University Press, 2007), 89, 98–109.

271 they rebelled three times: Vilhelm Moberg, *A History of the Swedish People*, vol. II, *From Renaissance to Revolution*, Paul Britten Austen, trans. (Minneapolis: University of Minnesota Press, 1973), 175–76.

271 the master miners of the late Middle Ages were granted the right: Gunnar Olsson and Burnett Anderson, *Stora Kopparberg: Six Hundred Years of Industrial Enterprise* (Falun, Sweden: Stora Kopparbergs Bergslags Aktiebolag, 1951), 13.

271 Loyalty to the guild transcended that to local law: Sven Rydberg, *The Great Copper Mountain: The Stora Story* (Stora Kopparbergs Bergslags Aktiebolag, 1988), 50.

271 These units, called "free companies": P. W. Singer, *Corporate Warriors: The Rise of the Privatized Military Industry* (Ithaca, NY: Cornell University Press, 2003), 22–26.

272 "Mercenaries and auxiliaries are at once useless and dangerous": Niccolò Machiavelli, *The Prince*, chapter XII (Harvard Classics, 1909–1914), www.bartleby.com/36 /1/12.html.

272 Sir Francis Drake and Sir Walter Raleigh: Peter Whitfield, *Sir Francis Drake* (New York: NYU Press, 2004), 29–36.

272 with the benefit of a navy partially provided by Louis de Geer: Peter H. Wilson, *The Thirty Years War: Europe's Tragedy* (Cambridge, MA: Belknap Press of Harvard University Press, 2009), 185, 299–407, 458.

273 Four out of every ten members of the British army were not British: Janice E. Thomson, *Mercenaries, Pirates, and Sovereigns* (Princeton: Princeton University Press, 1996), 28–29.

273 "From this moment until such time as its enemies shall have been driven": Quoted in Christon I. Archer et al., *World History of Warfare* (Lincoln: University of Nebraska Press, 2008), 790.

274 The French army swelled from 290,000 men to 700,000: John J. Mearsheimer, *The Tragedy of Great Power Politics* (New York: W. W. Norton, 2003), 283–84.

274 he used the state's resources to field an army: Philip Bobbitt, *The Shield of Achilles: War, Peace, and the Course of History* (New York: Alfred A. Knopf, 2002), 162.

274 This led to the passage of the Neutrality Act in 1794: Thompson, *Mercenaries, Pirates, and Sovereigns*, 78–81.

275 France's grew from 132,000 after Napoleon's defeat to 544,000 by 1880: Mearsheimer, *Tragedy of Great Power Politics*, 303.

275 While Prussia's army had been 130,000 men: Paul Kennedy, *The Rise and Fall of the Great Powers* (New York: Vintage Books, 1987), 154.

275 Later they served in the Landwehr: E. J. Hobsbawm, *Nations and Nationalism Since 1780: Programme, Myth, Reality* (Cambridge: Cambridge University Press, 1990), 83; Kennedy, *Rise and Fall of the Great Powers*, 182–91.

275 the United States emerged as a stronger union: Kennedy, *Rise and Fall of the Great Powers*, 178–82, 206–9.

276 By 1910, the Russians had 1.2 million men in their regular army: Mearsheimer, *Tragedy of Great Power Politics*, 303, 320.

278 Wilson's rules envisioned a League of Nations: Bobbitt, *Shield of Achilles*, 471.

278 In the U.N. Charter: United Nations Charter. "Chapter VII: Action with Respect to Threats to the Peace, Breaches of the Peace, and Acts of Agression," United Nations, www.un.org/en/documents/charter/chapter7.shtml.

279 In 1986 the court went further: *The Republic of Nicaragua v. The United States of America*, 1986 I.C.J. 520, www.icj-cij.org/docket/files/70/6503.pdf.

279 a wide prohibition against the use of force "has the nature of a preemptory norm": Natalino Ronzitti, "The Current Status of Legal Principles Prohibiting the Use of Force and Legal Justifications of the Use of Force," in Michael Bothe, Mary Ellen O'Connell, and Natalino Ronzitti, eds., *Redefining Sovereignty: The Use of Force After the Cold War* (Ardsley, NY: Transnational Publishers, 2005): 91–110, 93.

279 the ICJ ruled against the United States: *Military and Paramilitary Activities In and Against Nicaragua (Nicaragua v. United States of America)*, Jurisdiction and Admissibility, 1984 ICJ REP.

279 the United States pressured a new Nicaraguan government to drop the case: Mark A. Uhlig, "U.S. Urges Nicaragua to Forgive Legal Claim," *New York Times*, September 30, 1990.

280 "at home and abroad, the Reagan Administration has made it clear": Quoted in B. S. Chimni, "The International Court and the Maintenance of Peace and Security: The Nicaragua Decision and the United States Response," *International and Comparative Law Quarterly* 35.4 (October 1986): 960–70, 965.

280 The Soviets vetoed the Security Council's resolution: Brendan I. Koerner, "Can You Bypass a U.N. Security Council Veto?" *Slate*, March 12, 2003.

280 When the United States invoked its "right of self-defense": Raymond Hinnebusch, "The Iraq War and International Relations: Implications for Small States," *Cambridge Review of International Affairs* 19.3 (September 2006): 451–63, 452.

280 many feel less free to do so: Hakan Wiberg, "The Security of Small Nations: Challenges and Defences," *Journal of Peace Research* 24.4 (December 1987): 339–63, 343.

280 seeking to pressure Libya's Muammar Qaddafi to desist: David D. Kirkpatrick, Steven Erlanger, and Elisabeth Bumiller, "Allies Open Air Assault on Qaddafi's Forces in Libya," *New York Times*, March 19, 2011, www.nytimes.com/2011/03/20 /world/africa/20libya.html.

281 America's interventions in Iraq and Afghanistan will cost: Joseph Stiglitz and Linda Blimes, "The Three Trillion Dollar War," *Sunday Times*, February 23, 2008, www.timesonline.co.uk/tol/comment/columnists/guest_contributors/article 3419840.ece.

281 Its closest rival, China, spends only one-tenth as much as does the U.S.: Global Firepower database, available at www.globalfirepower.com/active-military-man power.asp.

281 The total defense spending of the remaining 175 countries of the world: Stockholm International Peace Research Institute's 2009 Year Book on Armaments, Disarmament, and International Security in 2008, summary available at www.globalissues .org/article/75/world-military-spending#WorldMilitarySpending.

281 It is estimated that the real dollar cost of new bomber aircraft: Thomas R. Cusack, "Sinking Budgets and Ballooning Prices: Recent Developments Connected to Military Spending," in Francis G. Castles, ed., *The Disappearing State? Retrenchment Realities in an Age of Globalization* (Cheltenham, England: Edward Elgar, 2007): 103–32, 121.

282 Only forty of almost two hundred countries have active forces: International Institute for Strategic Studies, *The Military Balance 2010: The Annual Assessment of Global Military Capabilities and Defence Economics* (New York: Taylor and Francis, 2010).

282 there are more admirals and generals in the Swedish military today: "Sweden Can No Longer Defend Itself," *The Local* (Sweden's News in English), May 15, 2008, www.thelocal.se/11782/20080515/.

282 the sixteenth century saw 34 such wars: Charles Tilly, *Coercion, Capital, and European States, AD 990–1992* (Malden, MA: Wiley-Blackwell, 1992), table 3.1, "Wars Involving Great Powers," 72.

282 "When the war of the giants is over": Winston Churchill, *Triumph and Tragedy* (New York: Houghton Mifflin Harcourt, 1986), 377.

283 that set in motion the first Anglo-Afghan war in 1839: Christine Noelle, *State and Tribe in Nineteenth-Century Afghanistan: The Reign of Amir Dost Muhammad Khan (1862–1863)* (London: RoutledgeCurzon, 2004), 38–56.

284 The conflict became the Soviet equivalent of Vietnam: Philip B. Heymann, *Living the Policy Process* (Oxford: Oxford University Press, 2008), 21–51, 64–82.

284 fewer members and affiliates than, say, the Swedish army: Deb Riechmannm "Petraeus: Al-Qaida Is Not on Rise in Afghanistan," Associated Press, April 10, 2011, www.azcentral.com/news/articles/2011/04/10/20110410afghanistan0410.html.

284 the U.S. Senate Foreign Relations committee has estimated that coalition spending in Afghanistan: Karen DeYoung, "Afghan Nation-building Programs Not Sustainable, Report Says," *Washington Post*, June 7, 2011.

285 The Ethiopians attempted to impose the fourteenth new government: Jeffrey Get-

tleman, "The Most Dangerous Place in the World," *Foreign Policy* (March/April 2009), www.foreignpolicy.com/story/cms.php?story_id=4682.

285 trying to contain them has motivated an effort incorporating support from the navies: Jeffrey Gettleman, "The Pirates Have Seized the Ship," *GQ*, February 2009, www.gq.com/news-politics/big-issues/200902/somalia-pirates; Jeffrey Gettleman, "Somali Pirates Get Ransom and Leave Arms Freighter," *New York Times*, February 5, 2009, www.nytimes.com/2009/02/06/world/africa/06pirates.html?scp=6&sq =gettleman+faina&st=nyt.

286 A report released in 1996 by the Department of Defense: "Improving the Combat Edge Through Outsourcing," a Department of Defense report, March 1, 1996, available online at www.defense.gov/speeches/speech.aspx?speechid=890.

286 The next year, the Defense Department's Quadrennial Defense Review announced: United States Department of Defense, "Report of the Quadrennial Defense Review" (DIANE Publishing, 1997), available online as a Google eBook, http://books .google.com/books?id=1buLAnPa0ZYC&source=gbs_navlinks_s.

286 And, as secretary of defense under George W. Bush, he would oversee: On September 10, 2001, Defense Secretary Donald Rumsfeld made a speech in front of twenty-three thousand Pentagon employees in which he declared that he wanted to "save" the Pentagon from its own wasteful bureaucracy. Remarks by Donald H. Rumsfeld, Secretary of Defense, at the DOD Acquisition and Logistics Excellence Week Kickoff at the Pentagon, September 10, 2001, www.defense.gov/Speeches/Speech .aspx?SpeechID=430.

287 "we crossed the Rubicon in 2002": Quoted in Allison Stanger, *One Nation Under Contract: The Outsourcing of American Power and the Future of Foreign Policy* (New Haven: Yale University Press, 2009), 87.

287 According to Stanger, over 80 percent of Department of Defense funds: Allison Stanger, "Addicted to Contractors," *Foreign Policy*, December 1, 2009, www.for eignpolicy.com/articles/2009/12/01/addicted to contractors.

287 Once a low-profile private security company that performed increasingly "mission-critical" assignments: Jeremy Scahill, *Blackwater: The Rise of the World's Most Powerful Mercenary Army* (New York: Norton Books, 2007), 69–72.

287 the company's work in Fallujah that day: Ibid., 91–104; Jeffrey Gettleman, "4 From U.S. Killed in Ambush in Iraq; Mob Drags Bodies," *New York Times*, April 1, 2004, www.nytimes.com/2004/04/01/international/middleeast/01IRAQ.html?scp=7&sq =blackwater%20fallujah&st=cse.

288 hiring 1.8 million new contract employees between 2002 and 2005: Stanger, *One Nation Under Contract*, 87.

288 when servicemen are injured in situations that "arise": Scahill, *Blackwater*, 251.

288 the company has also asserted that its employees are not liable: Jeffrey Rosen, "Contractors Status in Iraq Hits Gray Area," *Sacramento Bee*, May 23, 2004.

289 L. Paul Bremer, the U.S. "viceroy" in Iraq who was famously protected: Alissa J. Rubin and Paul von Zielbauner, "Blackwater Case Highlights Legal Uncertainties," *New York Times*, October 11, 2007.

289 The U.S. Justice Department avoided wading into these waters until September

2007: Ginger Thompson and James Risen, "Plea by Blackwater Guard Helps Indict Others," *New York Times*, December 8, 2008.

289   Al Clark, a former mentor of Prince's [Blackwater's CEO], quit because of a difference: Scahill, *Blackwater*, 103.

289   Other instances have seen contractors illegally inflate their invoices to the governments: Rajiv Chandrasekaran, *Imperial Life in the Emerald City* (New York: Vintage Books, 2006), 155–161; in April, the Fourth Circuit Court of Appeals reinstated a jury verdict holding the firm liable for five false claims under the False Claims Act, overruling the trial judge's limit on potential damages. See Ellen Nakashima, "Court Revives Suit Over Iraq Work, Door Could Be Opened for Other Fraud Cases," *Washington Post*, April 11, 2009.

289   In Africa, the exploits of another private contractor named Executive Outcomes: Deborah D. Avant, *The Market for Force: The Consequences of Privatizing Security* (Cambridge: Cambridge University Press, 2005), 10–15, 82–98; Singer, 110–15.

290   EO warned this would lead to problems for the government: Avant, *Market for Force*, 82–89.

290   another problem cited by Stanger: Stanger, *One Nation Under Contract*, 91–92.

290   And in August 2009, two former Blackwater employees testified in federal court: Jeremy Scahill, "Blackwater Founder Implicated in Murder," *The Nation*, August 4, 2009; see also CNN.com "Ex-guards' Statements Implicate Blackwater Founder in Iraq Crimes," CNN, August 4, 2009, www.cnn.com/2009/US/08/04/iraq.blackwater.lawsuit/index.html.

291   Allegedly, unlike the program initially reported by Panetta: Jeremy Scahill, "The Secret U.S. War in Pakistan," *Nation*, November 23, 2009, www.thenation.com/doc/20091207/scahill; see also Adam Ciralsky, "Tycoon, Contractor, Soldier, Spy," *Vanity Fair*, January 2010, www.vanityfair.com/politics/features/2010/01/blackwater-201001.

291   the attack would not have been possible without support from Siemens: Saeed Kamali Dehghan, "Iran Accuses Siemens of Helping Launch Stuxnet Cyber-attack," *Guardian*, April 17, 2011, www.guardian.co.uk/world/2011/apr/17/iran-siemens-stuxnet-cyber-attack.

292   the case in rural Brazil in which women of the peasant network Via Capesina: "Stora Enso's Brazilian Imbroglio," Forbes.com, March 5, 2008.

292   Protesters allege that the reason: "What You Should Know About Stora Enso," Friends of the Earth International, available online at www.foei.org/en/resources/publications/pdfs/2010/what-you-should-know-about-stora-enso/view.

10   Supercitizens and Semi-States

295   We live in a time when people are losing confidence: "Remarks as Prepared for Wal-Mart CEO and President Lee Scott at the Wal-Mart U.S. Year Beginning Meeting," July 30, 2008, http:walmartstores.com/pressroom/news/7896.aspx.

295   Wal-Mart Stores, Inc., has revenues higher than the GDP: Authors Tracey Keys and Thomas W. Malnight write in their report "Corporate Clout: The Influence of

the World's Largest 100 Economic Entities" that "in 2009, Wal-Mart Stores had revenues exceeding the respective GDPs of 174 countries including Sweden, Saudi Arabia and Venezuela and employed over 2 million people, more than the entire population of Qatar." Available online at www.strategy-dynamics.com/features /shapers-and-influencers/66-corporate-clout-the-influence-of-the-worlds-largest -100-economic-entities.

295 BlackRock, controls assets greater than the national reserves of any country on the planet: Sheelah Kolhatkar and Sree Vidya Bhaktavatsalam, "The Colossus of Wall Street," *Bloomberg Businessweek*, December 9, 2010.

295 the Gates Foundation, spends as much worldwide on health care as does the World Health Organization: Both the Gates Foundation and the World Health Organization spend about $800 million on global health issues each year. Scott T. Firsing, *Disturbing Times: The State of the Planet and Its Possible Future* (Johannesburg: 30° South Publishers, 2008), 47; Tom Paulson, "Gates Foundation Out to Break the Cycle of Disease," *Seattle Post-Intelligencer*, December 8, 2003.

296 Whether or not there was ever a truly Westphalian moment: Stephen D. Krasner, "Compromising Westphalia," *International Security* 20:3 (1995–96): 115–16.

297 having been introduced in a report to the U.S. Congress in 1934: "National Income, 1929–32." Division of Economic Research, Bureau of Foreign and Domestic Commerce. Senate Document Number 124, 73rd Cong., 2nd sess. (January 4, 1934), http://library.bea.gov/u?/SOD,888.

297 its inventor, Simon Kuznets, noted: Ibid. 5–7. Kuznets's exact words were, "The valuable capacity of the human mind to simplify a complex situation in a compact characterization becomes dangerous when not controlled in terms of definitely stated criteria . . . Thus, the estimates submitted, in the present study define income in such a way as to cover primarily only efforts whose results appear on the market place of our economy . . . Economic welfare cannot be adequately measured unless the personal distribution of income is known . . . The welfare of a nation can, therefore, scarcely be inferred from a measurement of national income as defined above."

299 median American incomes have fallen more than 7 percent: Timothy Noah, "The Great Divergence," *Slate*, September 3, 2010, www.slate.com/id/2266025/entry /2266026/.

299 Even John Locke, who famously enumerated: John Locke, *Second Treatise of Civil Government* (chapter 5, section 27), www.constitution.org/jl/2ndtr05.htm.

300 According to the economist Carol Graham: Carol Graham, "Happiness Economics: Can We Have an Economy of Well-being?" voxeu.org, July 31, 2011, www.voxeu.org/index.php?q=node/6819.

300 Graham admits that it's a challenge: Carol Graham, interview with the author.

300 the United States is currently ranked 127th in real GDP growth: "Country Comparison: GDP—Real Growth Rate," *CIA World Factbook*, www.cia.gov/library /publications/the-world-factbook/rankorder/2003rank.html.

301 When *Newsweek* ranked the "world's best countries": "Interactive Infographic of the World's Best Countries," *Daily Beast*, April 2010, www.thedailybest.com/news week/2010/08/15/interactive-infographic-of-the-worlds-best-countries.html.

301 In the 2011 Quality of Life Index by Nation Ranking: "2011 Quality of Life Index," *Nation Ranking* website, June 3, 2011, http://nationranking.wordpress.com/2011 /03/06/2011-qli/.

301 the Economist Intelligence Unit has the top American entry at: "Vancouver Still World's Most Livable City," Reuters, February 21, 2011, www.reuters.com/article /2011/02/21/us-cities-liveable-idUSTRE71K0NS20110221?pageNumber=1.

301 Mercer's Quality of Living Survey has the first U.S. entry at: "Quality of Living Worldwide City Rankings 201—Mercer Survey," Mercer website, May 26, 2010, www.mercer.com/press-releases/quality-of-living-report-2010#City_Ranking _Tables.

301 *Monocle* magazine showed only three U.S. cities: "The Livable Cities Index—01 Helsinki," *Monocle*, issue 45, vol. 3 (July/August 2011), www.monocle.com/Maga zine/volume-05/issue-45/.

301 which ranks twenty-eighth on the Sovereign Fiscal Responsibility Index: T. J. Augustine, Alexander Maasry, Damilola Sobo, and Di Want, "Sovereign Fiscal Responsibility Index 2011," *Stanford University International Policy Studies Program* report, March 25, 2011, http://publicpolicy.stanford.edu/system/files/A%20Sover eign%20Fiscal%20Responsibility%20Index%20Full%20Report.pdf.

302 Hans Morgenthau, the father of modern international relations theory, developed: Richard L. Merritt and Dina A. Zinnes, "Alternative Indexes of National Power," in Richard J. Stoll and Michael D. Ward, eds., *Power in World Politics* (Boulder, CO: Lynne Rienner Publications, 1898), 11–12.

302 Clifford German's formula for assessing national power: Ashley J. Tellis, Janice Bially, Christopher Layne, and Melissa McPherson, *Measuring National Power in the Postindustrial Age* (Santa Monica, CA: RAND, 2000), 28–29.

302 Wilhelm Fucks's approach that used: Ibid., 29.

302 the regression analyses of Alcock and Newcombe: Ibid., 29.

302 the Correlates of War Project looking at demographic: Merritt and Zinnes, "Alternative Indexes of National Power," 16.

302 Wayne Ferris and Ray Cline offered approaches: Ray S. Cline, *World Power Trends and U.S. Foreign Policy in the 1980s*, 2nd ed. (Boulder, CO: Westview Press, 1980), 12.

303 Number of employees, value of assets, and other measures make a difference: In fact, the Forbes 2000 ranking of the world's biggest companies ranks them based on a composite score of sales, profits, assets, and market value. See Scott DeCarlo, "The World's Leading Companies," Forbes.com, April, 21, 2010.

303 Exxon has more clout than say, Guatemala: ExxonMobil does arguably wield more clout than Guatemala in court. See for context, "A $16 Billion Problem," *Newsweek*, July 24, 2008.

304 Those pillars are the ability to make and enforce its laws: Historians and political scientists generally define states based on these criteria: "As is well known, the state is the only institution that can legitimately use force, and it has a monopoly on all forms of noneconomic coercion. Its legitimacy rests on its own laws and on agreements it makes with other states. Through these means, a state can fulfill its functions: ensuring domestic and foreign security, enforcing the law and promoting justice,

clears

withholding and redistributing portions of the gross domestic product, and developing and implementing economic and social policies." Sergei Rogov, "The Functions of a Contemporary State: Challenges for Russia," *Russian Social Science Review* 49.2 (March–April 2008): 4–5.

306 In 2009, fourteen states were listed as critical: *Foreign Policy* website, "2009 Failed States Index." The Failed States Index excludes fifteen U.N. member states: four European microstates (Andorra, Liechtenstein, Monaco, and San Marino), four Caribbean island nations (Dominica, St. Kitts and Nevis, St. Lucia, and St. Vincent and the Grenadines), and seven Pacific island nations (Kiribati, Marshall Islands, Nauru, Palau, Tonga, Tuvalu, and Vanuatu). Available at www.foreignpolicy.com /articles/2009/06/22/2009_failed_states_index_interactive_map_and_rankings.

306 But only ten navies in the world have even one aircraft carrier: WorldWideAircraftCarriers.com, "Where Are the Carriers?" (commissioned/operational carriers only), www.worldwideaircraftcarriers.com/.

306 The U.S. Navy has eleven carriers: U.S. Navy Fact File, "Aircraft Carriers—CVN," available at www.navy.mil/navydata/fact_display.asp?cid=4200&tid=200&ct=4.

306 larger than the total annual military budget of all but eleven nations: GlobalSecurity .org, "World Wide Military Expenditures," available at www.globalsecurity.org /military/world/spending.htm.

306 larger than the 2008 GDP of all but eleven countries: International Monetary Fund, "World Economic Outlook Database, October 2009: Report for Selected Countries and Subjects," available at http://imf.org/external/pubs/ft/weo/2009/02 /weodata/index.aspx.

306 full list of fourteen states considered to have failed: "2009 Failed States Index." Additionally, all fifteen U.N. member states not measured in the Failed States Index can safely be considered semi-states.

306 the twenty-three states that have GDPs bigger than the annual: "Global 500 (2009)," *Fortune*, on money.com, available at http://money.cnn.com/magazines /fortune/global500/2009/full_list/.

307 According to the IMF, a GDP of $458 billion: International Monetary Fund, "World Economic Outlook."

307 All twelve also have significant voting power in the IMF: "IMF Executive Directors and Voting Power," available at www.imf.org/external/np/sec/memdir/eds.htm.

307 and the World Bank: "International Bank for Reconstruction and Development: Subscriptions and Voting Power of Major Countries," available at http://sitere sources.worldbank.org/BODINT/Resources/278027-1215524804501/IBRDCoun tryVotingTable.pdf.

307 four are listed as "borderline" in the Failed States Index: "2009 Failed States Index."

307 but among the next group, only Australia, Korea, and the Netherlands are: Global Security.org, "World Wide Military Expenditures."

308 64 percent of all foreign exchange holdings are held in dollars: IMF website, "Currency Composition of Official Foreign Exchange Reserves," through 2009 QIII, available at www.imf.org/external/np/sta/cofer/ eng/cofer.pdf.

308 given up monetary control to the European Central Bank, as have semi-states: CIA

World Factbook, "Field Listing—Currency Code," available at www.cia.gov/library/publications/the-world-factbook/fields/2065.html.

309 countries like Saudi Arabia, the United Arab Emirates, and Oman have currencies pegged to the dollar: "GCC Defends Dollar Peg, Single Currency Deadline," May 11, 2008, available at www.arabianbusiness.com/518871-gulf-to-keep-dollar-pegs-2010-single-currency-plan.

309 85 percent of the countries on the planet are not represented within it: Tan Sri Lin See-Yan, "The Pittsburg G-20 Summit—Has It Worked?" *Star* (Malaysia), October 3, 2009, http://biz.thestar.com.my/news/story.asp?file=/2009/10/3/business/4817217&sec=business.

309 according to *Fortune* magazine's Global 500 list: "Global 500," at CNN Money, available online at http://money.cnn.com/magazines/fortune/global500/2010/.

309 *all five hundred* would rank in the top one hundred countries according to the World Bank: "Gross Domestic Product (2009)," The World Bank: World Development Indicators database (September 27, 2010), available online at http://siteresources.worldbank.org/DATASTATISTICS/Resources/GDP.pdf.

309 Stora Enso, the multinational most readers never heard of: In 2009, Stora Enso's net sales were 11 billion euros ($17 billion U.S.), "Stora Enso Oyj," Lexis Nexis Academic Snapshot, www.lexisnexis.com.proxy.uchicago.edu/us/lnacademic/search/companyDossiersubmitForm.do.

309 the characteristics that give corporations their special advantages: Brian Lane, "The Abuses of Corporate Personhood," *USA Today*, May 2004, available online at http://findarticles.com/p/articles/mi_m1272/is_2708_132/ai_n6019798/?tag=content;col1.

310 Using annual sales as a criterion, the one-thousandth-largest company in the world: If you rank *Forbes*'s list of "The Global 2000" companies by sales, the one thousandth company is Owens-Illinois. Its annual sales in 2010 were $7.07 billion. "The Global 2000," *Forbes* (April 21, 2010), www.forbes.com/lists/2010/18/global-2000-10_The-Global-2000_Sales_10.html.

310 That company's sales were larger than the GDPs of countries like Malta: "Gross domestic product (2009)," The World Bank: World Development Indicators database.

310 For those who fear that state-owned companies are dominating: Scott DeCarlo, "The World's Leading Companies."

310 Each of the world's ten biggest companies in terms of number of employees: "Global 500 (2010): Top Companies: Biggest Employers," *Forbes*, available online at http://money.cnn.com/magazines/fortune/global500/2010/performers/companies/biggest/.

310 supports an employee/family community of eight to ten million, which is about the size of Austria: The populations of Austria, Switzerland, and Israel are 8,217,280, 7,639,961, and 7,474,052 respectively. CIA World Factbook, "Country Comparison: Population," available online at www.cia.gov/library/publications/the-world-factbook/rankorder/2119rank.html.

311 Wal-Mart serves 200 million people a week: Wal-Mart website, http://walmartstores.com/aboutus/.

311 Royal Dutch Shell provides fuel to approximately ten million customers a

day: "Shell Case Study: Balancing stakeholder needs," The Times 100, available online at www.thetimes100.co.uk/case-study–balancing-stakeholder-needs–76 -403-1.php.

311 Toyota sells more than seven million cars a year: Toyota sold 7,237,00 in FY2010, www.toyota-global.com/sustainability/sustainability_report/highlights_in_fy2009 _economic_aspects/financial_results.html.

311 AXA has almost 100 million insurance clients: "The AXA Group at a Glance 2010," 4. Available at www.axa.com/lib/axa/uploads/depliantinstitutionnel/2010/AXA _IDcard_2010_VAb.pdf.

311 Royal Dutch Shell alone produces 2 percent of the world's oil and 3 percent of the world's gas: "Shell Case Study: Balancing Stakeholder Needs."

311 BlackRock has $3.3 trillion under management: Kolhatkar and Bhaktavatsalam, "The Colossus of Wall Street."

311 China and Japan's combined reserves are $3.6 trillion: CIA World Factbook, "Country Comparison: Reserves of Foreign Exchange and Gold," www.cia.gov /library/publications/the-world-factbook/rankorder/2188rank.html.

311 The top twenty countries in the world in terms of currency reserves: CIA World Factbook, "Country Comparison: Reserves of Foreign Exchange and Gold."

311 The top 125 asset managers each control the same amount: Global 2000, "The World's Biggest Public Companies," Forbes, filtered by industry (Investment Services), available online at www.forbes.com/global2000/list?industry=Investment %20Services&state=All&country=All.

311 Each of the top twenty-seven banks in the world controls over $1 trillion in assets: Global 2000, "The World's Biggest Public Companies," Forbes, the Global 2000 filtered by industry (Major Banks) and ranked by assets, available online at www .forbes.com/global2000/list?ascend=false&sort=companyAssets1&industry=Major %20Banks.

311 the Gates Foundation puts as much money in the field each year as the World Health Organization: Scott T. Firsing, Disturbing Times: The State of the Planet and Its Possible Future (Johannesburg: 30° South Publishers, 2008), 47; Tom Paulson, "Gates Foundation Out to Break the Cycle of Disease," Seattle Post-Intelligencer, December 8, 2003.

311 the total annual giving to philanthropy of all Americans is about $300 billion: "5 Questions for Vartan Gregorian, President and CEO, Carnegie Corporation of New York," Philanthropy News Digest, October 12, 2009, http://foundationcenter .org/pnd/fivequestions/5q_item.jhtml?id=268900010.

311 the top four hundred American taxpayers, who had total adjusted income of $138 billion: Carol J. Loomis, "The $600 billion Challenge," Fortune at CNN Money, June 16, 2010, http://features.blogs.fortune.cnn.com/2010/06/16/gates-buffett -600-billion-dollar-philanthropy-challenge/.

312 many of these organizations are providing vital social services: Risto Karajkov, "The Power of N.G.O.'s: They're Big, But How Big?" Worldpress.org, July 16, 2007, www.worldpress.org/Americas/2864.cfm.

312 the U.S. federal budget is estimated to be in excess of 24 percent of U.S. GDP: The

White House website, "The President's Budget for Fiscal year 2010," www.whitehouse
.gov/omb/budget.

313 the ability to shift domiciles in order to avoid tax consequences has already been
cited: "Out of the Door: Tax Treatment Tempts Businesses to Move Country,"
Financial Times, May 5, 2008, www.ft.com/cms/s/0/0401152c-1ad4-11dd-aa67
-0000779fd2ac.html?nclick_check=1.

313 Vince Cable, treasury spokesperson for the opposition Liberal Democrats, attacked the moves: Ibid.

313 "The global market has increasingly taken on the role of a regulator of sover-
eignty": Walter C. Opello, Jr., and Stephen J. Rosow, *The Nation-State and Global
Order: A Historical Introduction to Contemporary Politics* (Boulder and London:
Lynne Rienner Publishers, 2004), 256.

314 it was that "supreme" leadership giving in to the demands of high powers on Wall
Street: See, for example, Richard McGregor, *The Party: The Secret World of China's
Communist Rulers* (New York: HarperCollins, 2010), chapter 7, "Deng Perfects
Socialism: The Party and Capitalism," 194–228.

314 Sweden's GDP in 2009 was $406 billion: "Gross Domestic Product 2009," World
Development Indicators database, http://siteresources.worldbank.org/DATA
STATISTICS/Resources/GDP.pdf.

314 Exxon's annual sales that year were $442 billion: ExxonMobil, Fortune 500 (2009),
available online at http://money.cnn.com/magazines/fortune/fortune500/2009
/snapshots/387.html.

314 While Exxon has 83,600 employees: ExxonMobil at a glance, Forbes.com, http://fi
napps.forbes.com/finapps/jsp/finance/compinfo/CIAtAGlance.jsp?sedol=2326618.

314 Exxon has 2.5 million shareholders: ExxonMobil website, www.exxonmobil.com
/Corporate/community_ccr_stakeholders.aspx.

314 ownership interest in forty-six refineries: "Global Capabilities for the 21st Century," ExxonMobil website, www.exxonmobil.com/Corporate/Newsroom/Publica
tions/XOMGlobalCap/page_5.html.

314 In 2006, Exxon's budgeted expenditures exceeded $400 billion: ExxonMobil 2006
Summary Annual Report, available online at http://exxonmobil.com/corporate
/files/corporate/xom_2006 SAR.pdf.

314 Sweden's budget is heavily dominated by entitlement spending: Erik Lundberg,
"The Rise and Fall of the Swedish Model," *Journal of Economic Literature* 23, no. 1
(March 1985): 10.

314 Sweden has embassies in about thirty countries: "Sweden Embassies Worldwide,"
www.allembassies.com/swedish_embassies.htm.

314 Exxon operates in almost every country worldwide: "Global Capabilities for the
21st Century," ExxonMobil website, www.exxonmobil.com/Corporate/Newsroom
/Publications/XOMGlobalCap/page_5.html.

314–15 Sweden's standing army is tiny, and its reserves, while consisting of: "Sweden"
CIA World Factbook, www.cia.gov/library/publications/the-world-factbook/geos
/sw.html.

315 notably in the province of Aceh in Indonesia. In 2000: "A Matter of Complicity?

ExxonMobil on trial for its Human Rights Violations in Aceh," International Center for Transnational Justice, October 27, 2008, www.ictj.org/en/news/features/2080.html.

315 Sweden was one of the leading nations in engineering the Kyoto Protocol: "Bildt Presents Foreign Policy in Riksdag," The Local, February 13, 2008, www.thelocal .se/9971/20080213.

315 "President Bush's decision not to sign the United States up": "Revealed: How Oil Giant Influenced Bush," Guardian, June 8, 2005, www.guardian.co.uk/news /2005/jun/08/usnews.climatechange.

315 Stora Enso's annual sales of $20 billion: "Stora Enso CEO Jouko Karvinen's Message to Shareholders at the Company's AGM," Storaenso.com, April 1, 2009.

315 Stora today has thirty-two thousand employees: Stora Enso Annual Report 2008, "a clear vision for a bright future," available online at www.storaenso.com/media -centre/publications/annual-report/Documents/SE_Annual_ Report_08_en.pdf.

315 It owns land the size of Qatar: Stora Enso, "Planting for our future," Sustainability Performance (2009), 16. Available online at www.storaenso.com/media-centre/pub lications/sustainability-report/Documents/S_Stora_Enso_ Sustainability_2009.pdf.

316 Stora providing housing, schooling, its own courts, and even its own military: Gunnar Olsson and Burnett Anderson, Stora Kopparberg: Six Hundred Years of Industrial Enterprise (Falun, Sweden: Stora Kopparbergs Bergslags Aktiebolag, 1951), 72–77.

316 Today's corporations often conduct something very much like their own foreign policy: "The Corporate Diplomats," Financial Times, November 23, 2009, www.ft .com/cms/s/0/8f03208e-d86a-11de-b63a-00144feabdc0.html.

316 "vanguard companies," by pursuing such high-minded goals: Rosabeth Moss Kanter, SuperCorp: How Vanguard Companies Create Innovation, Profits, Growth, and Social Good (New York: Cross Business, 2009).

316 According to a 2008 report issued by the Committee Encouraging Corporate Philanthropy: Committee Encouraging Corporate Philanthropy, "Giving in Numbers, 2008 Edition," 4. Available online at www.hepdata.com/pdf/GivinginNumbers 2008.pdf.

317 The United Fruit Company was a trailblazer, literally and figuratively: Peter Chapman, Bananas: How the United Fruit Company Shaped the World (Edinburgh: Canongate, 2007), 30, 47.

318 "United Fruit . . . possibly launched more exercises in 'regime change'": Ibid., 7.

318 the company teamed up with another big fruit provider and supported Dávila's overthrow: Peter J. Dosal, Doing Business with the Dictators: A Political History of United Fruit in Guatemala (Oxford: SR Books, 2005), 81.

318 when the socialist Salvador Allende arrived on the scene in 1970 as a presidential candidate: Edward Boorstein, Allende's Chile: An Inside View (International Publishers, 1977), 260.

319 explosive reports in The Washington Post by columnist Jack Anderson: Brent Fisse and John Braithwaite, The Impact of Publicity on Corporate Offenders (SUNY Albany, 1983), 124.

319 agreed to focus on placing economic pressures on Allende: Boorstein, Allende's Chile, 85.

319 Orlando Letelier, Allende's ambassador to Washington, who was later murdered, characterized the coup: Naomi Klein, *The Shock Doctrine: The Rise of Disaster Capitalism* (New York: Henry Holt, 2008), 86.

319 "In the Eisenhower period we would be heroes": Kissinger TelCon 9/16/73, available online at www.gwu.edu/~nsarchiv/NSAEBB/NSAEBB255/19730916KP5.pdf.

320 "We didn't do it. I mean we helped them": Ibid.

320 "You read a book from beginning to end": Quoted in Jack Stack and Bo Burlingham, *A Stake in the Outcome: Building a Culture of Ownership for the Long-Term Success of Your Business* (Random House Digital, 2003), 36.

320 Shell Oil had "access to everything that was being done": *The Guardian* published the cable online at www.guardian.co.uk/world/us-embassy-cables-documents/230356.

320 In a cable dating from 2009, Robin Sanders, the U.S. ambassador to Nigeria, writes: Smith Lagos, "Cables Reveal Shell's Grip on Nigerian State," *Guardian*, December 9, 2010.

320 "Shell is everywhere. They have an eye and an ear": Quoted in ibid.

320 the fact is that the oil industry in Nigeria has extraordinary clout: Amnesty International, *Nigeria: Petroleum, Pollution and Poverty in the Niger Delta* (Amnesty International Publications, 2009), 9. Available online at www.amnesty.org/en/library/asset/AFR44/017/2009/en/e2415061-da5c-44f8-a73c-a7a4766ee21d/afr440172009en.pdf.

320 Shell's own estimate is that its venture in the country: Royal Dutch Shell website, www.shell.com.ng/home/content/nga/aboutshell/at_a_glance/.

321 according to the Wikileaks information, Shell requested sensitive information: Smith Lagos, "Cables Reveal Shell's Grip on Nigerian State", *Guardian*, December 9, 2010.

321 a region that is home to over thirty million people and has been called: Amnesty International, *Nigeria*, 9.

321 the U.N. Development Program describes the region as suffering: UNDP, *Niger Delta Human Development Report*, 2006.

321 Transparency International in 2004 ranked Nigeria's then president Sani Abacha: Transparency International, TI Global Corruption Report 2004, www.transparency.org/publications/gcr/gcr_2004#download.

321 "although Shell operates in more than 100 countries": Quoted in Kristin Sharon Shrader-Frechette, *Environmental Justice: Creating Equality, Reclaiming Democracy* (Oxford: Oxford University Press, 2002), 118.

321 "some 13 million barrels of oil have been split in the Niger Delta": Amnesty International, "Nigeria," 13.

321 "a corporation is the property of its stockholders": Quoted in Joel Bakan, *The Corporation: The Pathological Pursuit of Profit and Power* (New York: Free Press, 2004), 34.

321 "we sometimes feed conflict": "Shell Admits Blame in Nigeria," CNN World, June 11, 2004.

321 These entrepreneurial states are typically small, but they can be seen as laborato-

ries: Klaus Schwaab, World Economic Forum, The Global Competitiveness Report 2010–2011 (Geneva, 2010), www3.weforum.org/docs/WEF_GlobalCompetitiveness Report_2010-11.pdf

323 **They have 8,900 employees, at the core of whom are a group of elite:** Katrina Brooker, "Can This Man Save Wall Street?" CNNMoney.com, October 29, 2008, http://money.cnn.com/2008/10/28/magazines/fortune/blackrock_brooker.fortune /index2.htm.

323 **"Currently BlackRock runs tens of millions of risk models a day":** Ibid.

325 **"the worst disaster and largest capitulation":** Winston Churchill, *The Second World War*, vol. 4, *The Hinge of Fate* (Houghton Mifflin Harcourt, 1986), 81.

325 **Singapore does not conform to Western standards of a free society:** Singapore's extraordinary transformation capacity has often been subject to intense criticisms by economists such as Paul Krugman, who, in his article, "The Myth of Asia's Miracle: A Cautionary Fable," *Foreign Affairs* 73, iss. 6 (November/December 1994), argues that "the growth of Lee Kuan Yew's Singapore is an economic twin of the growth of Stalin's Soviet Union—growth achieved purely through mobilization of resources."

326 **"a very Asian model, a Singaporean capitalism":** Kishore Mahubani, interview with the author, 2010.

326 **"We have seen the defects in Anglo-American capitalism":** Tharman Shanmuga-rantnam, interview with the author, 2010.

326 **"offer what every citizen wants":** Quoted in John Kampfner, *Freedom for Sale: Why the World Is Trading Democracy for Security* (New York: Basic Books, 2010), 30.

326 **a systematic national effort to develop and update a national competitiveness strategy:** John W. Thomas and Lim Siong Guan, "Using Markets to Govern Better in Singapore," Working Paper Series rwp02-010 (Cambridge: Harvard University, John F. Kennedy School of Government, 2002), 18.

327 **"the cure to all this talk is really a good dose of incompetent government":** Quoted in Seth Mydans, "Singapore announces 60 percent pay raise for ministers," *New York Times*, April 9, 2007, www.nytimes.com/2007/04/09/world/asia/09iht-sing .3.5200498.html?_r=1.

327 **"makes use of the market concept to impose incentives":** Thomas and Guan, "Using Markets to Govern Better in Singapore," 17.

327 **Health care, housing, and education services are all provided via user-pay market mechanisms:** M. Ramesh, "Social Security in Singapore: Redrawing the Public-Private Boundary," *Asian Survey* 32, no. 12 (December 1992): 1,100.

327 **(The stimulus was $15 billion, 6 percent of GDP, and included):** Siow Yue Chia, "Singapore Weathers the Crisis and Prepares for a Stronger Year," *East Asia Forum*, January 12, 2010, www.eastasiaforum.org/2010/01/12/singapore-weathers-the -crisis-and-prepares-for-a-stronger-year/.

327 **Its GDP per capita is $62,200, fifth in the world:** "Singapore," CIA World Factbook, www.cia.gov/library/publications/the-world-factbook/geos/sn.html.

327 **one of the lowest unemployment rates in the world:** Ibid.

327 offers the thirteenth-highest life expectancy and is ranked sixth in health system performance: World Health Organization, World Health Report 2000, Health Systems: Improving Performance, www.who.int/whr/2000/en/.

327 rated number one among the world's easiest places to do business: "Doing Business 2007: How to Reform," World Bank, 2007, available online at www.doingbusiness.org/reports/global-reports/doing business-2007.

327 the second-freest economy in the world: Index of Economic Freedom, Heritage Foundation, 2011, available online at www.heritage.org/index/ranking.

327 "Singapore is the best-managed company in the world": Stewart Brand, review of *Strategic Pragmatism: The Culture of Singapore's Economic Development Board*, by Edgar H. Schein, Global Business Network website, http://web.archive.org/web/20050414192858/http:/www.gbn.com/BookClubSelectionDisplayServlet.srv?si=248.

329 Today only 25 percent of the country's revenues are derived from oil and gas: CIA World Factbook: United Arab Emirates, 2010, available at www.cia.gov/library/publications/the-world-factbook/geos/ae.html.

329 From construction to engineering, from information technologies to the experimental "green city" of Masdar: Christopher M. Davidson, *Dubai: The Vulnerability of Success* (New York: Columbia University Press, 2008), 1.

329 developing major sovereign wealth funds that redirect national wealth: See, for example, Edwin M. Truman, "Sovereign Wealth Funds: The Need for Greater Transparency and Accountability," Peterson Institution for International Economics Policy Brief (August 2007), 1, www.iie.com/publications/pb/pb07-6.pdf.

329 The World Bank currently lists the UAE in third place in terms of its ease of trading: "Doing Business 2011: United Arab Emirates, Making a Difference for Entreprenuers," The International Bank for Reconstruction and Development/World Bank (2011), 2, www/doingbusiness.org/~/media/FPDKM/Doing%20Business/Documents/Profiles/Country/DB11/ARE.pdf.

329 The World Economic Forum ranks it third: World Economic Forum, The Global Competitiveness Report 2010–2011, 38.

329 The country's per capita income is eighteenth in the world: CIA World Factbook: United Arab Emirates, 2010.

329 it is clear that the country is being prudent and creative in terms of diversifying: Christopher M. Davidson, "The Impact of Economic Reform on Dubai," in A. Ehteshami and S. Wright, eds., *Reform in the Middle East Oil Monarchies* (Reading, UK: Ithaca Press, 2008), 158.

330 ranked sixth in the world in capacity for innovation and twenty-fourth in overall competitiveness: The World Bank, *Doing Business 2011: Israel*; World Economic Forum, The Global Competitiveness Report 2010–2011.

330 "a hybrid socialist-nationalist ideology": Ofira Seliktar, "The Israeli Economy," in Robert Freedman, ed., *Contemporary Israel* (Boulder, CO: Westview Press, 2009), 159.

330 "the most socialist economy outside the Soviet bloc": Ibid.

331 by 1985 a major reform, called the Economic Stabilization Plan, was under way:

Stanley Fischer, "The Israeli Stabilization Program, 1985–86," *American Economic Review* 77, no. 2 (May 1987): 275–78, 276.

331 By 2008, the Israeli public sector was down to being "just" 45 percent of GDP: Rafi Melnick and Yosef Mealem, "Israel's Economy: 1986–2008," Jewish Virtual Library Publications, June 2009, 5, www.jewishvirtuallibrary.org/jsource/isdf/text/anthologytoc.html.

331 Israel "has the highest number of start-ups in the world per capita": Karlin Lillington, "What Ireland Has to Learn from Israel's High-Tech Companies," *Irish Times*, June 26, 2010, www.irishtimes.com/newspaper/weekend/2010/0626/1224273322693.html.

331 Israel has more tech companies listed on the NASDAQ stock exchange: Ibid.

331 More than 40 percent of industrial output is now directed at exports: Melnick and Mealem, "Israel's Economy," 2.

332 Israel attracted VC (venture capital) investments thirty times greater than did Europe: Lillington, "What Ireland Has to Learn from Israel's High-Tech Companies."

336 According to the *Oxford English Dictionary*, the word "international": "International," Oxford English Dictonary Online, 2011.

11 ■ Competing Capitalisms

338 "The widely held perception": Dennis C. Blair, "Annual Threat Assessment of the Intelligence Community," Testimony to the Senate Select Committee on Intelligence, Washington, D.C., February 12, 2009, 2.

338 There is a runestone in the fields near Vasteras in Sweden: "Vs Fv1988;36" in Scandinavian runic-text database, www.nordiska.uu.se/forskn/samnord.htm.

339 One Viking leader, Ingvar the Far-Travelled, was famous for: Kathryn Hinds, *Barbarians: Vikings* (Tarrytown, NY: Marshall Cavendish, 2010), 57.

339 he had "never seen more perfect physical specimens": Thomas J. Craughwell, *How the Barbarian Invasions Shaped the Modern World: The Vikings, Vandals, Huns, Mongols, Goths, and Tartars Who Razed the Old World and Formed the New* (Beverly, MA: Fair Winds Press, 2008), 140.

344 Peter Jay commented to the BBC in September 2008: "Viewpoints: Where Now for Capitalism?" BBC News, September 19, 2008, http://news.bbc.co.uk/2/hi/7621771.stm.

345 wrote one columnist for London's *Guardian* newspaper: John Gray, "A Shattering Moment in America's Fall from Power," *Guardian*, September 28, 2008.

345 "certainly not too soon to look beyond the current crisis" "Wall Street Casualties," *New York Times*, September 15, 2008.

345 "there will be a big demand for a major policy change": "Viewpoints: Where Now for Capitalism?"

345 "The U.S. will lose its status as the superpower of the world financial system": William L. Watts, "German Finance Minister Criticizes Lax Regulation, Focus on Short-term Profit," MarketWatch, September 25, 2008, www.marketwatch.com/story/us-to-lose-financial-superpower-status-german-finance-minister.

345 "the all-powerful market that is always right": Quoted in "It Is Time to Put Finance Back in Its Box," *Financial Times*, April 13, 2009.

345 George Osbourne joined the chorus of doubters: "Let Us Put Markets to the Service of the Good Society," *Financial Times*, April 13, 2009.

345 "belief in deregulation had been shaken": Edmund L. Andrews, "Greenspan Concedes Error on Regulation," *New York Times*, October 24, 2008.

345 central bank policies "would be more powerful if coordinated": "The Credit Crunch: World on the Edge," *Economist*, October 2, 2008.

346 The BBC saw the changes as a watershed: Paul Reynolds, "New World Order Emerges from Chaos," BBC News website, April 2, 2009, http://news.bbc.co.uk/2/hi/business/7979918.stm.

346 Massive government stimulus programs amounting to hundreds of billions or trillions of dollars: Andrew Batson, "China Sets Big Stimulus Plan in Bid to Jump-Start Growth," *Wall Street Journal*, November 10, 2008.

347 have falsely conflated economic growth with economic well-being: See Arthur C. Brooks, *The Battle: How the Fight Between Free Enterprise and Big Government Will Shape America's Future* (New York: Basic Books, 2010).

348 who, in 2001, published: Peter Hall and David Soskice, *Varieties of Capitalism: The Institutional Foundations of Comparative Advantage* (Oxford: Oxford University Press, 2011).

349 he will have to raise $750 million to $1 billion to hold on to the office: Ken Thomas, "Obama, Dems Hoping to Raise $60M by Late June," Associated Press, June 2, 2011, www.msnbc.msn.com/id/43250286/ns/politics-decision_2012/t/obama-dems-hoping-raise-m-late-june/.

349 the traditional American "Lockean liberal" ideal: John B. Judis, "Anti-Statism in America," *New Republic*, November 11, 2009, www.tnr.com/article/anti-statism-america.

350 an economy that is likely to pass the United States in size in purchasing power parity terms by 2016: Brett Arends, "IMF Bombshell: Age of America Nears End," MarketWatch, April 26, 2011, http://finance.yahoo.com/banking-budgeting/article/112616/imf-bombshell-age-america-end-marketwatch.

350 which translates in the eyes of many others as "capitalism with Chinese characteristics": Yasheng Huang, *Capitalism with Chinese Characteristics: Entrepreneurship and the State* (Cambridge: Cambridge University Press, 2008).

350 referred to by Lawrence Summers as forming the core of an emerging Delhi Consensus: C. Raja Mohan, "Raising the Game in Asia," IndianExpress.com, October 25, 2010, www.indianexpress.com/news/raising-the-game-in-asia/701978/4.

350 Germany has outperformed not only all the other major countries of Europe: Nicholas Kulish, "Defying Others, Germany Finds Economic Success," *New York Times*, August 13, 2010.

352 perhaps 400 million Chinese have been lifted out of poverty: United Nations Industrial Development Organization, *Industrialization, Environment and the Millennium Development Goals in Sub-Saharan Africa* (UNIDO, 2004), 85.

352 In 2010 it passed Japan to become the world's second-largest economy: David Barboza, "China Passes Japan as Second-Largest Economy," *New York Times*, August 15, 2010.

352 It holds the world's largest reserves of foreign capital, with the total now exceeding $3 trillion: "Country Comparison: Reserves of Foreign Exchange and Gold," *CIA World Factbook*, www.cia.gov/library/publications/the-world-factbook/rankorder /2188rank.html.

353 not majority owned by the state account for two-thirds of output: "Let a Million Flowers Bloom," *Economist*, March 10, 2011, www.economist.com/node/18330120 ?story_id=18330120.

353 according to one South Korean estimate, they contribute almost three-quarters of Chinese GDP: Ibid.

353 While this approach has a name suggesting it is part of a plan, "one eye open, one eye shut": "Bamboo Capitalism," *Economist*, March 10, 2011, www.economist.com /node/18332610.

353 with more than 180,000 demonstrations reported in the last year alone: Didi Kirsten Tatlow, "Indifference as a Mode of Operation at China Schools," *New York Times,* May 18, 2011, www.nytimes.com/2011/05/19/ vworld/asia/19iht-letter19 .html.

353 the editors of *The Economist* to conclude that "capitalism with Chinese characteristics": "Bamboo Capitalism."

354 Four hundred million Indians, for example, still live without regular access to electricity: World Bank website, http://web.worldbank.org/WBSITE/EXTERNAL /TOPICS/EXTENERGY2/0,,contentMDK:22855502~pagePK:210058~piPK:210062 ~theSitePK:4114200,00.html.

354 Fifty million Brazilians, almost a third of the population, live below the poverty line: Alain Rouqie, "Brazil, a South American State Among the Key Players," in Christopher Jaffrelot, ed., *Emerging States: The Wellspring of a New World Order*, Cynthia Schoch, trans. (New York: Columbia University Press, 2009), 98.

354 it ranks 73rd on the Human Development Index: Human Development Report 2010, "The Real Wealth of Nations: Pathways to Human Development" (UNDP, 2010), http://hdr.undp.org/en/media/HDR_2010_EN_ Complete_reprint.pdf.

354 Brazilian poverty, which fell from 22 percent to 7 percent: "Lifting Families Out of Poverty in Brazil—Bolsa Familia Program," *World Bank*, September 27, 2010, http://web.worldbank.org/WBSITE/EXTERNAL/COUNTRIES/LACEXT /BRAZILEXTN/0,,print:Y~isCURL:Y~contentMDK:20754490~menuPK:2024799 ~pagePK:141137~piPK:141127~theSitePK:322341,00.html.

355 continued foreign investment in Brazil that reached record levels by the time he left office: Riordan Roett, *The New Brazil* (Washington, D.C.: Brookings Institution Press, 2010), 91–95.

355 In a speech in Mumbai in 2010, Larry Summers argued: Vikas Bajaj, "In Mumbai, Adviser to Obama Extols India's Economic Model," *New York Times*, October 15, 2010, www.nytimes.com/2010/10/16/ business/global/16summers.html.

355 India also still has a shrinking but notable group of "public sector undertakings": "Public Sector Undertakings in India," http://india.gov.in/spotlight/spotlight _archive.php?id=78.

356 The roots of this approach are in the almost four and a half decades of social demo-cratic policies: Uma Kapila, *India's Economic Development Since 1947* (New Delhi: Academic Foundation, 2008).

356 what one leading Indian businessman has referred to as "Gandhian engineering": Abhishek Malhotra, Art Kleiner, and Laura W. Geller, "A Gandhian Approach to R&D," *strategy+business*, August 24, 2010, www.strategy-business.com/article /10310?gko=516c7.

356 it demanded bank equity in exchange for its investment, thus ensuring a return for the Swedish people: Carter Dougherty, "Can the U.S. Learn Any Lessons from Sweden's Banking Rescue?" *International Herald Tribune*, September 22, 2008.

356 "If I go into a bank, I'd rather get equity": "Sweden's Model Approach to Financial Disaster," *Time*, September 24, 2008.

357 "despite its reputation for austerity, Germany has been for more willing": David Leonhardt, "The German Example," *New York Times*, June 7, 2011, www.nytimes .com/2011/06/08/business/economy/08leonhardt.html.

358 "There's a pervasive sense in the United States that government and the economy": Jia Lynn Yang, "Where Germany, U.S. Differ: How Much Should Government Steer the Economy?" *Washington Post*, June 7, 2011.

358 "It is true that other countries are more comfortable with this thing called 'indus-trial policy'": Ibid.

359 managing city-sized development issues in places like Suzhou: Chen Wen and Sun Wei, "Recent Developments in Yangtze River Delta and Singapore's Investment," in Saw Swee-Hock and John Wong, eds., *Regional Economic Development in China* (Singapore: ISEAS Publishing, 2009), 168–70.

360 more like the role the U.S. government has historically played: Jeff Madrick, *The Case for Big Government* (Princeton, NJ: Princeton University Press, 2009).

361 the soil of Falun had finally given up its last bit of ore: The mine officially ceased operations in 1992. "Stora Enso History," Stora Enso website, http://81.209.16.116 /WebRoot/503425/Taso2_ content_siivottu.aspx?id=515562.

361 It had hints of Hoffmann's fictional story: E.T.A. Hoffmann and R. J. Hollingdale, *Tales of Hoffmann: The Mines of Falun* (New York: Penguin Group, 1982), 336–40.

361 as the former Swedish finance minister Par Nuder noted: Par Nuder, interview with the author, 2010.

Acknowledgments

Eric Chinski is one of the world's very best editors, and while it is very clear that that is just what I require, I'm not sure why I got lucky enough to have the opportunity to work with someone who possesses such skill, wisdom, wit, and infinite reserves of patience. However, it's the kind of good fortune life has taught me to accept without questioning. I'm immensely grateful for the opportunity to work with him again on this book, and the same can be said for all his colleagues at Farrar, Straus and Giroux, led by Jonathan Galassi and including especially Jeff Seroy and his team and Gabriella Doob, who provided guidance, essential humor, and encouragement at critical junctures.

I would probably not have met Eric, the folks at FSG, or anyone else involved in the publishing community were it not for my friend and agent, Esmond Harmsworth. It was his idea that I start writing books a while back, and it was his guidance that made fulfilling that particular lifelong aspiration possible. The more books I write, the more I owe him, but that's a business model we both can live with, and more a reflection of sincere gratitude than any commercial transaction.

I must also thank Jessica Mathews and the wonderful people at the Carnegie Endowment for International Peace for providing such terrific support throughout the writing of this book. It has been a privilege to be a visiting scholar at Carnegie for so many years—this being my fourth book written during the decade or so I have been affiliated with the endowment.

Not only has Carnegie continued to offer the ideal work environment, excellent resources, and a great team of researchers, but much of my interest in the area that is the subject of this book was inspired by thinking done by Jessica herself. As I mentioned earlier in the book, her *Foreign Affairs* article "Power Shift" made a very important contribution in this area, almost as great for me as did the conversations I have been fortunate enough to have with her over the years on that and related subjects. She has been a great president at Carnegie, built the organization into being truly the first global think tank, and remained a leading thinker in her own right, and she has done all that while cultivating exceptional work and great loyalty from her team. Among the members of that team, great thanks go to my dear friend Moises Naim, who first led me to Carnegie; to Uri Dadush, who offered especially pertinent ideas regarding this book; and to Paul Balaran, who is Carnegie's secret weapon, masterfully overseeing its daily operations.

In the same vein, I must also thank at the outset Bernard Schwartz, whose generous contribution has made my work and that of my research team at Carnegie possible for the last several years. Having been a remarkably successful and visionary businessman, Bernard has also devoted many years to providing sage advice to America's leaders. He is humane, insightful, and fearless, and I'm even more grateful to have him as a friend than as a benefactor.

The real work behind this book was done not by me but by a team of researchers who have made the process of writing *Power, Inc.* such a pleasure that I (almost) hate to see it end. While these young, gifted rising stars undoubtedly signed on to this job to learn something or to burnish already excellent academic credentials, they should know that over the course of this project, I have learned far more from them than they may accidentally have gleaned from me.

Leading this team was Chris Zoia, who persevered during those long spells when we were digging into distant history and who regularly found nuggets of solid gold near those veins of copper along which we were excavating. He brought to the project editorial gifts, humor, grace under pressure, and management abilities he probably didn't know he had at the outset. He is destined for great things, and I'm exceptionally fortunate to have had the opportunity to collaborate with him these past couple of years.

Chris had a number of especially effective associates throughout the process, and all made material contributions to this book. One was Jonathan Ross, now a practicing attorney, who came to us during a year off between his time at law school and his job and who was both a research star and someone who offered great insights and lively discussions that helped improve the book in myriad ways. Another was May Sabah, who put in not one but two tours of duty and contributed sound, smart, skillful research as well as uplifting energy and unfailing good spirits throughout. Heather Horn also made great contributions during her time as the project's lead researcher, especially in the area of European history, in which she excels, as did Robyn Mak, who made terrific contributions on everything from the history of Sweden to the story of rising economies in Asia. Jared Miller and Susanne Mueller also provided important research papers and useful perspectives during their briefer but nonetheless much appreciated associations with the project.

Elly Page, lead researcher on my last book, *Superclass*, kicked off the process on this one too, and frankly, we wouldn't have gotten here without her. She's a terrific friend, now also an attorney; I am proud to have had the chance to be associated with her over two projects and hope there will be more in the future.

Beyond this team, a small group of friends have played an absolutely essential role as advisers, confidants, and inspirations throughout the process of preparing this book. My business partner, Dr. Jeffrey E. Garten, has forgotten more about business, government, and the relationship between business and government than I will ever know, and I am grateful beyond words for having had the opportunity to work with him in the Clinton administration; at our company, Garten Rothkopf; and most of all, over countless breakfasts, lunches, and dinners, talking, schmoozing, contemplating the world, and getting the chance to see where his great mind has been—especially since he usually arrives at those places well ahead of the rest of the world. Truly, working with him over the past two decades has been one of the singular privileges of my life.

In the same vein, I am exceptionally grateful to my other colleagues at Garten Rothkopf, led by the smart and capable Claire Casey, and our partners at the law firm of Steptoe & Johnson, notably Ambassador Susan Esserman, Alfred Mamlet, and the indefatigable Harold Freilich (also my tennis partner, so I know just how indefatigable—and charitable—he really is), for their support.

For the past several years, I have had the privilege of writing for *Foreign Policy*, blogging daily for their award-winning website. I certainly don't do this for the money. The main reason I do it is that I enjoy so much working with the great editors there, notably the wonderful and gifted Susan Glasser, the mastermind of *Foreign Policy*'s recent successes, and the especially great and pop culturally attuned Becky Frankel. Hilda Ochoa-Brillembourg, Mary Choksi, Deb Boedicker, and the team at Strategic Investment Group, as well as Antoine van Agtmael at Emerging Market Management, have also been both valued friends and colleagues whose thinking has helped shape key ideas in this book.

While my other friends don't face my colleagues' burden of having to work with me daily, they have all done more than their fair share to provide me with guidance, ideas, and counsel during the preparation of this book. Tom Friedman of *The New York Times* has been an intellectual coconspirator and great pal for many years now and was especially helpful in working through some of the core ideas of this book. So too was his colleague and another great friend for the past nearly two decades, David Sanger, who offered many great ideas and a much-needed acid wash to peel away what was unnecessary in some of mine. Completing the *New York Times* trifecta was Helene Cooper, still another much-valued friend who happens to work at that newspaper. I have known Helene just as long as I've known the other two guys, and she was also very generous in sharing her very good thoughts and ideas throughout this project. Ed Luce, *Financial Times* columnist and terrific author, probably had to endure more conversations about this project than anyone else, and he was helpful in every one of them. Displaying similar generosity and also offering vital advice and insights were (in alphabetical order): Nancy Birdsall of the Center for Global Development; Steve Clemons of the New America Foundation; Jeffrey Goldberg of *The Atlantic*; Bob Hormats, currently Under Secretary of State for Economic Affairs and formerly of Goldman Sachs; Rob Shapiro of Sonacon, LLC. Anne-Marie Slaughter, formerly of the State Department and now back at Princeton; Debora Spar of Barnard College; and Allison Stanger of Middlebury College. I should also note that my friend Philippe Bourguignon offered not only great contributions but for a crucial period his wonderful home at the Miraval Resort in Arizona to enable me to finish a key draft of the book.

During the course of preparing for and later writing this book, I interviewed and spoke with scores of people from business, government, and academia. Some of those interviews were off the record or on background, so I can't cite the individuals who shared their time with me, but I do want to express my thanks to them. I also want to be sure to note that the views expressed in this book do not necessarily represent those of the people I can acknowledge. That said, the book would not have been possible without the generous access and thoughts provided by Lewis Alexander, Neil Allen, Celso Amorim, Charlene Barshefsky, Don Baer, Sandy Berger, Lael Brainard, L. Paul Bremer, Ian Bremmer, Richard Burns, Kurt Campbell, Steve Case, Ambassador Heng Chee Chan, Nelson Cunningham, Dan DiMicco, Niall Ferguson, Carol Graham, Ambassador Hussain Haqqani, Fred Hochberg, Walter Isaacson, John Judis, Susan Levine, David Lipton, Mack McLarty, Luis Alberto Moreno, Michael Oren, Antonio Patriota,

Karen Poniachik, Clyde Prestowitz, Dylan Ratigan, Jim Rogers, Francisco Sanchez, David Sandalow, Roger Sant, Klaus Schwab, Meera Shankar, Thomas Shannon, Tharman Shanmugarantnam, Joseph Stiglitz, Lawrence Summers, Julia Sweig, Arturo Valenzuela, Mauro Vieira, Timothy Wirth, and Daniel Yergin. I would also like to offer special thanks to two men who helped shaped my thinking for much of my adult life and who died during the preparation of this book. Ambassador Richard Holbrooke and the former U.S. representative Stephen Solarz were among the best international thinkers and leaders of their generation, and I remember both with admiration, appreciation, and fondness.

Naturally, the greatest thanks of all must go to my family. My parents regularly encouraged, coaxed, goaded, and inspired me along the way to getting this book done, and I must say my dad's particular enthusiasm for the idea was one of the leading reasons I did this book when I did. My mom proved once again to be a fantastic editor, both in her review of the manuscript and in terms of the little editor's voice that she embedded in my head when I was in a preconscious state (which could have been at almost any time in the past half century).

My daughters, Joanna and Laura, are not only the inspiration for everything I do, they are the reason I have the courage to undertake any creative venture, because I know that no matter how that particular venture may turn out, I have already been associated with the creation of two masterpieces. I know everyone else thinks their children are special and best. But mine actually are, and the rest of the world is just going to have to learn to deal with it.

Finally, I want to offer special thanks to the person who deserves the most gratitude of all, my wife, Adrean. As it happens, she lives her professional life at the intersection of government and business. This book is therefore largely written for her, not only in the hope that it might offer a glimpse into an aspect or two of what she does for a living, but as certain proof that her profession is in fact, contrary to popular belief, the world's second oldest. She has been unwaveringly supportive throughout this project, as she has been in all things throughout our time together. She is a wonder and a joy. And after all she has done for me, perhaps this book will allow me to return the favor and help her with one of the great challenges she faces in life. You see, she has trouble sleeping some nights . . .

Index

merchant class, rise of, 66–70
Metternich, Prince Klemens Venzel von, 136, 137, 141, 142, 146–47
Mexico, 157, 351
Micklethwait, John, 20
Mill, John Stuart, 156
mills, 68–69
Mir Jafar, 117
monetary union, European, 255, 259
money, history, 234–35
Monroe, James, 174
Montesquieu, 102
More, Sir Thomas, 3, 12, 13
Morgan, John Pierpont, 213, 246–49, 343
Morgan Stanley, 254, 263
Morgenthau, Hans, 302
Morse, Samuel, 199
mortgage-backed securities, 261
Muller, Ronald E., 20
multinational corporations: as of 1848, 201; as alienation target, 333; current numbers, 201; first enterprises, 200–201; impact of globalization, 216–23; nonaligned nature, 14, 20, 320–21; Singer Company as early example, 207–10; world's first, 160
Mun, Thomas, 238
Muscovy Company, 42, 83

Napoleonic wars, 135–37
National Economic Council, U.S., 231, 259
national security, as public-private power issue, 31, 286–91
nation-states: characteristics, 17; as defined by Treaty of Westphalia, 46, 47–48; four basic components, 170; impact of globalization, 196–97; modern, emergence, 22; need for more effective international cooperation, 31–32; see also countries
nautical technologies, 83, 199
Nawab of Carnatic, 116
Netanyahu, Benjamin, 331
Netherlands: and corporate relocations, 313; as maturing society today, 301; supports colonies in American Revolution, 130

Neutrality Act, 274
Newcombe, Alan, 302
New Deal, 250
Newton, Isaac, 109
New York Central Railroad, 158
Nicea, Council of, 51
Nigeria, 306, 310–22, 351
Niles, Nathaniel, 176
Nixon, Richard, 251, 252–53, 319
Nogaret, Guillaume de, 66
nongovernmental organizations (NGOs), 189, 311–12
Norris, Frank, 12
North, Lord, 122
North Korea, 302, 306
Norway: on Human Development Index, 354
Nuder, Par, 228–29, 267, 361–62
Nye, Joe, 31

Obama, Barack, 21, 189, 231
Occupational Safety and Health Act, 184–85
"Occupy Wall Street" protests, 8
Octopus, The (Norris), 12
Offenbach, Jacques, 40
Ogier, Charles, 91, 93
Olof Skotkonung, King of Sweden, 32, 34, 107
Olsdotter, Margareta, 40
On Liberty (Mill), 156
Opel (automobile), 217
Opello, Walter, 313
Organization for Economic Co-operation and Development (OECD), 330
Osbourne, George, 345
Oscar I, King of Sweden, 167
Osnabruck, Westphalia, see Westphalia, Treaty of
Ottoman Turks, 84
outsourcing, 286–87
Owens-Illinois, 310
Oxenstierna, Axel, 92–93

Paine, Thomas, 103, 126
Palme, August, 169